Casebook in Public Budgeting and Financial Management

Edited by CAROL W. LEWIS
The University of Connecticut

and A. GRAYSON WALKER, III

PRENTICE–HALL, INC., Upper Saddle River, New Jersey 07458

Library of Congress Cataloging in Publication Data
Main entry under title:

Casebook in public budgeting and financial management.

Bibliography.
Includes index.
1. Finance, Public—Case studies. 2. Budget—Case studies.
3. Local finance—Case studies. I. Lewis, Carol W.
(Carol Weiss) [date] II. Walker, A. Grayson.
HJ141.C37 1984 350.72 83-21235
ISBN 0-13-115402-8

to our students

©1984 by Prentice-Hall, Inc., Upper Saddle River, NJ 07458

Editoral supervision and interior design: Serena Hoffman
Cover design: Ben Santora
Manufacturing buyer: Ron Chapman

PRINTED IN THE UNITED STATES OF AMERICA

10 9 8 7 6 5 4

ISBN 0-13-115402-8

Prentice-Hall International (UK) Limited, London
Prentice-Hall of Australia Pty. Limited, Sydney
Prentice-Hall Canada Inc., Toronto
Prentice-Hall Hispanoamericana, S.A., Mexico
Prentice-Hall of India Private Limited, New Delhi
Prentice-Hall of Japan, Inc., Tokyo
Pearson Education Asia Pte. Ltd., Singapore
Editora Prentice-Hall do Brasil, Ltda., Rio de Janeiro

CONTENTS

Part II: *ANALYTIC METHODS AND APPROACHES*

Part III: FINANCIAL MANAGEMENT

PREFACE

There lurks a suspicion that the sentimentality associated with acknowledgments is precipitated chiefly by the relief felt when an entire project is completed. That relief undoubtedly is shared by the several dozen colleagues who contributed their time and resources to this enterprise.

The contributing authors submitted themselves willingly to initial guidelines, subsequent deadlines, interactive field tests, and repeated rewrites with the good grace and humor that are essential ingredients in such a complex undertaking. The shared purpose—generating a useful resource for professional training—stayed foremost in everyone's mind and bolstered cooperative working relationships all along the way. It has been an especially rewarding experience to work with them over the past two years.

Those who contributed their research and writing are acknowledged directly in the citations. However, the traditional, formal mode of citation and attribution does not readily recognize other types of assistance and support. Here is the opportunity to express sincere appreciation to other participants on this labor.

Field testing made significant contributions to the usefulness and precision of many cases and represents an integral component of the project. This burden fell primarily upon the students in graduate seminars in public budgeting at The University of Connecticut over the last several years. Students worked through guidelines, evaluated cases, pinpointed problem areas, omissions, and ambiguities, and enthusiastically participated in the intellectual and methodological development of the project. Some undergraduate classes participated as well, although to a much lesser extent. This experience enabled us to learn from each other, both about budgeting and about pedagogy. Our appreciation is also extended to Douglas Fox, John Swain, and Elaine Johansen, who ran some cases through the field tests with their classes. Elaine Johansen also helped design the evaluation instrument.

The University of Connecticut, through the Department of Political Science, the Institute of Urban Research, and the Graduate Research Foundation, provided assistance generously and continuously. Correspondence, telephoning, duplicating, collating, mailing, and typing went on—and on!—throughout the project, from development to field testing to wrap-up. Even special thanks are inadequate for the support provided by Helen Hauschild and Florence Selleck. Joe Shurkus did some bibliographic research and proofreading, and Katharine Holmes and Helen Rambush typed the final manuscript with care and patience.

Morton J. Tenzer, Director of the Institute of Urban Research, and other colleagues supplemented the institutional support with rigorous intellectual demands and a measured dose of encouragement when it was needed. Particular thanks are extended to: John Garmat, Paul Epstein, and the others who helped in soliciting potential authors and case materials for review and possible inclusion; Ken Euske, who added his arguments for a field test component and who turned out to be right; Donald Levitan and Thomas Lynch, who shared their thoughts on the teaching and writing of cases; Dennis Heffley and Peter Barth, who read case material in draft and made comments and suggestions; and several other colleagues at The University of Connecticut and elsewhere, who added to the quality of the product and the pleasure of the project. Stephen P. Weitz played his special part with persistence and fortitude, thereby helping to move the manuscript to publication.

It also is gratifying to note the generous assistance and supportive cooperation of: International City Management Association; Municipal Finance Officers Association; National Association of State Budget Officers; National Association of Counties; Rousmaniere Management Associates; Council on Municipal Performance (N.Y.C.); Price Waterhouse and Company; Peat, Marwick, Mitchell and Company; Hartford National Bank; *State and Local Government Review; Midwest Monitor; The Bond Buyer;* the U.S. Departments of Commerce, Housing and Urban Development, and Treasury; the Town of Arlington; and numerous other publishers, associations, agencies, and state and local governments.

In truth, a casebook of this scope would not have been possible at all without the cooperation and collaboration of the many authors, contributors, and participants. Insofar as this casebook contributes to the profession and to the literature, that contribution is theirs.

Carol W. Lewis

I appreciatively acknowledge the contributions of Marion R. Walker, Frank K. Gibson, and my students.

A. Grayson Walker, III

INTRODUCTION

THE CASE, CASE METHOD, AND CASEWORK

PURPOSE

Were the world of public policy a simple place, neatly partitioned into recognizable and routine tasks, cases would be unnecessary, and perhaps remain unwritten. Instead, complex challenges demand sophisticated initiatives and responses from trained, thoughtful professionals with the capacity to recognize a nascent problem, define and refine it, and then resolve it efficiently, effectively, and democratically.[1] On-the-job responsibilities routinely require a sensitive and sensible combination of abstract theory on the one hand and decisive judgment and practical knowledge gleaned from actual experience on the other. We have no confidence that informed analysis and decision-making capacities will in some way guarantee right answers and good decisions in public policy. We are confident, however, that without these skills and capacities, we are guaranteed the opposite.

The case method is one way of providing some of the analytic techniques, technical skills, and problem-solving experiences with which to meet these admittedly formidable expectations. It is a pedagogically flexible means of bridging the distance from the classroom to the field.

THE CASE

A case is a controlled exercise in experiential learning. It is a statement of a problem that leads to a decision. The readers encounter a concrete and frequently complex situation in the form of a real-world problem and the decisions associated with its resolution. Because the readers participate in problem solving under simulated field conditions, they learn by doing—and with minimal personal and public risk.

Nevertheless, the experience is highly controlled. Cases tend to highlight drama and conflict for communication purposes and, therefore, rarely deal with nondecisions, cooperation, or the more mechanical tasks which are part of any job or profession.[2] Often, cases are vivid, detailed, and personalized—peopled with personalities or, sometimes, even with characters. Role conflict and attributed quotes, motivations, or perceptions add drama and human interest, which are useful as learning, retention, and writing tools. After all, a case's power is derived in no small measure from the sense of realism and immediacy communicated to the reader. It has been said that a "case is really a distinct literary form . . . which may have an important

---

[1]According to Woodrow Wilson, "The principles on which to base a science of administration for America must be principles which have democratic policy very much at heart." From "The Study of Administration," *Political Science Quarterly* II,2 (June 1887): 16.

[2]Nondecisions have proven extremely difficult and rarely successful subjects for cases, perhaps because cases revolve around decisions. Similarly, purely hypothetical cases rarely work as well as real-world circumstances, perhaps because the need for detail introduces too many possibilities for error and omission.

analogy to a detective story."[3] Art plays a large part in any drama, and cases may draw upon hypothetical or actual events and personalities and are either attributed or anonymous as to locale and actors, as dictated by the purpose of the case and the need for a reader's involvement.

Stylistically, cases range from the purely descriptive to the highly analytic. The treatment varies according to the preferences of the author and the logic of the circumstances. Some possibilities are: chronology; budget cycle phases; implementation stages; actors, role, agencies; different problem definitions; and, possibly, cost impact or analytic progression, such as toward increasing sophistication. Each case can be approached from any one of several angles. Personal style and training objectives determine whether the writer traces, for example, the roles of selected actors or the formal resolution (statute passed, regulation approved). Bibliographic references are unnecessary and are considered by some as inappropriate to cases.

Another source of control stems from the task or participatory element and the intensity of engagement called for in cases. In general, there are three basic types of cases: the decision-forcing, the evaluative, and the model. Table I.1 lists each case in this casebook by type.

The *decision-forcing* or *issue case* presents a problem, and readers are asked to make recommendations and devise an appropriate solution or set of solutions. The problems may be posed in a straightforward fashion and readers asked to answer them. Alternatively, the problem may be left wholly for readers to identify and then resolve. In the decision-forcing case, participation in problem solving is high and direct but, especially when the problem is left undefined, there is less control over the learning experience. It is, in effect, an exercise performed under simulated but

highly selected field conditions. By posing a problem and then offering a solution, case no. 8 illustrates how this type of case works.

The second type is the *evaluative* or *descriptive case*, which requires readers to assess a decision already made and described in the narrative. While there is less direct involvement in this second type, where a reader is more an observer than an affected participant, the low personal investment offers an opportunity to make low-cost judgments about decisions and to examine their normative and other implications. The very nature of this type of case encourages open-ended discussions and creative approaches to diverse situations. The first evaluative case (no. 2) in this casebook illustrates the approach within the text of the case itself. Both traditional and innovative decision-making techniques and their consequences can be explored in this type of case, even by the novice or less technically-proficient reader. This is a real advantage, given the frequently technical nature of the subject matter. It can be intimidating enough without always demanding decisions from readers, as the decision-forcing type of case does. Both the decision-forcing and evaluative types do demand some degree of active participation in applied problem solving.

The *model* type of case is a more passive learning device. Usually, the problem is presented, the situation is unambiguous, and the reader is walked through, step-by-step, to a resolution. It is a particularly efficient mode of presenting a specific analytic, methodological, or otherwise technical skill in an applied format. Because the learning objective is limited, so too is the learning tool. It is used in this casebook to introduce basic documents (nos. 1, 9, 12), accounting information, and certain methodologies; two of the latter (nos. 19 and 21) are followed by decision-forcing cases that require application of the model's methodology.

In theory, cases can cover a range of topics as broad as the field itself. However, cases usually depict only selected aspects of reality. They do so in order to provide struc-

[3] "McNair on Cases," Intercollegiate Case Clearing House, Boston, Mass., #9-372-303, unpaginated. Reprinted from the *Harvard Business School Bulletin*, July-August 1971.

TABLE 1.1.　Case Types

Case	Type	Case	Type
1	model	20	decision-forcing
2	evaluative	21	model
3	evaluative	22	decision-forcing
4	model	23	evaluative
5	evaluative	24	decision-forcing
6	decision-forcing	25	evaluative
7	decision-forcing	26	evaluative
8	decision-forcing	27	evaluative
9	model	28	model
10	decision-forcing	29 A	evaluative
11	decision-forcing	29 B	decision-forcing
12	model	30	evaluative
13	evaluative	31	decision-forcing
14	evaluative	32	decision-forcing
15	evaluative	33	evaluative
16	model	34	evaluative
17	evaluative	35	evaluative
18	decision-forcing	36 A	decision-forcing
19	model	36 B	evaluative

ture and direction for learning purposes. This artificially but purposefully narrowed focus highlights general principles, certain techniques, and various problem areas. Yet it is almost as difficult to delineate strict boundaries for each case as it is to separate distinct issues and influences in the field. At some point, the boundaries are arbitrary and, in any text, represent no more than better or worse editorial choices.

There is yet another choice that involves "better" or "worse." Surely, it is preferred that a case illustrate the "better" rather than the "worse" approaches and techniques. Cases are designed as concrete, applied, controlled exercises in problem solving. Their substance usually illustrates some basic theme, analytic technique or concept, or some combination of these in an on-the-job setting. The promotion of the better, the more useful, more appropriate—this limitation hardly circumscribes discretion. It seems only reasonable that a "how-to" training tool should build an analytic foundation and body of simulated experience from the overall perspective of "better."

Each case is geared to certain learning objectives and tasks that further control the learning experiences through careful selectivity—the author's, the instructor's, and the reader's. Field tests suggest that the more varied the objectives and tasks in a single case, the more manipulation of data and ideas required, and the more active participation demanded, the more likely are users to evaluate the case as relatively "difficult." Objectives may range from introducing concepts or setting up analytic parameters to undertaking the analysis and resolving the problem. (See Table I.3, on pp. 12, 13.)

CASE STRUCTURE

The world is hardly equivalent to a case study. Should State X index the income tax? Mandate GAAP? Lease or buy that hardware? What's to be done about that audit, that bond rating, cash shortfall, revenue gap? These are closer to the ways in which the field is structured for a practitioner. Although it is expected that the problem-solving skills developed through the case method ultimately will be transferred to the field, it is recognized that even the most elaborate technical training tools are no substitute for on-the-job experiences.

Cases, by their very structure, screen, organize, and simplify information, interactions, and environmental influences. Since it is up to the practitioner to make these choices in the field, repeated exposure to basic analytic techniques and their consequences is a matter of some professional and pedagogical importance. The underlying structure of the case study illustrates the techniques and consequences.

Cases contain five basic structural components: a problem statement; actors and their roles; context and constraints; information, problem-solving methodology, and decision-making process; and the resolution in the form of the decision made or recommended. Of the five, the first and last are the most important. An applied problem and an identifiable, empirical decision distinguish the case as a genre. Furthermore, they are most likely to serve as the core of the discussion. Although it may be argued that the problem is most important because it is the analytic foundation—problem solving begins with problem recognition and definition—problem definition is only one part of problem solving. The five components together not only represent the structural components of a case, but can be usefully applied to analyzing various problem-solving situations. The components all warrant consideration in some detail.

Problem Statement

Every case treats two problems—the generic one and the one specific to the circumstances delineated in the case. The general problem may be fully articulated or, by contrast, never recognized by the actors. The specific problem may be described as an obvious, objective problem, a consensual problem understood by all actors, or as several different problems subjectively defined by individual actors at various stages of the case. Problems change, not only over time as the actors change, but

also across institutions and in response to significant events, over which the actors may exert little or no control. Interrelated problems may be perceived as a single set (suggesting a systemic solution) or never differentiated sufficiently for concrete action. Conversely, a single problem may be broken down to conform to serial steps in, for example, a legally prescribed process or a decision tree. Identifying a problem, defining it, and understanding how it surfaces and changes constitute the first steps toward resolving that problem.

Actors and Their Roles

Few decisions in public life or, for that matter, in any complex organization are made solely by one individual. In fact, there may be a large number of actors, only some of whom hold government positions and all of whose activities are examined from the perspective of the problem and decision. Criteria for identifying main actors include self-perception, ascription by other actors, formal–legal status, or observer recognition.

Organizational relationships, personal characteristics, prior training, past experiences, and other factors which impinge upon an individual's behavior may be as significant in a case as in the field. For the purposes of a case, a particular set of behavioral expectations defines a role. Leader, staff, consultant, innovator, compromiser, mediator—these are just a few of the many possibilities that may arise. Some roles, of course, are specific to budgeting and financial management, such as the spending advocate in a line agency or the naysaying role of the central staff budgeteer. (See case no. 3, for example.)

A case, like any other set of circumstances, may not contain a stable array of actors and roles. The focus may shift, the problem be redefined, or personal turnover may singularly affect the problem and the decision. Discrepancies in perceptions about roles are one important source of contention in human affairs, and budgeting does not escape the human condition, no matter how sophisticated the techniques. These discrepancies affect judgments about predictability, reliability, and trust in interpersonal and institutional relationships. Professional ethics also contribute to the pattern of behavior. The role of ethics is explored in several cases, especially those dealing with the potential conflict among the careerist, technical, and political criteria underlying decision making in the public arena (nos. 2, 3, 6, 7, 11). Furthermore, individuals act on the basis of what they believe to be so, rather than on the basis of some "objective reality" as written, for example, into budgets, work plans, or personnel schedules (nos. 7, 8, 29, 30).

Context and Constraints

No concrete problem can be resolved fully if it is divorced from its environment. This component of a case represents, in a sense, the reader's analysis of the field conditions that affect the problem. Relevant contexts include, but are not limited to: bureaucratic organizations (line agency, central staff); nonhierarchic (intergovernmental, interagency, interbranch, public–private activities); zero sum and non-zero sum contexts; and crises (where time is a significant factor).

Whatever the context, no activity and certainly no public activity is entirely free from constraints. There are three main types of constraints material to budget cases: environmental (e.g., legal, financial, political); organizational (e.g., incentives, autonomy, communication flows); and circumstantial (e.g., timing, personalities). Resources represent the flip side of constraints, since a fundamental constraint on behavior is the resources each main actor can bring to bear and the actor's willingness to do so in the given situation. Any objective or perceived change in context or constraints can affect a problem and, therefore, the decision. Issues such as revenue-raising capacity and inflation illustrate this point.

Information, Problem-Solving Methodology, Decision-Making Processes[4]

Information—appropriate or inappropriate, adequate or inadequate—is always applied to problem solving and decision making. Budgeting and financial management can be defined as a flow of information, so it is hardly surprising that the appropriateness, adequacy, timeliness, formating, reliability, and accuracy of information as well as access to that information are often critical to understanding a problem and developing a solution. (See Table I.2 on pp. 10, 11 for those cases in which the flow of information is particularly important.) Indeed, information may even constitute the substance of the problem (as in nos. 30, 31, 32, for example). Some cases, like field experiences, may contain too much information in the form of either quantified data or description, or both. That information may be extraneous, inconsistent, redundant, or trivial. Selecting the information to be brought to bear in any given case is, therefore, an analytic exercise directly related to problem definition and resolution.

While readers soon recognize that there is never enough information on which to base an unqualified decision, they are trained simultaneously to overcome the immobility that this recognition can induce. The emphasis is on action, while allowing for the possibility of imperfection. Indeed, the human capacity for error may prove to be one of the few limitless resources we have at our command. The key is to find that point of flexibility nestled somewhere between indecision and rigidity. Flexibility is structured right into the case method (see the fifth component— decision or resolution) and summed up as a

---

[4]These three elements are joined here into a single component because they rarely are assigned equal weight in any one case, and they are related logically and frequently empirically. Field tests have indicated that it is difficult and not altogether useful to distinguish strictly among these three elements.

commitment to ongoing evaluation, even of our own decisions.

Another critical element is the political and administrative decision-making processes, by which public budgeting and financial management also can be defined. These processes can be approached either chronologically or logically as part of the analysis. Alternatively, the processes may be considered as part of the context in which problems are identified and resolved or as part of the problem itself (nos. 8, 14, 15, for example). Jurisdictional fragmentation or functional specialization may conjure up the importance of decision-making processes.

The problem-solving methodology must take these processes into account. The methodology itself may reflect a relatively sophisticated, innovative technique or a more traditional, limited strategy which searches for ostensibly reasonable or comfortably familiar alternatives. Readers may find themselves raising questions about the reasonableness and professional responsibility of those seeking million-dollar solutions to hundred-dollar problems. Most options fall somewhere between a unique linear program and doing what one did last year or for the last problem. It may be useful to classify the strategies in various ways, such as adverse or cooperative negotiation, *quid pro quo* bargaining, cost avoidance, optimization, and so on.

Decision or Resolution

This is the action component for the reader, whether the reader devises a solution or assesses various alternatives presented. Frequently, a solution is neither "right" nor "wrong." Rather, the problem-solving methodology and the decision itself are evaluated in terms of more or less appropriate, better or worse. The reference points for the evaluation are a decision's appropriateness to the circumstances (the second, third, and fourth components) and a decision's logical relationship to the problem statement (first component). In decision-forcing cases, the reader

evaluates alternatives and selects one. In evaluative cases, the reader makes a judgment about someone else's decision; when the actual decision, as described in the case, departs from the author's or reader's preferred solution (no. 8, for example), part of the task may be to explain or justify the difference. Whether explicit or implicit, formal or informal, evaluation is part of the case method.[5]

In sum, the structure of the case generates a set of questions: Under these circumstances and given this problem, what should be done? Was the resolution appropriate to the circumstances and useful in dealing with the problem? What other options are available? What does the reader recommend?

THE CASE METHOD

The case method is defined from a reader's viewpoint as an experiential learning device and as a technical training tool. To "do" a case usually means to provide a recommended solution for a decision-forcing case or an evaluation of a decision or resolution for an evaluative case. Frequently, but *not* invariably, the discussion opens with the discussion leader raising one or two questions: "What is the problem here?" or, "What is your recommendation?"

Although readers can work through each case by keeping these questions in mind or by identifying and analyzing each of the five structural components, the analytic method, specific tasks, and group discussions necessarily follow the contours established by the discussion leader. As a highly individualistic, flexible instrument, the case method is best tailored to diverse goals, personal styles, and methodological preferences. Therefore, it can be expected to vary substantially from one situation to another. Just as there is no single

---

[5]The model, the more passive type of case, need not and usually does not directly involve evaluation of alternatives. Rather, a specific technique is applied. Of course, it is possible to evaluate the technique itself.

best way of working through a case, there is no single best way of teaching all cases.

Group interaction is yet another source of variation in using the case method. The case method offers the opportunity to use human nature and group dynamics to create a positive, active, and even enthusiastic training setting for examining this complex, technical subject. This point is illustrated by the fact that, as group dynamics change, the role of the discussion leader changes.

The general task of the discussion leader is to keep the discussion focused on the target topic and to keep the group moving toward a resolution in terms of the specific assignment. A primary role is that of a facilitator who keeps the session on track while promoting a consensus (or at least helping to identify points of absolute disagreement). The facilitator moves the discussion from problem to resolution, but this may be done in different ways. One way is to chart the major steps in the process as they arise in the discussion; another is to note the significant events and the reactions of main actors. Documentation or financial interactions can be traced. A chronological or analytic format may be used. It is also possible simply to outline the case according to structural components or other factors. Yet role playing may develop during the course of the discussion or through manipulation by various actors. Advocates, critics, and compromisers may speak up. Not all the posturing is built into the case; some derives from group interaction. By choosing the role of devil's advocate, a discussion leader may head off satisfaction with a simplistic analysis or a resolution that is considered, for one reason or another, unacceptable. The leader may even have to play pacifier and cool down a heated debate.

Despite the individualism and flexibility associated with the case method, there are three basic steps to follow in sequence: the first is to read the case; the second is to repeat the first; and the third is to repeat the second as the reader begins the analysis.

The pedagogical utility of the method often is most apparent for pre-entry students with limited or no field exposure. These individuals have yet to see themselves with either red or black ink on their hands. While the advantage of simulated field experience for pre-entry students is not being disputed, our field tests suggest that the case method is also meaningful to in-service and mid-career participants. Many are seeking to "tool-up" or to obtain a more precise picture of where they and their work fit into the overall field of public budgeting and financial management. Many regard general theory and abstractions with impatience born of daily pressures and skepticism related to their search for tools immediately or at least potentially applicable to the problems coming across their desks.

Readers' varying background and professional goals, of course, generate different learning needs, but, whatever the objective and whatever the substantive issue, the orientation of each case in this casebook is that of a professional practitioner. The obvious problem is that there are many perspectives to this orientation. The case method is well-suited to dealing with this. Different cases illustrate the different realities readers may face—in the budget bureau, operating agency, legislature, executive office, investment community, and with the taxpaying public.

It is desirable and possible to investigate these perspectives simultaneously and in a way that emphasizes the mutuality among public administrators. As a budgeteer learns to apply procedures to the environment, the actors, and their goals, other public administrators learn to relate public programs to resource allocation and management, to budget strategy, and to financial realities. As an academic field of study and as a profession, public budgeting and financial management draws its meaning from public programs and public goals. These programs and goals in turn are shaped and implemented by professionals in budgeting and financial management. Budgeting and program management need not and, for that matter, should not be isolated from each other. The case method, with its multiple perspectives, is ideal for keeping these activities within a broad public context.

There is an inherent disadvantage to this approach about which case readers should be aware from the outset. Cases deal with a generic problem or principle, as well as with a configuration of circumstances peculiar to an individual case. A case can be used to illustrate or illuminate a general problem or principle. A single case can serve to corroborate dramatically and concretely the general assertion. But it can do no more. To generalize from a single case involves a logical fallacy (perhaps on the order of one of the seven deadly sins) that smacks of stereotypical reasoning. Only the general case informs the particular and guides interpretation and action. The case method is not a series of markers on the road to theory.

The case method *is* an experiential learning device and technical training tool. As such, it has a major, inherent advantage. It emphasizes analytic skills which undoubtedly will be exercised during the course of a career in complex public organizations. It also aims at developing problem-recognition, problem-solving, and decision-making skills. These skills, the "survival skills" of budgeting and financial management no less than of other areas of public administration, are fostered by practice.

THE CASEBOOK

The casebook is organized around the main functional issues into which the study of public budgeting and financial management is traditionally divided. Part I (nos. 1–16) introduces the profession and its basic documents. It presents the decision-making processes and extends the view to include control aspects and intergovernmental dimensions. By the conclusion of Part I, the reader has been familiarized with the control *troika* (the three basic

documents—the budget, financial statement, audit report), the fundamentals of government accounting (also an important part of no. 36A, at the state level), and some of the professional pressures.

Part II (nos. 17–24) looks at some of the techniques and problems of expenditure analysis at various levels of difficulty. Benefit-cost analysis and performance measurement are relatively standard professional tools. Personnel costs and inflation are chosen as especially significant for contemporary budgeting and financial management and are examined in detail. Obviously, both budgeteers and program managers are affected by these factors.

The area of financial management, Part III (nos. 25–32), is relatively new and relatively technical. Risk and credit issues are set out in detail; unfortunately, cash management is touched upon only briefly. Other areas, such as pension administration and tax administration, are omitted; these cases, it seems, have yet to be written. Any definition of professional management surely includes a proactive element, and this is presented in Part III through cases evaluating financial condition and forecasting techniques.

Part IV (nos. 33–36) presents budget reform and cutback management as issues of current concern. The first issue is likely to be with us forever, and the second is unlikely to evaporate in the near future. There is no case on ethics simply because, for readily understandable reasons, no case was forthcoming.

The inclusions and omissions, then, are not foreordained but are the product of editorial decisions, author availability, and field-test processes combined with the hard-hitting realities of page limitations and calendar deadlines. The organization of the casebook suggests the broad parameters of the field. Yet the boundaries change—over time, across jurisdictions, and in response to the actual problem confronting the practitioner.

In addition, there are many other sources from which cases involving public budgeting and financial management can be drawn. Cases on budgeting and financial management are sprinkled throughout general texts on public administration and collections of cases.[6] The Intercollegiate Case Clearing House is another source. (See case no. 18.) Yet another is the multivolume study of case-related resources published by The Curriculum Development Project of Boston University's School of Management.[7] The Public Policy and Management Program for Case/Course Development is a program of the Council on Public Policy and Management (Cambridge, Mass.). If the experience of several professional associations and public agencies is any indicator, case materials will continue to be developed. The International City Management Association has used a variation of "City of Smithville" (no. 32) in its own training; "The Asphalt Paradox" (no. 7) was developed for and used in training programs for the U.S. Department of Housing and Urban Development; and a variant of Minnesota's cutback managment case (no. 36A, B) has been used by the National Association of State Budget Officers in their training. Versions of several other cases in this casebook were initially produced for professional training purposes in one setting or another.

Each chapter focuses primarily on the area described by the chapter heading in the casebook. Because of the fluid boundaries separating issue areas and case topics, many choices were involved. By and large, the choices are supported by the extensive, usually formal field tests which were conducted for 27 of the 36 cases. Field testing involved pre-entry and in-service participants in academic and professional training settings. (Many cases were subjected to repeated testing in different settings.) Participants identified key issues and themes, sometimes before and sometimes after the group discussions. In this way, they both identified new thematic classifications and fine-tuned earlier ones. By drawing heavily upon the field results, we organized the cases into chapters according to function. Because the topics range beyond the single one indicated by a chapter heading. Table I.2 shows cross-references. The table describes each case by key issues; more detailed descriptions can be found in the chapter introduction. Table I.2 also relates each case to general themes that characterize the literature and the profession. These themes include: control, planning, and management orientations of public budgeting and financial management;[8] and the professional, political, intergovernmental, and informational dimensions of decision making.

Each case is geared to certain learning objectives that are incorporated into the learning experience through careful selectivity — the author's, the instructor's, and the reader's. Table I.3 associates nine such learning objectives with the cases. These objectives, like the dominant issues and characteristic themes, were identified and then substantiated

[6]Among these are: David Besnick, *Public Organizations and Policy, An Experiential Approach to Public Policy and Its Execution* (Glenview, Ill.: Scott, Foresman and Co., 1982); Dennis R. Briscoe and Gene S. Leonardson, *Experiences in Public Administration* (North Scituate, Mass.: Duxbury Press, 1980); Robert T. Golembiewski and Michael White, *Cases in Public Management* (Chicago, Ill.: Rand McNally, various editions); Nicholas Henry, *Doing Public Administration: Exercises, Essays, and Cases* (Boston, Mass.: Allyn and Bacon, 1978); Frederick S. Lane, ed., *Managing State and Local Government: Cases and Readings* (New York: St. Martin's Press, 1980); Thomas D. Lynch, ed., *Contemporary Public Budgeting* (New Brunswick, N.J.: Transaction Books, 1981); David R. Morgan, *Managing Urban America: The Politics and Administration of America's Cities* (North Scituate, Mass.: Duxbury Press, 1979); Richard J. Stillman II, ed., *Public Administration, Concepts and Cases*, 2nd ed. (Boston, Mass.: Houghton Mifflin, 1980).

[7]Frederick O'R. Hayes, "Cases in Public Sector Budgeting," Boston University, School of Management, Public Management Program, Curriculum Development Project, 1979. Also by the same author and project, see "Curriculum Needs in Public Sector Budgeting, A Conference Report," April 4, 1980. See also from the same project, Ronald M. Joseph, "Cases in Public Sector Financial Management (except budgeting)," August 1981.

[8]Allen Schick, "The Road to PPB: The Stages of Budget Reform," *Public Administration Review* 26 (December 1966): 243-58.

TABLE 1.2. Key Issues and Themes

Case	Issue	Themes a	b	c	d	e	f	g
1	Introduction to budget document	x						x
2	Political context of effective analysis; job of budgeteer	x	x		x	x	x	x
3	Role and personality conflict; job of finance officers	x			x	x		x
4	Federal budget calendar; budget and accounting cycles	x						
5	Federal appropriations process	x				x	x	
6	State legislative budget office	x	x		x	x		
7	Strategic choice in municipal expenditures; cost avoidance; economy vs. efficiency		x		x	x		x
8	Strategic choice in municipal revenues, uncertainty		x			x	x	x
9	Introduction to financial statement; municipal fund accounting, GAAP	x						x
10	Federal budgeting and accounting concepts	x						
11	Management response to audit, municipal; GAAS	x		x	x	x		x
12	Introduction to audit letter	x						
13	State appropriations process and intergovern-mental financial interdependency	x	x			x	x	x
14	Intergovernmental grants and municipal budget process	x	x	x			x	x
15	State legislature and revenue mandate on municipalities	x				x	x	x
16	Fiscal impact model of mandates for municipalities	x	x	x			x	x
17	Federal benefit-cost analysis of municipal facility and interaction of affected leaders			x	x	x	x	x
18	Technical aspects of benefit-cost analysis of lease/buy decision; discounting	x		x				x
19	Methodology for costing labor contract; roll up, wage and salary, fringe benefits	x	x	x				x
20	Application of #19	x	x	x				x
21	Town's use of concept of inflation and com-municating with the public				x	x		x
22	Methodology for using price indices; inflation		x					x
23	History of performance measurement in municipal budgeting; efficiency and effectiveness			x		x		x

TABLE 1.2.—*Contd.*

Case	Issue	a	b	c	d	e	f	g
24	Effectiveness measures and strategic planning		x	x		x		x
25	Risk; innovation; cost savings			x				
26	Risk; innovation; cost savings			x				
27	Developing countywide program			x				
28	Variance analysis methodology			x				
29 A	Municipal bonding process; disclosure			x				x
29 B	Developing credit ratings			x				x
30	Accuracy and serendipity in budget estimates; need to disaggregate data		x		x	x		x
31	Revenue and expenditure forecasting techniques and problems		x					x
32	Choosing evaluative indices for hypothetical municipality		x	x				x
33	Political criteria for assessing budget reform		x			x		x
34	Planning-budgeting interface and implementation of budget reform		x	x	x	x		x
35	Evaluation of municipal budget process; decentralized and centralized management approaches to budgeting	x		x				x
36 A	State accounting procedures; revenue elasticity; fiscal and economic projections	x	x	x	x			x
36 B	Developing effective cutback strategy		x	x				x

Key: a = control   e = political dimensions
     b = planning   f = intergovernmental dimensions
     c = management   g = role of information
     d = professionalism

through field testing with an evaluation instrument and post-mortem reviews.

Altogether, the cases display different, even competing views of the field of public budgeting and financial management—its processes, principles, problems. There are even different definitions of the subject. This collection would present problems of integration were it not for the fact that the diverse approaches and emphases are not actually contradictory. They rather supplement each other. Public budgeting and financial management, as presented in this casebook, is no more varied or complex than the work world and challenges the professional will encounter.

TABLE 1.3. Learning Tasks and Objectives

Item	Case									
	1	*2*	*3*	*4*	*5*	*6*	*7*	*8*	*9*	*10*
Organize data sets	x						x		x	x
Perform basic calculations							x			x
Operationalize concepts for problem solving (concrete application)	x	x		x	x	x	x	x	x	x
Access information	x							x	x	
Process information	x			x				x	x	
Resolve problem						x	x	x		x
Analyze relationships	x	x	x			x	x	x	x	
Master definitions and/or concepts	x	x	x	x	x	x	x	x	x	x
Apply analytic method or technique										

Item	Case									
	11	*12*	*13*	*14*	*15*	*16*	*17*	*18*	*19*	*20*
Organize data sets						x		x	x	x
Perform basic calculations						x		x	x	x
Operationalize concepts for problem solving (concrete application)	x		x	x	x	x	x	x	x	x
Access information	x					x		x	x	x
Process information	x					x		x	x	x
Resolve problem	x							x		x
Analyze relationships	x	x	x	x	x	x	x		x	x
Master definitions and/or concepts	x	x	x	x	x	x	x	x	x	x
Apply analytic method or technique						x		x	x	x

TABLE 1.3.— *Contd.*

Item	21	22	23	24	25	26	27	28	29A	29B
					Case					
Organize data sets		x						x		x
Perform basic calculations		x						x		
Operationalize concepts for problem solving (concrete application)	x	x	x	x			x	x	x	x
Access information	x									x
Process information		x		x				x		x
Resolve problem		x		x						x
Analyze relationships	x	x	x	x	x	x	x	x	x	x
Master definitions and/or concepts	x	x	x	x	x	x	x	x	x	x
Apply analytic method or technique		x						x		x

Item	30	31	32	33	34	35	36A	36B	
				Case					
Organize data sets	x	x	x				x	x	
Perform basic calculations		x					x	x	
Operationalize concepts for problem solving (concrete application)	x	x	x			x	x	x	
Access information		x			x		x	x	
Process information	x	x	x				x	x	
Resolve problem		x	x				x		
Analyze relationships	x	x	x	x	x	x	x	x	
Master definition and/or concepts		x	x			x	x	x	
Apply analytic method or technique		x	x				x	x	

CHAPTER ONE

THE BUDGET AND BUDGETEERS

A behavioral definition of public budgeting and financial management suggests a broad view of the profession, that is, what budgeteers and finance officers do. Figures 1.1 and 1.2 depict the framework of this central staff function in local jurisdictions.[1] There are, however, other participants whose primary job responsibilities revolve around tracking, allocating, or analyzing the financial, labor, or material resources that are budgeted. Some line agencies have an individual designated as "budget officer" or a unit responsible for drawing up the agency budget request, providing supporting analysis, and overseeing implementation and reporting. Many of these individuals have perceived their work as part of the profession of budgeting and financial management rather than as only, or even primarily, associated with the line agency.[2]

The work of budgeting and financial management is not a static set of tasks fixed for all time by formal organizational lines. The field has grown at least as fast as government, itself. As government has expanded in intricacy and scope, the budget and finance function has also expanded in many jurisdictions as the central, overarching staff. Evaluation, performance auditing, planning, program research, data processing, and a full range of other administrative and support services may fall under departmental auspices. On the other hand, when competition for scarce resources increases, resource allocation becomes a singular, generalized concern and the function (along with its staff) "enjoys" added preeminence. It is truly a "survival skill."

It is the budget that is at the center of all this activity and concern. The first case introduces the budget as a document and poses the basic questions with which budget analysis begins. As a model case, "How to Read a Budget" relies upon a traditional mode of analysis that focuses on "the significant difference."[3] It walks the reader through a modified

[1]See also Lennox L. Moak and Kathryn W. Killian, *Operating Budget Manual* (Chicago, Ill.: Municipal Finance Officers Association, 1963), pp. 30-33.

[2]Robert A. Walker, "William A. Jump: The Staff Officer as a Personality," *Public Administration Review* 14 (Autumn 1954): pp. 233-246.

[3]This approach is sometimes referred to as "incrementalism," which is the subject of a now vast literature. See especially Aaron Wildavsky, *The Politics of the Budgetary Process* (Boston, Mass.: Little Brown, various editions).

program budget, that is, a program budget supplemented with line-item detail.

The role of the budgeteer is introduced in the second case, "Budget Examination and Politics." As the first evaluative case, it contains illustrative observations within the text itself. The case describes what

FIGURE 1.1.   General organization chart, department of finance.

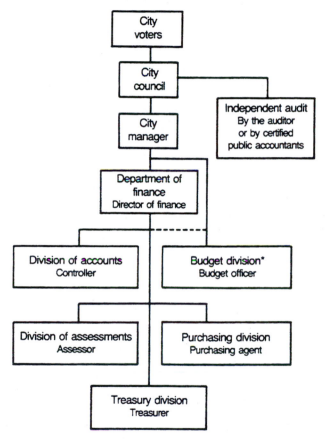

*The dotted line between the director of finance and the budget officer indicates that the latter is often primarily responsible to the chief administrator, being physically located in the finance department to prevent the duplication of records. In many cities the finance director handles the budget.

Source: Leonard I. Ruchelman, "The Finance Function in Local Government," in *Management Policies in Local Government Finance*, ed. by J. Richard Aronson and Eli Schwartz (Washington, D.C.: International City Management Association, 1981), p. 18. Courtesy of International City Management Association.

may very well be the inescapable tension between political and technical criteria in decision making. Certainly, the professional budgeteer works precisely at that interface between politics and analysis. The capacity to deal with ambiguity and competing standards and to entertain limited expectations about the impact of analysis is presented as an important professional asset.

The last case in this chapter describes an interplay of individuals in an environment characterized by fragmented authority. There are

FIGURE 1.2. Detailed organization chart, department of finance, showing typical functions and activities.

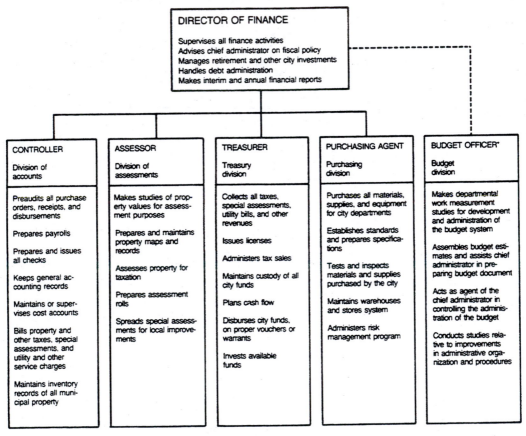

*The dotted line between the director of finance and the budget officer indicates that the latter is often primarily responsible to the chief administrator, being physically located in the finance department to prevent the duplication of records. In many cities the finance director handles the budget.

Source: Leonard I. Ruchelman, "The Finance Function in Local Government," in *Management Policies in Local Government Finance,* ed. by J. Richard Aronson and Eli Schwartz (Washington, D.C.: International City Management Association, 1981), p. 18. Courtesy of International City Management Association.

many participants, many perspectives, and many goals to budgeting and financial management. It is reasonable, then, to expect some exposure to role conflict, interpersonal conflict, and goal conflict. The case suggests that a skill might be developed to avoid conflict or to handle it.

All three cases involve local government, which dominates the field by sheer numbers. Other cases dealing with budget and financial management as a profession include nos. 6, 7, 11, 17, and 30.

1

How to Read a Budget *

An operating budget is a reflection of a government's financial plans—in its basic form, a listing of anticipated revenues and planned expenditures in the coming year. Although in a more complex form, a budget may contain a great volume of supporting information, readers of budgets should remember that no amount of this information changes the basic form, which should make any budget easy to read and understand. The degree to which it clearly presents its basic message is a measure of the value of the budget document.

Although supporting information is intended to add a more thorough understanding of the government's plan and purpose, it can and often does confuse the reader. However, the absence of supporting information leaves the reader uninformed and dubious about the budget's content and may spur his inquiry. We will explore in this chapter the elements of a representative budget document,[1] the type of information it presents and omits, and the deductions a reader can draw from it, together with examples of analysis that the reader could conduct.

This chapter is not intended to pass judgment on budget types or present alternate forms. It is intended only to help you, as the reader, better understand the budget example.

*By James D. Carney and Stanley Schoenfeld, Peat, Marwick, Mitchell & Co. Courtesy of Peat, Marwick, Mitchell & Co.

[1]A modified program budget, prepared for a city of 200,000 people, has been used in the various exhibits in this chapter. Despite its programmatic structure, this budget can also be viewed organizationally, because at the lowest level, the program elements are identical with organizational elements. The example also lists line item data by object of expenditure. Although other types of exhibits could have illustrated a traditional line item approach or a classic program budget, the selected budget contains elements of both and is representative of most budget documents in current use.

ELEMENTS OF A BUDGET DOCUMENT

Budget documents come in all sizes and formats, ranging from concise pamphlets to tomes several inches thick. Fortunately for the reader, they almost all contain four basic sections.

Budget Message

The budget message is generally a narrative preface to the document highlighting the economic climate, community service priorities, special circumstances, general constraints on budget building, and key changes in the budget, both financial and programmatic. It is normally prepared and signed by the government's chief executive, elected or appointed, and is often the only narrative analysis of the planned change included in the budget. The other sections of a budget are most typically in tabular form.

Summary Schedules

This section usually immediately follows the budget message and contains several schedules summarizing the budget. The exact number and type of schedules included will vary with legal requirements, which classification structure in use (i.e., program, organization, line item), and with the preferences of the government.

The following summary schedules are the most commonly used:

> property tax calculation (Exhibit 1)
> total revenues and expenditures (Exhibit 2)
> total expenditures by classification structure (Exhibits 3, 4)
> total revenues by source (Exhibit 7)
> expenditures by fund—used in govern-

ments with multiple fund structures (Exhibit 9)

In addition to these five general summaries, individual budgets may often contain other summary schedules of data related to items such as budgeted positions and prior-year fund balances.

For comparison, the document will often show both appropriated and actual prior-year budgets and expenditures, if available.

Detailed Schedules

This section presents the most detailed data. The government normally organizes detailed schedules according to the classification structures it uses. These structures will generally be one or more of the following:

program — type of service delivered (e.g., fire protection, snow removal)
organization — unit of organization delivering services (e.g., public works department, crime prevention unit)
object of expenditure (line item) — type of goods and services to be purchased (e.g., personnel services, office supplies)

In addition to planned expenditures by major classification (Exhibit 8), these schedules may furnish successively lower levels of detail within classifications (Exhibits 5, 6). They may also display expanded information on intended results (service objectives), the current year's achievements, and the planned method of reaching the service objectives (the service plan). Sometimes they show revenues generated by the program or department or expenditure budgeted elsewhere but attributable to the program (e.g., fringe benefits). Comparative data on prior budgets and requested budgets are also generally supplied.

The following detailed schedules are among the more commonly used:

Exhibit 8 — Detailed budget by classification (program and object): summary of a program by sub-programs.

Exhibit 5 — Detailed budget by classification (program and object): summary and sub-program by program element.
Exhibit 6 — Detailed budget by classification (program, organization and object): lowest level of detail — program element, department, object detail.

Supplemental Data

This last section contains any additional information the government chooses. Placed here because it does not fit appropriately into other sections, it will vary widely from government to government. The most common supplemental schedules are

unappropriated funds — a schedule of revenues and expenditures for a self-supporting activity not formally budgeted, such as an airport.
ordinances — the enabling legislation for adopting the budget, authorizing expenditures and levying taxes.
capital outlays — a schedule of planned capital outlays, which may also include the funding source (i.e., bonds, notes, or current revenue).
debt service — a schedule of debts, planned interest, and principal payments.
trust and agency funds — a schedule of assets held for others under specific instructions. These assets may include funds for retirement systems or funds donated to a local government to purchase something as a commemoration.
grants — a schedule of revenues received from outside sources (usually a higher level of government) to undertake specific programs or activities for a fixed period of time. These may also not be formally budgeted.

HOW TO UNDERSTAND A BUDGET

The title *How to Read a Budget* implies more than just a cursory review of the document. It really means *How to Read and Understand a Bud-*

get. To understand a budget, the reader needs to analyze its contents, but such analysis need not imply sophisticated techniques. Indeed, the reader can readily understand a great deal without much effort. The observation notes included with each exhibit are examples of very basic but important analysis a reader can use to understand a budget. By synthesizing various items of information, identifying gaps in data, and noting unexplained changes, the reader can draw even further deductions.

When analyzing a budget, keep the following general rules in mind:

Focus your examination on the largest dollar amounts. Small items, unless of specific interest, are not material to understanding.

Look at absolute as well as relative percentage changes. Although an item may increase by only seven percent, if the amount is in the millions the change can be very significant.

If you cannot find information on an area, ask about it; don't assume you lack the skills to locate it. The data may not be supplied when perhaps it should be. Indeed, it may be intentionally omitted to make understanding more difficult.

Look for trends over several years. Year-to-year changes, both large and small, may be misleading since they can be caused by one-time circumstances.

Review revenues as well as expenditures. They are equally important.

Try to understand something about the background of each item. Certain revenues, such as sales tax receipts, grow with inflation and the economy. Others, such as license fees, will tend to be flat in the absence of specific changes. Expenditures in certain areas, such as education, may be largely for personnel, but in others, such as road maintenance, the distribution should be balanced with material and equipment purchases. Any deviation from the expected should be questioned.

QUESTIONS

The general questions that the budget reader should attempt to answer to better understand it are examined below. They are:

1. How is the property tax rate changing?
2. Is the budget in balance, and has it been balanced in prior years?
3. How is the program expenditure plan changing?
4. Which department expenditure plan is changing the most?
5. Which program element is changing the most?
6. What is happening in the program element expenditure plan?
7. How is the revenue plan changing?
8. How are the individual revenue sources changing?

Each of these questions is answered for the sample budget. The analysis should be read in conjunction with the cited exhibit. An analytical reading of a budget will usually raise questions that cannot be fully answered by reading the budget alone; sometimes the budget message may supply the answer, but sometimes it does not. In order to facilitate scanning, the material is formatted as follows:

question
exhibit where data may be found
comments regarding analysis
unanswered questions (if any)

The exhibits include notes defining elements of the schedule and observations derived from a careful reading. (See pp. 25–35.)

1. HOW IS THE PROPERTY TAX RATE CHANGING? [See Exhibit 1.]

Comments:

The Property Tax Calculation schedule shows that the overall combined tax rate is increasing by $2.94 per thousand dollars of assessment, or a 4.3 percent increase. It shows that the city has two separate tax rates, one for general city purposes and the other for education. Although the general city rate is declining by $1.86 per thousand (9.2 percent), note that the actual tax levied ($13,035,648) declines by only 7.4 percent. This difference is because total assessments are increasing by 1.9 percent, enlarging the base for the rate calculation. Indeed, as happened in 1979-80, the rate can decline while the total tax levy increases.

In addition, the combined tax rate is increasing, because the education property tax rate is increasing by $4.80 per thousand (9.9 percent).

By looking at other data on the schedule, another fact becomes apparent. While both the general city and school *expenditures* are increasing, only general city *revenues* are increasing; school *revenues* are not. Therefore, all education expenditure increases must be funded through a local property tax rate increase.

Unanswered Questions:

What is the dollar impact of the tax rate on an average property owner in the community?

How does the tax rate compare to other neighboring communities?

Why are school revenues declining?

Can education expenditures be further reduced to minimize the tax rate increase?

How does the tax rate increase compare to other measures of change, such as, (a) added or reduced service? (b) increases in school population? (c) inflation rate fluctuations?

2. IS THE BUDGET IN BALANCE AND HAS IT BEEN BALANCED IN PRIOR YEARS? [See Exhibit 2.]

Comments:

A budget is balanced when planned expenditures equal anticipated revenues; most governments are required by law to submit a balanced budget. The manager's budget column shows that total revenues and total expenditures are equal, and hence the sample budget is balanced, as was also the prior year's budget (1979-80).

The actual operating results for 1978-79, however, show that revenues exceeded expenditures by $1.47 million. This differential does not mean the budget for that year was out of balance; it means rather that the actual result of the year's operations was a surplus of revenues over expenditures, generally a positive indication of performance.

Similar information could also have been estimated for 1979-80, but it was not. Such an estimate of actual operating results for the preceding year would be useful in assessing how realistic the new budget is.

Unanswered Questions:

What items legally must be budgeted?

Are any expenditures and revenues not budgeted?

How was the prior-year surplus achieved?

3. HOW IS THE PROGRAM EXPENDITURE PLAN CHANGING? [See Exhibit 3.]

Comments:

The schedule entitled *Summary of Budget by Program and Sub-program* is the most useful of the summary schedules available to answer this question. It displays areas of expenditure by service with a reasonable amount of detail. Total expenditures increased by $7,091,709 (7.4%) compared to 1979-80.

By examining the change in each program and within programs and sub-programs the reader can begin to isolate those areas where significant changes are occurring. For example, when comparing program areas to those in 1979-80, five are increasing, two are declining and one is new. Of those, public safety has increased the greatest percentage (18.8%). When examining the sub-programs within public safety, two areas emerge with major increases–fire prevention and control (25.8%) and traffic safety (53.2%). Note, however, that in absolute dollars, fire protection's increase is much larger–$1.5 million compared to $300,000 for traffic safety. In addition, both programs had lower budgets in 1979–80 when compared to actual expenditures of 1978–79. This discrepancy may suggest that these areas were underbudgeted in 1979–80 and that the current increase is a two-year catch-up attempt. By examining each program, the reader may isolate areas for more careful review of their detailed budgets.

Unanswered Questions:

Is the new program area being added to the budget or is that item a separate identification of a program previously grouped elsewhere? If so, why?

Why are the transportation and public safety administration sub-programs eliminated, and where are these expenditures now reflected?

4. WHICH DEPARTMENT EXPENDITURE PLAN IS CHANGING THE MOST? [See Exhibit 4]

Comments: (See also Exhibit 8.)

The schedule of departmental expenditures ignores programs and sub-programs. It is worth noting that "finance" is both the title of a department and a sub-program (see Exhibit 3). This is unnecessarily confusing.

The Community Development Department has grown 20.5 percent over 1979–80, although much less than the departmental request, which was an increase of 46.6 percent over 1979–80. This change suggests that functions and services are being added.

Two departments, Legislative and Law, show higher manager's budgets than the departments requested, although by small amounts. Managers are usually faced with limiting spending plans or at least making choices between competing needs, so it is unusual to see increases in departmental requests unless the government is moving an activity from one department to another. The occurrence is sufficiently unusual to warrant further inquiry.

The Parks, Recreation, and Conservation Department has had its budget reduced for two consecutive years, although it requested a substantial increase. The planned reduction may imply a reduction of service and/or a deferral of maintenance.

Unanswered Question:

What services will the new Community Services Department provide?

5. WHICH PROGRAM ELEMENT (LOWEST ORGANIZATIONAL UNIT IN BUDGET) IS CHANGING THE MOST? [See Exhibit 5.]

Comments:

There are four program elements within the Finance Department: Purchasing, which is increasing at a 19.1 percent rate, the Comptroller's Office which is increasing at a 14 percent rate, and Budget and Assessment, which are increasing at very modest rates. While the manager's increase in the budget sub-element is only 1.5 percent, the increase in 1979–80 is 62.1 percent over 1978–79. A change of that magnitude usually implies either an increase in staff or a transfer of staff and function from one organization to another.

The forecasted expenses for 1979–80 are 4.7 percent less than the adopted budget. Most of that reduction is in personal services—indeed, the forecasted expenses for personal services for 1979–80 are less than the actual expenses in 1978–79.[2] The manager's budget shows a decrease on each line from the department request.

[2]The manager's budget is 12.5 percent higher than the 1979–80 budget but 18.4 percent higher than the forecasted expenses.

Unanswered Questions:

What did the manager eliminate from the department request?

What staffing or organizational change resulted in the personal service budget fluctuation?

6. WHAT IS HAPPENING IN THE PROGRAM ELEMENT EXPENDITURE PLAN? [See Exhibit 6.]

Comments:

The information for program elements is the lowest level of detail in the budget, and is also for the organization unit. Exhibit 6 shows the purchasing unit's budget. The commentary indicates that the print shop has been added to this program element, which may account for the almost thirty-four percent increase. However, no definite statement is made.

The largest increases are in wages, indicating that people are being added to the unit.

Interestingly, the final budget is higher than that requested, suggesting that the decision to add the print shop was made by the city manager and not the department. Note also that the miscellaneous categories are being dropped.

Finally, the fact that the forecast expenses are significantly lower than budgeted in 1979–80 suggests that positions were budgeted but not filled.

7. HOW IS THE REVENUE PLAN CHANGING? [See Exhibit 2.]

Comments:

In addition to the changes in property taxes discussed in question 1 above, other revenue sources are changing, and, in fact, the change in the property tax in part depends on what happens to all other revenues, since property tax is used to balance revenues with expenditures.

Generally the other revenue sources fall into four categories:

Special taxes — These are taxes from which the government receives all or a portion of the receipts. The government may or may not control the tax rate and base. Most tax receipts are subject to economic conditions.

State and federal aid — These are revenues received for both general and special purposes. Most often they will be controlled by the government providing the funds.

Department revenues — These revenues, usually controllable, result from department operations, including fees, charges, fines, etc.

Other revenues and credits — These revenues and credits do not fall into any of the above categories.

Of the six other revenue categories shown in Exhibit 2, four are increasing while two are declining. The decline in *state and federal aid* — *education* is interesting because overall, *state and federal aid* — *general* is increasing sharply. This discrepancy may indicate that aid to education is being capped or limited for some reason. The second declining revenue source is *revenue from other funds*.

Unanswered Questions:

Why is aid to education declining, especially in view of the increases in other aid? Are revenues declining in all other funds, or only in specific funds?

8. HOW ARE THE INDIVIDUAL REVENUE SOURCES CHANGING? [See Exhibit 7.]

Comments:

To answer the above question, each category of revenue should be reviewed. In Exhibit 7 all categories of general fund revenue are increasing, with state and federal aid increasing the most, proportionately. However, within this category, most sources are stable, and only state revenue sharing is increasing dramatically. It is also the largest source of state and federal aid.

Under special taxes, a new real estate transfer tax is planned. The sales and use tax, the largest of all general fund revenues, is increasing at 10.4 percent.

Departmental revenues, the smallest category, is relatively stable, with several new types of revenues shown.

The other revenues and credits category has perhaps the largest number of changes. We can note two new revenue sources, one of which, maintenance of state and county roads, should perhaps be shown under state aid or departmental revenues. Most significantly, sale of real estate is large and increasing. Revenues from the sale of any assets are one-time revenues and because of this, are not wise to budget as a revenue source, especially if significant. The following year either an asset of similar worth must be sold or another source must be found to replace the revenues. The city may have a problem next year. Finally, the reserve for uncollected taxes, which is used to offset delinquency, is increasing more than the total tax levy, indicating that greater tax delinquency is expected.

Unanswered Questions:

What is the exact source of the new revenues shown?

What is the real estate to be sold and how will this revenue be replaced or offset next year?

Why is state revenue sharing increasing when other aid is stable?

Once these questions have been answered, the budget reader can feel certain in identifying:

how many dollars the government is spending for what services
what has changed significantly from year to year
what factors most affect revenues and expenditures
what additional questions still may need answering

Two additional exhibits (Exhibits 8 and 9) have been included.

EXHIBIT 1
Property Tax Calculation

Schedule shows the calculation of the tax rates for the general city and education. The latter is broken out by law.

Assessments—increasing

Education revenues declining causing tax rate to increase

Tax rate — City's rate declining

Education rate increasing

PROPERTY TAX CALCULATION

(City Fiscal Year July 1, 1980 – June 30, 1981)

	1978-79 Actual	1979-80 Budget	1980-81 Manager's Budget
① General City Appropriations	$47,302,801	49,365,935	52,500,894
② Less: General City Revenues	33,348,147	35,285,877	39,465,246
③ Tax Levy - General City	13,954,654	14,080,058	13,035,648
④ Assessed Valuation - City	685,721,795	694,564,649	708,207,188
⑤ Tax Rate - General City	$20.35	$20.27	18.41
① Education Appropriations	43,193,746	46,550,000	50,506,750
② Less: Education Revenues	12,415,000	12,297,867	12,135,921
③ Tax Levy - Education	30,778,748	34,252,133	38,370,779
④ Assessed Valuation - Education	697,776,795	706,709,649	720,338,988
⑤ Tax - Education	$44.11	$48.47	$53.27
⑥ Combined Tax Rate	$64.46	$68.74*	$71.68*

*Note: Tax Rate based on $1,000 of assessed valuation.

II

DESCRIPTION:

To estimate the tax rate the schedule takes the total expenditures ① less the total revenues excluding the property tax level ② to compute the amount of tax to be raised ③ This is divided into the total assessment ④ for the tax to establish the tax rate per $1000 of assessment ⑤

Note that Education's assessments are higher than the general city due to fewer exemptions

The two rates are summed to show an approximate rate per $1000 ⑥

EXHIBIT 2

Summary of Revenues and Expenditures

Schedule summarizes total revenues and expenditures as well as the change in the tax rate.

DESCRIPTION:

Title of schedule should describe content

Comparative data for two years

Revenue Sources

Expenditure by program

OBSERVATIONS:

Property tax for city purposes is declining

Property tax for education is increasing

State and Federal aid to education is declining

Revenue from other funds is declining

Revenues equal expenses—budget is balanced

Major expenditure change areas are:

Education

Public Safety

Undistributed

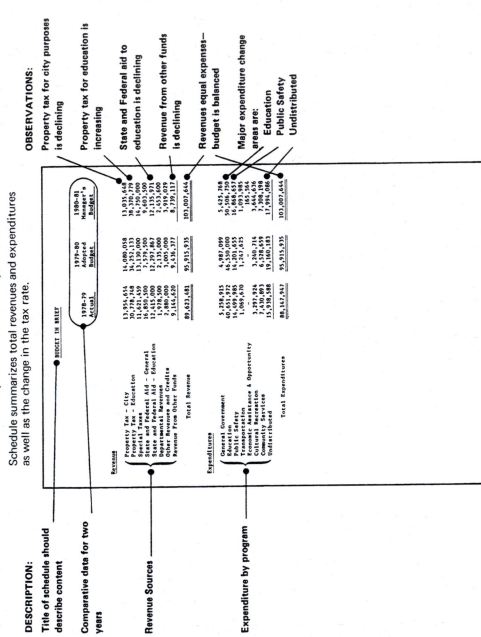

BUDGET IN BRIEF

	1978-79 Actual	1979-80 Adopted Budget	1980-81 Manager's Budget
Revenue			
Property Tax - City	13,954,654	14,080,058	13,035,648
Property Tax - Education	30,778,748	34,252,133	38,370,779
Special Taxes	11,621,459	13,130,000	14,750,000
State and Federal Aid – General	16,850,500	7,579,500	9,603,500
State and Federal Aid – Education	12,415,000	12,297,867	12,135,971
Departmental Revenues	1,978,500	2,135,000	2,453,600
Other Revenues and Credits	2,880,000	3,005,000	3,919,029
Revenue From Other Funds	9,144,620	9,436,377	8,739,117
Total Revenue	89,623,481	95,915,935	103,007,644
Expenditures			
General Government	5,258,915	4,987,099	5,425,768
Education	40,651,972	46,550,000	50,506,750
Public Safety	14,499,985	14,201,655	16,868,959
Transportation	1,069,670	1,247,635	1,093,985
Economic Assistance & Opportunity			165,564
Cultural Recreation	3,297,924	3,240,714	3,644,636
Community Services	7,430,893	6,528,659	7,308,198
Undistributed	15,938,588	19,160,183	17,994,086
Total Expenditures	88,147,947	95,915,935	103,007,644

EXHIBIT 3

Expenditure by Program

Schedule shows expenditure by program only. It does not distinguish fund or organization.

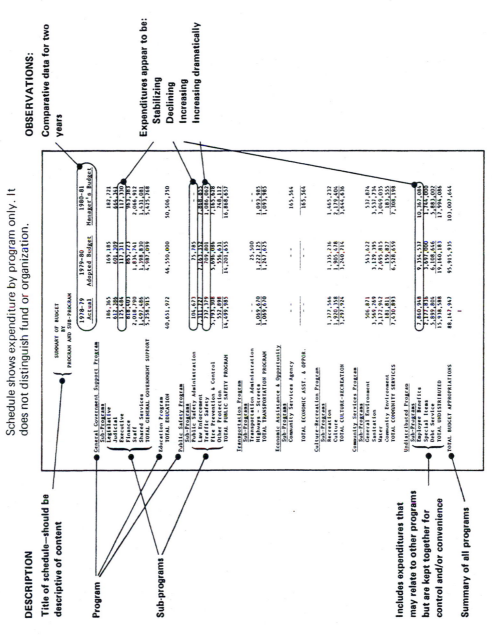

DESCRIPTION

Title of schedule—should be descriptive of content

Program

Sub-programs

Includes expenditures that may relate to other programs but are kept together for control and/or convenience

Summary of all programs

SUMMARY OF BUDGET BY PROGRAM AND SUB-PROGRAM

	1978-79 Actual	1979-80 Adopted Budget	1980-81 Manager's Budget
General Government Support Program			
Sub-Programs			
Legislative	186,365	169,185	182,721
Judicial	612,286	601,309	664,361
Executive	125,484	117,311	117,330
Finance	818,401	865,773	961,383
Staff	2,018,790	1,834,741	2,066,912
Shared Services	1,497,486	1,398,830	1,431,081
TOTAL GENERAL GOVERNMENT SUPPORT	5,258,915	4,987,099	5,425,768
Education Program			
TOTAL EDUCATION	40,651,972	46,550,000	50,506,750
Public Safety Program			
Sub-Programs			
Public Safety Administration	104,673	75,785	-
Law Enforcement	311,721	7,161,152	7,868,855
Traffic Safety	732,379	709,801	1,086,062
Fire Prevention & Control	5,793,308	5,696,086	7,165,678
Other Protection	552,898	556,631	748,112
TOTAL PUBLIC SAFETY PROGRAM	14,499,985	14,201,655	16,868,657
Transportation Program			
Sub-Programs			
Transportation Administration	-	25,500	-
Highways - Streets	1,069,670	1,222,125	1,093,985
TOTAL TRANSPORTATION PROGRAM	1,069,670	1,267,625	1,093,985
Economic Assistance & Opportunity			
Sub-Programs			
Community Services Agency	-	-	165,564
TOTAL ECONOMIC ASST. & OPPOR.	-	-	165,564
Culture-Recreation Program			
Sub-Programs			
Recreation	1,377,566	1,335,236	1,465,232
Culture	1,920,358	1,905,478	2,179,404
TOTAL CULTURE-RECREATION	3,297,924	3,240,714	3,644,636
Community Services Program			
Sub-Programs			
General Environment	506,871	563,622	537,874
Sanitation	3,569,269	3,129,395	3,537,734
Water	3,172,942	2,695,815	3,049,035
Community Environment	181,811	159,827	183,555
TOTAL COMMUNITY SERVICES	7,430,893	6,528,659	7,308,198
Undistributed Program			
Sub-Programs			
Employee Benefits	7,860,948	9,354,537	10,367,084
Special Items	2,177,835	1,697,000	1,744,000
Debt Service	5,899,804	6,108,646	5,883,002
TOTAL UNDISTRIBUTED	15,938,588	19,160,183	17,994,086
TOTAL BUDGET APPROPRIATIONS	88,147,947	95,915,935	103,007,664

EXHIBIT 4

Expenditure by Department
(Organization Unit)

DESCRIPTION:

Organization unit

Schedule shows departmental expenditures for the general fund only. Expenditures from other funds are shown in Exhibit 9. Expenditures by Fund; but not by department, an inconsistency in preparation.

OBSERVATIONS:

An additional element of comparative data as compared to Exhibit 2

Growing

Stabilized

Declining for two years

Departmental requests have been reduced by over $2 million

New department

Summary of General Fund expenditures by department

GENERAL FUND
DEPARTMENTAL EXPENDITURES

Departments	1978-79 Actual	1979-80 Adopted Budget	1980-81 Dept. Request	1980-81 Manager's Budget
Legislative	380,122	$ 368,886	405,928	417,008
Executive	312,236	291,645	389,810	325,431
Finance	1,060,141	990,653	1,173,691	1,160,944
Assessment	183,395	168,700	203,098	175,841
Development	576,295	649,591	952,428	782,846
Law	307,980	311,769	333,671	338,571
Civil Service	75,811	65,291	77,984	67,293
Judiciary	612,386	601,309	742,051	664,341
Public Works	6,339,206	5,995,660	6,923,592	6,101,655
Youth Services Agency	363,275	351,732	355,104	353,604
Veterans Service	31,684	31,897	36,693	36,429
Engineering	400,158	371,259	640,686	385,550
Budget	63,163	102,413	103,994	103,993
Parks, Recreation & Conservation	1,366,424	1,325,236	1,689,624	1,314,032
Police/Fire	13,987,344	13,686,003	16,521,260	14,877,032
Community Services	0	0	165,564	165,564
TOTAL	26,059,620	$25,312,044	30,725,178	27,270,132

VII

EXHIBIT 5

Detail Budget by Classification (Program and Object)

Schedule shows expenditures for subprogram by line item and program element.

DESCRIPTION:
Department

OBSERVATIONS:

The Finance program is comprised of four organization units

Budget had a major increase in prior year

SUMMARY OF SUB-PROGRAM EXPENDITURES

PROGRAM: GENERAL GOVERNMENT SUPPORT	Bk. 1000	Department FINANCE			
SUB-PROGRAM: FINANCE	Bk. 1300	Fund GENERAL		Bk. A	

MAJOR OBJECT OF EXPENSES	1978-79 ACTUAL EXPENSES	1979-80 ADOPTED BUDGET	FORECAST EXPENSES	1980-81 DEPARTMENT REQUEST	MANAGER'S BUDGET
100 - Personal Services	725,496	753,978	716,850	877,839	848,878
200 - Equipment	9,351	0	0	0	0
300 - Materials & Supplies	6,680	8,575	7,675	8,975	8,375
400 - Other Expenses	76,876	103,170	97,305	109,685	106,130
TOTALS	818,403	865,723	821,830	996,499	963,383

COMMENTARY

The Finance Sub-Program provides a full range of financial and related services required for the operation of the City government.

Program Element Expenditures

Element Code	Program Element	1978-79 Actual Expenses	1979-80 Adopted Budget	1980-81 Manager's Budget
1315	Comptroller Office	481,760	497,602	567,993
1340	Budget	63,163	102,413	103,993
1350	Purchasing	90,085	97,008	115,556
1355	Assessment	183,395	168,700	125,841
	Total Finance	818,403	865,723	963,383

FORM 03

A19

Program element code

Program element

The units within the Finance Department

29

EXHIBIT 6

Detailed Schedule by Classification
(Program, Organization & Object)

Lowest level of detail in budget: program element, department, object detail

DESCRIPTION:

Program Element

Department

Budget year salary range for positions

Number of individuals in position

Position Title

Civil Service Pay Grade

OBSERVATIONS:

- Data presented for first time by organization
- Lowest level of detail provided in budget

This data shown for information. Does not summarize into expenditure data presented

SUMMARY OF PROGRAM ELEMENT EXPENDITURES

PROGRAM	NO.	Program Element		NO.	1350
GENERAL GOVERNMENT SUPPORT	1000	PURCHASING		NO.	
SUB-PROGRAM	NO.	Department	FINANCE		
FINANCE	1300	Fund	GENERAL		A

| | 1978-79 | 1979-80 | | | 1980-81 | |
MAJOR OBJECT OF EXPENSES	ACTUAL EXPENSES	ADOPTED BUDGET	FORECAST EXPENSES	DEPARTMENT REQUEST	MANAGER'S BUDGET
100 - Personal Services	80,458	85,083	75,570	97,776	163,876
200 - Equipment	278	0	0	0	0
300 - Materials & Supplies	2,166	2,500	2,100	2,330	2,200
400 - Other Expenses	7,183	9,425	8,660	8,670	9,480
TOTALS	90,085	97,008	86,330	108,796	115,556

COMMENTARY

The Purchasing Office procures all materials, supplies, equipment and services for the City Government and serves as the Administrative Staff for the Board of Contract and Supply. The Purchasing Office: prepares specifications and advertisements for all public bids, solicits and accepts all public advertised bids, acts as secretary in the preparation of all agendas for meetings of the Board of Contract and Supply, prepares all purchasing contracts, and administers all purchasing contracts. Print shop functions have been assumed by this program element.

1980-81 Salary Schedule

| No. | Title | Grade | Range | |
			From	To
1	Director of Purchasing	VIII	21,000	23,378
2	Assistant Purchasing Agent	V	11,003	13,378
1	Senior Clerk	IV	7,718	9,234
1	Senior Typist	IV	7,718	9,234
1	Junior Stenographer	III	7,718	9,234
1	Junior Typist		7,174	8,524
1	Printer			11,700
1	Printer-Helper			9,900

30

EXHIBIT 6 (Con't)

Detailed Objects of Expense

DESCRIPTION:

Hourly employees

Seasonal hourly employees

OBSERVATIONS:

This page presents detailed objects of expenditure. Note: 101, 102, 103 equal 100-Personal services total presented on previous page.

Categories of miscellaneous supplies are being eliminated, which is appropriate given the other detailed categories used.

DETAIL OF PROGRAM ELEMENT EXPENDITURES

PROGRAM	No.	Program Element	No.
GENERAL GOVERNMENT SUPPORT	1000	PURCHASING	1350
SUB-PROGRAM	No.	Department	
FINANCE	1300	FINANCE	
		Fund	No.
		GENERAL	A

ANALYSIS OF OBJECTS OF EXPENSE

CODE	DESCRIPTION	1979-80 BUDGET	1980-81 MANAGER'S BUDGET
101	Salaries	84,083	81,276
102	Wages	0	21,600
103	Special Services	1,000	1,000
	Total Personal Services	85,083	103,876
301	Office Supplies	2,000	2,300
313	Miscellaneous Supplies	500	0
	Total Materials and Supplies	2,500	2,300
402	Telephone	825	750
403	Printing	2,500	3,350
405	Postage	1,800	1,700
407	Maintenance and Repair - Equipment	300	300
410	Mileage Allowance	400	380
416	Advertising	150	50
419	Miscellaneous Expense	250	0
424	Maintenance Office Equipment	500	500
425	Subscriptions and Publications	1,500	1,500
440	Photo Copy Service	1,200	1,000
	Total Other Expenses	9,425	9,480
	Total Purchasing	97,008	115,556

EXHIBIT 7

Revenues by Source

This schedule shows general fund revenues by type (tax, aid, direct user charge) and source (kind of tax or aid)

DESCRIPTION:

Taxes from which the government receives revenues

Direct aid received by the government from the State and Federal government

Special purpose aid usually distinguishable by description that identifies a specific activity or program. Funds are provided to run the program described

OBSERVATIONS:

Largest single revenue

Special purpose state aid, no allowance for cost increases

GENERAL FUND - ANTICIPATED REVENUES
1979/80 vs. 1980/81

	1979/80 Budget	1980/81 Manager's Budget
SPECIAL TAXES		
Supplemental R/E Taxes	25,000	70,000
Utilities - Gross Receipts	380,000	420,000
Municipal Housing (In Lieu)	75,000	10,000
Sales and Use Tax	11,500,000	12,700,000
Raceway Admissions Tax	1,150,000	1,200,000
Real Estate Transfer Tax	--	350,000
Parking Tax	--	--
TOTAL SPECIAL TAXES	13,130,000	14,750,000
STATE AND FEDERAL AID		
State Revenue Sharing	7,000,000	8,800,000
Youth Projects - Recreation	40,000	45,000
Youth Projects - Youth Board	75,000	75,000
Mortgage Tax Aid	225,000	325,000
Loss of Railroad Tax Revenue	105,000	110,000
Veterans Service Agency	7,500	7,500
Civil Defense	20,000	45,000
Environmental Protection	100,000	100,000
Recreation for the Elderly	7,000	6,000
Community Services Projects	--	50,000
Child Development Program	--	40,000
TOTAL STATE AND FEDERAL AID	7,579,500	9,603,500

EXHIBIT 7 (Con't)
Revenues by Source

Departmental revenues generally result from user charges, fee, fines, etc. made by the department

Other revenues and credits is a miscellaneous catch all for items of revenues not otherwise classifiable

OBSERVATIONS:

Most stable of revenue sources declining

Major non-repetitive revenue—where will funds come from next year?

Lost source of revenue

Increase in reserve for uncollected taxes may indicate increasing tax delinquency

GENERAL FUND - ANTICIPATED REVENUES
1979/80 Vs. 1980/81

	1979/80 Budget	1980/81 Manager's Budget
DEPARTMENTAL REVENUES		
Boiler Inspection	2,500	2,000
Building Department	150,000	150,000
City Clerk	80,000	110,000
City Court	1,000,000	1,300,000
Engineering	325,000	225,000
Recreation	200,000	250,000
Public Safety	75,000	125,000
Public Works	300,000	265,000
Zoning Board	2,500	5,600
Consumer Protection	--	12,000
Comptroller	--	9,000
TOTAL DEPARTMENTAL REVENUES	2,135,000	2,453,600
OTHER REVENUES AND CREDITS		
Maintenance of State and County Roads	--	100,000
Interest on Taxes	225,000	225,000
Rents on City-Owned Property	100,000	100,000
Parking Authority	110,000	110,000
Sale of Real Estate	1,150,000	1,634,029
Special Assessments	190,000	--
Interest on Investments	400,000	450,000
Reserve for Uncollected Taxes	830,000	1,100,000
Loss of Track Revenue - OTB	--	200,000
TOTAL OTHER REVENUES AND CREDITS	3,005,000	3,919,029
GRAND TOTAL - GENERAL FUND	25,849,500	30,726,129

XI

EXHIBIT 8

Detail Budget by Classification (Program & Object)
Summary of a Program by Sub-Programs

Schedule shows expenditures for a program and its subprograms, also for line items.

DESCRIPTION:

Program name

Program number

Fund name

Major object classifications—
types of goods and services
purchased

Sub-Program Code

Sub-Program
The sub-programs which
comprise the program

OBSERVATIONS:

Forecast expenses are usually
based on latest actual and a
forecast to year-end

A general statement regarding
the nature of the program.
May not be included in a line
item budget. May also be
considerably expanded to
include the intended results
or service objectives, the
prior and/or current year
achievement and the method
to be used to achieve the
objectives, also called the
service plan.

SUMMARY OF PROGRAM EXPENDITURES

PROGRAM	Bt.	Fund		Bt.	
GENERAL GOVERNMENT SUPPORT	1000	GENERAL		A	

	1978-79 ACTUAL EXPENSES	1979-80 ADOPTED BUDGET	1979-80 FORECAST EXPENSES	1980-81 DEPARTMENT REQUEST	1980-81 MANAGER'S BUDGET
MAJOR OBJECT OF EXPENSES					
100 - Personal Services	4,002,721	3,896,094	4,157,396	4,708,814	4,176,288
200 - Equipment	37,840	770	190	24,820	200
300 - Materials & Supplies	432,914	392,355	405,139	532,220	465,370
400 - Other Expenses	779,321	697,880	775,490	840,960	783,910
TOTALS	5,252,796	4,987,099	5,338,215	6,106,814	5,425,768

COMMENTARY

The General Government Support Program provides a full range of
management and support activities necessary for the efficient and effective
conduct of City operations.

SUB-PROGRAM EXPENDITURES

SUB-PROGRAM CODE	SUB-PROGRAM	1978-79 ACTUAL EXPENSES	1979-80 ADOPTED BUDGET	1980-81 MANAGER'S BUDGET
1000	Legislative	180,246	169,185	182,721
1100	Judicial	612,386	601,309	664,341
1200	Executive	125,484	117,311	117,330
1300	Finance	818,403	865,723	963,383
1400	Staff	2,018,791	1,834,741	2,066,912
1600	Shared Services	1,497,486	1,398,830	1,431,061
	Total Government Support	5,252,796	4,987,099	5,425,768

A1

FORM 6-1

EXHIBIT 9

Expenditures by Fund

DESCRIPTION:

Schedule shows expenditures for each fund and equals the total appropriation shown in Exhibit 1. Funds are generally self-explanatory

Total departmental expenditure in general fund— see total in Exhibit 4

Total appropriation ties to total expenditures in Exhibit 2

OBSERVATIONS:

New fund—where were expenditures last year?

Was budget too low last year?

Largest area of growth

This recapitulation is intended to be used in connection with Exhibit 1 PROPERTY TAX CALCULATION. The total is composed of all funds except Education. (Verify the total)

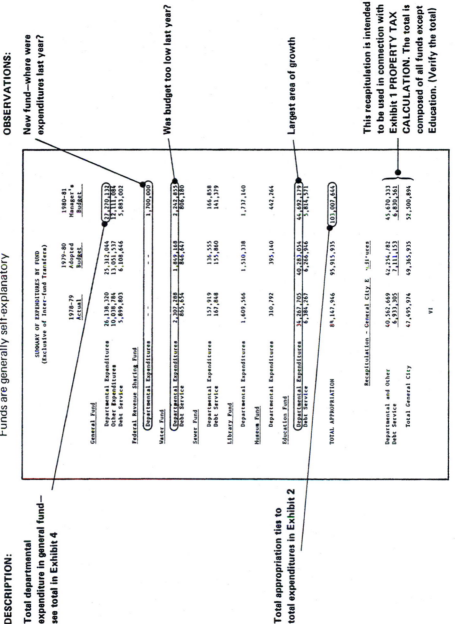

SUMMARY OF EXPENDITURES BY FUND
(Exclusive of Inter-fund Transfers)

	1978-79 Actual	1979-80 Adopted Budget	1980-81 Manager's Budget
General Fund			
Departmental Expenditures	26,138,320	25,312,044	27,270,132
Other Expenditures	10,038,784	13,051,537	12,111,084
Debt Service	5,899,803	6,108,646	5,883,002
Federal Revenue Sharing Fund			
Departmental Expenditures	--	--	1,700,000
Water Fund			
Departmental Expenditures	2,307,288	1,849,168	2,242,855
Debt Service	865,654	846,647	806,180
Sewer Fund			
Departmental Expenditures	157,919	136,555	166,858
Debt Service	167,848	155,860	141,379
Library Fund			
Departmental Expenditures	1,609,566	1,510,338	1,737,140
Museum Fund			
Departmental Expenditures	310,792	395,140	442,264
Education Fund			
Departmental Expenditures	34,267,705	40,283,054	44,692,179
Debt Service	6,384,267	6,266,946	5,814,371
TOTAL APPROPRIATION	89,147,946	95,915,935	103,007,664

Recapitulation - General City Expenditures

Departmental and Other	40,562,669	42,254,782	45,670,333
Debt Service	6,933,305	7,111,153	6,830,561
Total General City	47,495,974	49,365,935	52,500,894

vi

35

2

Budget Examination and Politics*

INTRODUCTION

At the nexus of analysis and politics is the budget examiner. The staff person—alter ego of the President, governor, or county manager—must be a career civil servant sensitive to the political winds affecting the examiner's ultimate boss and an expert capable of a wide variety of analytical skills. Policy making and analytical expertise come together in the government's budget office which prepares the chief executive's recommended budget and then insures that the established legislative and executive policy is carried out by the various agencies of government.

What happens in a budget office? The following are two brief cases of what happened regarding two policy questions in two separate governments: one involved the U.S. Office of Management and Budget; the other involved the Broward County Florida Office of Management and Budget. The cases are not meant to be representative but they are illustrative of the challenge, excitement, and frustration when one mixes analysis and policy. Explaining that emotion-laden world in a textbook is impossible. Hopefully, these cases will bring to the student a better understanding of the human process called budgeting.

OMB BUDGET EXAMINATION

The Problem

In the fall of 1979 and early 1980, OMB budget examiner Alan Rhinesmith started to notice an alarming development in the U.S. Department of Housing and Urban Development. The nation was experiencing significant

*By Thomas D. Lynch, Florida International University.

oil and heating cost increases due to the Arab oil embargo. One consequence was a parallel increase in fuel cost for federally subsidized public housing. This situation was dramatically presented in a January 1980 meeting with public housing authority representatives in Rhinesmith's office. He argued that public housing authorities, like other Americans, had to watch their heating costs. They said that such was practically impossible in light of the following factors:

strong vocal resistance from tenant organizations
the threat of and actual legal suits when thermostats were lowered
technical problems involving expensive construction remedies
a lack of staff or inadequate training of staff to help them implement conservation practices

In the summer of 1980, Rhinesmith went on a field trip to the Atlanta regional office of HUD. One HUD engineer was especially critical of existing HUD public policy. That conversation plus discussions with Atlanta housing authority personnel confirmed the worst fears of the examiner. Essentially, HUD and local housing officials had no way of controlling or lowering heating costs. Officials kept poor records and metering by units did not exist. Even if cost saving could be implemented, that fact would only be reflected in the overall housing authority's heating bill; thus, incentives could not be used to reward the conscientious tenants. Atlanta officials explained the need for a congressional appropriation supplement to cover this unanticipated extra fuel cost. But they were not able to explain how better management could minimize fuel cost increases.

HUD was aware of the problem and even had a research project addressed to devising engineering solutions. HUD had a three-year energy-consumption report which included recommendations on improving conservation through structural improvements. In fact, a HUD Office of Policy Development and Research study dated March 31, 1980 and entitled "An Evaluation of the Physical Condition of Public Housing Stock" was useful to Rhinesmith as an examiner. The report said: "Given that a substantial portion of the public housing stock was designed in a cheap energy era, and that funding limitations have precluded the implementation of a total energy-conservation program, the potential for saving remains substantial."

Budget Supplemental

On July 10, 1980, HUD Secretary Moon Landrieu requested that the Carter Administration request a $277 million supplement for public housing operation subsidies. The 1980 budget assumed a $785 million subsidy for 1980 and an $862 million subsidy for 1981. The increases were assumed to be 20% in 1980 and 8.8% in 1981, but the actual increase was 29%. Since Congress does appropriate money for operating subsidies, this budget item is "controlled"; but politically cutting off the heat would place any administration in an apparent Simon Legree position. Thus, how could the Carter Administration or Congress say "no" to the supplemental?

The Carter Administration did not say "no," but it did not act. The problem was inherited by the new Reagan Administration. The Reagan Administration decided upon a $113.8 million request, forcing the housing authorities and Congress to address this question of heating costs. HUD had little immediate success in encouraging individual energy conservation. It could have meant a savings of $140 million, but, unfortunately, in 1981 incentives did not encourage tenant or management energy conservation. However, HUD did agree to a modernization program which could lead to energy savings. Fortunately, the previous year's energy crisis did not extend into the Reagan Administration. Circumstances, therefore, made the band-aid solution adequate, especially in the context of dramatic domestic-program cutbacks in the new conservative Republican administration. Interestingly, the OMB recommended a dramatic cut in public housing subsidies in the next budget year.

Observations

Budget examination does not take place in isolation from events in society as a whole. The public-housing heating-cost crisis is a part of the larger nationwide energy crisis. The critical view of public housing costs is also a reflection of the general Reagan Administration approach to budget priorities for the nation. Rhinesmith had to be aware of those factors in order to be an effective and responsive budget examiner.

In addition, analysis of information is critical. Budget submissions, talks with local public-housing representatives and HUD headquarters and field staff, HUD research reports, and sensitivity to both congressional and executive persons are all important in doing the job of a budget examiner. The submissions and the conversations enable the OMB examiner to determine HUD's current inability to encourage meaningful heating-cost savings. Longer term solutions were needed and the examiner was able to encourage their utilization. On the other hand, external factors are critical and may lead one to realize that there is no good short-term solution as was the situation here.

Clearly, ultimate political values superseded other considerations in this case. The transition permitted the Carter Administration to pass on the problem. The Reagan Administration's desire to cut domestic programs, especially of a welfare character, was the critical political value in this case situation. Apparently the examiner's role was to assist the political leadership to make more intelligent decisions within the political agenda of the elected and appointed political actors.

AN INTERGOVERNMENTAL HEALTH BUDGET

Background

In 1980–81, Broward County, Florida was a fast-growing urban county faced with the twin problems of growth and tight budgets at the state and local levels and government retrenchment at the federal level. In 1980, County Administrator Graham Watt instructed his Office of Budget and Management and all county administration personnel to develop a "maintenance of effort" budget for 1981.

Health was one functional set of government programs which was marked by complex intergovernmental relations. In the county, there were several tax-supported public hospitals which operated as independent governments. Also there was the state Department of Health and Rehabilitative Services (HRS), District X, which exactly coincides with the boundaries of Broward County. Finally, there was a Broward County Health and Medical Department headed by R.P. Kelley. The state District X HRS Health Department was responsible for clinics, health education, food inspections of those who sell food, testing water supplies, ambulance inspections, and day-care inspections. The county unit was responsible for primary health-care services, animal control, mosquito control, alcohol and drug abuse, rehabilitation, mental health services, and emergency medical services.

The financial arrangements were equally complex. The funding for the state health department came from federal, state, and county funds. The funding for county health services came mostly from county *ad valorem* taxes, but some came from user charges which went into a special Capital Maintenance Trust Fund earmarked for capital purchases. The state law establishing this county fund, however, did say that no more than 50 percent of it could be used for operating expenses. Although the transfer payments were important, 80 percent of the resources of the county's

Health and Medical Department came from county sources.

Round One

In May 1980, the county health department submitted its budget to the County Office of Budget and Management. By July 15, the County OMB had to submit a budget recommendation through the County Manager to the county elected Board of Commissioners. The May submission by the Health Department was a 9 percent plus increase, and OMB felt that the budget request was beyond a "maintenance of effort level." In June, a meeting was held with the county commissioners after which a 3.3 percent decrease across each department was decreed. Kelley felt that given inflation, this decrease meant cutting services. As a former director of the state HRS district office, he was familiar with the state's effort, and he decided that cuts were best made in the county's contribution to the state's health department.

The county OMB budget analyst, James W. Seuffert, had analyzed the state's budget request, which was channelled through Kelley's office. This analysis was difficult because the state was not obligated and did not provide budget justification data in the same manner as county offices. For example, there were (1) no computer salary forecast, (2) no "actuals" for the year prior to the current year, (3) no audit trial for personnel changes, (4) poor output measures, (5) no information on actual personnel attrition, and (6) limited access to financial information. Nevertheless, a budget review was possible by examining (1) the current year budget information, (2) comparing personnel detail with organizational charts, and by (3) comparing funding levels by various programs for the current and budget year.

The conclusion reached by Seuffert was that the state health department would be receiving a 9 percent funding increase from all sources, which was higher than comparable county programs. The local contribution would be an increase of a little over 6 percent. Overall, there would be fourteen new positions with $90,000 being shifted from the capital outlay fund to recurring operating expenses. Over fifteen positions were upgraded with a high number in overhead administrative activities in spite of some shifting of positions from one section to another. Thus, the county OMB concurred that the county contribution to the state health department was too high and a cut was appropriate. Moreover, an examination of the contributions made by other Florida counties showed that the county was more generous than most other Florida counties.

Round Two

At this point, an important development occurred which illustrates the unique character of intergovernmental programs. The recently approved state budget had appropriated extra funds to the health departments, but they said in their appropriation law, "In order to receive the increased per capita state funding appropriated in this specific appropriation, each county shall continue to provide at least the same level of contribution to the county health unit trust fund in the 1979–80 to fiscal year." This meant that unless the county contributed the same amount of money as in 1980 to the state health department, the department would lose $162,000. Obviously, Broward County residents would significantly lose health services because of a minor cut in the county contribution.

Now, the county OMB staff and Kelley were in disagreement. The county OMB did not wish to lose $162,000 state money for Broward residents, and the county health director did not wish to cut his own program for the sake of a less efficient state health program. Seuffert proposed a unique "solution" by suggesting tht the county contribution come from both the general fund and the Capital Outlay and Maintenance Trust Fund (CMTF).

The OMB suggestion must be understood in the context of the developing Florida tax revolt. The general fund received much of its money from the property tax, thus any program funded from the general fund would be under more pressure to be within budgeted targets. If a program can be partially or fully funded from some other source such as user fees, then intense political pressure would be relieved. On the other hand, the CMTF was meant to be used primarily for capital purchases and this proposal might violate that policy and deplete resources for capital projects. For that reason, Kelley opposed the OMB suggestion.

Seuffert carefully examined the CMTF revenue forecasts, checked the county ordinance carefully, and prepared a stronger argument for using the CMTF. The forecasted fund balance was about $1.3 million. After careful examination. Seuffert concluded that because the FY 1980 fund revenues were understated, the fund could be used for the planned purposes as well as a one-time contribution to the state health trust fund for operation of the state district health department. The wording of the ordinance did permit use of the money in this manner. Therefore, Seuffert was able to argue for a one-time, non-precedent-setting use of that county user fee fund.

The policy outcome went in favor of OMB. Kelley eventually agreed with the county OMB recommendation and the commissioners in early September 1980 did approve the OMB recommendation. The extra revenue from the fees did materialize and the 1980 fees were not increased. However, in 1981 fees were increased. The long-run effect was an extra $250,000 in annual revenues for health-care services for Broward residents. The less than ideal administrative cost of the state district health—from the Broward County perspective—was not resolved in the 1981 budget year, but it continued to be an issue in future budget years. For example, the 1982 budget year was affected by the Reagan budget cuts, the national recession, and a local taxpayer revolt. Thus, a "maintenance-of-effort" policy in 1981 became an approximately 5 percent cut policy in 1982, and a cut of 20 percent was considered for 1983. Obviously, the state health department partially funded by county funds remained a prime candidate for cutting.

Observations

Budget examination at the local level is much more detailed and certainly as complex as the federal counterpart. Management is a key consideration in deciding budget cuts, and in this case, the budget analyst did not look for the most effective way to manage county funds. In periods of tight budgets, the budget analyst is especially encouraged to find less expensive ways to provide government services. However, the intergovernmental political realities took priority over concern for efficiency. Losing $162,000 of state money was an overriding factor. That the analyst could challenge the user fee revenue forecast was also significant. This case illustrates how analysis and budget examination might and might not make a difference in policy outcomes. The analysis, which showed that the state health district department could get by with less money, did not result in less county money for that unit. However, the OMB user fee forecast probably did contribute to the county commissioner's decision not to cut the county contribution to the state health unit. Analysis is ammunition in the policy-making process. As in a battle, though, sometimes the ammunition is effective and sometimes not.

CONCLUSIONS

The work of budget analysts is both frustrating and exciting. The most significant policy medium for government in most situations is the budget, and the budget analyst is *the* administrative expert in that medium. Policy-making and analytical expertise come together in OMB. Decision making is often influenced by analysis. Although not always influential and even sometimes ignored, the analyst does often make a political difference. Rhinesmith helped OMB and HUD officials realize that some type of reasonable managerial control over public heating costs was important. Seuffert reinforced the importance of good management in health programs and helped discover a means to avoid losing state money for the county. Although not asked in the interviews, both Rhinesmith and Seuffert were obviously excited about the role they played in their case situation; but they were obviously somewhat frustrated by the realities of the political process.

Budget analysis is a combination of professional expertise and dealing with political realities. To be effective, the analyst must bring a wide range of analytical talents to his or her job. Reading organization charts, forecasting revenues and expenses, forecasting personnel levels, recognizing too much overhead, dealing with and properly understanding clientele and agency professionals are a few of the analytical skills necessary to do the job. Beyond those skills, the analysts must also be able to relate intelligently to the dynamic realities of politics. Transition politics will delay decisions. Political values will cut programs regardless of the positive or negative conclusions of the analysts. Losing money from the state, federal, or private sector will often override concerns for efficiency. Since political realities tend to overcome analytical purity, a pragmatic and existential professional philosophy will best serve analysts.

Budget examination is at the nexus of analysis and politics. Thus, it will always be challenging, exciting, and frustrating.

3

*This City Has Two City Managers**

Shortly after his arrival in late 1971, Flint's new city manager began preparing his first budget. To perform this responsibility properly, he needed comparisons of planned versus actual revenue received during the current fiscal year, as well as revenue forecasts for the next several fiscal years. He therefore sent a memorandum to the Finance Department requesting this information.

To the manager's surprise, the finance director responded by saying that no such information was available. Subsequently, he learned that crude revenue forecasts had in fact been prepared and that monthly revenue data were available to the finance director on tally sheets which he kept in his desk.

*Reprinted by permission from Brian W. Rapp and Frank M. Patitucci, *Managing Local Government for Improved Performance: A Practical Approach* (Boulder, Colorado: Westview Press, 1977), p. 195.

The manager decided to visit the finance director personally to see if he could get the information he needed. Under the city charter, the finance director held a council-appointed position on a par with that of the city manager. In view of this, and of the fact that the finance director had been in his job for almost twenty-five years, the manager decided that the problem was merely one of protocol; a personal visit would solve it.

At their meeting, the manager asked if he could review the revenue-control sheets in order to better prepare the city's budget. The finance director admitted that some of the information had been compiled, but refused to part with it. "What you must realize," he told the manager, "is that in Flint the finance director is a second city manager. My job is to conserve city revenue and your job is to try to spend it."

CHAPTER TWO

THE DECISION-MAKING PROCESS

Decision-making processes are designed to produce choice, the necessity for which is determined by universal, permanent scarcity. The two in conjunction generate the likelihood of competition and the potential for conflict. Any decision-making process is geared to reduce conflict to acceptable, if not reasonable, proportions by imposing structure, regularities, expectations, laws, and other limitations. A decision-making process can be described in behavioral terms: the demands made upon it (and those excluded); the actors participating as individuals and offices; and the rules (formal and informal, explicit and implicit, obeyed and ignored) that order the process and confine the choice. Consequently, the incentives and disincentives operating toward or against agreement are a critical aspect of the process; some kind of choice is, after all, the desired output.

Decision-making processes in budgeting and financial management are no different at this level of generality, although from a normative perspective they are aimed at the authoritative allocation of resources among public purposes. Scarcity is a dominant theme in the budgeting literature—demands upon the public treasury almost always outstrip the resources available to meet them. Added to this apparently infinite variety of demands is a large number of interacting individuals and institutions. They operate within a fragmented governmental structure characterized by limited authority and limited power. Also, behavior is limited. A diverse (and yes, sometimes contradictory) set of legal, social, economic, and political rules and constraints establish boundaries while at the same time introducing competing values into the process. Because decision makers depend upon the cooperation of others to reach agreement, negotiation is fostered. If a budget is to be produced and if government operations, programs, and payrolls are to continue, then agreement is necessary.

The effects of mutuality and competition show up in the frequently abrasive interplay between executive and legislative institutions as they compete for power over authoritative allocations. In most U.S. governments today, decision making in budgeting and financial management is predominantly executive in character. Commonly, the executive budget process consists of four stages: executive formulation and submission to the appropriating body; legislative review and appropriation; executive implementation; audit and evaluation. The steps in the process are not quite as discrete as this implies. The process is interactive and recursive, and the stages for one fiscal period (most commonly, a twelve-month fiscal year) overlap each other and the stages in other fiscal cycles. By tracking a fictitious financial transaction in the U.S. Department of the Interior's budget, case no. 4 (model type) lays out the chronology in the federal budget process. It is supplemented by charts that describe the phases of the federal budget process. Calendars and chronology are particularly important in light of the fact that steps in the process, deadlines, and timetables are so frequently mandated by statute, executive regulation, and sometimes even by charter provisions.

The use of the fiscal year itself has analytic and decision-making implications, as illustrated most markedly in case no. 7. Logically, efficient management should be designed to conform to strategy rather than to the budget calendar or fiscal year. By looking at the longer range (for example, cases nos. 31 and 32), decision makers can devise and then implement solutions which break out of the analytic limitations imposed by the annual budget cycle. Improved management techniques, like improved work methods in case no. 7, take time and planning, and need not be constrained by the fiscal year. On the other hand, a major advantage of the limited focus and limited timeframe is that frequent agreement is required throughout the negotiations by set dates. It breaks the budget problem down into manageable fragments and reduces the potential for conflict as it limits the stakes, the problem, and, thus, the choice.

The cases in this chapter describe the decision-making processes at the federal (no. 5), state (no. 6), and local (nos. 7 and 8) levels of government. In doing so, they depict both frictions and an underlying drive toward compromise. In cases 5 and 6, the focus is on legislative-executive relations, the impact of professional staff, and the development of an effective role for the legislature in the budget process. In looking at the role of Congress in the federal budget process, case no. 5 introduces basic terminology and illustrates some complex aspects of the authorization–appropriation process. These include: appropriations and authorizations; budget uncontrollability; jurisdictional conflicts among committees; and the whole realm of legislative budgeting. In addition to taking a close look at budgeting in Georgia's state legislature, case 6 examines the impact of professional staff organized in a legislative budget office, time limitations on legislators as decision makers in the budget process, and legislative–executive relations. Case no. 5 is evaluative, and case no. 6 adds related problems to the treatment.

Case no. 7, "The Asphalt Paradox," presents a municipal budget problem concerning the mode of expenditure and overall fiscal planning. From another perspective, it raises the question of competing professional roles. Note, moreover, that in this instance no strategies for making use of efficiencies were chosen; furthermore, there was no attempt to bring the choice to the attention of the appropriate decision makers (the city manager and the council). An interesting point made is that it is cheaper to be rich than to be poor. This decision-forcing case illustrates that, because of the way the efficiency value is calculated, the dollar benefit always increases when services are increased. Therefore, the more services are increased, the higher the calculated benefit–although a jurisdiction may not be able to afford the reduction in unit cost or the increase in service. There is a step intervening between identifying efficiency improvements (here, "cost avoidance") and implementing them; that step involves determining how to take those benefits.

Case no. 8, a problem-solving case, also deals with strategic choice at the local level of government, but this time on the revenue side of the ledger. Local decision makers are faced with making decisions that will be binding for a decade and making those decisions under conditions of great uncertainty. Their adopting simplifying assumptions and limited time horizons illustrate a rather common approach to decision making. This case, by offering a solution to the problem it poses, illustrates how a decision-forcing case works.

Related cases include cases nos. 13, 14, 33, 34, 35. All deal to some extent with aspects of the decision-making process in budgeting and financial management.

4

Tracking a Financial Transaction Through the Federal Budget and Accounting Calendar *

BACKGROUND

The Department of Interior's FY 1981 budget includes an appropriation request of $4.4 million for the maintenance, janitorial, and security services of the John F. Kennedy Center for the Performing Arts.

The following fictitious example, intended to track a typical item through the federal budget and accounting system, zeroes in on the sequence of financial events.

INTRODUCTION

Described below are twenty significant events of the federal budget and accounting cycle, in chronological order. You are to read each paragraph and fill in an appropriate heading best describing the event. Your headings then can be matched with the appropriate number on the chart to show the timing and relationship of federal budget and accounting functions.

1. _____

    Description: The head of the security force at the Kennedy Center currently has twenty full-time employees. On the basis of an increase in scheduled performances for next fiscal year, a trend toward increased attendance at Center activities, and a greater petty vandalism problem, the security chief believes five additional full-time guard positions are needed. Five positions are considered

adequate to allow full coverage at all Center entrances/exits and more frequent observations of the parking garage and rest-room facilities where vandalism has been occurring. The security chief develops an estimate of $105,000 to include personnel compensation and benefits and uniform allowances for the five positions.

2. _____

    Description: The director of the Kennedy Center regularly receives operating cost reports and estimates of additional funding needs for review and approval. Already aware of the need for additional protective officers because of previous discussions with the security chief, the requested five positions are approved.

3. _____

    Description: The Budget Office, National Parks Service, Department of Interior, performs budget and accounting services for the Kennedy Center. The Budget Office reviews the Kennedy Center budget and recommends the additional amount for approval by the Director, National Parks Service, and the Secretary of Interior.

4. _____

    Description: The five positions and related funds for the Kennedy Center are approved by top management and are included within a departmental budget justification, along with other similar organizations which are included in Interior's budget, such as the Heritage Conservation Commission.

*By Charles Falvey. Courtesy of Management Sciences Training Center, U.S. Office of Personnel Management, Washington, D.C..

5. _____

Description: On September 15, the Office of Management and Budget receives for review the Department of Interior's budget justification (and budget schedules). An OMB budget examiner reviews the department's request, arranges and attends OMB department budget hearings, and prepares recommendations to the director of OMB on the increases being requested.

6. _____

Description: During December the OMB director meets with the president to discuss agency budget requests. Although several requested program increases for the Department of Interior are not approved, the Kennedy Center increase is allowed.

7. _____

Description: On January 23rd the president gives his State of the Union address to a joint session of Congress. He outlines several legislative proposals which are included in the president's budget, as transmitted to Congress the following day.

8. _____

Description: The second week in March the House Appropriation Subcommittee having responsibility for the Department of Interior holds hearings. The secretary, director of the National Parks Services, and other officials attend.

9. _____

Description: About a month following House hearings, the Senate Appropriation Subcommittee considers Interior's budget. The Kennedy Center item is briefly touched upon in discussions.

10. _____

Description: Interior's House Appropriation Subcommittee drafts an appropriation bill for consideration and passage by (1) the full House Appropriations Committee and (2) the House of Representatives.

11. _____

Description: The Senate Appropriation Subcommittee for the Department of Interior and related agencies similarly drafts its version of an appropriations bill. The Senate Appropriation Committee and the full Senate consider and debate the bill.

12. _____

Description: Because minor variations exist between the House and Senate bills, a conference committee is appointed composed of representatives of the House and Senate appropriation subcommittees having jurisdiction over the bill. The conferees reach agreement on the bill, both Houses of Congress approve, and the enrolled bill is forwarded to the president for signature. An additional $105,000 for the Kennedy Center is included in the final appropriation bill.

13. _____

Description: The president signs the appropriation bill for the Department of Interior on October 1. A public law number is assigned.

14. _____

Description: The Department of Treasury issues to the Secretary of Interior a one-page document stating the congressionally approved amounts for each appropriation account.

15. _____

Description: Within ten calendar days after approval of the appropriation, the department submits a quarterly distribution of obligations to be incurred for each appropriation account under the operations planned during the year.

16. _____

   Description: The Kennedy Center director delegates authority to incur obligations during the first quarter to the respective operating officials in charge of the maintenance, janitorial, and security services. This action is a regular part of the administrative control system for the use of budgetary resources. Approximately one-quarter of the $105,000 in additional funds is being made available to the security chief.

17. _____

   Description: The security chief promptly hires the new employees. They are given their work schedules, are placed on the payroll, and begin work.

18. _____

19. _____

   Description: Upon receipt and utilization of the employees' services, the agency's accounting records technically reflect what two entries?

   Note: In the case of personnel compensation and benefits, agency accounting records reflect answers 17, 18, and 19 simultaneously. Given the case of contractual services or a large printing order, however, a clear distinction would be evident among the terms.

20. _____

   Description: Payday arrives. Kennedy Center employees paid from this appropriation are given green U.S. Government paychecks.

FIGURE 4.1. Budget and Accounting Calendar, FY 1981: Significant Events.

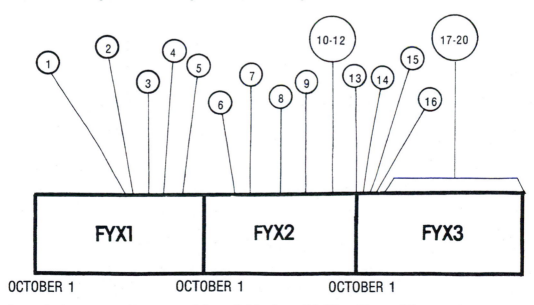

Source: Provided courtesy of Management Sciences Training Center, U.S. Office of Personnel Management.

FIGURE 4.2. Federal Budget Cycle

PHASE 1 – EXECUTIVE PREPARATION AND SUBMISSION

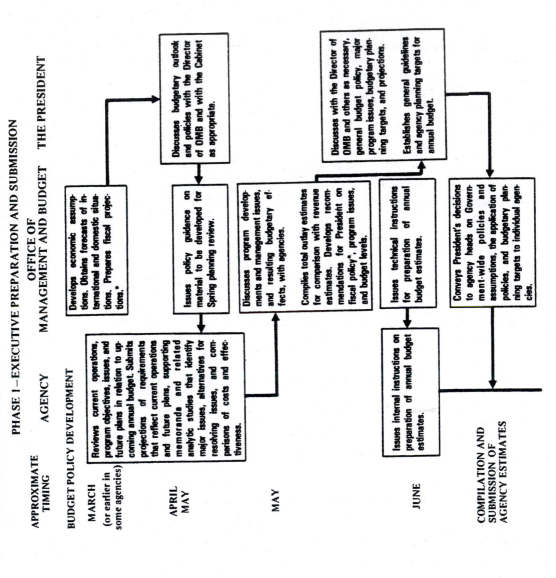

APPROXIMATE TIMING	AGENCY	OFFICE OF MANAGEMENT AND BUDGET	THE PRESIDENT

BUDGET POLICY DEVELOPMENT

MARCH (or earlier in some agencies)

Reviews current operations, program objectives, issues, and future plans in relation to upcoming annual budget. Submits projections of requirements that reflect current operations and future plans, supporting memoranda and related analytic studies that identify major issues, alternatives for resolving issues, and comparisons of costs and effectiveness.

Develops economic assumptions. Obtains forecasts of international and domestic situations. Prepares fiscal projections.

Discusses budgetary outlook and policies with the Director of OMB and with the Cabinet as appropriate.

APRIL MAY

Issues policy guidance on material to be developed for Spring planning review.

MAY

Discusses program developments and management issues, and resulting budgetary effects, with agencies.

Compiles total outlay estimates for comparison with revenue estimates. Develops recommendations for President on fiscal policy*, program issues, and budget levels.

Discusses with the Director of OMB and others as necessary, general budget policy, major program issues, budgetary planning targets, and projections.

Establishes general guidelines and agency planning targets for annual budget.

JUNE

Issues internal instructions on preparation of annual budget estimates.

Issues technical instructions for preparation of annual budget estimates.

Conveys President's decisions to agency heads on Government-wide policies and assumptions, the application of budgetary planning targets to individual agencies.

COMPILATION AND SUBMISSION OF AGENCY ESTIMATES

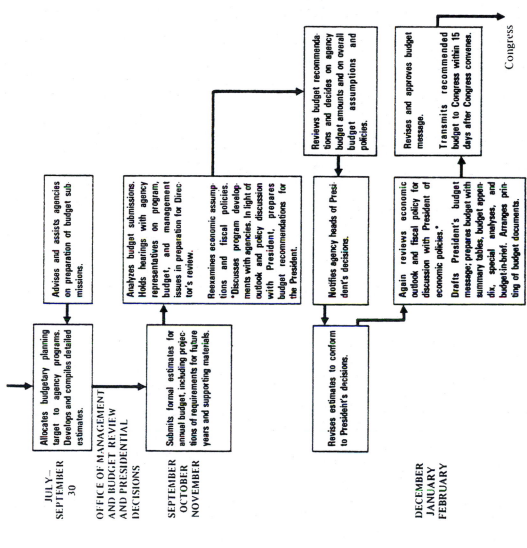

JULY—
SEPTEMBER
30

Allocates budgetary planning target to agency programs. Develops and compiles detailed estimates.

Advises and assists agencies on preparation of budget submissions.

OFFICE OF MANAGEMENT AND BUDGET REVIEW AND PRESIDENTIAL DECISIONS

SEPTEMBER
OCTOBER
NOVEMBER

Submits formal estimates for annual budget, including projections of requirements for future years and supporting materials.

Analyzes budget submissions. Holds hearings with agency representatives on program, budget, and management issues in preparation for Director's review.

Reexamines economic assumptions and fiscal policies. *Discusses program developments with agencies. In light of outlook and policy discussion with President, prepares budget recommendations for the President.

Reviews budget recommendations and decides on agency budget amounts and on overall budget assumptions and policies.

Notifies agency heads of President's decisions.

Revises estimates to conform to President's decisions.

DECEMBER
JANUARY
FEBRUARY

Again reviews economic outlook and fiscal policy for discussion with President of economic policies.*

Drafts President's budget message; prepares budget with summary tables, budget appendix, special analyses, and budget-in-brief. Arranges printing of budget documents.

Revises and approves budget message.

Transmits recommended budget to Congress within 15 days after Congress convenes.

Congress

*In cooperation with the Treasury Department and Council of Economic Advisers

PHASE 2—CONGRESSIONAL BUDGET PROCESS

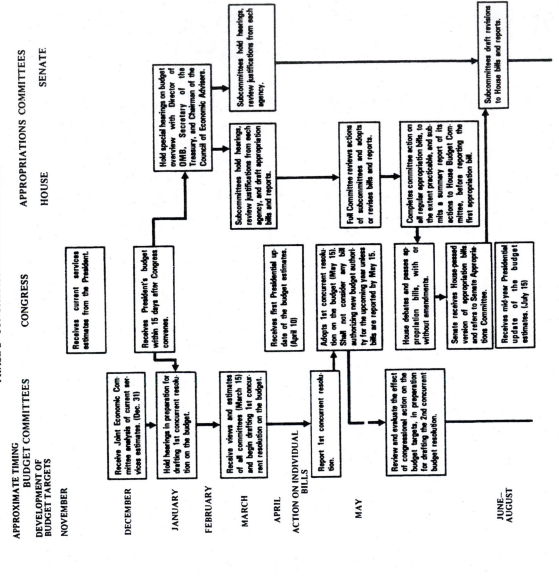

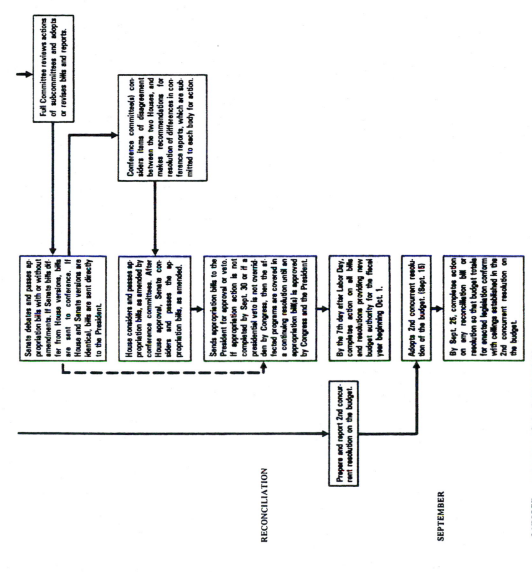

Full Committee reviews actions of subcommittees and adopts or revises bills and reports.

Conference committee(s) considers items of disagreement between the two Houses, and makes recommendations for resolution of differences in conference reports, which are submitted to each body for action.

Senate debates and passes appropriation bills with or without amendments. If Senate bills differ from House versions, bills are sent to conference. If House and Senate versions are identical, bills are sent directly to the President.

House considers and passes appropriation bills, as amended by conference committees. After House approval, Senate considers and passes the appropriation bills, as amended.

Sends appropriation bills to the President for approval or veto. If appropriation action is not completed by Sept. 30 or if a presidential veto is not overridden by Congress, then the affected programs are covered in a continuing resolution until an appropriation bill(s) is approved by Congress and the President.

By the 7th day after Labor Day, completes action on all bills and resolutions providing new budget authority for the fiscal year beginning Oct. 1.

Adopts 2nd concurrent resolution of the budget. (Sept. 15)

By Sept. 25, complete action on any reconciliation bill or resolution so that budget totals for enacted legislation conform with ceilings established in the 2nd concurrent resolution on the budget.

Prepare and report 2nd concurrent resolution on the budget.

RECONCILIATION

SEPTEMBER

OCTOBER   NEW FISCAL YEAR BEGINS OCTOBER 1

51

PHASE 3 –IMPLEMENTATION AND CONTROL OF ENACTED BUDGET

APPROXIMATE TIMING

TREASURY- GENERAL
ACCOUNTING OFFICE

AGENCY

OFFICE OF
MANAGEMENT AND BUDGET

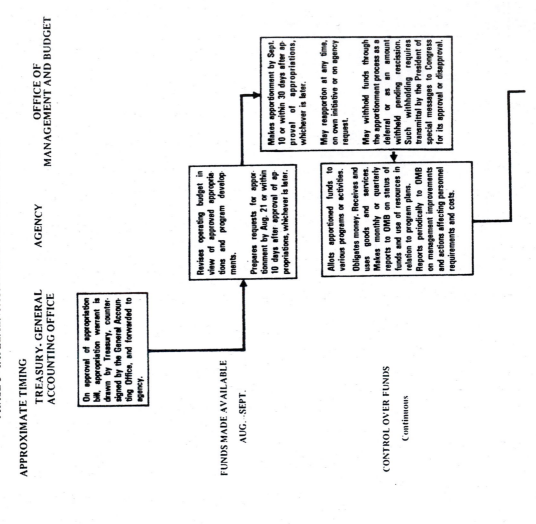

FUNDS MADE AVAILABLE

AUG.-SEPT.

On approval of appropriation bill, appropriation warrant is drawn by Treasury, countersigned by the General Accounting Office, and forwarded to agency.

Revises operating budget in view of approved appropriations and program developments.

Prepares requests for apportionment by Aug. 21 or within 10 days after approval of appropriations, whichever is later.

Makes apportionment by Sept. 10 or within 30 days after approval of appropriations, whichever is later.

May reapportion at any time, on own initiative or on agency request.

May withhold funds through the apportionment process as a deferral or as an amount withheld pending rescission. Such withholding requires transmittal by the President of special messages to Congress for its approval or disapproval.

CONTROL OVER FUNDS

Continuous

Allots apportioned funds to various programs or activities.

Obligates money. Receives and uses goods and services.

Makes monthly or quarterly reports to OMB on status of funds and use of resources in relation to program plans.

Reports periodically to OMB on management improvements and actions affecting personnel requirements and costs.

EXPENDITURE OF FUNDS

As bills become payable

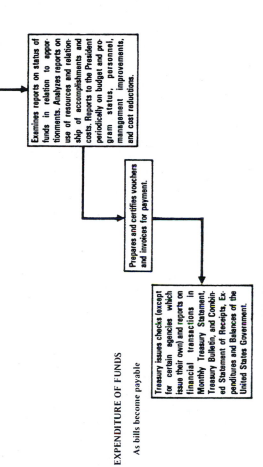

Prepares and certifies vouchers and invoices for payment.

Treasury issues checks (except for certain agencies which issue their own) and reports on financial transactions in Monthly Treasury Statement, Treasury Bulletin, and Combined Statement of Receipts, Expenditures and Balances of the United States Government.

Examines reports on status of funds in relation to apportionments. Analyzes reports on use of resources and relationship of accomplishments and costs. Reports to the President periodically on budget and program status, personnel, management improvements, and cost reductions.

PHASE 4—REVIEW AND AUDIT

APPROXIMATE TIMING AGENCY OFFICE OF MANAGEMENT AND BUDGET

TREASURY-GENERAL ACCOUNTING OFFICE

PROGRAM EVALUATION, MANAGEMENT APPRAISAL, AND INDEPENDENT AUDIT

Periodic

General Accounting Office performs independent audit of financial records, transactions, and financial management, generally. "Settles" accounts of certifying and disbursing officers. Makes reports to Congress including reports on special messages on deferrals and proposed rescissions.

Reviews compliance with established policies, procedures, and requirements. Evaluates accomplishment of program plans and effectiveness of management and operations.

Reviews agency operations and evaluates programs and performance. Conducts or guides agencies in organization and management studies. Assists President in improving management and organization of the executive branch.

Source: *A Glossary of Terms Used in the Federal Budget Process and Related Accounting, Economic, and Tax Terms,* 3rd ed. (Washington, D.C.: U.S. General Accounting Office, March 1981), PAD–82–27, pp. 8–13.

5

*The 1980 Reauthorization of General Revenue Sharing**

INTRODUCTION

The rules of the House and Senate provide for a division of labor between authorization committees, which establish the basic legislative authority for programs, and the appropriations committees, which provide the financial resources necessary to implement them. Although the rules of the two bodies describe a simple, two-step procedure for the funding of programs, actual practice is far more complex.

Jealousies over institutional prerogatives run high in the Congress. Committees are wary of encroachment of their legislative jurisdiction. Thus, the division of labor between authorization and appropriations committees is a perennial source of tension between these committees. Proposals to fund programs without an authorization, or proposals to establish programs which don't require annual appropriations, can be expected to (and do) meet with vigorous opposition. This tension between these committees is not merely of interest as a matter of internal congressional politics. It has potential substantive consequences because of the respective roles of the committees in the congressional spending process.

The conventional wisdom about congressional spending is that authorization committees tend to be advocates of spending, whereas the appropriations committees have historically played the role of guardians of the purse and have been more resistant to spending increases. The House Appropriations Committee in particular has historically seen its role as one of reducing appropriations. The

Senate Appropriations Committee has generally been more willing to grant budget authority than has the House Committee. But both House and Senate Appropriations Committees view with displeasure any proposals to fund programs which circumvent the regular appropriations process. Such proposals are usually given the derogatory label of "backdoor financing," because by sneaking in the "backdoor," they escape the scrutiny of the appropriations committee, particularly that of the House, where for years programs have experienced cuts well below what the authorizing committees would prefer. Backdoor financing is part of the more general problem of "uncontrollability" in the federal budget, which has become so prominent in recent years. Over 75 percent of the federal budget is technically uncontrollable. This uncontrollability, which removes budget items from the regular appropriations process, takes on a variety of forms, such as entitlement authority, contract authority, trust funds, or permanent appropriations.

An example of an entitlement which is also a permanent appropriation is the General Revenue Sharing (GRS) Program. The nature of the funding of the revenue sharing program has been controversial since its enactment in 1972. When the program came up for reauthorization in 1976, the funding mechanism was debated again, and in 1980, when revenue sharing was again up for reauthorization, the funding issue arose once more in the context of a more general debate over the reauthorization of the state share of the GRS program. The 1980 reauthorization of GRS for the states serves to illustrate some of the issues and controversies which arise in the authorization–appropriation nexus. To provide a context for that decision, it is useful to

*By John R. Gist, Virginia Polytechnic Institute and State University.

review the controversy surrounding the initial enactment of GRS as an entitlement and the arguments associated with that decision.

(*Author's note*) After this case was written, Congress decided not to include funding for the state portion of revenue sharing in the FY1982 and 1983 budget resolutions. At the time of publication, reauthorization for FY1984 and beyond was not yet enacted. The case, nonetheless, reflects a recurrent issue in the congressional appropriations process.

HISTORICAL BACKGROUND

The State and Local Fiscal Assistance Act of 1972 authorized what is commonly known as the General Revenue Sharing Program, although the words "revenue sharing" do not appear in the legislation. The initial legislation authorized the expenditure of $30.2 billion over the period from 1972 to 1976 for fiscal assistance to the states and over 38,000 units of general purpose local government. In 1976, after considerable debate, the program was reauthorized at an amount of $25.6 billion for an additional 3 3/4 years, until September, 1980, when fiscal year (FY) 1980 ended. In December of 1980, over two months into FY 1981, Congress again reauthorized GRS, with substantial changes in the provisions for the state share.

Revenue sharing was perhaps the central component of the Nixon Administration's "New Federalism," an attempt to provide local officials with greater discretion over the use of federal aid. GRS is an *entitlement* program, which means that, if states and local governments meet the criteria set forth in legislation, they are automatically eligible for funds, without submitting an application; they are legally "entitled" to them. Although the term "entitlement" program has been applied to revenue sharing as well as other intergovernmental grant programs, such as Community Development Block Grants (CDBG) and Comprehensive Employment and Training Act (CETA) grants, it has generally been associated with federal programs which benefit *individuals*, such as Social Security, Medicare, Medicaid, and food stamps.

In recent years, individual entitlements have been the fastest growing component of the federal budget. One important reason for this is that many of these entitlements are "indexed" to the rate of inflation, which means that benefit payments are adjusted periodically to keep pace with the overall rate of price increases in the economy. These cost-of-living adjustments (or COLAs, as they are often called) have been incorporated into Social Security, Medicare, civilian retirement, Supplemental Security Income, food stamps, and other programs, causing these entitlements to escalate in response to the double-digit inflation our economy has endured for nearly a decade. Another factor in these escalating costs is that the annual appropriation for these entitlements is open-ended or indefinite, in that it depends on how many individuals qualify for assistance.

Revenue sharing differs from individual entitlements in that it has no COLA and its annual appropriation is a definite, fixed amount. Nevertheless, the entitlement aspect of the funding has contributed greatly to the lack of enthusiasm for revenue sharing on the part of many members of Congress, but for reasons other than escalating costs. As an *entitlement* to cities, there is no opportunity for representatives to claim credit for obtaining revenue sharing funds for cities in their districts, whereas mayors, city councils, governors, and legislatures can get credit for *spending* the money.

Revenue sharing, besides being an entitlement, is also a formula grant, because the amount of federal funds going to each jurisdiction is determined automatically by formula. It thus removes congressional discretion from the allocation process. The formula has been a very contentious issue since the inception of the program. Another issue of considerable significance in the initial enactment was how funds would be made available for the program. In the original proposal of the Nixon Administration, revenue sharing funds were to be obtained by earmarking a fixed percentage of federal income tax receipts to be put into a trust fund. This mechanism was expected to create an expanding sum of money as the economy grew. The trust fund mechanism would make GRS an "uncontrollable," since the money would be available without going through the regular appropriations process. The direct link with federal revenue that was originally proposed provided some justification for bypassing the appropriations committees.

However, the final legislation dropped the direct revenue link by providing for a definite annual amount of money but calling it a "permanent appropriation," even though the authorization was set to expire in 1976. Since permanent appropriations do not go through the appropriations committees, this designation constituted an attempt to bypass the regular appropriations process, even without the direct revenue link. This controversial maneuver led to charges that the powerful tax writing committees which had jurisdiction over revenue sharing—the House Ways and Means Committee and the Senate Finance Committee—were usurping the prerogatives of both the House and the Senate Appropriations Committees. Senator John McClellan of Arkansas, chairman of the Senate Appropriations Committee, stated the issue succinctly:

> It is clear that the Appropriations Committee would have a particular concern in any effort to circumvent its jurisdiction, whether it be a trust fund device or some other form of backdoor financing. Otherwise, it would be possible for legislative committees, through the use of such techniques, to completely vitiate the jurisdiction of the Appropriations Committee. By providing for appropriations in every bill granting legislative authority for such appropriations, legislative committees could negate the need for subsequent appropriation acts.[1]

The strongest argument *in favor* of making revenue sharing a permanent appropriation was made by Rep. Barber Conable (R–N.Y.), in the context of a general statement about the authorization–appropriation process:

> (You) said at one point that Congress should not give up its prerogatives, but should go through something like the appropriation process. Do you not think one of the important parts about any plan for the aid of other levels of government should be dependability, that we should have somehow something on which they could count?
>
> One of the great problems of the categorical grant programs has been that we have told them that we are going to authorize X dollars, and many unsophisticated people at lower levels of government considered that a promise, and then we have delivered about 35 cents instead, leaving them with very high expectations and with commitments of their own constituencies.[2]

In the Senate, Russell Long, who chaired the Finance Committee, which had jurisdiction over revenue sharing, argued that

> to subject this program to the vicissitudes of annual appropriations is to destroy at least half of the value of the revenue sharing program. The very essence of revenue sharing is that here are funds which the local governments can definitely plan upon and take into account in their budgetary consideration.[3]

Thus, proponents of the funding procedure were arguing for a dependable, certain source of revenues on which local governments could count. Subjecting revenue sharing to annual review by the Senate and House Appropriations Committees would necessarily increase uncertainty. Opponents did not disagree with this point, but argued that to deprive the appropriations committees of their jurisdiction over the budget would not only

---

[1]*U.S. Congressional Record*, 92nd Congress, 2d Session, September 7, 1972, S 14289.

[2]U.S. Congress, House of Representatives, Hearings before the Committee on Ways and Means on State and Local Fiscal Assistance Act, 92nd Congress, 1st Session, p. 921.

[3]*U.S. Congressional Record*, 92nd Congress, 2d Session, August 18, 1972, S 14002.

risk loss of control of the budget, but also vitiate the most important power of the Congress itself.

Given the interest of the appropriations committees in maintaining their authority over spending, their members might be expected to be more opposed to the funding mechanisms of the revenue sharing plan than other members of Congress. Only in the Senate, however, was an amendment proposed dealing solely with the issue of the funding mechanism; in the House, the only opportunity for members to express dissatisfaction with the funding procedure was on a motion to end debate on a "closed rule," which would prevent amendments to the bill and thus deprive members of an opportunity to alter the funding procedure on the floor of the House.

The results of the vote in the Senate can be seen in Table 5.1, which compares the votes of the full Senate with the votes of the Senate Appropriations Committee. The amendment lost 34–49, but the Appropria-

tions Committee voted unanimously (20–0) in support of it, with nine of the eleven total Republican yes votes coming from the committee.

Table 5.2 shows the results of the House vote on the motion to end debate on the closed rule prohibiting amendments. If members had wished to amend the funding procedure of revenue sharing, we would have expected them to vote "no" on this motion, because it would prevent them from doing so. The House voted 223–185 to end debate, with the Republicans strongly in favor (113–57) and the Democrats opposed (110–128). However, a majority of the House Appropriations Committee members from both parties voted against ending debate which suggests the influence which committee loyalty had. Even committee Republicans, whom we would normally expect to support a bill sponsored by a Republican administration, voted against it.

In 1976, when revenue sharing was reauthorized, the funding mechanism was again subjected to efforts in both House and Senate to substitute annual appropriations for

TABLE 5.1. **Comparison of Senate and Appropriations Committee Vote on Annual Appropriations for Revenue Sharing Programs, 1972**

		Total	Dem.	Rep.
Senate	Y	41.0% (34)	46.9% (23)	32.4% (11)
	N	59.0 (49)	53.1 (26)	67.6 (23)
		- - - - 100% (83)	- - - - 100% (49)	- - - - 100% (34)
Appropriations Committee	Y	100.0 (20)	100.0 (11)	100.0 (9)
	N	0.0 (0)	0.0 (0)	0.0 (0)
		- - - - 100% (20)	- - - - 100% (11)	- - - - 100% (9)

TABLE 5.2. Comparison of House and Appropriations Committee Vote on Motion to End Debate on Closed Rule for Revenue Sharing Debate, 1972

		Total	*Dem.*	*Rep.*
House	Y	54.7% (223)	46.2% (110)	66.5% (113)
	N	45.3 (185) - - - - 100% (408)	53.8 (128) - - - - 100% (238)	33.5 (57) - - - - 100% (170)
Appropriations Committee	Y	19.6% (10)	13.3% (4)	28.6% (6)
	N	80.4 (41) - - - - 100% (51)	86.7 (26) - - - - 100% (30)	71.4 (15) - - - - 100% (21)

the entitlement. Although the results of the 1976 votes (see Table 5.3) suggest less consensus among appropriations committee members than there had been in 1972, these members were still much more in favor of annual appropriations than the other members of their respective parties.

Thus, despite concern over increasing uncontrollable spending and consistent deficits in the federal budget, efforts to treat revenue sharing like a regular program subject to a separate annual appropriation met with even less success in 1976 than in 1972. The situation would be slightly different in 1980.

1980 REAUTHORIZATION

When revenue sharing came up for its second reauthorization in 1980, external conditions were far different from what they had been in 1972. The economy had been through the deep recession of 1974–75, and another was forecast for 1980. Although the federal deficit

was sizeable even in 1972, fiscal pressures had grown much more severe by 1979 due to sustained high inflation, high interest rates, and high unemployment. Conditions were equally bleak for local governments in 1979 because, despite tremendous increases in federal aid during the Carter Administration, one city after another was faced with actual or potential defaults, employee layoffs or closing of schools due to increased costs.

The states, however, appeared to be in much better fiscal circumstances. Whereas in the early 1960s only thirty-three states had income taxes and thirty-four had sales taxes, by 1980 forty-four states had income taxes, forty-five had sales taxes, and forty-one had both. Their revenue structures were consequently much more elastic, meaning that their revenues would grow more rapidly with growth in the economy. The aggregate state budget surplus was over $7 billion. In 1979, nineteen states reduced personal income taxes and fourteen reduced sales taxes; still no state had a deficit, thirty-five had surpluses in excess of

TABLE 5.3. House and Senate Votes on Amendment Providing for Annual Appropriations for Revenue Sharing, 1976

			Total	Dem.	Rep.
	House	Y	38.1% (150)	48.9% (129)	16.2% (21)
		N	61.9 (244)	51.1 (135)	83.8 (109)
(a)			- - - - 100.0 (394)	- - - - 100.0 (264)	- - - - 100.0 (130)
	Appropriations Committee	Y	64.7 (33)	82.4 (28)	29.4 (5)
		N	35.3 (18)	17.6 (6)	70.6 (12)
			- - - - 100.0 (51)	- - - - 100.0 (34)	- - - - 100.0 (17)
	Senate	Y	18.4% (14)	23.9% (11)	10.0% (3)
		N	81.6 (62)	76.1 (35)	90.0 (27)
(b)			- - - - 100.0 (76)	- - - - 100.0 (46)	- - - - 100.0 (30)
	Appropriations Committee	Y	47.8 (11)	60.0 (9)	25.0% (2)
		N	52.2 (12)	40.0 (6)	75.0 (6)
			- - - - 100.0 (23)	- - - - 100.0 (15)	- - - - 100.0 (8)

5 percent, and nineteen had surpluses in excess of 10 percent of expenditures. These macroeconomic conditions led members of Congress to question seriously the wisdom of continuing revenue sharing with the states.

But there were political factors which were influential as well. In 1979, the fervor to balance the federal budget in order to combat inflation reached a peak. The state governors, through the National Governors Association, went on record insisting that the president and the Congress exercise fiscal restraint and balance the federal budget. Also, by 1979, thirty state legislatures passed resolutions calling for a constitutional convention for the purpose of passing an amendment requiring that the federal budget be balanced, only four states short of the number required. These persistent cries for reductions in federal spending angered members of Congress who saw it as an example of biting the hand that feeds. State governors benefited from federal revenue sharing and then criticized Congress for not balancing the budget. It should have come as no surprise that one of the first programs Congress suggested be cut in order to attain balance in the federal budget was revenue sharing with the states.

As early as March of 1979, the Joint Economic Committee, which has no authority to introduce legislation, recommended that Congress reduce or eliminate the state share of revenue sharing. When the House and Senate Budget Committees began marking up their first concurrent resolutions on the budget in 1979, each deleted the state share from the revenue sharing program, but it was later restored. President Carter's initial budget message for FY 1981 contained requests for both the local and state share of general revenue sharing. But within two months, in an effort to balance the federal budget for FY 1981, the president reversed himself and proposed that the state share of $2.3 billion be eliminated. Since the loss of the state shares would clearly affect the states' ability to provide assistance to their own local governments, (estimates of how much revenue sharing money the states "pass through" to local governments range from 40 percent to 60 percent of the total state allocation), Carter also requested an additional $500 million for FY 1981 and 1982 for transitional assistance to local governments.

House Action

Carter's quick turnabout was mild, however, compared to an extended series of reversals and flip-flops which the Congress did in 1980 over the reauthorization of revenue sharing. It began in the House Government Operations Committee's Subcommittee on Intergovernmental Relations. In the early summer of 1980, after first excluding the states from the program, the subcommittee decided to exclude them only for fiscal 1981 and leave them in for 1982 and 1983. However, on June 24, on the last day of markup session, the subcommittee again reversed itself and cut the states out entirely. This was consistent with the preferences of the chairman of the Government Operations Committee, Rep. Jack Brooks (D-Texas), who has opposed revenue sharing since its inception.

However, when the bill went to the full committee on July 1, Rep. Ted Weiss (D-N.Y.) offered an amendment, which restored the state share for 1982 and 1983 and subjected the state funds to annual appropriation. This amendment, to the dismay of Chairman Brooks, was accepted on a 21–15 vote. State revenue sharing was in again, at least temporarily.

However, the battle in the Government Operations Committee was not over. After the vote on the Weiss amendment, Chairman Brooks adjourned the markup for the Fourth of July recess, perhaps in hopes of allowing opponents of state participation, such as the Carter Administration, to marshal their forces. If so, the strategy worked. Within a month after the July 1 vote, which included the states, the full committee reversed itself and voted by an almost identical margin—20–15—to exclude them entirely.

Due to election year campaigning, Congress adjourned before it was able to consider the reauthorization of revenue sharing. This and other pending legislation, especially the FY 1981 budget resolution, forced the Congress to reconvene after the November election, the first "lame duck" Congress in nearly half a century. The revenue sharing versions sent to the floors of the House (HR 7112) and Senate (S 2574) differed fundamentally on the questions of length of authorization, the status of the state share and how it would be financed. The House extension was for three years and excluded the states completely; the Senate bill extended GRS for five years through FY 1985 and excluded the states only from the FY 1981 budget because provisions of the Congressional Budget Act of 1974 prevented its inclusion for the fiscal year already begun.

In House floor consideration of HR 7112, two matters received by far the most attention — state participation in revenue sharing and the retention of entitlement financing for the program. These two issues were related because the proposals to restore state participation after 1982 also removed the entitlement for states. But the issue of entitlement was also raised in regard to the entire program. As in 1972 and 1976, efforts were made to subject the program to annual appropriations.

The state share issue resurfaced immediately when Rep. Wydler (R–N.Y.) offered a substitute measure, which restored the states' $2.3 billion share of the revenue sharing program for 1982 and 1983, and rejected the entitlement aspect of the program for the states, as the Senate bill did. State revenue sharing funds would be subject to discretionary annual appropriations, whereas local governments would still enjoy the security of an entitlement.

True to form, Rep. Brooks made a last ditch effort to delete the states from the program by proposing an amendment which would have deleted the state share from Wydler's measure also. The amendment was rejected on a 158–215 vote, with a majority of Democrats in favor and a majority of Republicans against. However, the House did agree to an amendment by Rep. Levitas (D–Ga.), which required each state government to refund or decline categorical grant funds on a dollar-for-dollar basis in order to obtain revenue sharing funds. Levitas argued as follows:

For every dollar that a categorical program is disavowed by a state because they do not want it and do not need it, to that extent they will receive general

revenue sharing money to spend as they so desire. It does it without adding to the budget, without adding to the deficit.[4]

The arguments in favor of the amendment were that revenue sharing better allows local officials to make their own decision about local priorities, that revenue sharing is an efficient, relatively inexpensively administered program, and that the dollar-for-dollar reduction would increase decentralization of government without adding to the federal deficit. Despite objections to the administrative problems the amendment would create for the Secretary of the Treasury and the Office of Revenue Sharing, the amendment passed on a voice vote.

Once the entitlement had been eliminated for the states, Rep. Boland (D–Mass.), chairman of the House Appropriations Committee, went a step further and proposed an amendment which read as follows:

. . . notwithstanding any other provisions of this title, no unit of local government shall be entitled to an allocation calculated on the basis of a funding level in excess of the amount appropriated under this sentence for the entitlement periods beginning in October 1 of 1981 and 1982.[5]

In other words, it subjected the entire program to annual appropriations. Boland argued in favor of greater budget control and for giving Congress the responsibility to determine the spending level every year. Clearly, Boland was arguing for his committee's prerogatives, the same arguments made eight years earlier.

The argument against him was the same too — revenue sharing must be an entitlement so that local communities can have certainty about their allocations and plan better. Rep. Wydler noted that, although committee

[4]*U.S. Congressional Record*, 96th Congress, 2nd Session, H 10599.

[5]*U.S. Congressional Record*, 96th Congress, 2d Session, H 10607.

prerogative and power were the motives for the Boland amendment, these were *valid* motives.

> *Maybe if I was a member of the Committee on Appropriations, I would agree with him (Boland), too. They get jurisdiction; they get a little more power over the program if the amendment is passed. That is all right. That is a perfectly legitimate motivation.*[6]

Unfortunately, because the Boland amendment was defeated on a voice vote, the vote cannot be compared with similar measures in earlier years. The vote on the Wydler substitute measure comes closest to representing a vote on entitlement funding versus annual appropriations, although it is mingled with the state funding issue. The vote on the Wydler measure is presented in Table 5.4. We see from the vote distribution that there was virtually no difference between the com-

[6]*U.S. Congressional Record*, 96th Congress, 2d Session, H 10610.

mittee and the rest of the House on the issue. We also see that the Republicans were for the first time more favorably disposed to removing the entitlement than the Democrats. Again, we cannot attribute this solely to the funding mechanism issue because it is inseparable from the state funding issue.

Senate Action

It took the Senate nearly a month to take up the revenue sharing measure after the House completed its action. When it did, on December 9, there was little time left before the planned adjournment, December 12, to make major changes or even to hope to reconcile the Senate Finance version with HR 7112. Due to the time constraints, the Senate began working on HR 7112, which now contained revenue sharing for the states for FY 1982 and 1983, instead of taking up its own bill with the five-year extension.

The issue of the state share and the

TABLE 5.4. Comparison of House and Appropriations Committee Vote on Wydler Measure Making State Revenue Sharing Subject to Annual Appropriation, 1980

		Total	Dem.	Rep.
House	Y	68.4% (255)	58.2% (138)	86.0% (117)
	N	31.6 (118)	42.8 (99)	14.0 (19)
		- - - - 100% (373)	- - - - 100% (237)	- - - - 100% (136)
Appropriations Committee	Y	66.7 (28)	55.6 (15)	86.7 (13)
	N	33.3 (14)	44.4 (12)	13.3 (2)
		- - - - 100% (42)	- - - - 100% (27)	- - - - 100% (15)

terms of state participation in revenue sharing recurred in Senate debate, but the results proved to be somewhat different. An amendment offered by Sen. Mitchell (D–Maine) would have included the states for FY 1981 as well as 1982 and 1983. But a motion by Senator Dole (R–Kan.) to table (kill) the Mitchell amendment was accepted on a narrow 47–44 vote. Although Mitchell moved to reconsider the vote, the motion to reconsider was also tabled, 46–45. Senator DeConcini (D–Ariz.), representing the antistate forces, then proposed an amendment excluding the states for FY 1982 and 1983, but it too was defeated, 26–56. In a significant reversal of the House, however, the Senate rejected the Levitas amendment on a voice vote. Concerned about the administrative feasibility of the trade-off idea, it instead voted to set up a pilot program to permit states to exchange categorical grants for revenue sharing. The Senate then passed revenue sharing on an 80–3 vote.

The next day, facing a Dec. 12 adjournment but unwilling to accept the Senate reversal of the Levitas amendment, Rep. Brooks offered a resolution (H. Res. 826) which accepted most of the bill but restored the Levitas amendment. Brooks, consistent with his opposition to revenue sharing, voted against his own resolution, which passed the House 337–19.

Neither the Senate nor the House is pleased about accepting an all or nothing proposition. But facing adjournment just a few hours away, the Senate had either to accept the House version or forego revenue sharing. It relented, accepting the bill on a voice vote.

CONCLUSION

The congressional action on the state portion of revenue sharing and the removal of the entitlement has some interesting implications. Because of the removal of the entitlement, Congress can conceivably fund all or *none* of the state share in the future. There is no commitment to the states. For this reason, political pressure will probably shift to the appropriations committees. The House Government Operations Committee and the Senate Finance Committee can disclaim responsibility because they reauthorized the state share, and they can argue that they helped the states but at the same time abided by congressional rules and comity by deferring to the appropriations committees. The lobbyist "monkey," it seems, is off the back of the members of the authorizing committees and on that of the appropriations committees.

Yet, the Levitas amendment provides that states will receive no net additional revenues as a result of the reauthorization. The intent of the amendment was to avoid adding to federal spending. Therefore, whether funds are appropriated or not will have no bearing on the amount of federal funds available to the states. The appropriations committees, therefore, can conceivably argue that since no states will lose revenues, there is no need for the appropriations committees to act.

On the other hand, the arguments for the Levitas amendment stressed the greater efficiency of revenue sharing over categorical grants and the value of decentralization. These are values which the Reagan Administration espouses and will most likely prod the Congress to implement. The effort to trade revenue sharing for categorical grants has potentially ironic consequences, however. The supporters of revenue sharing praised the cost-efficiency of its administration and its tiny bureaucracy. Yet the Levitas amendment, which these supporters approved, leaves the problem of administering the amendment up to the Secretary of the Treasury. The amendment contains no definitions or procedures. Thus, the bureaucracy will be given the task of writing regulations for and carrying out the intent (to the extent it can be discerned) of the Levitas amendment. The low administrative cost of revenue sharing, which was an important justification for the tradeoff amendment, will inevitably increase, not because of a fondness for regulations by federal bureaucrats, but because of a well-intentioned but poorly conceived congressional amendment.

Finally, the reauthorization of revenue sharing has partly reestablished the jurisdiction of the appropriations committees. Whether this will set a precedent for the removal of the entitlement provision from the local share after 1983 will probably depend more on the nation's fiscal health than on the arguments or blandishments of the appropriations committees. As we have seen, their appeals for their jurisdictional prerogatives have not been heeded in the past, except when external economic and political factors provided additional justification for restoring their jurisdiction.

FOR DISCUSSION

1. It might appear that a dollar of revenue sharing is equal to a dollar of categorical assistance, according to the Levitas amendment. But categorical grants are usually matching grants which require some local contribution, whereas general revenue sharing does not. What fiscal advantages might there be for local governments to choose revenue sharing rather than categorical grants?

2. What alternative procedure might be devised which would assure localities of the amount of funds they would receive while still making revenue sharing an annual appropriation?

3. Aside from reducing the uncertainty of local officials about the annual *amount* of revenue sharing funding, what other motive which was not stated in the case might exist for making revenue sharing a permanent appropriation?

4. What are some of the implementation problems that are created by the Levitas amendment?

GLOSSARY OF TERMS*

Appropriation An authorization by an act of Congress that permits Federal agencies to incur obligations and to make payments out of the Treasury for specified purposes. An appropriation usually follows enactment of authorizing legislation. An appropriation act is the most common means of providing budget authority, but in some cases the authorizing legislation itself provides the budget authority. (See "backdoor authority".)

Authorizing legislation Substantive legislation enacted by Congress that sets up or continues the legal operation of a Federal program or agency either indefinitely or for a specific period of time or sanctions a particular type of obligation or expenditure within a program.

Backdoor authority Budget authority provided in legislation outside the normal (appropriations committees) appropriations process. The most common forms of backdoor authority are authority to borrow and contract authority.

Concurrent resolution on the budget A resolution passed by both Houses of Congress, but not requiring the signature of the President, setting forth, reaffirming, or revising the congressional budget for the United States government for a fiscal year. The first, due by May 15, establishes the congressional budget targets for the next fiscal year; the second, scheduled to be passed by September 15, sets a ceiling on budget authority and outlays and a floor on receipts. Additional concurrent resolutions revising the previously established budget levels may be passed by Congress at any time.

Contract authority Statutory authority that permits obligations to be incurred in advance of appropriations.

Entitlements Legislation that requires the payment of benefits (or entitlements) to any person or unit of government that meets the eligibility requirements established by such law. Authorizations for entitlements constitute a binding obligation on the part of the Federal Government, and eligible recipients have legal recourse if the obligation is not fulfilled.

*Source: *A Glossary of Terms Used in the Federal Budget Process and Related Accounting, Economic and Tax Terms* 3rd ed. (Washington, D.C.: U.S. General Accounting Office, March 1981), PAD–81–27.

Permanent authority Budget authority that becomes available as the result of previously enacted legislation (substantive legislation in prior appropriation act) and does not require current action by Congress.

Uncontrollability The inability of Congress and the President to increase and decrease budget outlays or budget authority in the year in question, generally the current or budget year. Relatively uncontrollable refers to spending that the Federal Government cannot increase or decrease without changing existing substantive law. For example, outlays in any one year are considered to be relatively uncontrollable when the program level is determined by existing statute or by contracts or other obligations. Controllability, as exercised by Congress and the President, is determined by statute. In the case of Congress, all permanent budget authority is uncontrollable. For example, most trust fund appropriations are permanent, as are a number of Federal fund appropriations and interest on the public debt, for which budget authority is automatically provided under a permanent appropriation enacted in 1849. In the case of the President, relatively uncontrollable spending is usually the result of open-ended programs and fixed costs (for example, social security, medical care, veterans benefits—outlays generally mandated by law), but also includes payments coming due resulting from budget authority enacted in prior years, such as entering into contracts.

6

The Legislative Budget Office in Georgia: A Study of Politics and Analysis *

Budgeting is among the most important of public sector activities. The budgeting process, especially during legislative appropriations hearings, focuses public attention on government and frequently exhibits controversy over the object and level of proposed expenditures. The budget document is important because it presents, in concrete terms, the policy directions and program goals that will guide future government actions.

At least since the Budget and Accounting Act of 1921, budgeting has largely been viewed as a tool for the executive to use in determining the direction of government policy. The National Association of State Budget Officers uses the following definition of an executive budget:

The governor's recommended program to the legislature for the forthcoming fiscal year expressed in dollar terms. This annual submission contains an overall plan of appropriations and expenditures as well as an estimate of anticipated income to meet them including, if necessary, proposed additional revenue sources necessary to insure a balanced budget as required by the state constitution. When passed by the legislature this becomes the "state budget."

As the one who prepares the budget document for legislative review, the executive sets the context of the exchange and thereby has a powerful tool to control the outcome of the appropriations process. Also, the executive commonly has a large staff agency to help with budget preparation. Legislatures usually have only meager staff support.

There have been several notable efforts at the federal level to increase legislative

*Michael J. Scicchitano, University of Georgia.

influence over the fiscal process. The 1946 Legislative Reorganization Act contained provisions for the preparation of a legislative budget which eventually failed. The 1974 Budget Act provided for the creation of budget committees in both chambers of Congress and establishment of the Congressional Budget Office. In spite of these efforts, the executive typically retains a dominant voice in the budget process.

This study will examine the Georgia General Assembly, which has grown from a "rubber stamp" legislature to one which has a substantial impact on fiscal decision making. An important factor in developing the influence of the General Assembly is its supporting staff agency, the Legislative Budget Office (LBO). It will be instructive to examine the LBO in operation to discover why it has been able to be effective and make a significant contribution to budgeting in the General Assembly. The LBO must produce an analytical and informational product in a highly political institution. The following case illustrates interactions between analytical and political aspects of legislative staff life in the budgetary process. Each aspect necessarily affects the other. The case (1) presents a brief history of budgeting and the LBO in Georgia; (2) examines in some detail a specific example of the LBO at work; (3) presents conclusions and illustrates generalizations.

BUDGETING AND THE LBO IN GEORGIA

The budget process in Georgia has traditionally been dominated by the executive. From the 1930's to the early 1960's the governor and the state auditor had almost total control of budget allocations. Legislators ultimately became dissatisfied with their insignificant role in the budget process. The first important step to correct this imbalance was the Budget Act of 1962, which more precisely defined the budgetary roles of the governor and the General Assembly.

An important provision of the 1962 act authorized the General Assembly to hire a legislative fiscal officer. This individual would provide much needed professional staff assistance for the appropriations committees. Because the members of the General Assembly could not decide upon an individual for this position or the precise role he or she would play, it remained vacant for several years. In 1970, however, Pete Hackney, at the time working for the governor's budget office, was hired. Hackney has retained this position.

At the time of his appointment, Hackney was an experienced budget analyst with an extensive knowledge of Georgia's fiscal system. He was the nucleus of what eventually became the Legislative Budget Office. The task of Hackney and the LBO was a difficult one. He had to provide professional support to a legislative appropriations process that had historically been dominated by the governor. Also, since the General Assembly meets only briefly each year, the annual work of the LBO culminates in a few short weeks of frantic activity in which the major budgetary decisions are made.

The immediate problem for Hackney was to serve not one master but two appropriations committees directly and the many members of the General Assembly indirectly. Service for Hackney meant being supportive of all members of the General Assembly and, specifically, locating funds for programs and projects in which legislators were interested. Because Hackney had come directly from the governor's budget office, he was able to be effective during his first year. Having helped to prepare the budget, he knew it sufficiently well to be able to "find" several million dollars which legislators used for their own projects.

The governor, however, still held a firm grasp on the budget process. Whenever a legislator would cut funds from a program to support a pet project, the governor would loudly proclaim that crucial operating funds had been removed from the program. The governor could then mobilize clientele support and public opinion to force legislators to rescind the cut. The governor was also able to intimidate legislators with his veto power. It took a brave or foolish legislator to push for a budget cut when he knew that the governor might veto one of his bills at a later date.

To circumvent this problem, Hackney, working closely with several legislators, devised what became known as the continuation budget. This document lists last year's programs and allocates enough money to fund them at current year costs. For example, if utility costs for a state facility increased by ten percent, that institution would receive operating funds equal to last year's amount plus the ten percent increase. Each state activity is automatically carried at last year's level of effort. The continuation budget established a new framework for budget politics. It was now impossible for the governor to declare that essential operating funds were being withheld from programs. Legislators were released from the possibility of intimidation and were able to appropriate funds above the continuation amount (improvements) for programs of their own.

THE LBO AT WORK — AFDC IN GEORGIA

This case study will examine the role of the LBO in providing funds for the Aid to Families with Dependent Children (AFDC) Program. This is an important social program in Georgia and consumes a significant amount of state resources. Currently, over 180 million dollars is spent annually on the AFDC program with a third of this money coming from the state budget. There are 85,000 active AFDC cases in Georgia. The program is administered locally in each of Georgia's 159 counties. Policy, rules, and regulations for the program, however, are established by the State Department of Human Resources in Atlanta. All administrative costs are paid by state and federal funds.

The AFDC program has grown greatly in the past decade from spending only about ten percent of state benefits to over fifty percent. Because of this rapid growth, there has been a strong desire among legislators to limit state expenditures on the AFDC program. There are two basic reasons for this concern. First, and most obviously, AFDC consumed considerable resources which could be spent on other programs or district projects. Second, many legislators, especially those from the more conservative, rural parts of the state, were ideologically opposed to "welfare."

Part of the LBO's job, which Hackney actively encourages, is to visit agencies to discover what problems exist and how effective the agencies have been. During some of these visits, caseworkers informed LBO staffers of one way to limit AFDC rolls. If caseworkers could spend sufficient time with certain recipients, they could get them back into the labor force by helping them locate an appropriate position or obtain needed vocational training. The caseworkers felt that they could be especially effective with those who had been out of work for only a brief time and still interested in returning to the labor force. The number of social workers was too small and the number of cases too high to permit them to spend the time necessary to find jobs for recipients. Through calculation of the number of AFDC recipients, caseworker loads, and the amount of time that should be spent with each case, the LBO determined that 244 additional caseworkers would be required to effectively reduce AFDC rolls.

Hackney approached the Georgia Department of Human Resources for support in hiring the additional 244 people. DHR officials were initially noncommital. Nothing happened on Hackney's plan until the autumn of 1978, when he met Ruth Lee who was the chief officer of the Georgia County Welfare Association. Hackney explained his plan for hiring the additional caseworkers and Lee was enthusiastic. The association soon gave its support for the plan.

Members of the County Welfare Association are "down home" folks to the state legislators and were thereby able to secure considerable support for Hackney's plan among members of the General Assembly. The DHR, however, especially Secretary Doug Skelton, was now firmly opposed to the hiring plan. Any available money for the AFDC program, Skelton felt, should be spent on benefits and not new staff positions.

Governor Busbee, realizing that there was strong legislative support for the hiring plan, was not as firmly opposed as Skelton. Busbee, however, felt that it was necessary to support his DHR secretary. The governor's budget agency, the Office of Planning and Budget (OPB) was also aware of the support for Hackney's plan in the General Assembly. Realizing that it had to back Skelton, at least tacitly, but not wanting to jeopardize a long-term relationship with the LBO, the Office of Planning and Budget took a less strident approach than DHR. By this time the lines for the conflict were drawn.

Confronted with considerable DHR opposition, Hackney had to decide how best to obtain funds for hiring the 244 caseworkers. Instead of approaching the problem directly, Hackney decided that an oblique approach would be more successful. Every January, the General Assembly passes the Supplemental Budget which is a mid-fiscal-year adjustment to shift surplus funds from some areas to more needy programs. In the January 1979 Supplemental Budget, Hackney, with legislative support, included $1.2 million for the 244 caseworkers. Only $300,000 of this figure was state money with the remainder contributed by the federal government. Since the state money was available and a relatively small expenditure and since there was a danger of losing the federal money if it was not used, this move was readily accepted by the General Assembly.

Hackney's reasons for this method of securing the necessary funding are as follows. First, this was the easiest means of getting the new positions into the budget. Subsequent budget decisions would be made not on the basis of a new item but rather as part of the continuation budget. Second, the federal money would not be available during the next fiscal year. While it was relatively easy to start a new program with the small state contribution, it would have been almost impossible to begin one requiring the full $1.2 million of state funds.

Having gotten the program started, the LBO now had to face the gauntlet of the regular appropriations hearings for the upcoming fiscal year (1979–80). The House was generally supportive of the plan. Some conservative rural legislators were opposed to the hiring of "social workers" and made fiery speeches to that effect on the floor. Hackney, realizing this, shrewdly called the new positions "county workers." There was hardly a legislator who opposed more jobs for his or her county. The Senate, however, has traditionally been more supportive of the governor and it was here that Skelton was successful. Skelton got the Senate to drop the hiring plan from the continuation budget. The $1.2 million state expenditure would now have to be considered as a totally new appropriation.

The differences between the two chambers on appropriations matters are resolved in a conference committee. Since Georgia is constitutionally prohibited from deficit spending, any conference agreement must balance gains and losses between chambers so as not to exceed the projected state revenues. Hackney, aware of this, prepares a list of "trades" between the two chambers. The conference committee usually accepts about 80% of his recommendations. In this instance, Hackney naturally included as one of the programs to be retained the hiring of the additional caseworkers. The final conference decision was thus resolved in such a manner that it did include funds for the 244 employees.

Still, the battle was not over. In Georgia, as in most states, the governor has the power of item veto. Realizing that Busbee would support Skelton and veto this appropriation, Hackney decided to "bury" the expenditure. Instead of leaving it in a separate account, Hackney had the funds for the 244 new employees placed in a general "grants for counties" classification which Busbee could not touch without killing several popular programs.

The impact of this program remains to be seen. In a new program of this type, there is always a lag between when the positions are funded and the personnel are hired and trained. Time must then be given for their efforts to produce results. Still, some preliminary studies by the LBO indicate that welfare costs are being somewhat reduced and this is a likely consequence of the new program.

CONCLUSION

This case study presents an example of how a legislative budget staff can be effective in a political environment. Much of this effectiveness can be credited to Hackney who, while being an activist director of the LBO, remains very sensitive to the needs and desires of legislators. In this instance, confronted with the problem of rapidly increasing AFDC costs, the LBO's analysis produced a solution with the cues supplied by the General Assembly. The major operational premises for the LBO are to be both supportive of legislators and the legislature and to locate funds for projects in which legislators have an interest. In trying to make funds available by eventually cutting AFDC rolls, Hackney was perceptive enough to select, among the many possible alternatives, one which would be of immense benefit to legislators. Members of the General Assembly could claim credit and gain political support for the additional jobs they had brought to their district.

This case illustrates several points. First, the Legislative Budget Office can be effective and its work can influence legislative appropriations decisions. Second, the nature of the analysis produced by the staff is determined by legislative needs and not by the comprehensive or programmatic criteria embodied in the rational problem-solving budgetary approaches such as PPBS or ZBB. Third, the staff must work in and between the House and

Senate. The budget staff thus serves both an integrative and analytical function. Budget staffs in legislatures can be effective if they orient their analytical products to the political needs of the legislative system.

At the beginning of this case it was suggested that there was an orientation toward executive budgeting in our governmental system. For example, most innovations to improve budgeting are developed for or by the executive. Yet, this case demonstrates that a legislative budget staff can be effective. Improving the capabilities of legislative budget staffs is an "innovation" that is a viable means of enhancing the fiscal process.

REFERENCES

BALUTIS, ALAN P., and BUTLER, DARON K., *The Political Pursestrings*. New York: Holsted Press, 1975. Case studies which examine the role of the legislature and its staff in the budget processes of seven states.

BOWHAY, JAMES H., and THRALL, VIRGINIA D., *State Legislative Appropriations Processes*, 1975. Lexington, KY: Council of State Governments. Good description of the legislative appropriations process in the fifty states with detailed profiles of fifteen states.

DOUBLEDAY, D. JAY, *Legislative Review of the Budget in California*, 1967. Berkeley, California: University of California Printing Department. An in-depth study of the legislative experience with the budget process in one state which devotes considerable attention to the role of the legislative staff analyst.

HREBNAR, RONALD J., "State Legislative Budgetary Review Processes," *Midwest Review of Public Administration* 9 (April–July, 1975): 133–44. An examination of the several information sources, including staff, of Washington State Legislators in the appropriations process.

ROBERTS, ALBERT B., "American State Legislatures: The Staff Environment," *Public Administration Review* 35 (September–October, 1975): 501–04. Discusses the possibilities for increased staff positions in state legislatures and their potential to play an active role in the policy process.

ROSENTHAL, ALAN, *Legislative Performance in the States* (Chapter 7). New York: The Free Press,

1974. Examines the use of and issues facing the staff in state legislatures with some emphasis on the fiscal process.

PROBLEMS

1. This case has presented one possible solution to controlling AFDC costs. Develop your own proposal for reducing AFDC costs while effectively meeting the needs of those who deserve assistance. Your reply should specify how we can identify those individuals who need aid as well as recipients who are ineligible. One method of saving money may be to reduce administrative costs. What alternative techniques and organizational approaches could be used to make the AFDC program both more efficient and effective?

2. As part of the national movement to reduce energy consumption, the governor of your state proposes that a new state energy agency be organized. This agency would be housed in the state capitol and institute state-wide programs, such as tax credits and loan incentives, to foster energy conservation. Legislators are also interested in saving energy but would rather see a program that would not add to the growth of the bureaucracy and would earn them political credit. The legislature proposes a decentralized program tied to an existing agency such as the county extension service. This program would not focus on a broad-based approach but on specific on-site activities, such as home-energy audits, educational presentations, and information packets on how to save energy in the home.

   As a staff member in a legislative fiscal office you must develop a proposal to fund the legislature's new program. How could you justify funding this program? What are its advantages and disadvantages, based on cost and effectiveness criteria, compared to the governor's program? How could you convince skeptical legislators of the worth of this program? What specific benefits would it supply to legislators? Could a compromise between the legislative and executive proposals be engineered that would satisfy both?

3. This case has demonstrated that the political aspects of a legislative fiscal officer's job are often as important as the technical. One of these political functions is to build support among other legislators for the budget alternative produced by the appropriations committees. What are some techniques that a budget officer could employ to build this support? Your reply should address at least the following aspects of a legislature: legislators' constituency needs and policy preferences, the tension between appropriations and authorization committees, differences between majority and minority members, and upper and lower chambers.

4. An effective budget staff person plays a difficult role. While being both technically and politically active in the budget process, she or he must not appear to assume the role of decision maker. If you were a legislative fiscal officer with more expertise about the budget than most legislators, how would you conduct yourself and your office so as not to encourage the resentment and hostility of legislators? You should respond by considering the many interactions of the legislative fiscal office with individual legislators, with appropriations committees in both chambers, with the appropriations' conference committee and with the executive branch on behalf of the legislature.

FOR DISCUSSION

1. How active should staff be in the operation of a legislature and the development and implementation of policy? Consider the factors of professionalism and time.

2. What are the advantages and disadvantages of the line-item veto for a state governor?

3. A "classic" view of legislative-executive relations in the budget process is one of distinct separation. In reality, such separation of responsibilities does not exist. What factors reduce the degree of separation? Consider the impact of staff interaction.

4. What problems stem from the fragmented nature of legislative budgeting? How can a legislature develop an effective role in the budget process?

7

The Asphalt Paradox*

Like many other jurisdictions, this city was in a tight fiscal squeeze. The budget officer saw the need for the city to save money and increase efficiency wherever possible. Through the chief executive, the budget officer called upon all departments to make existing resources go as far as possible.

The city committed a large proportion of its budget each year to resurfacing streets and highways, which the city did with its own work force. The city government did not want to cut this program because the streets generally were considered to be in bad shape — with many cracks and potholes. Poor street conditions were one of the biggest sources of citizen complaints.

An industrial engineer was assigned to the resurfacing program to see if it could be made more efficient. The engineer's initial analysis indicated the following:

The program had an operating efficiency of $17,500 per lane-mile resurfaced; this unit cost was based upon

$10,000 labor cost per lane-mile

$7,500 asphalt cost per lane-mile.

At the current rate of productivity per labor-hour, the city's resurfacing crews would be able to resurface 75 lane-miles in one year.

After carefully charting out the entire resurfacing process, work sampling the resurfacing crews in action, and analyzing the results, the engineer determined that it was possible, in a relatively short time, to improve the schedule of delivery of asphalt, vary the size of resurfacing crews to meet the needs of each job, and improve work methods. The engineer concluded such changes would increase the productivity of the resurfacing labor force by 33 percent in the first year of implementation alone. His conclusions were as follows:

The existing resurfacing work force would be able to resurface 100 lane-miles in a year.

The unit cost of labor would be reduced to $7,500 labor cost per lane-mile.

The program's operating efficiency

*By Paul D. Epstein, Division of Government Capacity Building, Office of Policy Development and Research, U.S. Department of Housing and Urban Development. Adapted from *Using Performance Measurement in Local Government: A Guide to Improving Decisions, Performance, and Accountability* (Washington, D.C.: HUD, 1981, draft), Chapter 4. Forthcoming under same title from Van Nostrand and Reinhold: N.Y., 1983. The author is currently manager of New York City's Citywide Productivity Program.

would improve considerably, as the total unit cost would be reduced by $2,500, the new unit cost being $15,000 per lane-mile resurfaced, based upon

$7,500 labor cost per lane-mile
$7,500 asphalt cost per lane-mile.

In seeking approval to implement the proposed resurfacing improvements, the engineer told the budget officer that the improvements would have an annual "efficiency value" of $250,000 to the city. This figure was based upon the benefit realized by resurfacing 100 lane-miles at a reduced unit cost.

The engineer calculated benefit as equal to the reduction in cost per lane-mile multiplied by the number of lane-miles resurfaced:

benefit = ($2,500)(100) = $250,000 "efficiency value"

Convinced by this argument, the budget officer supported the engineer's recommendations to the chief executive who, in turn, approved them. The chief executive was pleased that the city might get 100 lane-miles resurfaced by the same crews that resurfaced only 75 lane-miles last year. The operations improvements were implemented quickly and smoothly. Labor productivity increased as predicted and the projected $2,500 reduction in unit cost resulted. By the end of the fiscal year, the resurfacing work force, without adding any staff, had resurfaced 100 lane-miles of streets and highways.

However, the budget officer was angry at the engineer by the close of the fiscal year. In fact, the budget officer was livid. He had expected a $250,000 benefit, but when all the bills were totaled, he decided the "improved" program had actually cost the city budget an additional $187,500. How had it happened?

Under the original program of resurfacing 75 lane-miles at a higher unit cost, the total costs would have been

Labor ($10,000 per lane-mile)(75 lane-miles)
= $750,000
Asphalt ($7,500 per lane-mile)(75 lane-miles)
= $562,500.
Total Cost = $1,312,500

Under the "improved" program of resurfacing 100 lane-miles at the lower unit cost, the actual costs were

Labor ($7,500 per lane-mile)(100 lane-miles)
= $750,000
Asphalt ($7,500 per lane-mile)(100 lane-miles)
= $750,000
Total Cost = $1,500,000

The result was a net increase in city expenditures of $187,500 ($1,500,000 − $1,312,500 = $187,500).

PROBLEM

Who was right? Was the engineer, who calculated a "benefit" of $250,000; or was the budget officer, who calculated an added cost of $187,500?

FOR DISCUSSION

1. How could a jurisdiction be tempted into taking a benefit it cannot afford? What sounds better, anyway—$250,000 worth of increased services or $187,000 in savings?

2. Given that increasing services generates a higher dollar "efficiency value," when should productivity gains be taken in the form of actual savings?

8

*The Management of Uncertainty: The St. Louis County Sales Tax**

In 1977, the Missouri legislature enacted a law permitting St. Louis County (a suburban county which does *not* include the City of St. Louis) to levy a 1% sales tax. Municipalities within the county already had such authority, but unincorporated areas of the county did not. The 1977 legislation, which was bitterly debated in the legislature, and which required referendum approval, specified that unincorporated areas, as well as all municipalities which had not previously levied their own sales tax, would be covered by the 1% county levy. Municipalities would receive revenue from total tax collections in the covered area proportionate to their share of population in the sales-tax pool.

Municipalities which had a previous sales tax were given the option of remaining on their own, in which case they would continue to receive sales-tax revenues based on sales within their own boundaries or joining the county pool. This arrangement was a compromise, adopted by proponents of the county tax measure in the legislature, in order to overcome objections from municipalities rich in potential sales-tax generating businesses. The details of the option, as finally enacted, were to give many St. Louis County municipalities some difficult choices in financial management in the years that followed.

For some municipalities, of course, the choice was easy. Those municipalities with large shopping centers within their boundaries naturally chose to retain their own sales-tax revenue. Indeed, it had been legislators from such communities who had been instrumental in assuring that the newly permitted county tax would continue to allow this option. Other

*By Andrew D. Glassberg, University of Missouri–St. Louis.

county municipalities, which had previously adopted their own sales tax, but which contained only tiny shopping districts, also had a clear choice. For them, it was an easy decision to opt to join the county pool as soon as possible.

For some municipalities in more marginal situations, however, the choice of own-source sales-tax revenues (Plan A) or county pool (Plan B), posed difficult choices, since the terms of the enabling legislation required them to make decisions which could be binding for a decade or more and which would have to be based on necessarily incomplete information.

The statute provided that in 1978 and 1979, municipalities which had their own sales taxes could join the county pool if they chose to do so. It was anticipated at the outset that many municipalities would indeed choose to do so, and the technical note which accompanied the passage of enabling legislation by the state listed twenty-seven county municipalities which would find it financially advantageous to make the switch.

The state enabling legislation required the adoption of a local ordinance and required that the decision be taken six months in advance of its date of implementation, but calculations as to whether it would be worthwhile for a municipality to join the county pool at the outset were relatively straightforward.

Using the state-prepared note, a municipality could easily compare the revenues it had received through its own-source sales tax with what it would have received had it been a part of the county pool. The only technical problems encountered in making such a calculation during the first two years of the law's effect would be the need to assume that other municipalities had made rational decisions and the possible need to anticipate any major new shopping projects scheduled for opening within the municipality's borders during the coming year. The first problem would be significant only in the most marginal cases, where the presence or absence of other municipalities in the county pool would affect per capita distribution and make the difference between utility in joining the county pool or remaining dependent on own-source sales-tax revenues.

The second problem, which could have arisen at the early stages of a municipality's decision making, would also be fairly simple. A municipality which anticipated the opening of an extensive shopping development within the year would have reasonably clear local knowledge of the pace of construction and plans for store openings through its building permit and licensing procedures and could estimate potential revenues that such new facilities might generate.

But the choices permitted by the state enabling law for 1980 and beyond were considerably more difficult. The 1977 state law indicated that the option exercised in 1980 would bind the municipality for the forthcoming decade. Decisions were required by July 1, 1980.

Of vital significance to these calculations were the assumptions that municipalities chose to make about the results of the 1980 census. Since distributions from the county pool are made on a per capita basis, a municipality would need to know not only its own projected population, but also the population patterns in the remainder of the county pool, both in other participating municipalities and in unincorporated areas. Unfortunately for municipal finance officers, no 1980 census figures were available at the time state law required that their decisions be made.

Interviews with municipal finance officers in several municipalities who took the opportunity in 1980 to switch out of the county pool indicated that the prime consideration was their estimate of population. That the size of the population would have a potentially

serious impact was well-known in St. Louis County. Most inner suburban municipalities were predicting stable or declining populations, while the county pool included large areas of unincorporated West County, which had been the focus of the most rapid development in the region through the 1970's. Many municipalities knew, therefore, that their share of sales-tax revenues through the county pool would decline as a result of the 1980 census; and they had some basis for estimating what "own-source" sales-tax revenue would be, since they knew their pre-1977 own-source tax-collection figures. On the basis of estimates of municipalities' likely post-1980 population and estimates based on previous own-source revenues, St. Louis County municipalities made individual decisions about whether to remain in the county pool or revert to their own, locally generated sales-tax collections for the 1980's.

PROBLEM

In the environment of uncertainty depicted in this case your task is to outline what factors municipalities might have wanted to consider in deciding whether to participate in Plan A (own-source revenues) or Plan B (county pool) for the 1980's. Remember that this decision must be made by a known deadline (July 1, 1980), but that no 1980 census data would be available for making this decision. The County Planning Department had made some population estimates, but municipal decision makers would have no way of knowing the accuracy of these estimates at the time when they were required to choose Plan A or B. Remember also that the choice made is, under current statutes, binding for the 1980's.

Municipalities have a population projection of uncertain accuracy. What else might they wish to consider?

Factors in Addition to Population Projections

1. Estimates could be made of the likelihood that other municipalities with rea-

sonable local sales-tax bases and population losses relative to the rest of the pool will withdraw. (This factor would work in favor of a decision to remain in the pool.)

2. Estimates could be made of the likelihood that any currently unincorporated county areas might incorporate and choose to rely on own-source revenue. Some media attention had been given to the possibility of incorporation of one area of rapid development surrounding a large regional shopping mall in an unincorporated area of the county. (Such an eventuality would reduce the sales-tax revenue in the county pool and would decrease the revenue shared with any municipality which remained in the county pool.)

3. Estimates could be made of the potential for differential growth of taxable sales within the municipality and elsewhere in the pool through the 1980's. (Such estimates might include factors such as development of additional retail sales facilities, differential population gain [or loss] through the 1980's, and differential changes in average income among clientele of the municipality's shopping districts [and therefore differential changes in sales-tax receipts]. Additionally, municipalities might have considered the potential for changes in shopping patterns [possibly as a result of changes in gasoline cost and availability].)

4. Estimates could be made of the potential for differential growth in certain types of sales-tax receipts through the 1980's. The Missouri sales tax applies to all food purchases, and municipalities with disproportionate shares of their sales in supermarkets would have different sales taxes from those of a municipality with a large "discount store," selling general merchandise.

5. Political estimates could be made as to the likelihood of the state again changing the list of items subject to the sales

tax. (Although elimination of the sales tax on groceries has been rejected by Missouri voters in the past, other tax changes have been made. A 1979 change, for example, exempted prescription drugs from the sales tax.) If a municipality made a political judgment that elimination of the grocery sales tax was likely, it might or might not decide to remain in the county pool, depending on the amount of its own-source tax share generated by groceries compared with that of the others in the county pool.

6. Political estimates could be made as to the likelihood of further changes in the patterns of Sunday store openings and the possible consequences of such changes for sales-tax collections. (Within the past two years, changes in union agreements in the St. Louis area permitted the opening of supermarkets for the first time on Sundays, but permission to open other types of retail establishments was defeated by referendum. If a municipality judged that other Sunday openings might eventually materialize, it would need to determine how changing patterns of sales would affect its benefit from participation in the county pool.)

Sequel — What the Municipalities Did

In practice, no municipality examined went beyond population projections in any systematic way in making its decisions, although some municipal treasurers did mention considering the stability of their municipality's own business district as a source for sales-tax revenues in the '80's.

What impediments were there to the consideration of other factors? One city manager produced the following catalogue when these options were reviewed with him:

Municipal decision makers may regard these variables as too unpredictable. Even population projections provided by county planning bodies have been subject to significant error. The additional factors described above may simply seem unknowable to many municipal officials.

Many of the factors listed above require estimates of decision making in other municipalities. Municipal officials vary in the extent to which they are familiar with the workings of other jurisdictions in their area and are wary of making assumptions about the outcomes of political–administrative interactions beyond their own turf.

Using complex models may increase decision-makers' anxiety, especially for officials who lack experience in comparing such statistics.

Many municipalities, especially those in the "inner ring" of suburbs, knew that the 1980 census results would have a variety of negative consequences for population-driven funding formulas, and sales-tax changes were only one of these. Such municipalities were also facing additional pressure because of changes in the socioeconomic composition of their populations. This combination of pressures produced a classic retrenchment environment, in which decision makers ordinarily feel heavily pressured by external forces and lack the time (and probably the enthusiasm) for complicated models, none of which will produce the "happy ending" of additional revenue. (For such municipalities, a "right choice" of sales-tax plans would only reduce the loss of revenue, not produce any improvement.)

Many, perhaps most, municipalities would be unable to perform calculations of this type by themselves. While external consulting firms are available for such purposes, many small municipalities have no experience in dealing with such organizations and few obvious sources of resources to pay the fees involved.

The combined effect of these factors, this city manager argued, leads municipalities to take the simpler decision route and ignore factors in addition to population projections.

One final consideration needs to be raised. A choice which is binding for a decade raises unusual problems in the "management of uncertainty" and also raises difficult issues of appropriate time horizons for municipal officials. Line decision makers simplified their problems by treating the sales-tax decision as a "snapshot" taken in 1980. It is, of course, a "moving picture" with consequences throughout the 1980's. Many of the "missing elements" listed above have the potential for producing a calculation that might show one choice as most advantageous in the early years of the decade, but another as more beneficial for the decade as a whole. While many technicians may be comfortable with making calculations on a decade-long basis, elected officials whose terms are never more than a fraction of such a period, are unlikely to be sympathetic with such extended time horizons. While the legislature was concerned with preventing a too-frequent change in pools by St. Louis County municipalities, it produced a procedure which was virtually guaranteed to result in a process of municipal decision making which omitted significant elements in producing the required local decisions.

CHAPTER THREE

BUDGETARY CONTROL AND FINANCIAL ACCOUNTABILITY

The purpose of control is to ensure the prudent and proper use of public monies, in particular those revenues raised by local taxes. Recent efforts to extend this "stewardship" to intergovernmental funds (for example, the audit requirement described in case no. 11) and the heightened concerns of the investment (no. 29) and professional (no. 14) communities with the fiscal viability (no. 34) of cities such as New York and Cleveland should not obscure the fact that conventional control endures as a traditional emphasis in budgeting and financial management.[1] It remains the predominant emphasis, although the initial aim has broadened from minimizing waste, fraud, and abuse to providing the necessary informational underpinning for effective operations (no. 10) and planning (nos. 32, 34). The issue, then, is accountability, in its broadest sense.

Most jurisdictions are subject to some combination of the many control mechanisms that have been developed. Some of these are relatively passive, formal requirements for information and documentation produced either for a central staff within a jurisdiction or for purposes of intergovernmental oversight.[2] Verified or documented compliance with legally mandated regulations and restrictions primarily depends upon record keeping and reporting rules; these include accounting standards, independent audit requirements, and standards for financial reporting and public disclosure. The Financial Accounting Standards Board, the American Institute of Certified Public Accountants, the National Council on Governmental Accounting, and other authoritative groups within the profession have developed sets

[1] Allen Schick, "The Road to PPB: The Stages of Budget Reform," *Public Administration Review* 26 (December 1966), 243–58.

[2] John E. Petersen, Lisa A. Cole, and Maria L. Petrillo, *Watching and Counting: A Survey of State Assistance to and Supervision of Local Debt and Financial Administration* (National Conference of State Legislatures and Municipal Finance Officers Association: October 1977).

of widely recognized professional standards.[3] Although adherence to these "generally accepted" prescriptions is less than what may be preferred,[4] their development represents more than merely cosmetic or symbolic change. A consensus has developed around the professional principles according to which the underlying mechanics, the building blocks of budgeting and financial management, are expected to operate. The mechanics and the generally accepted principles are introduced in the cases in this chapter. (For disclosure standards, see case no. 29.[5])

Segmentation of responsibility and authority, another important control device, creates a structure of checks and balances which is intended to reduce the likelihood of fraud, waste, and abuse.[6] Prudential financial management requires that a number of individuals and offices be involved in each process. This approach, however, increases the complexity of the process and may induce delays and redtape, especially in conjunction with internal procedures or administrative requirements through which funds also are controlled. Examples here include position controls, competitive bidding, multiple sign-offs, formal designation of contract or obligating authority, apportionment, allotment, and encumbrance procedures, and the like.

Personal liability is yet another control mechanism, and such a serious one that it is not uncommon for the finance officer in a locality to be bonded. A description of the federal Antideficiency Act suggests the seriousness of this control mechanism:

[It] prohibits any officer or employee of the United States from making or authorizing obligations or expenditures under any appropriation or fund in excess of the amount available . . . . Any Government employee who violates this law will be subject to appropriate administrative discipline, including, when circumstances warrant, suspension from duty without pay or removal from office. Penalties for those who knowingly

---

[3]The major authoritative sources are National Council on Governmental Accounting, *Governmental Accounting, Auditing and Financial Reporting* (Chicago: Municipal Finance Officers Association, 1980) and Committee on Governmental Accounting and Auditing, American Institute of Certified Public Accountants, *Audits of State and Local Governmental Units* (New York: AICPA, 1974). Supporting sources include: James M. Williams, "Accounting, Auditing and Financial Reporting," in *Essays in Public Finance and Financial Management, State and Local Perspectives*, ed. by John E. Petersen and Catherine Lavigne Spain (New Jersey: Chatham House Publishers, 1978), pp. 86-94; and William W. Holder, "Local Government Accounting," in *Management Policies in Local Government Finance*, 2nd ed., ed. by J. Richard Aronson and Eli Schwartz (Washington, D.C.: International City Management Association, 1981), pp. 414–32.

[4]*How Cities Can Improve Their Financial Reporting* (U.S.A.: Ernst & Whinney, 1979).

[5]See also the disclosure guidelines of the Municipal Finance Officers Association and Coopers & Lybrand and The University of Michigan, *Financial Disclosure Practices of the American Cities, A Public Report* (U.S.A.: Coopers & Lybrand, 1976).

[6]*Enhancing Government Accountability* (New York: Price Waterhouse & Co., 1979).

and willfully violated the law include, upon conviction, fines up to $5000 or imprisonment for not more than two years, or both.[7]

Thus, personal integrity is no less an important component of financial control than are the more mechanical aspects like accounting and reporting.

Each case in this chapter begins with a general introduction to the admittedly technical topic. Emphasis in the chapter is on principles and concepts, as well as on encouraging mastery of a body of information. Case no. 36A applies the principles to state budgeting.

Case no. 9 describes the basic accounting controls and financial-reporting requirements that constitute "generally accepted" principles and practices (see Preface to case no. 9) applicable to local jurisdictions. This model case introduces the concept of "reporting entity," the basis of accounting, fund structure, encumbrances, and other relatively technical and, for budgeteer and program manager alike, absolutely necessary aspects of the subject. Several of the features which distinguish governmental accounting are explored in depth in case no. 9: governmental accounting segregates resources by funds; it draws upon budgets, which are the official financial plan, with the force of law; the method of accounting varies by fund, and the generally accepted basis of accounting for the general fund is modified accrual. The model takes the reader through the primary financial reporting document, the balance sheet.

Case no. 10 introduces some federal budgeting and accounting concepts and, through a series of exhibits, interrelates costs, accrued expenditures, and obligations and outlays. The federal fund and account structure is described through a problem-solving case that requires the recording of transactions and the calculation of account balances. Given the effort to avoid forfeiture, the possibility of reprogramming funds, and personal liability, it is only reasonable that a program manager should want information on unobligated allotment. Minimally, this information precludes violation of the Antideficiency Act.

Case no. 11, "Evergreen's Audit," deals with the financial and compliance audit and "generally accepted auditing standards" (GAAS) and explores the appropriate management response to an audit. This descriptive case is expanded by case no. 12, a model illustrating the main features of the auditor's report. Both cases treat independent audits at the municipal level of government.

[7]Joint Financial Management Improvement Program, General Accounting Office, *Financial Handbook for Nonfinancial Executives in the Federal Government* (Washington, D.C.: GPO, March 1981).

9

*Understanding Local Government Financial Statements**

PREFACE

One important information source available to citizens attempting to determine how their local government is managing its financial affairs is the government's annual financial report. Although the reports are public information and can be extremely enlightening, they have not been generally utilized by private citizens because they are considered complex and confusing to those with little or no governmental accounting background. Even someone who is adept at reading the balance sheets and income statements of commercial enterprises may have difficulty with government financial reports because of differences in terminology, format, and types of statements encountered.

Accounting has been called the language of business. It is also the language of government and, like any language, it can reveal much to those who understand it. This guide has been written to help you, the concerned citizen, understand and analyze the language of your local government's financial statements. The guide will not make you an expert on government financial reporting, but after a brief study you should have a sense of what the financial statements can tell you. This guide will also enable you to ask informed questions of appropriate government officials.

Accounting principles or standards for local governments are established by the National Council on Governmental Accounting (NCGA), an organization formed under the sponsorship of the Municipal Finance Officers

Association (MFOA).[1] MFOA membership is comprised principally of finance directors of state and local governments. NCGA principles are included in a publication entitled *Governmental Accounting, Auditing and Financial Reporting*, also known under the acronym GAAFR. The principles in GAAFR have been recognized by the American Institute of CPA's as representing generally accepted (most preferred) accounting principles (GAAP) for local governments. However, largely because state governments have the right to establish accounting standards to be followed by their constituent governments, compliance with NCGA principles, while increasing, has often been discouraged by existing state laws or regulations.

The most frequently encountered exception to GAAP basis financial statements is "cash basis" reporting which presents only receipts and disbursements. In contrast GAAP for government involves reporting "revenues" and "expenditures" under the modified accrual basis and "income" and "costs" under the full accrual basis of accounting. The latter two bases will be described in greater detail in the following discussion. Generally speaking the "cash basis" of accounting is *not* considered to fairly present the results of operations or financial position of an entity, in either the commercial or governmental environment. Its principal advantage is viewed by some as its inherent simplicity.

[1] At the time of this writing a "Government Accounting Standards Board" (GASB) will take over the work of NCGA and is expected to operate similar to, and in concert with, the Financial Accounting Standards Board (FASB), which sets accounting principles for the private sector.

The financial statements and accounting principles described and discussed in this guide are based upon NCGA pronouncements; however, because the guide is intended to increase understanding of the contents of governmental reporting, we have taken considerable liberty in presenting the format of the sample financial statements to which our comments will apply.

The following presentation emphasizes the two aspects of local government financial reporting considered most significant by finance officers and government managers—results of operations as represented by comparison of budget to actual revenues and expenditures and—financial position as represented by a summary of the government's assets and liabilities in a balance sheet.

Included at the end of this guide is a short bibliography for those who wish to delve further into the subject of government accounting.

THE FINANCIAL REPORTING ENTITY

Commercial accounting usually presents the results of transactions for a "single economic entity" such as a corporation (including all of its subsidiaries and divisions), a partnership, or a sole proprietorship. Identification of what constitutes the commercial economic entity is usually based on "investment" or "ownership" criteria.

Government accounting usually presents the results of the transactions of the organization's various projects and activities in "funds," i.e., groups of related accounts. Separate funds are usually established for specific types of activities. Determination of what constitutes all of the funds of the governmental entity is usually based on "control" criteria, i.e., the extent to which the city controls an activity through budgets, personnel policies, etc.

THE BASIC FUNDS

Funds are divided into three broad categories:

1. *Governmental funds:* The resources in these funds are intended to be expended within a specific period of time, usually a budget year. These funds are accounted for on the modified accrual basis of accounting and accordingly, as further described later, allocation of costs, such as depreciation among accounting periods, is not practiced in these funds. Rather, the funds generally measure the flow of resources (revenues and expenditures) into and out of the funds.

2. *Proprietary funds:* The resources in these funds are not meant to be exhausted within a specific time period. Their activities more closely resemble ongoing businesses in which the purpose is to conserve and add to basic resources while meeting operating expenses from current revenues. For this reason, proprietary fund financial statements are concerned with measuring costs (e.g., depreciation) and operating results. Therefore, they apply commercial accrual accounting principles and their reports closely resemble commercial financial statements. Usually the intent of the proprietary activity is to break even or recover the cost of operations.

3. *Fiduciary funds:* These funds are used to account for those activities in which a governmental unit is acting as a trustee or agent for other individuals, or governments. They are used to demonstrate how the governmental unit carried out its fiduciary responsibilities with regard to the assets entrusted to it.

These broad categories are further broken down into fund *types*.

Governmental funds:

1. *General fund:* Includes all general government financial operations which are not accounted for by any other fund type. Revenues in this fund would be derived from taxes, fees, and other sources which are not designated for any specific purposes (e.g., income and property taxes, license fees). These revenues are utilized for general ongoing government services such as administration, maintenance, and police and fire protection.

2. *Special revenue funds:* Account for the expenditure of revenues which have been provided to the government for specific programs or projects (excluding expenditures for building programs and major equipment purchases or any other similar undertakings, usually classified as a capital project). An example of a special revenue fund activity would be the accounting for revenues and expenditures under a federal grant for a research or training program.

3. *Capital projects funds:* Account for the collection and disbursement of revenues from a variety of sources (bond proceeds, loans, or grants) for the purposes of building or purchasing major capital assets, such as schools, public buildings, or recreational facilities.

4. *Special assessment funds:* Account for revenues and expenditures related to improvements, maintenance, or repair to public property for which assessments are levied against the property owners who are expected to directly benefit from the services or improvements. For example, a special assessment for installing sidewalks is usually levied against the property owners on whose property the walks are installed.

5. *Debt service funds:* Account for resources set aside to make interest and principal payments on long-term debt.

Proprietary funds:

6. *Enterprise funds:* Account for activities which are usually self-sustaining prin-

cipally through user charges for services rendered. Such activities include the operation of water supply and sewerage plants, hospitals, and transportation systems.

7. *Internal service funds:* Account for services performed by one local government organization or department for another. Often such services include maintenance and repair of vehicles by a centralized garage or operation of a data processing center.

Fiduciary funds:

8. *Trust and agency funds:* Account for collection and disbursement of assets held in trust by a government for another individual or group of individuals, or another government agency. Typical examples of trust and agency funds include pension funds in which the city is administering retirement plans on behalf of its employees, and scholarship funds in which the city awards scholarships to specified individuals in accordance with the terms of a scholarship trust agreement entered into with a donor.

In practice a local government, although maintaining only one general fund, may establish any number of special revenue, capital project, special assessment, debt service, enterprise, internal service, and trust and agency funds to account for its many separate projects and activities.

One of the most significant recent reporting changes introduced by NCGA was to require the combining of similar fund *type* activities (e.g., all special revenue, enterprise, capital projects, etc.) in general purpose financial reporting. Previously, combining of individual funds was not considered appropriate.

NON-FUND ACCOUNT GROUPS

In addition to the previously described funds, local governments also maintain separate memorandum accountability for general government fixed assets and long-term liabilities, known technically as account groups.

In the accounting for governmental funds fixed asset acquisitions are recorded as expenditures and borrowings as revenues. Accordingly, the commercial accounting procedure of recording them as assets and liabilities is not practiced. However, to establish accountability these transactions are recorded in memorandum form in account groups known as the *General Fixed Assets Group of Accounts* and the *General Long-term Debt Group of Accounts*. As depicted later in the sample financial statements presented herein, fixed assets and long-term debt are recorded in these account groups by means of contra account posting in account group balance sheets, the offset to fixed assets being the "investment in fixed assets" and the offset to long-term liabilities being the "amount to be provided from future revenues for payment of principal on bonds." While a summary of account group changes should be presented in statement or footnote form, an operating statement has no applicability to account groups.

FOOTNOTES

Most government financial reports contain extensive footnotes which include further explanatory information about specific areas of the financial statement. For example, the footnotes will usually indicate the type of funds established by the government and a brief description of the basis of accounting for each fund type and other significant accounting policies. Footnotes usually also include information on loan covenants, commitments and contingencies. It is a good idea to read the footnotes in conjunction with the financial statements in order to obtain a more complete understanding of your government's financial position and results of operations.

THE MEASUREMENT FOCUS

If you are a stockholder in a corporation, you are entitled to receive its annual report containing financial statements, which will tell you how well the company has accomplished its primary objective—making a profit. The income statement will reveal the size of the profit or loss. The balance sheet will tell you the composition of the company's assets and liabilities, as well as the amount of the stockholders' equity or accumulated worth.

Although you may not receive them as a matter of course, as a stockholder, that is, "taxpayer," in your local government, you should read its financial statements. If you do, you will find that they are more detailed and cumbersome than typical corporate financial statements. You will also learn that because the purpose of government reporting differs from that of a commercial enterprise, the information required to judge how well a government is accomplishing its objectives also differs.

Government operations are not intended to make a profit. Instead, its primary financial function is to use the funds it acquires from a variety of sources (e.g., income and other taxes, bond proceeds, state and federal grants) to provide services to its citizens according to a predetermined plan and within approved budgetary constraints. There is no single figure or amount which provides a measure of overall government performance. However, a government's general financial operations can be evaluated through a detailed comparison of actual performance with its adopted budget. Government financial statements are intended to facilitate such a detailed comparison.

In addition to the distinction which exists between the "profit" and "budgetary" bases of reporting it should be recognized that, as previously noted, government operations are reported on either the "modified accrual" (general government activities) or "accrual" (business-like activities of government) bases of accounting. Alternatively, commercial accounting employs only the accrual basis of accounting. The following discussion describes the unique attributes of the "modified accrual" basis, an understanding of which is essential to proper interpretation of government financial statements.

THE UNIQUENESS OF "MODIFIED ACCRUAL" GOVERNMENT FUND ACCOUNTING

The modified accrual basis of accounting used to account for activities of governmental funds has as its primary purpose the measurement of the flow-of-funds into and out-of the governmental unit. It is *not*, however, cash basis accounting. To understand the implications of modified accrual accounting it is best to relate it to the more frequently encountered accrual accounting applied to commercial entities. The following is a discussion of the principal modifications which are made to accrual accounting principles to arrive at governmental fund "modified accrual" principles.

Accounting for "Expenditures" Rather Than "Costs"

In commercial accounting, the determination of costs for a particular year is important because profit, of course, is measured by income earned less costs incurred. In governmental fund accounting it is the *expenditure* of funds within a particular year rather than *cost* which is important because government operations and related budgets are usually based on expenditures or use of resources.

A good example of the distinction between *costs* used in commercial accounting and *expenditures* used in governmental accounting is provided by the accounting for fixed assets acquisitions.

Since fixed assets acquired by a commercial entity are used to generate products or services and thus income, *cost* is spread out, or depreciated, over the years during which the assets are expected to be revenue producing. Depreciation as a *cost* is not particularly useful in government accounting, because assets are not typically revenue producing. The primary focus of government is on the *expenditure* for the asset, and whether the current budget for asset purchases was exceeded. Accordingly, the acquisition price is reflected as an *expenditure* in governmental funds in the year of purchase.

Accounting for "Encumbrances" and "Available Revenues"

Encumbrances

Encumbrances are commitments for expenditures for which goods or services have not been received at the time financial statements are prepared. They may be in the form of purchase orders or contracts for goods and services. In budget to actual comparisons, expenditures are often adjusted for encumbrances because budgets are usually approved on an encumbrance or obligation basis rather than a pure expenditure or disbursement basis.

Another of the recent accounting changes promulgated by NCGA prohibits showing encumbrances as though they were expenditures, except in budget–actual comparison statements. Because of many years of use in the preparation of governmental budgets, total disappearance of encumbrance accounting from government accounting is not expected to be rapid.

Available Revenues

The character of governmental revenues is different from that of commercial income. For example, income, sales and real estate taxes are not earned by producing goods or providing services. Rather, these revenues are usually assessed on an annual basis. Because of the flow-of-funds focus of government accounting there is a tendency to report revenues conservatively by only recognizing in the operating statement that portion of revenues which will be collected within the fiscal year, or soon enough thereafter (usually 60 days), to meet expenditures of the fiscal year just ended. Such revenues are commonly referred to as "available" (to meet expenditures) revenues. For example, property taxes which may have been levied but are not expected to be collected in time to pay current bills are recorded as "deferred revenue" in the government's balance sheet and as revenues in the period in which they meet the "available" test.

Accounting for Only Current Expenditures

Because governmental accounting focuses on changes in spendable financial resources, only those expenses that will be paid currently are recorded in governmental funds, i.e., expenses that have been incurred in the operation of the government that will be paid within the fiscal year or shortly thereafter. Those expenses that will be paid at a later time are considered long-term in nature and in the past, only disclosed in notes to the financial statements. In keeping with this expenditure philosophy, the cost related to unfunded (unpaid) pension liabilities, as well as for unpaid sick and vacation pay, are recorded in the period when cash payment or funding is required rather than the period in which benefits are earned. The amounts of earned but unpaid or unfunded pension, sick leave, and vacation benefits usually aggregate very material unrecorded liabilities for most government entities. The NCGA has under consideration a proposed change in its standards which would require recording such long-term liabilities in the general long-term debt group of accounts.

Recording Debt Proceeds as Operating Revenues

Since governmental accounting is concerned primarily with the flow-of-funds into and out-of the government, the proceeds of *long-term debt* raised for construction and other purposes is recorded as revenue in governmental funds. The long-term liabilities are recorded only in memorandum form in the general long-term debt group of accounts. However, *short term* debt of governmental funds, usually in the form of notes secured by a pledge of current revenues to be received, are not recorded as revenues but rather are recorded as liabilities, as is the practice in commercial accounting. Accordingly, the reader of governmental financial statements should be aware that the fund balance of governmental funds has been increased by the amount of long-term debt proceeds which require repayment in subsequent years.

The characteristics described above are the major distinctions between the so-called "modified accrual" basis of accounting used to record general government operations and the "accrual" basis used in commercial accounting and by governments to record their commercial or business-like proprietary fund activities.

AUDITOR'S REPORT

Your government's financial statements may be accompanied by a report of an independent public accountant or other auditor. This report should state whether the financial statements are presented in accordance with generally accepted accounting principles. Any significant deviations from generally accepted accounting principles should be discussed in the auditor's report and amplified where appropriate in the notes to the financial statements. In addition, the auditors should identify any limitations imposed upon their ability to perform generally accepted auditing procedures and the impact of those limitations or any other unusual factors on their opinion on the fairness of the financial statements.

Keep in mind that it is the primary role of the independent public accountant to express an opinion on whether the financial statements *present fairly the entity's results of operations and financial position in accordance with generally accepted accounting principles.*

A MODEL PRESENTATION

Now that we have discussed briefly the theory and general concepts of governmental accounting, let's look at an example of its practical application.

Annual financial reports of governments usually contain a substantial volume of financial presentations, including statistical data, individual fund, combining, and combined fund type financial statements and footnotes. We will concentrate on only two of the most frequently encountered financial statements in local government annual financial reports— (1) the Combined Balance Sheet for All Fund Types and Account Groups; and (2) the Statement of Revenues, Expenditures, and Encumbrances and Changes in Fund Balance— Budget and Actual.

The example statements illustrated in Exhibits I and II may not look exactly like those produced by your local government. Jurisdictions often employ variations in terminology and format. However, after examining the exhibits and studying the referenced explanations of terms and classifications (many of which have been described in the preceding pages), you will know what to look for in your government's statements and have a basis for recognizing and understanding any differences.

Once you know how to interpret and use your local government's financial statements, they can represent a concise and readily accessible method of evaluating your government's financial condition and detecting potential problems. This introduction to the language of government accounting should assist you in becoming an informed and active participant in your local government's financial affairs.

STATEMENT OF REVENUES, EXPENDITURES AND ENCUMBRANCES, AND CHANGES IN FUND BALANCE— BUDGET AND ACTUAL (EXHIBIT I)

The most frequently analyzed financial statement in local government is the Statement of Revenues, Expenditures, and Encumbrances and Changes in Fund Balance—Budget and Actual, which provides four important measurements:

1. revenues actually received against budgeted revenues

2. actual expenditures and encumbrances against the budgeted expenditures and encumbrances

3. total actual expenditures and encumbrances against total actual revenues

4. the changes in fund balance available for expenditure in future years

This statement (Exhibit I) can provide a wealth of information if it is correctly interpreted. A discussion of what it reveals about your government's financial operations follows. Examine the statement and identify the following symbols:

(A) *General fund:* This statement is for the general fund which accounts for administrative and typically recurring government services (e.g., police, fire, welfare, etc.).

(B) *For the year ended December 31, 19X2:* Since this is an annual statement, it presents summary figures for the total fiscal year's operations.

(C) *Revenues:* All significant sources from which the government's general fund received revenue during the year are identified.

(D) *Expenditures and encumbrances:* Since local governments are typically organized by function, financial statements are usually organized to summarize expenditures and encumbrances, both actual and budgetary, by major functional activity.

(E) *Budget:* This column shows the estimated revenues which were expected to be collected by source and the amount of estimated expenditures and encumbrances allocated to operations by function. Ideally these two estimated figures should agree since the objective is usually a perfectly balanced budget.

(F) *Expenditures:* These figures represent, for each function, the amounts actually expended for goods and services received during the year.

(G) *Encumbrances:* These amounts represent the contractual commitments to acquire

EXHIBIT I
(A) **General Fund**
Statement of Revenues, Expenditures, Encumbrances
and Changes in Fund Balance
Budget and Actual
(B) **For year ended December 31, 19x2**

	(E) Budget	(F) Actual Expenditures	(G) Actual Encumbrances	(H) Total Actual	(I) Budget Variance Favorable (Unfavorable)
(C) **Revenues**					
Property taxes	$2,633,000			$2,570,000	$ (63,000)
License and permit fees	230,000			212,500	(17,500)
Intergovernmental revenues	750,000			736,000	(14,000)
Service charges	66,000			67,250	1,250
Fines and forfeitures	80,000			80,850	850
Miscellaneous	41,000			40,120	(880)
Total revenues	3,800,000			3,706,720	(93,280)
(D) **Expenditures and encumbrances**					
General government	861,000	$ 478,260	$393,820	872,080	(11,080)
Public safety (police and fire)	445,500	382,380	67,250	449,630	(4,130)
Highways and streets	186,000	162,200	21,170	183,370	2,630
Building inspection and maintenance	85,350	72,920	11,450	84,370	980
Sanitation	84,000	80,200	3,180	83,380	620
Culture	92,000	81,300	17,800	99,100	(7,100)
Health	101,000	111,800	6,720	118,520	(17,520)
Welfare	106,000	136,300	3,850	140,150	(34,150)
Recreation	64,150	59,920	3,580	63,500	650
Education	775,000	712,000	64,800	776,800	(1,800)
Debt Service	1,000,000	1,000,000		1,000,000	—
Total expenditures and encumbrances	3,800,000	$3,277,280	$593,620	3,870,900	(70,900)
(J) Excess (deficiency) of revenues over expenditures and encumbrances	—			(164,180)	$(164,180)
(K) Unreserved fund balance, beginning of year	306,180			306,180	
(K) Unreserved fund balance, end of year	$ 306,180			$ 142,000	

See text for explanation of letter symbols

goods or services which were *not* received at year end. These amounts are included in the budget—actual financial statements as though they were expenditures if, as is customary, the government's budget is approved on an encumbrances or obligation basis.

(H) *Total Actual:* Under "revenues," the amounts in this column represent revenues collected or currently receivable from each source, which is compared with budgeted revenues. For the items under "expenditures and encumbrances" (D) this column contains the total of the "expenditures" and "encumbrances" columns, which is compared with the budgeted amounts for each function.

(I) *Budget Variance—Favorable (Unfavorable):* This column compares actual and estimated revenues and actual and budgeted operating expenditures and encumbrances.

(J) *Excess (deficiency) of revenues over expenditures and encumbrances:* Under Column (E) (Budget) there is no excess or deficiency of revenues over expenditures and encumbrances because the budget was prepared on the basis that "revenues" and "expenditures and encumbrances" would be balanced.

Under Column (H) (Total Actual), the figure on this line indicates that revenues fell short of operating expenditures by $164,180. This figure was computed by subtracting total "expenditures and encumbrances" from total "revenues."

Under Column (I), the identical figure is arrived at by adding the net amounts under total revenues and total expenditures and encumbrances. It can be seen that the overall operating deficit is composed of a *net* $93,280 short-fall in expected revenues and a *net* $70,900 overexpenditure of budgeted operating expenditures and encumbrances. A line-by-line analysis of this column, of course, will pinpoint the causes of these differences.

(K) *Unreserved Fund Balances, beginning and end of year:* The unreserved fund balance is usually comprised of the government's inception to date excess of revenues over operating expenditures and encumbrances. It has been built-up over the years. Annual surpluses (i.e., more revenues than expenditures and encumbrances) increase its size. Conversely, the fund balance will be decreased by operating deficits (i.e., more expenditures and encumbrances than revenues). Deficits may even completely eliminate the balance. A series of deficits may produce a negative fund balance. When this happens, it should be a signal to the reader that liabilities exceed assets, a condition usually associated with insolvency.

WHAT THE STATEMENT OF REVENUES, EXPENDITURES AND ENCUMBRANCES AND CHANGES IN FUND BALANCE—BUDGET AND ACTUAL, CAN TELL YOU

The major point to remember when reading this or any other financial statement is not to jump to conclusions.

These statements provide summary fund information about 365 days of complex operations and financial transactions, by a variety of government departments and functions. They can alert you to potential trouble spots which you could not otherwise identify except by wading through a myriad of vouchers, invoices, memoranda, journals and ledgers.

Consider an example from the statement on Exhibit I. From reading the statement you can see that this year the general fund had an operating deficit of $164,180. Further analysis shows that the deficit is attributable to two factors: (1) a short-fall in revenues, primarily in the area of property taxes, and (2) overexpenditures in certain areas, especially welfare and health.

The statement indicates that in spite of

the current year's deficit the fund has a $142,000 balance of resources available at the end of the year. However, should the government incur another deficit in the following year the fund balance could be eliminated, or, worse yet, a deficit fund balance could be created, in which case fund liabilities would exceed assets.

Questions such as the following may occur to you now:

> Are the over-expenditures and the short-fall in revenues unusual or significantly large?
> Has there been an increase in government spending this year?
> If so, is it a new phenomenon or has the increase in spending been a trend in recent years?

You may find answers to these questions by comparing this year's statement with statements for past years, which should be available in previously issued annual reports.

Assume that your review of prior years' statements indicates that (1) the revenue short-fall and the overexpenditures this year were indeed unusual and by comparison relatively large, and (2) government spending has been increasing significantly over the past five years.

It will now be necessary to search for causes and explanations from a variety of sources: city officials, newspapers, citizens groups, published reports of the various government departments. Was the revenue short-fall caused by a high delinquency rate, poor collection procedures, or a faulty estimate of expected revenues? Is the problem expected to recur, and is there a solution? Are the over-expenditures attributable to wasteful spending, poor estimates of the city's needs in certain areas, inflation, market conditions, or special situations? If the latter, has the situation passed, or will it continue? Will government spending keep rising and can the city handle the increasing financial burden?

You have already developed a great number and variety of questions about your government's financial condition. You might never have become concerned had you not taken a few moments to read the Statement of Revenues, Expenditures and Encumbrances and Changes in Fund Balance — Budget and Actual.

COMBINED BALANCE SHEET (EXHIBIT II)

Every local government's annual financial report should include a combined balance sheet (illustrated in Exhibit II) showing the year end financial position of governmental, proprietary, and fiduciary fund types, and account groups. This combined balance sheet may be supported by many other statements and schedules detailing the operations of individual funds. But the balance sheet by itself gives you a "snapshot" of your government's overall financial condition.

While the numerous columns and categories under "Assets" and "Liabilities and Fund Equity" make the statement look formidable, it is not nearly as complicated as it seems at first glance. Each column usually represents the financial position of numerous funds combined by fund types. In our illustration the balance sheet reflects only one fund of each fund type.

The columns have been arranged so that all governmental funds are grouped together, as are all proprietary funds, fuduciary funds and the two non-fund account groups. A discussion of what the balance sheet can tell you about your government's overall financial position follows the description of the references in Exhibit II.

(A) *Cash and Investments:* Most governments pool or combine idle cash of different funds to the extent permitted by law in order to obtain maximum earnings on investment and minimize the number of separate disbursement bank accounts. Investments can be made by all fund types. They represent the placement of otherwise idle cash into an earnings capacity.

EXHIBIT II
Combined Balance Sheet
All Fund Types and Account Groups
December 31, 19x2

| | | GOVERNMENTAL FUNDS | | |
| | General Fund | Special Revenue Fund | Special Assessment Fund | Capital Projects Fund |
ASSETS		City Parks Fund	Sidewalk Installations	Civic Center
(A) Cash and investments	$2,350,000	$ 80,000	$26,000	$40,000,000
(B) Accounts receivable				
(C) Taxes receivable	395,000			
(C) Assessments receivable			16,500	
(D) Due from other funds	16,000			
(E) Due from state government	374,000	55,000		
(E) Due from federal government	200,000	450,000		
(F) Inventories	45,000			
(G) Fixed assets, at cost less accumulated depreciation				
(H) Amount to be provided from future revenues for payment of principal on bonds				
(I) Amount available in debt service fund for payment of principal and interest				
Total Assets	**$3,380,000**	**$585,000**	**$42,500**	**$40,000,000**
LIABILITIES AND FUND EQUITY				
Liabilities:				
(J) Accounts payable	$1,219,000			$ 1,120,000
(K) Notes payable				
(K) Bonds payable				
(D) Due to other funds	16,000	$ 12,000		
(L) Other liabilities	38,000			
(C) Deferred revenue	395,000		$16,500	
Total Liabilities	**1,668,000**	**12,000**	**16,500**	**1,120,000**
Fund equity:				
(M) Investment in general fixed assets				
(N) Retained earnings				
Fund balances:				
(O) Reserved for encumbrances	1,525,000	520,000	23,400	2,500,000
(F) Reserved for inventories	45,000			
(P) Unreserved	142,000	53,000	2,600	36,380,000
Total Fund Equity	**1,712,000**	**573,000**	**26,000**	**38,880,000**
Total Liabilities & Fund Equity	**$3,380,000**	**$585,000**	**$42,500**	**$40,000,000**

See text for explanation of letter symbols.

| | PROPRIETARY FUNDS | | FIDUCIARY FUND | ACCOUNT GROUPS | |
Debt Service Fund	Enterprise Fund — Muncipal Water Utility	Internal Service Fund — Central Purchasing Agency	Trust and Agency Fund — Scholarship Fund	General Fixed Assets	General Long-term Debt
$1,000,000	$ 115,000 77,000	$ 83,000	$3,544,000		
		16,000			
	1,240,000 (450,000)	214,000 240,000 (28,000)		$47,580,000	
					$38,420,000
					1,000,000
$1,000,000	$ 982,000	$525,000	$3,544,000	$47,580,000	$39,420,000
	$ 10,000 2,000 36,000 4,000	$ 23,000			$39,420,000
	52,000	23,000			39,420,000
				$47,580,000	
	930,000	502,000			
$1,000,000			$3,544,000		
1,000,000	930,000	502,000	3,544,000	47,580,000	
$1,000,000	$ 982,000	$525,000	$3,544,000	$47,580,000	$39,420,000

(B) *Accounts receivable:* In commercial accounting the term describes amounts yet to be collected from customers who have purchased goods and services on credit. In this example the amount applies only to the Municipal Water Utility, which bills customers for services just as a commercial entity does. Accordingly, these accounts receivable represent an asset of the water utility.

(C) *Taxes and assessments receivable:* Taxes and assessments receivable are monies that various property owners owe to the local government for property taxes and property assessments. If they are not expected to be received in time to pay current liabilities, i.e., their due dates are beyond 60 days after the end of the fiscal year, the revenues are recorded in the balance sheet in an account called "deferred revenue." The reader is thereby advised that receivable amounts are outstanding which will be collected at some point in the future, but they will not be considered "revenue" until the year in which collected.

(D) *Due from other funds or to other funds:* Although each fund is a separate and distinct accountability unit, transfers of monies between funds sometimes occur. Rather than net (offset) the amounts due to and from other funds, amounts are shown separately in order to maintain the integrity of each fund. For example, although the amounts shown as due to and due from other funds by the general fund are equal, the funds that are due amounts from the general fund are different from those which owe amounts to the general fund. A close inspection indicates that the general fund has amounts due from the special revenue and enterprise funds and has amounts due to the internal service fund.

(E) *Due from state or federal government:* Because these items often represent a major receivable, they are generally classified separately on the balance sheet. The receivables typically represent amounts due under grant or entitlement programs.

(F) *Inventories/reserved for inventories:* As you may have noted, all previously discussed assets either represent cash or are convertible into cash which will be available for future operations. Inventories, however, constitute supplies and other materials which will be consumed in future operations and do not comprise a spendable or appropriable revenue. To highlight that fact, a portion of the fund balance is reserved to identify that it has already been dedicated to a specific end use.

(G) *Fixed assets at cost, less accumulated depreciation:* As discussed previously, the purchase of fixed assets by governmental and proprietary funds is accounted for differently. Fixed assets which are acquired in general government operations are recorded as expenditures in governmental funds, and memorandum accountability recordkeeping is established in the general fixed assets group of accounts. The enterprise and internal service funds, on the other hand, capitalize fixed assets, depreciate them, and consider their net value as a component of fund equity. Typically a breakdown of the nature of the assets, e.g., property, plant and equipment, will be provided either in the financial statements or footnotes.

(H) (I) (K) *Amounts to be provided or available:* These accounts provide information on the size of the city's long-term debt, how much has been set aside to retire the debt, and how much remains to be provided from future years revenues. Reference to item **(K)**, "notes payable" and "bonds payable" indicates a total bonds payable liability of governmental funds (exclusive of proprietary fund amounts) of $39,420,000. Item **(I)** indicates by memorandum entry that $1,000,000 has already been set aside in the debt service fund (see separate debt service fund). However, $38,420,000 needs to be raised in the future to service the debt.

Refer back to "Debt Service" expenditures on the Statement of Revenues, Expenditures, and Encumbrances and Changes in Fund Balance — Budget and Actual, which shows a large appropriation ($1,000,000 in column (**H**)), which is the annual transfer to the debt service fund for debt retirement. A large annual appropriation like this will likely continue until the bond issue has been retired.

(**J**) *Accounts payable:* These are outstanding bills which the various funds have incurred for goods or services received but have not yet paid. They will usually be paid within 60 days after the year end.

(**K**) *Notes and bonds payable:* While the government's general long-term debt is accounted for in the general long-term debt group of accounts previously discussed, enterprise and internal service funds account for their long-term debt in the conventional commercial accounting manner as direct fund liabilities in the balance sheet.

(**L**) *Other liabilities:* These represent miscellaneous liabilities of the respective funds for such items as payroll withholding, deposits, etc.

(**M**) *Investment in general fixed assets:* This amount represents the aggregate original or estimated cost of fixed assets acquired and in use in general government operations.

While some would contend that this amount represents a significant factor in evaluating the entity's equity, it should be remembered that it is usually stated at original (undepreciated) cost or estimated value.

(**N**) *Retained earnings:* This term is used in commercial accounting to denote the entity's cumulative excess of income over expenses since the date of inception of operations, net of any dividends or distributions to owners. It has the same connotation in enterprise and internal service fund accounting.

Because of its very nature municipally owned proprietary activities do not usually have outside investors and as such they do not issue stock. Any investment required by the general government at inception or during the operation of the activity would be recorded in a "contributed capital" account within the equity section of the balance sheet as would any capital contribution received from senior governments in the form of capital grants or assistance.

(**O**) *Reserved for encumbrances:* As previously described, encumbrances represent commitments for anticipated expenditures. (Refer to (**G**) in Exhibit I for an explanation of the reason for their inclusion in that statement.) However, since they do not represent incurred liabilities at the balance sheet date (goods and services not received), they are reflected in the balance sheet as a reservation of fund balance rather than as a liability.

(**P**) *Unreserved fund balance:* The aggregate fund balance which represents the excess of assets over liabilities (or vice versa if an accumulated deficit) can be broken down into several components. A segment may be "reserved" as a means of identifying portions of the balance set aside to meet other operational restrictions such as in the example, the reserves for encumbrances (**O**) and inventories (**F**). The remainder is identified as unreserved, and is intended to identify the net assets or resources available for use in future operations. The unreserved fund balance is usually used to meet unexpected expenditure requirements (supplemental budget amendments) or to reduce future years' budget requirements.

However, a word of caution is in order. As previously discussed, long-term loan proceeds requiring future repayment are recorded as revenues when received, and accordingly, have increased the unreserved fund balance. Likewise, long-term liabilities for items such as vacation, pension and self-insurance, which represent a claim on the government, are not recorded in governmental funds. A reference back to the asset side of the balance sheet and consideration of any "amounts *to be* provided," and a reference to the footnotes to the financial statements for other outstanding commitments may be prudent in any evaluation of the unreserved fund balances and future financing requirements.

WHAT THE COMBINED BALANCE SHEET CAN TELL YOU

You can learn a geat deal about your government's financial condition from the combined balance sheet if you examine it systematically with an inquisitive mind. Some of your questions might be:

How financially "healthy" are the various funds?
Is my government's financial position better, the same, or worse than it was a year ago?
How much of a financial burden has this year's operations placed on future years, and is that burden manageable?

First, glance at the fund balance for each fund to see whether it is positive or negative. The fact that all of the fund balances are positive may be superficially reassuring, but you should not stop there. While positive, the fund balance may have decreased from last year, an indication of potential problems.

Additionally, you should look closely at the composition of the assets of each fund type. Remember that assets within a fund are usually restricted to use in that fund. Also, assets in governmental funds should be rela-

tively liquid or available and readily convertible into cash. If they are not liquid or available you should expect to find an offsetting reserve or deferred revenue such as is illustrated in items Ⓒ, Ⓞ and Ⓕ in Exhibit II. (Only liquid or available assets of governmental funds should be included in the unreserved fund balance.)

Next you can look to the fund liabilities to determine whether assets are sufficient to pay liabilities or whether additional revenues must be generated for this purpose. A positive unreserved fund balance usually indicates sufficient assets to meet liabilities.

Also, most funds have "interfund receivables" (item Ⓓ, Exhibit II). Those receivables are only available assets if the debtor fund has the ability to currently pay the creditor fund. You should make inquiries about large amounts of interfund receivables and payables that appear to remain unpaid from year to year.

Next, look at the proprietary fund balance sheets. They should include long-term assets, such as fixed assets, and all long-term liabilities of those funds, such as bonds and notes payable. Since proprietary funds are accounted for like commercial entities, their balance sheets should reflect all assets and liabilities both short and long-term, in order to present a total picture of the fund's financial position. In our example, Exhibit II, the proprietary funds show equity (retained earnings) which appear to represent a healthy financial position of those funds. However, it might be appropriate to inquire about the intended future use of the resources (assets) represented by the large retained earnings.

Fiduciary fund balance sheets present assets held in trust on behalf of others. Accordingly, there should rarely be deficit fund balances in these funds.

Finally, remember that the account groups represent memorandum accounts only; they are not funds. They should be evaluated together with the governmental funds to which they are related.

For example, by itself the size of the

government's general long-term debt cannot be considered either a positive or negative indicator. It must be judged in terms of what led to its incurrence, whether the debt was necessary, and whether it can be repaid without placing an undue strain on operations or the taxpayers.

The annual contribution of approximately $1,000,000 to the debt service fund to repay the debt comes from general fund revenues, that is, from your taxes. Given the condition of the general fund, the annual contribution is likely to be a heavy financial burden on you as a taxpayer. Although there is little you can do about a previous bond issue, you can closely monitor your government's future borrowing activity and judge each prospective bond issue on its individual merits. What is the intended use of the bond proceeds? What is the repayment period? Are revenues available to meet debt repayment without appreciably increasing future tax rates?

Answers to these and other similar inquiries do not come easily, but hopefully this guide has at least helped you identify the important questions — a formidable beginning in the quest to improve the accountability of your government.

BIBLIOGRAPHY

There are many books, articles and reports available in the field of governmental accounting. The following bibliography presents a selection of basic, authoritative works which can provide any citizen with a further understanding of the theoretical and practical aspects of the subject.

American Institute of Certified Public Accountants, *Audits of State and Local Governmental Units*. New York, 1974. Sets forth AICPA position on state and local government financial reporting plus brief discussions of the evolution of governmental accounting, governmental accounting principles and concepts, and budgeting procedures. May be purchased from the AICPA, 1211 Avenue of the Americas, New York, N.Y. 10036.

FREEMAN, ROBERT J., and LYNN, EDWARD S., *Fund Accounting: Theory and Practice*. Englewood Cliffs, N.J.: Prentice-Hall, Inc., 1974. Exhaustive treatment of all aspects of fund accounting.

National Committee on Governmental Accounting, *Governmental Accounting, Auditing and Financial Reporting*. Chicago, 1968. An authoritative and widely accepted treatment of governmental accounting and reporting principles, generally referred to as GAAFR or "the blue book."

> *Statement 1, Governmental Accounting and Financial Reporting Principles*. Chicago, 1979. An update, clarification, and codification which modifies slightly some of the 1968 GAAFR principles.
> *Statement 2, Grant, Entitlement, and Shared Revenue Accounting by State and Local Governments*. Chicago, 1979. Presents appropriate accounting for these types of revenue.
> *Statement 3, Defining the Governmental Reporting Entity*. Chicago, 1981. Establishes criteria for determining which organizations, functions, and activities should be included in the general purpose financial statements of a governmental unit.

> May be purchased from the Municipal Finance Officers Association, 180 North Michigan Ave., Chicago, Ill. 60601.

Municipal Finance Officers Association, *Governmental Accounting, Auditing and Financial Reporting*. Chicago, 1980. An unofficial, but widely recognized interpretation of Statements 1 & 2. May be ordered from MFOA.

10

Simple Agency
Federal Budgeting and Accounting Concepts:
Obligations, Accrued Expenditures, Costs, and Outlays*

INTRODUCTION

The time at which transactions are recorded in the budget is of major significance. Prior to 1956 when Public Law 84–863 was enacted and before specific provision was made to require accrual accounting, budget data were primarily expressed in terms of appropriations, obligations, and disbursements. Since implementation of several of the recommendations of the President's Commission on Budget Concepts, disbursements are not referred to as outlays. These concepts continue to be significant.

Obligations measure the use of budget *authority* (e.g., appropriations) granted by Congress to legally commit the government. Careful records of obligations must be maintained to assure that the authority granted by the Congress is not exceeded.

Outlays measure cash requirements to pay the government's bills and are needed by the Treasury in order to manage cash balances and determine Treasury borrowing requirements. Cash receipts and cash outlays are also used to measure the budget surplus or deficit of the government.

If these two major concepts served for years as budgetary measures, why have two additional concepts on how to measure budget transactions been actively pursued?

The two additional concepts are *costs* (also called accrued costs or applied costs), which have already been incorporated in most of the program and financing schedules, and *accrued expenditures*, which are not yet reflected in the budget, but are being reported to the Treasury and are under consideration for use as an additional budget measure.

These concepts reflect a recording of transactions between the time an obligation is incurred and the disbursement to pay for that obligation. The new measures have these advantages:

1. *Program costs* measure the goods and services used or consumed in carrying out operations of programs. Measuring programs in terms of costs has three advantages:

   a. Costs (inputs) can more readily be compared to program accomplishments (outputs) without distortions between accounting periods. This is so because costs exclude materials purchased but not used and contracts made but not performed. In business-type and in some appropriation schedules, costs also exclude capital equipment, except as charged through depreciation, and increases in accrued leave which will be paid in future years.

   b. Costs can be used to compare similar organization units, or similar jobs, products, or services even though different practices as to the accumulation of inventory, use of equipment, or payments to contractors are employed.

   c. Costs include property or service donated without charge, thus mea-

*By Edward Murphy. Courtesy of Management Sciences Training Center, U.S. Office of Personnel Management, Washington, D.C.

suring more accurately resources actually used.

All these factors improve management control over the program by more accurate measures of inputs. They permit the Executive and Congress to prevent undue accumulation of inventories and undelivered orders. They also are more accurate in relating the dollar measures of activities in the program and financing schedule to the program performance shown in the narrative statement in the budget and the more detailed justifications submitted to OMB and the Congress.

Congress recognized the desirability of cost-based budgets when it enacted Public Law 84–863 in 1956, which requires cost-based budgets when agencies have their accounts on an accrual basis.

2. Accrued expenditures differ from disbursements in that they include accounts payable and other accrued liabilities and exclude unearned advances. Measuring budget expenditures in terms of accrued expenditures has these advantages:

   a. Accrued expenditures reflect the point in time at which the government actually incurs a liability requiring immediate or eventual payment, including constructive delivery in the case of work performed by contractors on a specific order. These expenditures, then, represent the best measure of the economic impact of the budget.

   b. Accrued expenditures measure more precisely the actual acquisition of goods and services by the government in any time period. They there-

fore reduce the distortion of the budget results by the possible payment or nonpayment of bills at the end of the fiscal year.

   c. Relating accrued expenditures to accrued receipts (revenues) gives a more precise measure of the budget surplus or deficit because amounts due to or owed by the government, whether or not collected in cash, would be included.

The President's Commission on Budget Concepts recommended that "Expenditures should be reflected in the budget and federal financial reporting when the government incurs liabilities to pay for goods and services—in other words, on an accrual rather than a cash basis."

It is important to have some understanding of these concepts whether your work is in budget, accounting, or program management. The following illustrations of these concepts will assist your understanding:

Table 10.1   Table comparing the time of the recording of a purchase in the accounting records with the time of the ordering, delivering, use, and payment for materials.

Table 10.2   Formula showing adjustments made to costs to arrive at accrued expenditures, obligations, and outlays.

Table 10.3   Example of monetary application of these concepts.

FOR DISCUSSION

1. Is this information meaningful to a program manager? Why?

TABLE 10.1   Timing of the Recording of a Purchase of Materials Under Accrual Method of Accounting

Transactions	Order is placed	Materials are delivered	Materials are used	Bill is paid
	Recorded in Accounting Records in Month in Which			
Placing an order for materials	as an obligation			
Materials delivered		as an accrued expenditure		
Materials used or consumed			as an applied cost	
Payment made for materials				as an outlay of cash

TABLE 10.2   Formula Relating Costs to Accrued Expenditures to Obligations and Outlays

Element/transaction	Description
COSTS	Goods and services applied or consumed (actual performance during period)
+ Net increases in inventories	Deliveries received have occurred in excess of use of items on hand
or	
– Net decreases in inventories	Use of items on hand has exceeded deliveries received
ACCRUED EXPENDITURES	Goods and services received. Accrued expenditures have occurred when goods are *received* whether consumed or placed in inventory
+ Net increases in undelivered orders	Orders have been placed in excess of deliveries received
or	
– Net decreases in undelivered orders	Deliveries have been received in excess of orders placed
OBLIGATIONS	Goods and services ordered. Obligations have been incurred for goods and services ordered whether received or not
– Net increases in unpaid obligations (unpaid, undelivered orders and accounts payable)	Obligations have been incurred in excess of payments
or	
+ Net decreases in unpaid obligations	Payments have been made in excess of new obligations incurred
OUTLAYS	Payments made

TABLE 10.3   Monetary Application of These Concepts

Element/transaction		Illustrative amounts	
Costs		$100	
Inventory level:			
Start of period	$10		
End of period	15		
Change in inventory level (Add increase, subtract decrease)		+5	(Have received more than used during year)
Accrued expenditures		105	
Undelivered orders:			
Start of period	12		
End of period	10		
Change in undelivered orders (Add increase, subtract decrease)		−2	(Have received more during year than ordered during year)
Obligations		103	
Unpaid obligations:			
Start of period	15		
End of period	12		
Change in unpaid obligations (Subtract increase, add decrease)		+3	(Have paid more during year than ordered during year)
Outlays		106	

SIMPLE AGENCY

Illustrating the Federal Fund and Account Structure

SIMPLE AGENCY was established by an Act of Congress to begin operations on October 1, 19X6. Following are SIMPLE AGENCY's transactions during the first quarter of fiscal year 19X7:

October 1, 19X6.   Congress passed and the president approved a $1,500,000 appropriation for the year for Simple Agency.

October 2, 19X6.   The Office of Management and Budget approved apportionment of $310,000 of the funds previously appropriated to Simple Agency.

October 3, 19X6.   The Director of Simple Agency allotted $300,000 to various operating units of the agency to finance operations for the first quarter of fiscal year 19X7.

October 5, 19X6.   Orders were placed with XYZ Company for materials and supplies estimated to cost $50,000.

October 8, 19X6.   Orders were placed with ABC Company for equipment estimated to cost $30,000.

October 20, 19X6.   All material and supplies ordered October 5, 19X6, were received together with a XYZ Company invoice, billing Simple Agency $50,000.

October 22, 19X6.   All of the equipment ordered on October 8, 19X6, was received accompanied by an invoice from ABC Company for $30,000.

December 1, 19X6.   Simple Agency paid XYZ Company $50,000 in payment of the billing received on October 20, 19X6.

December 3, 19X6.   Simple Agency paid ABC Company $30,000 in payment of the billing received on October 22, 19X6.

Required:

A.   Determine as of October 31, 19X6, the status of funds as follows:

1. Unapportioned Appropriations _____
2. Unallotted Apportionments _____
3. Unobligated Allotments _____
4. Undelivered Orders _____
5. Expended Appropriations _____

B.   Determine as of October 31, 19X6, the Agency's
1. Obligational Authority _____
2. Unexpended Appropriation _____

Note: Use the following worksheet to record the transactions and calculate the account balances as of October 31.

WORKSHEET FOR SIMPLE AGENCY

				BUDGETARY ACCOUNTS						
	Fund Balance	Unapportioned Appropriations	Unallocated Apportionments	Unobligated Allotments	Undelivered Orders	Accrued Expenditures	Accounts Payable	Materials & Supplies	Equipment
Oct. 1									
Oct. 2									
Oct. 3									
Oct. 5									
Oct. 8									
Oct. 20									
Oct. 22									
Balance									
Dec. 1									
Dec. 3									

11

Evergreen's Audit *

INTRODUCTION TO AUDITING

In 1976, the U.S. Congress amended the General Revenue Sharing Program (originally enacted in 1972) to require state and local recipients to be audited at least once every three years. (Congress tightened the requirement in 1980 to at least once every two years.) The audit was to be performed by professionally qualified accountants and done in accordance with professional auditing standards. In addition, the audit was to examine every aspect of the recipient organization—a significant expansion upon earlier federal grant and entitlement audit requirements, which permitted the audit to be restricted to a specified stream of funds or a specified department or program.

The 1976 amendment ushered in a massive wave of professional auditing of state and local governments. Many localities had not been audited professionally for many years—if at all. Thousands of local officials had to learn the concepts and terminology of auditing and accounting, in order to make sure their community complied with the GRS audit requirement.

GAAS

In the technical language of the amendment, the audit was to be performed in accordance with "generally accepted auditing standards." These standards, developed and under continual review by the American Institute of Certified Public Accountants, are mainly pro-

*By Rousmaniere Management Associates, 111 Washington Street, Brookline, MA., 1981. Portions of this case are drawn from research conducted in part with the financial assistance of a grant from Aetna Life and Casualty Foundation to the Council on Municipal Performance, 84 Fifth Avenue, New York, N.Y.

cedural rules about investigating and reporting on the financial report of an audited organization. (The 1976 amendment stopped short of prescribing accounting rules. The GRS recipient was still permitted to prepare its financial reports as it wished.)

The most established type of audit defined by GAAS—and the type prescribed by the GRS audit requirement—is a financial and compliance audit. Financial auditing basically consists of a systematic examination and evaluation of the financial systems, transactions, and accounts of an organization in order to offer an opinion of the "fairness" or reliability of its financial statements. The compliance aspect is to ensure that an organization is following the laws and ordinances that govern the handling of its general finances, such as those pertaining to tax levies, spending, investing, and borrowing.

Internal Control Review

When conducting a financial and compliance audit the accountants review the internal controls of the audited organization. The internal controls are the systems an organization has established to (1) prevent fraud and waste; (2) ensure accuracy of the accounting and other operating data; (3) promote adherence to state policies; (4) further the efficiency of operations; and (5) ensure conformity with applicable laws. Systems devised to achieve the first two objectives are often referred to as accounting controls; the latter three aims are often referred to as administrative controls. To comply with GAAS in a narrow and literal sense, the accountants may concentrate on examining the accounting controls. But in most audited organizations the accounting and administrative controls overlap extensively, so the accountant examines the entire body of internal controls.

This internal control review is but one of several steps in arriving at a professional judgment regarding the "fairness" or reliability of the financial reports of the audited organization. For local governments, the internal control review can be an end in itself—a source of valuable observations about the strengths and weaknesses of financial management practices. Many local officials are more interested in the accountant's evaluation of internal controls than they are in the accountant's opinion about the financial reports. Accountants, in response to this interest, usually prepare a separate, informal report on internal controls, in which they list the major weaknesses they have found alongside their recommendations for remedial action. This informal report often is referred to as the "letter to management," or simply the management letter.

The executives within the audit organization may have extremely contrasting points of view about the management letter. As is often the case, the letter may dwell upon technical and narrowly defined problems, which may be important to a few middle and lower level managers but of no practical relevance to the rest of the bureaucracy. However, sometimes the accountant may include in the management letter observations about major system problems. There is a high probability this will happen if the accountants are performing their first audit of the community and if a number of major system problems in fact exist. In these cases the accountants usually prefer to put their reservations on record. Executives generally aligned with the status quo may view these observations as a threat; executives who are more willing to promote or accept change may view the observations as a refreshing breath of fresh air. In any event, the management letter provides an excellent opportunity for a fresh, objective analysis of the auditee's management practices and operations.

The case which follows draws upon an actual professional audit of a large American city. Conducted in 1978, it was the first professional audit of the city's more than 150-year history. The case is written from the perspective of a middle-level manager whose job is affected by the contents of the accountants' management letter.

EVERGREEN'S AUDIT

In late May, 1979, Susan Dewing received a memorandum from her boss, the budget director of the city of Evergreen. The memorandum asked Susan to recommend what the director should do about the management letter, which the city's accountants had recently submitted in final form.

Susan joined the city about the time the audit began, that is, a year ago. Her assignments generally dealt with developing procedures for improved budgetary analysis and improved interim-year spending controls. As part of her work, she built up an introductory knowledge of the accounting system of the city.

The unit she worked in was commonly perceived within City Hall as favoring greater application of advanced analytic methods in financial management. The Budget Office of the city falls within the Finance Department. Other units of the Finance Department include Auditing, Purchasing, Systems and Procedures, and Data Processing.

Susan was aware that the budget director's management priorities were as follows: (1) improve the quality of personnel/payroll data used in annual budgetary analysis, forecasting of employee benefits, and labor contract negotiations; (2) improve the quality of budgeting of data processing; and (3) impose a quarterly allotment system to control interim spending.

Moreover, Susan was aware that the mayor, who was deeply engaged in a campaign to be reelected in a September primary, was unenthusiastic about the audit, so that neither he nor his aides had shown any interest in the management letter.

She felt that she first had to sort out the short- and long-run implications of the audit and the management letter for the mayor and the budget director. How might their goals (what she knew and could infer) be influenced by the management letter? How could they best take advantage of it? She also had to consider her own position and future within the city. How might the management letter be used to improve her standing with City Hall?

She sketched out on a pad a crude list of alternative steps that could be taken by the city in response to the management letter. These steps were not mutually inclusive. The list was for her a starting point for preparing a report to her boss:

OPTIONS: postpone until after primary
              initiate in-house task forces
              hire consultants or use the
                  accountants to follow up
              think of more

The more she thought about the problem of what to do with the management letter, the more she began to entertain simultaneously two entirely contradictory questions about the management letter: Was it a vehicle for management reform or a terrorist bomb?

The audit of the city was for the fiscal year ending June 30, 1978. As is typical in first-time audits of large government organizations, the audit work extended over a year, starting in early 1978 and ending in the spring of 1979. The accountants prepared and submitted a draft management letter in January, 1979. They submitted a revised and final version of the management letter in May, 1979. The city released copies of the management letter to the press in June.

A summary of the management letter, observations about payroll- and vendor-payment practices, and a brief, incomplete assessment of executive responses to the observations are included below.

Payroll

Over 70 percent of the expenditures of the city was payroll. In a bewildering variation in form and period of payment, city employees, the accountants discovered, were paid on one of four days in the week, and on a weekly, semiweekly, or monthly basis. The accountants found that current practices had resulted in delayed payments to new employees, payments to employees who had been terminated, incomplete processing of federal income tax forms and other deductions, payroll charges to incorrect budget codes, and unnecessary clerical costs.

In the first steps of the payroll cycle, employees had been hired and the specific information on their employment was entered in the central payroll register. The accountants found that since there was no effective integration of the personnel department (the department which had hired the employee) and the payroll department (the department that paid the employee), there were delays in putting new employees on the rolls.

Time sheets, while filled out by several thousand workers, were worthless indicators of employee performance. Many line managers routinely signed payroll authorizations without ascertaining whether employees showed up for work. The payroll department, for its part, did not have a list of authorizing line managers' signatures and therefore could not determine whether the signatures on authorization forms were legitimate.

Once payroll information was prepared by the audit division of the payroll department, the data were put into the city's computer to produce paychecks. The city ran an "exception based" payroll system whereby the payroll master data files on the computer were designed to produce paychecks on schedule unless there were any exceptions or changes. The payroll audit division did not, as a practice, check the computer files to determine that only changes authorized by them were made to the files and that all of their authorized changes were in fact made.

Procedures for distributing checks invited theft or manipulation of the system. According to the accountants, any employee could pick up checks for his or her department at the Treasury Department window. Batches of checks were delivered to employees on the street by unbonded employees. During the audit, there was a holdup of a city paycheck distributor.

These weaknesses in controls over payroll struck some city executives as rather trivial, resulting in inconvenience to employees and, at worst, a potential loss of a relatively limited amount of funds. However, the new budget director felt that failure to enforce detailed controls at the mundane level of daily payroll operations compromised the city's capacity to manage its financial affairs at higher levels. For example, the city had a residence requirement for employees. Neither the personnel nor the payroll department made a serious effort to verify reported residences. Furthermore, there were serious inaccuracies in the personnel data, as evidenced by the return by the Postal Service of one tenth of the W-2s mailed by the payroll department. Unfortunately for the city, these files were the primary source of information used to project the future costs of payroll increases and changes in benefits.

Vendor Purchases

Three hundred steps were required to order, receive, and pay for goods from vendors. This maze of controls resulted in delays, high costs, and poor vendor relations. They did not prevent major scandals from occurring, for example, in the award of contracts to the departments which managed the city's parks and tax-title property. Delays of three to four months in paying bills alone were frequent. The city's internal auditor estimated that each purchase order cost the city about $40 to $50 to process.

Many departments failed to maintain inventory records and to order in economical quantities, the accountants found. In addition, the accountants found that some departments irrationally awarded contracts to lowest bidders who were almost certain to fail to deliver, while other departments clung to extremely precise specifications and selected high bidders.

The most serious weakness in vendor purchases was in the inordinate processing delays which occurred throughout. One cause of delay was chronic confusion over who was responsible for certifying the availability of funds. Line department managers believed that the budget department, when notified of a requisition order, checked for availability of funds. Budget Department personnel, however, contended to the accountants that their job was only to certify that the correct appropriation account was charged. As it happened, neither line nor budgetary officials were authorized to reserve funds formally. That was the job of the Auditing Department, which would reject requisition orders (already weeks or months old) for which funds were not available at the time the Auditing Department matched the order with the appropriate records.

Vendors were selected through a highly formalized and time consuming competitive bidding process, supervised by the city's Purchasing Department. After this department would designate an awardee, it would prepare a formal letter of award which it would send to the mayor's office by way of the city's legal department. The accountants estimated that it took an average of 25 days after the preparation of the award letter by the Purchasing Department for the mayor to sign the letter.

The order for the desired goods still could not go out until a formal contract was signed. There was no uniform contract and weeks would go by as supporting documents and required signatures were collected and reviewed by the law and auditing departments. Only after their review was complete could the line agency manager place an order.

These delays, justified on the grounds of statutory requirements, discouraged many vendors from bidding and drove bid prices up to include implicit financing charges. The delays abused the patience of the better quality city executives. Some executives had already concluded that procedural difficulties in vendor purchases contributed to the poor performance record of the city's data processing

---

PRESS RELEASE

City Public Affairs Office
Contact: Joel Berman
Hold until 4:00 p.m., Wednesday, June 16, 1979

Mayor Edward Silvers received this morning the official management report of the city's auditors, McHenry & Co.

At a meeting attended by Mayor Silvers, Robert Crum, partner in McHenry & Co., and Eileen Raymond, the director of finance, Mayor Silvers received a brief presentation of the major findings and recommendations of the auditors.

According to Mr. Crum, the auditors found no major problems in the financial administration of the city, and they were impressed by the dedication and talents of city employees.

Mayor Silvers and the finance director expressed their appreciation of the professionalism of the auditing team headed by Mr. Crum.

The finance director will review the management report with city personnel and will report back to the mayor within two weeks.

---

department, since municipal data processing shops typically depend very heavily on outside vendors to provide equipment, maintenance, and consulting. The problems with vendor purchasing had persisted because no city department or key official had been sufficiently motivated and influential to streamline controls.

BIBLIOGRAPHY

American Institute of Certified Public Accountants, *Codification of Statements on Auditing Standards*. New York, 1977.

_____, *Auditing of State and Local Governmental Units*. New York, 1974.

Comptroller General, *Standards for Audit of Governmental Organizations, Programs, Activities, and Functions*. Washington, D.C.: GPO, 1981.

PROBLEM

Write Ms. Dewing's memorandum. What recommendations should be made to the budget director?

12

*The Auditor's Report Analyzed**

The auditor refers to a table of contents where you can learn what funds and account groups have been audited. Further description of the locality's system of funds usually is included in the first note to the financial statements, "summary of significant accounting policies."

If the auditor does not follow generally accepted auditing standards (because, for example, records were not made available), he so states.

If the auditor believes that the financial statements conflict with generally accepted accounting principles in a way that would mislead the reader, he identifies the departures in one or more separate paragraphs at this point.

"Present fairly" can be taken to mean "present in all material respects" or "reliably show."

The auditor identifies the time period to which the statements and his opinion apply.

The auditor states that the statements conform with generally accepted accounting principles. Had he audited the statements in light of another body of accounting principles, he would state as much.

Last year's statements can be compared with this year's statements without having to adjust for accounting changes.

February 20, 19X9

To the City Council:

We have examined the financial statements of the various funds and account groups of the City of X for the year ended December 31, 19X8, listed on the *foregoing table of contents.* Our examination was made in accordance with *generally accepted auditing standards*, and accordingly included such tests of the accounting records and such other auditing procedures as we considered necessary in the circumstances. In our opinion, the financial statements listed in the aforementioned table of contents *present fairly the financial position of the City of X at December 31, 19X8, and the results of its operations for the year ended* in conformity with *generally accepted accounting principles* applied on a basis *consistent* with that of the preceding year.

Sisson, Dewing & MacLeish

*Reprinted from Peter F. Rousmaniere, ed., *Local Government Auditing, A Manual for Public Officials* (New York: Council on Municipal Performance, 1979) p. 12. Courtesy of Council on Municipal Performance, 84 Fifth Avenue, New York, N.Y..

CHAPTER FOUR

INTERGOVERNMENTAL DIMENSIONS

The intergovernmental dimensions of budgeting and financial management have become increasingly important over the last few decades. More recently, efforts have been underway to redefine and redistribute fiscal and functional responsibilities among governments. This "new federalism" has reestablished intergovernmental relations as a locus of political turmoil. The importance of this concern is reflected in some notable administrative and political responses to systemic changes over the last decade and more. Elected and appointed officials may find themselves spending more of their time on intergovernmental issues than ever before. Complaints are heard about a plague of rules, regulations, and requirements imposed by one government upon another. Some cities have opened offices in their state capital and in Washington in order to track and lobby for specific legislation and grant monies. Grant offices have been authorized and staffed in many jurisdictions and "grantsmanship" has developed into an area of professional expertise. Many additions to the literature in recent years, in the form of handbooks, guidebooks, newsletters, and scholarly writings, also attest to the significance of these intergovernmental dimensions.[1]

---

[1]Some of these sources include: Advisory Commission on Intergovernmental Relations, *Significant Features of Fiscal Federalism* (Washington, D.C.: GPO, annual editions) and *A Catalogue of Federal Grant-in-Aid Programs to State and Local Governments: Grants Funded FY 1981*, M–133 (February 1982); publications of the Government Finance Research Center of the Municipal Finance Officers Association, such as its series entitled "Elements of Financial Management" and *Resources in Review* (a publication of the Local Government Financial Management Capacity Sharing Program of the U.S. Department of Housing and Urban Development) and John E. Petersen, Wayne Stallings, and Catherine Lavigne Spain, *State Roles in Local Government Financial Management: Nine Case Studies* (undated report); U.S. Department of the Treasury, *Federal Aid to States, Fiscal Year 1981* (Washington, D.C.: GPO, February 1982); and Financial Management Project, National League of Cities, *Financial Management Digest* series (Washington, D.C.: U.S. Department of Housing and Urban Development, Office of Policy Development and Research). More general sources are: George F. Break, "Intergovernmental Finance," in *Essays in Public Finance and Financial Management, State and Local Perspectives*, ed. by John E. Petersen and Catherine Lavigne Spain (New Jersey: Chatham House Publishers, 1980), pp. 95–104; "Intergovernmental Fiscal Relations," Part Three, in *Management Policies in Local Government Finance*, ed. by J. Richard Aronson and Eli Schwartz (Washington, D.C.: ICMA, 1981), pp. 213–73; and sources cited in bibliographies accompanying the cases in this chapter.

The complexities and inconsistencies on the fiscal side of intergovernmental relations reflect the fluidity of the intergovernmental system. The fiscal decisions evolve in response to larger fluctuations in public policy. These zigzags have been termed, variously, "layer cake," "marble cake," "picket fence," and, currently, the "new federalism." Each represents a tangled set of interrelationships, many of which are incongruent and even contradictory. Flexibility has been purchased at the cost of predictability. In fact, an earlier case (no. 8) illustrates how uncertainty is generated by complex financial interdependency. Financial and program planning are necessarily short-term and difficult in an evolving system. Furthermore, the changes suggest a deep-rooted ambivalence in a political system in which traditional attachment to local autonomy vies with concern for fiscal and service capacity.

In some measure, that ambivalence toward financial interdependency is reflected also in the proliferation of rules, regulations, and requirements that characterize the grants and oversight processes. Interestingly enough, the need for heightened financial accountability (see Chapter 3) in the intergovernmental financial system is noted in a report to the New York State Legislature in 1891:

> *There can be no wise legislation with reference to the government of the cities, unless it be possible for the officers of this State, and especially for the legislature and the governor, to be able at all times to know with definiteness and certainty the facts relative to the general condition of municipal administration in each of the cities, and more particularly, the exact financial situation of each and all of them.*[2]

This concern for accountability and, derivatively, credibility, is, then, a consistent one.

The first case in this chapter describes how the Oklahoma state legislature tried to establish legislative budget control over federal funds received each year. Case no. 13 is an evaluative one that focuses in detail on the issues of authority, control, and planning capacity. It presents an overview of the issues surrounding federal aid to state governments. (It is an interesting counterpoint at the state level to the federal perspective described in case no. 5.) The extensive introduction examines fiscal, administrative, and policy planning effects; some technical issues such as fungibility and reimbursables are introduced. The authors suggest that the best single measure of reliance of one government level upon another is intergovernmental transfers as a percentage of own-source revenues; they argue that reliance is the critical factor for understanding financial interrelationships. The case is particularly instructive because many jurisdictions are attempting to subject intergovernmental revenue sources to the regular appropriations process as a control and planning vehicle.

[2]Cited in Advisory Commission on Intergovernmental Relations, *City Financial Emergencies* (Washington, D.C.: GPO, 1973), p. 66.

Case no. 14, "Municipal Budgets and Grants: A Marriage of Convenience," describes how budgeting, financial management, and the grants process interact in two New England municipalities, Rutland, Vermont, and Worcester, Massachusetts. Control and planning again are the focus in this evaluative case. The author emphasizes that the dynamics of federalism, especially its grant component, require an integrated management and delivery center to seek funds, assure compliance with regulations, and then manage the grant for financial and programmatic purposes. The case presents an overview of recommended practices in grant administration (Grant Management Information System) and relates these practices to sound financial management, as represented by the Certificate of Conformance issued by the Municipal Finance Officers Association. This case also includes a useful glossary.

Case no. 15, "Democracy Is a Messy System," is an evaluative case that traces the legislative history of a statutory, state-mandated revenue loss during a period of intensive activity. The case emphasizes the legal constraints on budgetary decision making and the political and intergovernmental context within which those decisions are made. It is followed by case no. 16, "Living with Mandates," developed for the National Association of Counties to exemplify a method for costing mandates. This fiscal impact model presents some interesting notions, such as "present preferred cost" and "displacement," the latter of which is also applicable to matching grants.

All three cases open with an introduction to the subject and conclude with a series of discussion questions. The appropriations, grants, and mandates cases are accompanied by suggestions for field research. These practical applications expose the researcher to the intergovernmental dimensions of budgeting and financial management. Related cases in the book include nos. 2, 5, 8, 17, and 36.

13

Gunfight at the OK Statehouse:
A Legislature's Duel with Federal Aid*

INTRODUCTION

The 1980 Oklahoma legislature experienced a marathon session which ran a full 90 days over a six and one-half month period—the limit set by state law. The legislature acted upon a number of critical issues such as bailing out a deficit-ridden welfare department, approving record high funding for state public schools, reapportioning congressional districts, and expending a large state surplus. Although these issues received the attention of front-page news stories, there was another critical issue that confronted the legislature that remained rather obscure: how to gain control over the federal funds that pour into the state each year.

On the next-to-last day of the legislative session, the Oklahoma lawmakers voted to override a governor's veto and thereby complete the passage of Senate Bill 326. This bill establishes a new bureaucratic apparatus that gives lawmakers oversight of federal funds. The story appeared in the *Daily Oklahoman*, a newspaper published in the state's capitol, Oklahoma City, but was buried on page 18 just above an advertisement for a two-step dancing contest.

The importance of the passage of this bill was neglected because of an unawareness of the critical nature of the related issues of federal funds and state budgets. In American governments, legislatures are the governmental bodies that have the ultimate budget power: the power to authorize and appropriate financial resources for a series of public

*By Anthony Brown, Oklahoma State University; Mark R. Daniels, The University of Connecticut; and John W. Swain, University of Nebraska–Omaha.

policies. This "power of the purse" defines in large part the formal authority of legislatures. But here is the crisis: Within the last decade the influx of federal funds into a state has challenged legislative budgetary control and in doing so has actually challenged the formal authority of state legislatures.

The purpose of this case study is to reveal the critical impact that federal funds have on state budgets and to illustrate the financial interdependency that characterizes the contemporary intergovernmental system by closely examining one state: Oklahoma. After a general examination of the extent and nature of federal funds in American state budgets, Oklahoma's particular experience will be related.

THE NATURE AND EXTENT
OF FEDERAL FUNDS AND
THE AMERICAN STATES

There are over 500 federal aid programs that give cash support to states and localities. These programs can be grouped into grants-in-aid, loans, and revenue sharing. During fiscal year 1981, almost $91 billion will be given by the federal government to states and localities, representing 32.8 percent, almost one-third, of their own-source revenue. This federal aid has made up for an average of 16 percent of total federal outlays during the 1970–80 decade. During that time, however, federal aid has constantly increased relative to state and local own-source revenue from about one-fifth in 1970 to almost one-third in 1980.

In fiscal year 1980, federal aid to state governments alone amounted to $61.9 billion and accounted for over one-fifth of total state revenue. At no time during the last decade did federal aid represent smaller than one-fifth of total state revenue. The highest amount of federal aid was $7.1 billion received by California, and the lowest amount of federal aid was $.21 billion received by Delaware.

But it is the extent to which federal funds represent a large part of a state's own-source revenue that best reveals the importance of federal aid in a state's budget. This is not only an issue of dollars, but also of a state's relative dependency on the federal government. While South Dakota receives only $.27 billion of federal aid, it nonetheless depends on the federal government for funds that represent a high of over 34 percent of its state revenue. Arizona receives $.54 billion from federal aid, yet this amount represents only a low of 17 percent of its state revenue. Thus, there is variation in the amount of federal aid received by a state and the extent to which a state is dependent on the federal government.

Not all federal aid to state governments is spent by the states. Some of the funds are "passed-through" to local governments that actually spend the money. The Advisory Commission on Intergovernmental Relations (ACIR) and the National Association of State Budget Officers surveyed budget officers in each state, asking questions relating to the pass-through issue for fiscal year 1974. Based on the states that responded to the survey, 59 percent of all federal aid is retained by the states for expenditure while 41 percent is passed-through to be expended by localities. State governments, then, are used by the federal government as a channel for funds to local governments.

THE EFFECTS OF FEDERAL AID ON STATE LEGISLATIVE BUDGETING

While the effects of federal aid on a state are numerous, they can be grouped in three categories of consequences: (1) policy determination effects; (2) fiscal policy effects; and (3) administrative effects.

Policy Determination Effects

The effects of federal aid on state policy planning depend upon the particular type of funds that are received from the federal government. Each state's share of revenue-sharing funds is based on a formula determined by Congress, and each state's legislature decides how its funds will be used. Revenue-sharing funds have generally been absorbed into a state's budget without serious planning problems. Loans also have little effect on state planning, for such funds are lent only for a fixed amount of time and must, of course, be repaid. Accounting for only 1.2 percent of all funds in 1980, loans are only a small part of federal aid and therefore have little overall influence on state planning.

The best-known type of federal aid is the grant, accounting for about 90 percent of all funds in 1980. There are two types of grants, block and categorical. Block grants are broad in scope and have funds attached to a general policy activity, while categorical grants have a particular focus and intended results and have funds attached to specific programs. While the block grants give the greater flexibility in planning than the categorical grants, both types of aid allow the federal government to dangle particular public policies in front of a state government like carrots in front of a horse. Grants have alerted state legislatures to what they see as a threat to their basic responsibility and accountability for establishing policy priorities. In other words, federal grants influence the determination of state policy by offering funds for certain policy priorities. While some federal aid is a gift to states based on complex formulas, most federal grants require that a state match the federal aid with a certain amount of state funds. In effect, grants lower the "price" of public policy, thereby making it fiscally attractive to a state government.

The Reagan Administration hopes to minimize the policy determination effects of federal aid through proposed cuts in federal grants. President Reagan's fiscal plan is a proposal to consolidate categorical grants into block grants in the areas of education, health, social services, manpower training and youth programs, welfare, and housing. The goal is to give states and local governments more discretion in the use of the funds at the same time that total federal grant funds are being sharply reduced.

Fiscal Effects

Discussions of the effects of federal aid on a state's fiscal policy generally conclude that the aid stimulates state spending. This stimulative effect occurs when a state raises its support for a federally funded program by more than the required matching amount. This usually means that a state must increase its own-source revenue to meet its increased spending. In this respect, the growth of state budgets and the increases in state income tax are attributable to some extent to the intergovernmental aid system.

Another effect of federal aid is the slow reimbursement a state receives from some federal programs. Federal grants often require that a state first set up and begin a program before the federal government will reimburse state spending. Slow reimbursement of course results in cash-flow problems for states.

Yet another effect is that of the lack of information about the amount of federal aid for state budget planners. State budget officers estimate federal aid for future fiscal years as part of overall budget estimation. Uncertainty about certain federal aid projects often leads state budget officers to misestimate future federal aid and, in doing so, misestimate future budgets.

A crucial effect is the separate bank account requirements for selected federal aid programs. Some state agencies receive, deposit in private accounts, and spend federal funds at their own discretion, ignoring state fiscal officers and appropriate legislative committees. Funds that are spent in a state, but are not controlled by state fiscal officers, are called uncontrolled funds. Such funds directly challenge the power of a state legislature to authorize and appropriate expenditures for a series of public policies.

State Administrative Effects

Federal aid requires detailed, diverse, and burdensome reporting requirements on how funds are spent. The reporting requirements demand great administrative effort by state employees, thereby imposing a burden on a state's bureaucracy.

The accounting system of a state is also affected by federal aids. Federal funds are fungible in that it is impossible to identify federal money once it is mixed with state money. Because of this fungibility, state funds may actually be used to support indirect costs involved in federal programs, such as group insurance and retirement benefits for state workers assigned to federally funded projects. States often find themselves funding the indirect costs of administering programs that the federal government initiated.

By far, the development of a professional bureaucratic complex is the biggest effect that federal aid has on state administration. The term "professional bureaucratic complex" identifies a network of state actors who exert collective influence on obtaining funding for their pet public programs. This network is composed of a few legislators on a relevant specialized subcommittee, spokespeople for a particular public program, and officials in an administrative agency. The bureaucratic complex works to insure that certain public programs are pursued by state governments. The network has considerable expertise within a certain policy area and has a self-interest in perpetuating certain public programs. The availability of federal funds allows the network to finance programs which the state legislature has refused to finance. The federal funds that are received bypass the state treasury, are not included in the state budget, and are deposited in a separate agency account.

Once a program has been financed by federal funds through the "end-run" efforts of the bureaucratic complex, the state legislature may find it difficult to deny state funds for continuance of the program at such time as federal funds might be cut or eliminated. State legislatures may find themselves, compliments of state administrators, with a program they previously voted against.

LEGISLATIVE CONTROL OF FEDERAL FUNDS: THE CASE OF OKLAHOMA

While it is interesting to know the nature and extent of federal funds and their impact on state budgetary power, it is nonetheless useful to discuss one state's experience with federal funds. It is hard to measure the extent to which Oklahoma relies upon federal funds for no one really knows how much pours into the state each year. Federal funding is shown in three places in the annual budget, and it is rare to find all three figures to be the same. The official accounting of federal funds is taken from a section entitled "Receipts from the Federal Government," and it is that section that is used here. As shown in Table 13.1, Oklahoma currently relies on the federal government for about one-quarter of its total revenue but has in the past received as much as one-third. This makes Oklahoma, then, more dependent on federal aid than 35 other states. As is also shown in Table 13.1, federal funds received by Oklahoma have more than doubled in the last decade and have increased by $200 million in the last recorded fiscal year.

This dependence on federal funds is not an isolated occurrence among state agencies. Over half of all state agencies are currently receiving federal funds and have for a number of years. Of the 73 agencies that received federal funds in fiscal year 1980, 28 of them received over a million dollars each. Table 13.2 indicates a considerable range of federal aid among the agencies in this "million dollar club." The 28th-ranked agency had only slightly over one million dollars in aid while the first-ranked agency had over $350 million. For three of these agencies—the Employment Security Commission, the Department of Education: Federal Programs, and the Board of Education: Indian Division—federal funds accounted for their total budgets.

Oklahoma's heavy reliance on federal funds causes it to suffer from all the ill effects of federal aid discussed above. As of fiscal year 1980, the only source of control that the state legislature had over federal funds was the State Grant-in-Aid Clearinghouse, located in the Department of Economic and Community Affairs (DECA). Through the A–95 Project Notification and Review System, all state agencies must notify the state clearinghouse of all efforts to obtain federal funds. Although this informs the legislature of attempts to receive funds, it does not give the legislature direct, formal control over federal funds.

This lack of legislative control led the chairman of the House Special Committee on

TABLE 13.1.   State of Oklahoma Receipts 1970–80 (millions)

Fiscal Year	Federal Government	Percent of all Collections	Total Receipts
1970	348.4	34.0	1,028.0
1971	398.3	35.0	1,139.0
1972	440.4	34.1	1,292.0
1973	491.8	34.8	1,412.2
1974	454.6	29.6	1,534.5
1975	542.8	29.4	1,845.1
1976	645.7	32.5	1,988.3
1977	668.4	30.7	2,200.8
1978	670.2	26.5	2,530.6
1979	668.9	23.9	2,797.5
1980	813.2	24.5	3,317.5

Source: Annual Budgets of the State of Oklahoma

TABLE 13.2.   The 1980 Million Dollar Club: Oklahoma Agencies Receiving One Million Dollars or More from the Federal Government

Rank	Agency	Amount (millions)
1	Department of Human Resources	353.2
2	Transportation Department	108.4
3	Employment Security Commission	81.7
4	Department of Education — Federal Programs	52.8
5	Economic and Community Affairs	39.5
6	Board of Education — School Lunch	36.0
7	General State Government	24.7
8	Department of Health	18.6
9	Oklahoma State University	13.8
10	Vocational and Technical Education	12.4
11	University of Oklahoma	11.9
12	Oklahoma Health Sciences Center	10.8
13	Tourism and Recreation	5.9
14	Crime Commission	4.9
15	Veterans Department	3.0
16	Agriculture Department	2.8
17	Board of Education — Indian Division	2.6
18	Langston University	2.2
19	Wildlife Conservation Commission	1.9
20	Indian Affairs Commission	1.7
21	Department of Mental Health	1.7
22	Regents for Higher Education	1.5
23	Oscar Rose Junior College	1.4
24	Civil Defense	1.4
25	East Central State University	1.3
26	Department of Energy	1.1
27	Library	1.0
28	Southeastern Oklahoma State University	1.0

Source: 1980 Budget of the State of Oklahoma.

Legislative Organization to request the State Legislative Council to study ways of increasing legislative accountability over federal funds. The Legislative Council contracted with the Bureau of Government Research at the University of Oklahoma, and eventually a report was issued. Larry Walker, a professor at the state university and director of the reporting team, wisely suggested that Oklahoma adopt the ACIR Model Legislation that would allow the legislature to appropriate federal funds. Its provisions include:

1.   legislative appropriation of all federal aid, except pass-through funds

2.   placement of all federal aid into the state general fund

3.   reduced state spending in the event of reduced federal aid and stable state spending in the event of increased federal aid

4.   establishment of a joint legislative committee with appropriation powers during the legislature's recess.

This legislation puts the power of the purse firmly in the hands of the legislature, for it would approve all appropriations involving federal funds. The expenditure of all federal funds could only be made by the state's finance director, not by a state agency acting out of a special account. It would also stabilize state spending in spite of the predominantly stimulative effects of federal aid. The joint committee would allow federal funds to be appropriated by the legislature even if the legislature is not in session.

Other suggestions of the Walker Report were less powerful but nonetheless provided the legislature with additional options. First, the legislature could require greater reporting requirements as part of the A–95 process. Second, greater dissemination of information about federal aid applications could be circulated in the legislature. Third, the legislature could hire more staff to oversee the grant applications of state agencies. Fourth, the legislature could establish a standing committee on federal–state relations. And fifth, the legislature could more effectively exercise its existing powers of review and prior clearance.

None of the Walker Report's recommendations were immediately acted upon. Ironically, the report itself was financed by federal funds received by DECA from the U.S. Department of Housing and Urban Development.

It was two years after the Walker Report

that action was taken by the legislature. In March, 1981, House Bill 1234 was voted out of the House Appropriations and Budget Committee. This bill sets up a process that would require each agency seeking federal money to submit a two-page notice of intent with the Legislative Fiscal Office and with the newly created Federal Assistance Management Division of DECA. The Legislative Fiscal Office would have 30 days to decide whether or not to approve of the application. Grants would be approved with the written signature of the speaker of the House and the Senate president *pro tempore*. The state finance director would not be able to process any claims for federal assistance without the approval of both these leaders. The measure proved very popular and inspired the Senate to introduce its own bill for controlling federal funds.

The efforts of both houses resulted in Senate Bill 326 being reported out of the Conference Committee and submitted to Governor George Nigh. This bill included aspects of the original House bill but added other elements that greatly increased legislative control. Exhibit 13.1 portrays an organizational flow chart for this bill.

EXHIBIT 13.1. Legislative Approval Process for Federal Aid Applications.

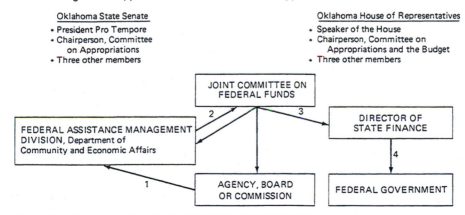

1. Agency, board, or commission submits application for federal assistance.
2. Application is reviewed by Joint Committee on Federal Funds.
3. If approved, application is signed by President *Pro Tempore* and Speaker of the House and sent to appropriate offices.
4. Director of state finance submits application to the appropriate federal granting agency.

A Joint Committee on Federal Funds was created which would consist of 10 members of the legislature, five from each house. The president *pro tempore* and the speaker of the House would both be *ex-officio* members and would appoint the remaining eight members every two years. Chairmanship of the committee would alternate between the president *pro tempore* and the speaker every two years. The Joint Committee would meet at least once a month when the legislature was out of session, with five members constituting a quorum. All state agencies that were applying for federal funds would have to submit the applications to a newly created Federal Assistance Management Division within DECA, which in turn would submit them to the joint committee. The joint committee would have 30 days to approve or disapprove an application. If 30 days expired without any action from the committee, then the application would be considered approved. Once an application was approved, it would be signed by the president *pro tempore* and the speaker, who would then send it to the requesting agency, the director of state finance, and the Federal Assistance Management Division. The only types of federal financial assistance exempted from the bill were assistance to Indian tribes and to the Oklahoma State Regents for Higher Education.

By late June it was clear that although the bill was popular with the legislature, it was not as popular with Governor Nigh: He vetoed it. Nigh called the bill "an inherent threat to representative government." Nigh explained that the Joint Committee was just another bureaucratic apparatus and that it would give total discretion for federal funds applications to as few as five legislators during legislative recesses. Nigh went on to say that the new bureaucracy would only serve to stall expenditures for necessary programs.

But House Speaker Dan Draper countered by calling the bill a step in the direction of fiscal accountability and predicted that both houses would override the veto. He was right: The veto was quickly overridden on the next-to-last day of the legislative session.

For now, the OK Statehouse Shootout was won by the state legislature. But as with most western duels, the ultimate winner can only be decided by history; apparent winners often become eventual losers. Only time can test whether or not the Oklahoma legislature's victory over federal aid will endure.

BIBLIOGRAPHY

Advisory Commission on Intergovernmental Relations, *Significant Features of Fiscal Federalism* (Washington, D.C.: Government Printing Office, 1981).

_____*The Intergovernmental Grant System as Seen by Local, State and Federal Officials* (Washington, D.C.: Government Printing Office, 1981).

HALE, GEORGE E., and MARIAN LIEF PALLEY, *The Politics of Federal Grants* (Washington, D.C.: Congressional Quarterly Press, 1981).

MAXWELL, JAMES A., and J. RICHARD ARONSON, *Financing State and Local Governments*, 3rd. ed. (Washington, D.C.: Brookings Institution, 1977).

WRIGHT, DEIL S., *Understanding Intergovernmental Relations* (North Scituate, Mass.: Duxbury Press, 1979).

FOR DISCUSSION

1. How closely did Oklahoma's Senate Bill 326 follow the ACIR's Model Legislation?

2. How much does Oklahoma's legislation affect the efforts of state budget officers, who are responsible for budget estimation, and the efforts of the state comptroller, who is responsible for the state's accounting system?

3. To what extent has the legislature controlled state spending by passing this bill?

4. Will this legislation minimize either federal-aid reporting requirements administered by the state's bureaucracy or the duplication of governmental services by the state bureaucracy?

5. What reasons might the governor have

had for his veto of the legislation in addition to the reason he publicly expressed?

6. The position(s) of the state professional administrators has not been expressed in this case. Would the members of the bureaucracy support or oppose the legislation, and what would be the main points of their argument?

7. Many state-elected officials feel that the federal government dictates public policies to the states through the federal-aid process. To what extent will this legislation help Oklahoma legislators assert their own policy priorities?

8. Does the legislature have the staff, expertise, and time to make informed, timely decisions about intergovernmental fiscal problems or projects?

9. How has the conversion from categorical grants-in-aid to block grants affected legislative authority in your state? How has this affected executive-legislative relations?

PROBLEM

Field Research Task. Investigate the flow of federal funds into either your state or local government. What proportion of total receipts does federal aid represent? What types of federal aid does the government receive? What process must applications for federal aid go through? To what extent is federal aid unaccountable to the legislative body? What changes could be made to help legislators control the flow of federal funds and make federal aid accountable to the appropriating body?

APPENDIX: ACIR MODEL LEGISLATION

(Title, enacting clause, etc.)

Section 1. [*Short Title.*] This act may be cited as the [state] Legislative Appropriation of Certain Federal Funds Act.

Section 2. [*Definitions.*] As used in this act:
(1) "Agency" means all state offices, departments, divisions, boards, commissions, councils, committees, [state colleges or universities,] or other entities of the executive branch, offices of the judicial branch, and offices of the legislative branch of state government.
(2) "Federal funds" means any financial assistance made to a state agency by the United States government, whether a loan, grant, subsidy, augmentation, reimbursement, or any other form except for federal pass-through funds to local governments and organizations which do not require state matching funds [or financial assistance to state colleges and universities].
(3) "State chief fiscal officer" means [appropriate official as designated by the state].

Section 3. [*Receipt of Federal Funds.*]
(a) As federal funds are received, they shall be deposited in and credited to the appropriate fund account and be available for appropriation by the legislature as part of the state's operating budget; furthermore, detailed and accurate accounting records shall be maintained for those federal funds.
(b) The provisions of subsection (a) of this section shall not apply in those cases where, by statutory enactment, the legislature has created a special fund or restricted receipt account and has specifically provided for an exclusive, special purpose, or other use of federal funds so long as those federal funds are used solely and exclusively for specific statutory purpose or purposes.

Section 4. [*Legislative Appropriation Authority* [*and Delegation Thereof*].]

(a) No state agency may make expenditures of any federal funds whether the funds are advanced prior to expenditure or as reimbursement, unless the expenditures are made pursuant to specific appropriations of the legislature or in accordance with subsection (d) of this section.

(b) If the federal funds received are less than the amount of the funds appropriated by the legislature according to this act and for a specific purpose, the total appropriation of federal and state funds allocated for that purpose shall be reduced in proportion to the amount of reduction in federal funds.

(c) If the federal funds received are greater than the amount of those funds appropriated by the legislature according to this act for a specific purpose, the total appropriation of federal and state funds for that purpose shall remain at the level designated by the legislature.

(d) When the legislature is out of session, [a committee designated by that body] [state chief fiscal officer] may act in its behalf to approve the expenditure of available federal funds and appropriate necessary state matching funds. However, the [designated committee] [state chief fiscal officer] shall act only in instances when new or additional federal funds are made available at such a time as to preclude the possibility of their inclusion in the budget bill under consideration in the legislature.

Section 5. [*Severability*.] [Insert severability clause.]

Section 6. [*Repeal*.] [Insert repealer clause.]

Section 7. [*Effective Date*.] [Insert effective date.]

Note: Those state officials considering this draft act should be aware that it is possible for language in Section 4 requiring decreased state expenditures under certain circumstances to be in conflict with federal maintenance-of-effort requirements. Clarifying language indicating that no such decrease should occur if it would jeopardize receipt of federal funds could be inserted in Section 4(b) and (c).

14

Municipal Budgets and Grants: A Marriage of Convenience*

INTRODUCTION

A significant portion of municipal revenues, for many communities, consists of "payments" from the state and federal government. The ever-increasing need for municipal governments to deal with rising needs and wants on behalf of its constituency coupled with their inadequate revenue base has forced them to look to a superior unit of government to supplement their resources. Over the last several decades the amount of federal (and state) monies turned over to local governments has risen dramatically to a point, in the 1980's, where it equaled almost a quarter of total state and local expenditures.

A municipality may receive aid for a wide range of programs including, but not limited to, aid for: housing, schools, streets, public works, economic development, conservation and recreation, and management assistance. And while the programs and dollar amounts vary according to program, fiscal year, community, etc., the precise nature of the concept does not. The concept has been generically referred to as an *intergovernmental transfer*.

The majority of these intergovernmental transfers comes from the federal government in the form of a grant-in-aid. The impact of these grants has been substantial on large and small municipalities alike.

The impact of intergovernmental assistance on local government is a mirror reflection of the quality of municipal planning and

*By Donald Levitan, Suffolk University. The author wishes to thank Mr. Ronald Graves, Rutland, Vermont, and Mr. Charles O'Conner, Worcester, Massachusetts, for their assistance in responding to never-ending requests for information.

management. Those communities who can establish and maintain an integrated planning and management process to deal with grants will incorporate them into municipal programs, rather than approach each grant on a singular or fragmented basis, and will benefit most from them.

Grants are not a free commodity; they make many municipalities a ward of the federal government, for grants bring a family of hungry mouths: rules, regulations, economic, and administrative costs. Unless grants are planned for, administered, and managed carefully, instead of being a boon they soon become a bane. The financial management system of a community thus becomes a significant factor in the planning and programming of grants. By examining this system, additional insight, it is contended, is gained into the management of grants.

All municipal grant recipients follow a similar set of laws, rules, and regulations in their quest for federal grants, for the rules are the same according to grant type and program. The difference, and there is one, is the manner in which a municipality establishes a management system *first* to seek and comply with the federal grants process and *second* to manage the grant on a programmatic and financial basis.

This study will focus on how two disparate communities followed this concept. It is, however, somewhat open-ended, allowing for comparison of both cities and further allowing, if desired, for added comparison of a third—a field study community.

Grants-in-aid: An Historical Perspective

Federal aid came with the establishment of our federal republic; the present federal grant system has its roots, however, in the Morrill

Act of 1862 with the establishment of land grant colleges. Until the early part of the 20th century, programs were few and far apart. In the early 1900's, grant programs expanded greatly with the emphasis on conservation and vocational education.

In the grey days of the 1930's, the federal government added to its aid programs and shifted emphasis. The federal government initiated massive aid programs to assist state and local governments which were unable to cope with the emerging urban malaise. These grants emphasized public works and welfare. In the post-war 1940's, federal aid was launched as a response to urban needs and technological changes. Subsequent decades mirrored what had preceded, and today the remnants remain. More and more programs were spun off and funded to deal with the impact of national programs and policy at the local level.

The 1980's brought a significant change in dollars and program concepts. Starting in the 1980's, and undoubtedly destined to continue throughout the decade, a shift from categorical or single-purpose grants to block or multifunctional programs has begun. We anticipate, in addition to program consolidation with less funds, the shifting of the program foci from the federal government to the 50 states. The states will have an increased role in the interpretation of national policy, establishment of programs, and the funding and evaluation of these programs.

The dynamics of federalism and the grant component require an integrated management and delivery center. And regardless of a diminution of funds, municipalities remain accountable for the stewardship of the program and for the dollars.

GRANT MANAGEMENT INFORMATION SYSTEM[1]

A.   General: A single centralized grants office should be established within the

[1]Donald Levitan, *Grants Management* (Newton, Mass.: Government Research Publications, in press).

municipality. This office would report to the municipal executive. It would be the responsibility of the Grants Office to:

1.   Assume the responsibility for soliciting and collecting information on various grants from all sources, governmental as well as nongovernmental. This information should be gathered on an ongoing basis.

2.   Maintain a grants library. This library should include information on grant sources and resources, applications, and reporting forms.

3.   Distribute and make available grants information to all governmental units within the municipality, as well as to those organizations which "provide" pertinent services to residents of the municipality.

4.   Establish uniform procedures and systems for grant applications on behalf of all who seek funds in the name of the municipality. These procedures and systems would be cognizant of all applicable laws, rules, and regulations of all governmental entities involved in the process, e.g., county, COGS, RPA, State, etc.

5.   Assist all governmental and nongovernmental units in grant preparation and submission rather than prepare the grant for said unit.

6.   Review and comment on all grant submissions including those made by a unit of municipal government and those made by a nongovernmental unit which might affect municipal finances, services, and/or residents of the municipality. The intent of this review and commentary is not central as much as it is compliance with item #4 above.

7.   Monitor fiscal and program compliance for those grants awarded to

units of the municipality as well as to all nongovernmental entities which receive municipal funds and/or which have delegated program responsibility from the municipality.

8. Periodically assess the program and financial impact of grant programs by examining:
   a) programs and fiscal compliance
   b) impact of program (grant) completion
9. Avoid infringing upon the responsibility for programs or finances of the designated governmental and/or nongovernmental units which possess same.
10. Insure that all grant records of programs and finances are maintained and retained, in accordance with municipal, state, federal, and other grant rules and regulations.

B. Frame of Reference. It is the responsibility of the Grants Office to:

1. Conduct an inventory of all grants affecting the municipality and ascertain the following for each grant:
   a) grant source
   b) grant purpose
   c) grant amount
   d) local share:
      1) dollars
      2) services-in-kind
      3) source
   e) grant manager (who will locate information)
      1) grantee
      2) grantor
   f) grant expiration date
2. Obtain a copy of each grant application, grant award, financial and reporting requirement, and forms for each grant identified above.
3. Maintain this information on a current basis, quarterly if possible.

4. Review, prior to submission, all grant reports from all governmental units and all nongovernmental units which utilize municipal funds within the grant program.
5. Prepare a report from the Grants Office for submission to the CEO yearly.

C. Financial Management

1. The budget of the municipality should reflect the receipt and impact of external funding.
2. The legislative unit, of the municipality, should appropriate all external sources of funding on a grant-by-grant basis within municipal units.
3. Procedures should be established for the timely and proper withdrawal of grant payment, including advances and reimbursements.
4. All grant budget submissions should be coordinated with the municipal budget.
5. The grant's financial impact, both direct and indirect, should be analyzed prior to budget interface.
6. Cash-flow projections should be prepared and maintained for each grant by the grant (program) manager.
7. All cash flow projections should be submitted to the CEO of the municipality for review and interface with the municipal accounting and financial reporting system.
8. All financial grant reports should be prepared and reviewed by the CEO.
9. A program audit for all grants should be conducted annually, as well as at the conclusion of each grant program, to measure financial operations and program results.
10. Financial reports, including

audits, should be made available to a wide range of users: government officials at all levels, grantors, civic groups, residents, and nonresidents.

D. Grant Administration and Management

1. All grant material, i.e., application, etc., should be made available to the executive and legislative unit.
2. All grants are to be reviewed by the Grants Office prior to "submission" to the CEO.
3. All grants should be reviewed and approved by the legislative unit prior to submission.
4. All internal (and external) controls, all grant procedures and systems, as well as their structure and function, are to be accessible to the legislative unit.
5. All grant reports, financial as well as programmatic, are also to be made available to the legislative unit.

RUTLAND, VERMONT

The Community

The city of Rutland, Vermont, is the second largest city in the state; the 1980 population was 18,153. Rutland is the county seat of Rutland County. The city consists of approximately 8 square miles and is the trading center for a region of over 125,000 people.

YEAR	POPULATION
1950	17,659
1960	18,325
1970	19,007
1980	18,153

Rutland is located, at the midpoint, north to south, of the state; it is 65 miles south of Montpelier, the state capital; 160 miles northwest of Boston, Mass.; 165 miles southeast of Montreal, Canada; and 100 miles northeast of Albany, N.Y. Rutland, a market center today, nicknamed the Marble City, is situated in a broad valley more known, today, for skiing rather than for quarrying.

Government Organization

Rutland is governed by a strong mayor with an 11-member nonpartisan aldermanic council elected at-large every two years. The other major elected officials are: assessor(s), treasurer, and constable/tax collector(s). The mayor appoints all other department heads. The schools are under the purview of an independent board of commissioners, who are elected also at-large every two years and possess fiscal autonomy in setting the school tax rate. (See Exhibit 14.1.)

The library is a quasi-multimunicipal entity serving and financed by two municipalities—the city of Rutland, as well as the town of Rutland. In addition to the library, there are several other significant quasigovernmental entities: Housing Authority, Redevelopment Authority, and an industrial, as well as a downtown, development corporation.

Financial and Budget Administration

In Rutland, municipal and school financial and budget administrative functions are somewhat decentralized under the direction of elected and appointed officials. For the municipal side—the mayor, city clerk, treasurer, and constable/tax collector. The mayor, with the assistance of the city clerk and treasurer, prepares the budget; the mayor submits the budget; the board of aldermen considers and enacts same; the treasurer is responsible for the programming of the budget and the collection of taxes; the constable/tax collector is responsible for the collection of delinquent taxes. The board of school commissioners establishes, enacts, and programs the school budget and the school tax rate with the collection of the revenue in the hands of the city treasurer.

The municipal, as well as the school, budget is unitary and includes personnel, equipment and supplies, capital improvements, etc. The budget cycle is as follows:

EXHIBIT 14.1. Table of organization, Rutland, Vermont.

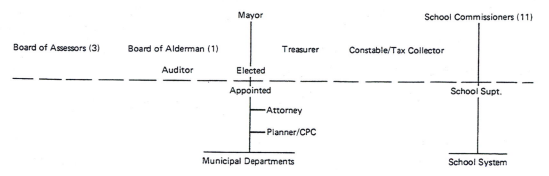

FISCAL YEAR JULY 1, 19—
TO JUNE 30, 19—

May	FY municipal budget requests submitted to mayor.
May 15 — June	Public hearing held on proposed budget.
Prior to 1st Mon. in June	Mayor submits his final budget to board of aldermen.
June 10	Board of aldermen considers budget, holds public hearing and enacts budget prior to June 10.
July 1	Fiscal year begins.

See Table 14.1 for the relationship between Rutland's budget and federal funds.

In the early 1960's, the city of Rutland was the only city in Vermont to achieve MFOA's Certificate of Conformance and over the years managed its finances consistent with GAAP. In their FY 1982 Annual Plan, the presentations will be consistent with Statement 1—National Council on Government Accounting.

Grant Administration

Prior to 1973, the city received little or no federal funds, with the exception of general revenue sharing. In 1973, a newly elected mayor appointed a city planning coordinator (CPC) to his staff. The person chosen was a resident of Rutland and had many years of experience with the state of Vermont in various intergovernmental positions.

TABLE 14.1. Rutland, Vermont

Fiscal Year	Municipal Budget (Total)	GRS*	Federal Funds: Other	Total	Federal Funds: Percent of Total Municipal Budget
1977	$ 9,353,898	$756,965	$1,267,272	$2,024,237	22
1978	9,651,941	809,588	2,380,949	3,190,537	33
1979	10,375,446	792,949	220,130	1,013,079	10
1980	11,183,501	775,659	217,960	993,619	9

*Does not include interest

In the city of Rutland, each municipal entity, as well as the schools, does its own program planning. As support staff of the mayor, the CPC (a single-person operation with a shared clerk/typist) became the Grants Office for all governmental entities, including the schools. CPC also became responsible for assisting and coordinating the quest for federal grants on behalf of all nongovernmental enterprises and individuals in/for the city.

CPC has been successful in bringing substantial sums of federal aid into the city on behalf of governmental as well as extragovernmental entities that are located in and provide resources for the city (see Table 14.1). As such, his office has become the Grants Office for the city *in toto*. He actively has sought funds and prepared and followed through on grant applications, while turning the programmatic and financial management of the grants over to line agencies, quasigovernmental agencies, and others. Record keeping and monitoring are decentralized to the unit receiving the grant, with financial reporting delegated to the city treasurer.

Once a possible grant source is isolated, CPC works with the responsible program official in preparing the grant application. In most cases, the initiation of the quest, as well as the grant preparation, originates with CPC. The program and financial components of the grant applications are submitted to the board of aldermen for their consideration and approval; a public hearing is held for all federal grants. Finances are folded into the municipal budget process. The local share of all federal grants is appropriated by the mayor and aldermen from general revenue sharing funds. All funds received are segregated into separate funds, according to the principles of GAAP, and presented in the annual financial report accordingly. Program reports are the responsibility of the entity which receives the funds, although in many cases assistance is sought and supplied by CPC. Financial reports follow the same process, with outside assistance the rule and the treasurer supplying the financial statistics for the report. The treasurer, in other words, implicitly assumes control of the financial component of all federal grants.

WORCESTER, MASSACHUSETTS

The Community

The city of Worcester is the second largest city in the state of Massachusetts, with a 1980 population of 161,799. Worcester is the county seat for the county of Worcester as well as the major community and only city in the Worcester SMSA. The city consists of slightly more than 37 square miles of land area and is a trading center for over six million people within a 50-mile radius.

YEAR	POPULATION
1950	203,486
1960	186,587
1970	176,572
1980	161,799

Worcester is located approximately 50 miles west of Boston (the state capital), 35 miles south of the New Hampshire border, and 25 miles north of Connecticut. Worcester, originally known as the City of Seven Hills, has capitalized on several factors, such as location and socioeconomic base, to become a major commerce–finance–education center for the state, second only to Boston. At present there are over 400 manufacturing firms and 3,100 nonmanufacturing firms located in the city, as well as 10 colleges with over 15,000 students. In 1980 Worcester was named as an "all-American city."

Government Organization

Worcester is governed by a nine-member city council and a city manager. The council is elected at-large on a nonpartisan basis every two years. The council, in turn, elects one of its members to serve as mayor and chairperson. The city manager is appointed by and

EXHIBIT 14.2. Table of Organization, Worcester, Massachusetts.

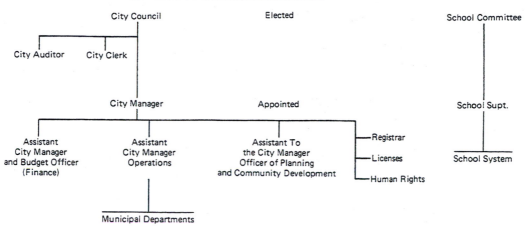

serves at the pleasure of the council. (The present city manager has held the position for 21 years!) The city manager then appoints all municipal department heads with the exception of the city clerk and auditor who are appointed by the city council.

There is an independently elected school committee, which possessed fiscal autonomy prior to the 1980 enactment of Proposition 2-1/2.[2] (See Exhibit 14.2.)

Financial and Budget Administration

The office of the assistant city manager and budget officer is the locus for assessment, treasury work, and budget administration. (The auditor, who reports to the city council, performs the audit functions.) This office is responsible for budget coordination, submission, and management. There are four components of this budget process:

> consolidated budget, which consists of all portions of the budget
> municipal operating budget

capital improvement budget
school budget

Budget preparation calls for the inclusion of the following components into the consolidated budget:

> capital improvement (CIP)
> maintenance program
> personnel program
> school budget
> miscellaneous

The budget cycle is as follows:

*FISCAL YEAR JULY 1, 19—
TO JUNE 30, 19—*

July–August–September	CIP input solicited and adjusted.
October	Maintenance (M) programs submitted.
November	Personnel (P) and Salary (S) information submitted.
December	M, P, and S updated.

[2]Prior to 1980, schools in Massachusetts possessed complete fiscal authority. In 1980, a constitutional amendment (Proposition 2-1/2) was passed which, among other things, did away with this independence and allowed for a more integrated municipal budget policy.

December	Draft budget prepared.
January to March	City manager reviews and prepares executive budget.
April	City manager submits budget to city council, which holds a public hearing and enacts budget; charter budget enactment must occur by May 15.
(by) May 15	City council approves budget.
July 1	Fiscal year begins.

See Table 14.2 for a display of Worcester's municipal budget, 1977–80.

Grant Administration

The grant function for the city of Worcester is divided between two units of government: the School Committee and the city manager and assistant city manager of the Office of Planning and Community Development. (See Exhibit 14.3.) The latter is also the chief planning office for the city. The school department possesses its own planning and grants component. Prior to the enactment of Proposition 2-1/2, the schools did not have to coordinate with their brethren on the municipal side regarding grants including application, local share, etc. (The school department was independent in almost all municipalities in Massa-

chusetts prior to Proposition 2-1/2.)

In 1972, various functions associated with planning, housing, urban renewal, and economic development were consolidated in the executive office of the City Manager, Office of Planning and Community Development (OPC). Prior to that date, these functions were fragmented throughout the municipality.

In charge of OPC is the director of community development and assistant to the city manager. At present OPC has five functional areas plus administrative staff, 40 professionals, and a support staff. OPC provides planning and grant support to all municipal governmental units (with the exception of the school as stated above) and to nonprofits when requested. Thus, OPC is the chief intergovernmental, grants, and planning office for the city of Worcester. OPC is a professional, multifunctional, centralized municipal grants office which seeks out, prepares and/or coordinates grant preparation; it manages programmatic and financial components of grants for all municipal units (including itself) and nonmunicipal entities.

In almost all cases, OPC has the responsibility for monitoring all federal grants coming into the city on behalf of governmental and nongovernmental units (where municipal resources are utilized in the grant program). In 1979, the city manager institutionalized this function by delegating this grant authority to OPC and mandating a grants inventory for the city. (See Appendix.)

As the lead agency for the city in grants, OPC will seek out grant sources and closely

TABLE 14.2. Worcester, Massachusetts

Fiscal Year	Municipal Budget (Total)	GRS*	Federal Funds; Other	Total	Percent of Municipal Budget
1977	$127,892,421	$4,611,761	$24,467,061	$29,078,834	22
1978	127,661,623	5,053,543	28,762,765	22,816,308	26
1979	132,502,727	4,913,896	35,981,265	40,805,161	31
1980	152,374,369	4,132,568	44,854,854	48,987,422	32

*Does not include interest

EXHIBIT 14.3. Executive Office of the City Manager–Office of Planning and Community Development, Worcester, Massachusetts.

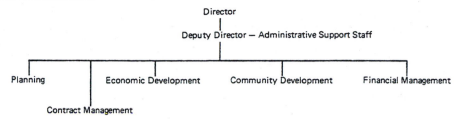

monitor funding. OPC may prepare the grant application *per se* or work in concert with a governmental/nongovernmental entity in the preparation and submission of the grant. In most cases, the latter is the path followed after the grant source has been legitimatized. In almost all instances, the nonprofits who deliver programs in Worcester are funded, in part, by the city. And, lastly, neither fees nor an indirect cost factor is charged for OPC assistance.

The grants (all grants) are submitted, as policy, to the council for their input and "permission to file." A public hearing is only held in the case of those grants which require it, e.g., general revenue sharing. However, a public hearing is mandatory prior to final consideration of the municipal budget.

In all cases, the grants financial component is folded into the municipal budget process. The local share for federal grants is appropriated from the general fund. All funds received are segregated into separate accounts within the budget program entity. Within OPC there is a financial management unit responsible for management of the financial aspects of all federal grants. (See above for exceptions.) Interim, annual, and financial reports on federal grants management are made available within the city's annual financial statement. Program reports are also the responsibility of OPC and made available to interested parties.

In 1981 the city of Worcester, Massachusetts, received the designation as an all-American city in acknowledgment of the strides made in community and economic development.

BIBLIOGRAPHY

JESSE BURKHEAD, *Grantee Budgeting for Federal and State Aid*, Occasional Paper Nos. 46 & 47 (New York: Syracuse University, Maxwell Metropolitan Studies Program, 1981).

Financial Management of Federal Assistance Programs (Washington, D.C.: OMB, 1981).

Guidelines for Financial and Compliance Audits of Federally Assisted Programs (Washington, D.C.: U.S.G.P.O., 1980).

GEORGE E. HALE and MARIAN LIEF PALLEY, *The Politics of Federal Grants* (Washington, D.C.: Congressional Quarterly, 1981).

DONALD LEVITAN, *Grants Management* (Newton, Mass.: Government Research Publications, in press).

_____, *A Guide to Grants: Governmental and Nongovernmental*, rev. ed. (Newton, Mass.: Government Research Publications, 1982).

National Council on Governmental Accounting, Statement 2: *Grant Entitlement, and Shared Revenue Accounting and Reporting by State and Local Governments* (Chicago: Municipal Finance Officers Association, 1979).

Office of Management and Budget (OMB) circulars (selected for their importance to governmental grants):

A-11	Preparation and Submission of Budget Estimates
A-21	Cost Principles for State and Local Governments (formerly FMC 73–8)
A-73	Audit of Federal Operations and Programs
A-87	Cost Principles for State and Local Governments (formerly FMC 74–4)
A-88	Coordinating Indirect Cost Rates, Audit, and Audit Follow-up at Educational Institutions

A–89   Catalog of Federal Domestic Assistance

A–95   Evaluation, Review and Consideration of Federal and Federally Assisted Programs and Projects

A–102   Uniform Administrative Requirements for Grants-in-Aid to State and Local Governments

A–110   Grants and Agreements with Institutions of Higher Education, Hospitals, and Other Nonprofit Organizations (Formerly FMC 73–7)

A–111   Jointly Funded Assistance to State and Local Governments and Nonprofit Organizations: Policies and Procedures

A–122   Cost Principles for Nonprofit Organizations

Treasury Department Circulars (TC) selected for their importance to government grants:

TC–1075   Regulations Governing Withdrawal of Cash from the Treasury for Advances Under Federal Grant and Other Programs

TC–1082   Notification of States of Grants-in-Aid Information

B. J. REED and ROY E. GREEN, *A Perspective on Small City Development: Local Assessments of Grant Management Capacity*, Urban Affairs Paper, Vol. 2, No. 3, Summer 1980.

Review Guide for Grantee's Financial Management Systems (Washington, D.C.: U.S.G.P.O., 1978).

DEIL S. WRIGHT, *Understanding Intergovernment Relations*, 2nd ed. (Mass.: Duxbury Press, 1982).

FOR DISCUSSION

1. Analyze and compare the grants system of each community to the Grants Management Information System (GMIS).

2. Analyze and compare the grants financial and budget organization/system of each community.

PROBLEM

Field Research Task. Select a study community and examine its grant management system utilizing the GMIS matrix and *then*
compare the results with the analysis completed here.

GLOSSARY OF TERMS

A. The following has been excerpted from Donald Levitan, *A Guide to Grants: Governmental and Nongovernmental*, rev. ed. (Newton, Mass.: Government Research Publications, 1982).

Grant, Grant-in-Aid   An assistance award in the form of dollars, product(s), or technical assistance. There are three general categories of grants — categorical, block, and revenue sharing:

Categorical   Grants allocated for a single purpose, via nationwide/regional competition.

Formula   Grants to states on a prescribed basis; the state may distribute "these" funds upon a state plan and they are then termed "pass-through" funds.

Block   Consolidation of categorical funds into a single, flexible grant program for distribution to the states.

General Revenue Sharing   Distribution of federal funds by formula (mathematical) to state, counties, and municipalities for their use with few restrictions.

Special Revenue Sharing   This program was the precursor of . . .

    Block Grants   Categorical grants blended into several multifunctional grants which are distributed to states.

Grantee   Person/organization receiving a grant.

Grantor   Organization giving a grant to a grantee.

B. The following has been excerpted from OMB circular A–11.

Grants-in-aid are defined as budget authority and outlays by the federal government in support of state or local programs of government operations or provision of services to the public.

For purposes of this classification, state or local governments include

a.   Puerto Rico, the Virgin Islands, and U.S. territories

APPENDIX A
ATTACHMENT TO EXECUTIVE ORDER #7
CITY OF WORCESTER, MASSACHUSETTS
RELATIVE TO GRANTS/PLANNING COORDINATION
EXECUTIVE OFFICE OF THE CITY MANAGER

Due to the increasing number of federal and state grant applications submitted by city departments and the need to provide coordination among the municipal planning agencies, the following grants coordination procedures shall be implemented immediately by offices within the Executive Office of the City Manager.

The grants coordination process shall be the primary responsibility of the Office of Planning and Community Development and shall require a four-step communication system between the sponsoring agency and the OPCD as outlined below. All executive offices shall also submit a schedule of grant intent on a yearly basis to allow the OPCD to document staffing requirements for grant reviews.

Step I: Notification of Intent

A notification of intent to file a grant shall be made to the OPCD a minimum of 10 working days prior to submission of the application (or preapplication, if required) to the grantor agency and should include sufficient information to determine the need for a preapplication conference. The "City of Worcester: Project Application/Profile Form" (attached) shall be a part of this notification. The sponsoring agency shall notify the appropriate state and regional clearinghouses at the same time (if the project is covered under the A–95 process) and shall include a copy of the letters submitted to these agencies in the intent letter.

Step II: Preapplication Conference

If determined to be necessary, the OPCD shall schedule a preapplication conference between the sponsoring agency and other departments which may be affected by the grant implementation. The proposed grant activity shall be discussed in relation to overall city planning goals/objectives/policies, local commitments required, and ongoing or proposed city programs.

An opinion by OPCD shall be made to the city manager following the preapplication conference. After the agency receives the opinion, it will prepare the final application for submission to the grantor agency. The OPCD's comment also be sent to the sponsoring agency, which has the option to forward a comment to the city manager on OPCD's opinion. If a negative is received, the agency shall seek specific instructions on filing the grant from the city manager.

Step III: Final Application Review

A final application review for the purpose of reviewing conformity to the original proposal and the application and grantor requirements, as well as the A–95 review comments, shall be held by OPCD.

As appropriate, the OPCD shall notify the city manager of any changes in the grant proposal. The sponsoring agency may then proceed to submit the proposal to the grantor agency.

Step IV: Grant Award/Evaluation Conference

Upon notification by the grantor agency of the status of the funding request, the sponsoring agency shall notify the OPCD. The grant award (or rejection) notification shall inform the OPCD of the feasibility of implementing the grant program, giving the grant amount (if different from the original request), the grant conditions, or any other deviations from the originally proposed package.

A final application profile form, if different from the original submission in Step I, will be completed and filed with the OPCD for the purpose of reporting on the intergovernmental grants received by the city on a yearly basis.

The Office of Planning and Community Development shall have the ongoing responsibility of maintaining a reporting system to track program progress and to advise the city manager of the status of each grant application and program on a regular basis. ●

b. Indian tribal governments when
    1. the legislation authorizing the payment includes such entities within the definition of eligible state or local units
    2. the tribal government acts as a nonprofit agency operating under state or local auspices
c. Quasipublic nonprofit entities, such as community action agencies, when the boards of such entities must either be elected in state or local elections or must include significant representation of state or locally elected officials.

Grants-in-aid include the following:

a. Direct cash grants to state or local governmental units, to other public bodies established under state or local law, or to their designee (e.g., federal aid for highway construction).
b. Payment for grants-in-kind, such as purchases of commodities distributed to state or local governmental institutions (e.g., school lunch programs).
c. Payments to nongovernmental entities when such payments result in cash or in-kind services or products that are passed on to state or local governments (e.g., payments to the Corporation for Public Broadcasting or to the American Printing House for the Blind).
d. Payments to regional commissions and organizations that are redistributed at the state or local level to provide public services.
e. Federal payments to state and local governments for research and development that is an integral part of the state or local government's provision of services to the general public (e.g., research on crime control financed from law enforcement assistance grants or on mental health associated with the provision of mental rehabilitation services). (See (i) and (j) below for exclusions related to research and development.)
f. Shared revenues, a subcategory of grants. Payment of these to state or local governments is computed as a percentage of the proceeds from the sale of certain federal property, products, or services (e.g., payments from receipts of Oregon and California grant lands) or are tax collections by the federal government that are passed on to state or local governments (e.g., internal revenue collections for Puerto Rico).

Excluded under this definition are

g. Federal administrative expenses associated with these programs.
h. Grants directly to profit-making institutions, individuals, and nonprofit institutions not covered above (e.g., payments to Job Corps centers and trainees).
i. Payments for research and development not directly related to the provision of services to the general public (e.g., basic research).
j. Payments for services rendered (e.g., utility services, training programs and expenses for federal employees, research and development for federal purposes conducted under contracts, grants, or agreements by such agencies as the National Institute of Health, the National Science Foundation, the Department of Energy, the National Aeronautics and Space Administration, and the Department of Defense).
k. Federal grants to cover administrative expenses for regional bodies and other funds not redistributed to the states or their subordinate jurisdictions (e.g., the administrative expenses of the Appalachian Regional Commission.)

Also excluded are loans to state and local governments. This category includes all loans (including repayable advances) to state and local governments as defined above. All programs not classified as either grants-in-aid (including shared revenues) or loans (including repayable advances) to state and local governments should be classified as "direct federal programs."

15

Democracy Is a Messy System *

INTRODUCTION

The distribution of functional and financial responsibilities among governments is not static, but evolves within a political tradition that simultaneously ascribes positive value to local discretion over local revenues and assigns a preeminent position to the state in the legal arrangements governing local activity. The mandate issue illustrates the intergovernmental context of budgeting and the dynamism, flexibility, and strains that context generates. Mandates are only one of the many components of the intergovernmental financial relationship, which is itself only one of many relationships, such as the political, legal, and administrative ones in the intergovernmental system.

Definitions and typologies vary, but the term generally refers to all requirements imposed by one level of government on another. They may be classified according to level of government (federal, state); basis of authority (constitutional, statutory, administrative, executive, or judicial); and functional type (service, personnel, government structure and process, environmental, and revenue loss). They also can be categorized by purpose, e.g., equity, standardization, and public safety. Some definitions include only direct obligations; broader definitions may include obligations imposed as conditions-of-aid. Mandates may impose service or cost obligations or require that a government refrain from certain activity or adhere to specific guidelines. Revenue restrictions and tax-and-expenditure limitations are revenue-loss mandates.

For the following fiscal impact model, a mandate is defined as "any responsibility, action, or procedure that is imposed by one sphere of government on another through constitutional, legislative, administrative, executive, or judicial action as a direct order or that is required as a condition-of-aid.[1]

The public controversy surrounding mandates is increasing along with their number and type. Many jurisdictions must contend with hundreds of federal and state mandates that together are perceived as a heavy administrative burden and a strain on already hard-pressed revenues. To some, mandates effectively substitute federal or state priorities for local ones while diminishing the possibility for electoral review of financial or programmatic decisions at any level of government. Similarly, it has been argued that mandates reduce local discretion over local budgets and increase budget uncontrollability. Mandates may especially benefit those special interest groups with the organization, access, information, and other resources that transcend the local jurisdiction. When the mandate issue is raised within the context of tax reform, as it was in California and Massachusetts, the controversy deepens.

Although it can be argued that compliance and compulsion are as much at issue as compensation, cost remains one of the principal objections to mandates. It is widely recognized that the costing of mandates is a time-consuming, expensive, and difficult task. Frequently, the need for costing outweighs the difficulties, and techniques, such as those in "Living with Mandates," are being developed for research and policy purposes. Of course, costing is immediately imperative if reimbursement or fiscal notes are adopted. It may be necessary in these instances to estimate initial and multi-year costs statewide or for each

*This case is based upon Carol W. Lewis, *State Mandates: Responsibility and Accountability in Massachusetts* (Boston: Massachusetts League of Cities and Towns, August 1978).

[1] *Living with Mandates: A Guide for Elected Officials* (Washington, D.C.: National Association of Counties, 1980), p. 11.

community or to apportion costs among several layers of mandates and to determine what a government would spend were there no mandated obligations. The goal, then, is reasonable estimation rather than precise calculation.

In addition to reimbursement procedures and fiscal notes, other policy alternatives have been developed to deal with the fiscal aspect of mandates. These include the permissive use of new or additional revenue sources, relaxation of existing revenue constraints and tax limits, and reliance upon an extraordinary legislative majority when statutory mandates have potentially substantial fiscal impact.

The policy of "deliberate restraint" as recommended by the Advisory Commission on Intergovernmental Relations is perhaps the most far-reaching because it affects more than just the fiscal aspect of mandates.

TERMS

Dillon's Rule. Municipal corporations owe their origin to and derive their powers and rights wholly from the legislature . . . . As it creates, so it may destroy. If it may destroy, it may abridge and control.

The *City of Clinton* v. *The Cedar Rapids and Missouri Railroad Company*, 24 Iowa 455 (1868).

Home Rule. The general court shall have the power to act in relation to cities and towns, but only by general laws which apply alike to all cities, or to all towns, or to cities and towns, or to a class of not fewer than two, and by special laws . . . .

Article 89 of the Articles of Amendment, Massachusetts Municipal Home Rule Amendment of 1966.

Strict construction of Dillon's Rule assigns sovereign authority to the state, which has the preeminent position in the state–local legal relationship. The state's authority to delegate specific powers, issue guidelines and directives, and compel or restrict activity by local government is only weakly circumscribed by the home rule provision.

Tax Abatement. "An official reduction or cessation of an assessed valuation for *ad valorem* taxation after the initial assessment has been completed."

Byrl N. Boyce, ed., *Real Estate Appraisal Terminology Book*. Cambridge, Mass.: Ballinger, 1975, p. 1.

REVENUE LOSS MANDATE

The property tax raised almost $2.8 billion in FY 1977 as the main source of general revenues for municipalities in Massachusetts. Property tax relief and tax reform proposals were being debated in a heated atmosphere that would soon produce a statutory appropriation and levy limit. That atmosphere also was marked by municipal officials' vocal opposition to state mandates and their imputed costs. In the town's 1977 annual report, Arlington's town manager noted: "The many programs mandated by the state legislature put such a severe strain on our property tax rate that town officials and the town meeting now control only approximately 30 percent of the town's total expenditures." One group of mandates—property tax abatements for individuals—clearly represented a substantial and increasing revenue loss to local governments across the state (see Table 15.1).

The property tax abatement for low-income elderly was one of the six abatements providing for no reimbursement from the state. Intending to adjust the arrangements for ineligibilities introduced whenever the recently court-ordered full-value assessments might bump against the dollar ceiling written into the 1963 enacting legislation, and in response to pressures from the Councils on Aging and the Executive of Elderly Affairs, legislative members of the 1977 session amended the statute (General Laws, Ch. 59, cl. 41, s. 6).

The original bill (H6509) introduced the option of disallowing the value of an individ-

TABLE 15.1.   Individual Abatements

	FY 1976	*FY 1977*
State appropriations (millions)	$ 3.464	$ 3.434
Taxes abated (millions)	62.215	75.778
Current net cost to localities		
in millions	58.881	72.283
as percent of tax levy	2.4%	2.6%

By state law, state appropriations for a given fiscal year are used to calculate the levy for that same fiscal year. Therefore, current net cost is calculated as total tax dollars abated minus state appropriations in the same fiscal year.

ual's house in the calculation of wealth (whole estate estimate of eligibility). It also proposed making benefits available sooner, at age 70, by shifting from the calendar to the fiscal year. In something akin, but not identical to, a fiscal note, the report from the Committee on Taxation included an estimate of tax rate increases attributable to the proposed change. Local input at this point was restricted to assessors.

After the House Committee on Taxation reported out the bill, it was amended on the floor to provide for reimbursement. As H6600, the amended bill went to Ways and Means, from which it was reported out in September 1977. The bill now included a $3 million cap on reimbursements. It amounted to an expanded version of an open-ended cost obligation imposed by the state on municipalities, with a dollar limit on the state's share of the cost.

The Department of Community Affairs' (DCA) legislative liaison, which tracks legislation, routinely notified the appropriate office in DCA. That office then examined the proposed legislation for its programmatic and financial effects. The office's memorandum of October 4, 1977 concluded that the bill would impose additional costs upon cities and towns without full reimbursement by the state. The costs of this single abatement in 1977 were put at $36.4 million, none of which was to be reimbursed under the proposed change. The memorandum went on to propose four policy alternatives, including increased reimburse-

ment authority, gubernatorial veto, shift from mandate to local option, and the incorporation of H6600 into an overall property tax relief package. In his memorandum later that month to the Senate Ways and Means Committee, DCA Secretary Flynn called attention first to the mandate feature of the proposal. The previous day he had sent DCA's information to Governor Dukakis and recommended the more comprehensive approach. (This approach would be the only formally announced by the governor as administration policy in his State of the State Address the next year.)

Thus, the thrust for reimbursement emanated from the House and the governor. According to the 1977 State of the State message, the critical factor for the governor was the reimbursement, not mandating *per se.* He said:

> *The legislative leadership and I are agreed that we will not mandate additional financial responsibilities on the cities and towns without the money to pay for them . . . . Where we mandate new programs, we will pay for them.*

The question of repealing or reducing the revenue loss mandate never arose, nor did the question of compensation for the original mandate.

In late fall, 1977, Senate Ways and Means reported out an elderly abatement bill authorizing the reimbursement of all additional costs up to a ceiling of $500 for each abatement. Reimbursement in this version was put at $10 million, compared with the $3 million in the House version. It still did not touch those revenue losses imposed by the 1963 legislation or the proposed cost increases due to the liberalization of age and wealth criteria. As DCA's memorandum of December 15 noted, the Senate version first expanded eligibility for the original abatement, then promised reimbursement for the difference between the 1963 basic abatement ($350, for which more elderly were to be eligible) and the new abatement ($500). Clearly, the costs of the abatement statewide and for individual communities would increase.

Cost estimates had become quite complex by this time and would become even more so. That is not to say that cost estimates would become more influential in the decision. Apparently, no systematic analytic support underlay the new reimbursement figure written into the third version that came out of the conference committee in December, 1977. It was proposed that up to $6 million be distributed by prorating the number of exemptions in each jurisdiction. It looked as if the conference committee had just about split the difference between the House and Senate versions, thereby making use of one of the most traditional modes of compromise.

According to DCA's analyses, $6 million was insufficient, and the reimbursement mechanism itself was faulty. Costs in different communities would vary with their assessment ratios. The analyses also suggested more straightforward methods by which the state could subsidize low-income, elderly homeowners and renters, e.g., income tax credit, the costs of which are not readily shifted to the property tax via a mandate. It was further noted that even the $10 million figure might not be enough to cover all additionally imposed costs; estimates ranged from $9 million to $35 million. DCA's cost estimates changed as they were increasingly refined, but costs remained largely unknown because of the change in the current eligibility criteria. It was only in the early winter that a consensus emerged that favored the lower end of the range.

Secretary Flynn recommended to the governor on December 28 that the bill be vetoed and a "viable and equitable . . . subsidy plan" be developed or, alternatively, that the bill be returned to the legislature with an amendment for increased reimbursement. Otherwise, his memorandum suggested, the change in the abatement statute would be regarded as a new state-mandated cost on municipalities.

Administration officials met with the representatives of both elderly and municipal organizations on February 1, 1978. This was the first formal contact between local officials and the administration on this matter. Except for this meeting and the information solicited from the assessors, very little local input was sought. The Joint Legislative Office of the Massachusetts Municipal Association provided memoranda and telephone contacts in opposition to the bill as it proceeded through the legislature. In the end, special interest advocacy groups were far more effective in lobbying on behalf of bread-and-butter issues critical to their constituents. (The director of the municipal organization later underscored the success of these groups in pressing their claims when he pointed out that by restricting mandates, "we eliminate the luxury of being a hero to advocacy groups but not accountable to the electorate.")

By the time this meeting took place, Bill 6600 had passed, with the $6 million reimbursement to take effect July 1, 1978. On January 11, the governor signed the bill, now Chapter 967 of the Acts and Resolves of 1977. In his 1978 State of the State message, the governor explained his position:

Unfortunately, the General Court has once again approved legislation imposing such burdens without providing sufficient funds to reimburse the cities and towns for the tax losses they will incur— this time by granting broader property tax abatements for senior citizens. I support liberalized tax abatements for the elderly, and I will sign the legislation later today.

However, I will not do so at the expense of our cities and towns. As part of my local aid package, therefore, I will submit a request for twelve million dollars to reimburse local communities for property taxes they will lose under this bill.

Evidently, the governor separated the mandate decision from the reimbursement decision and, while favoring the former, insisted upon full reimbursement of additional costs in accordance with estimates provided by DCA and the Massachusetts Council on Aging.

Early in January, 1978, it appeared that the governor would request the $12 million. However, when the administration filed H1, it requested only $10 million. This still amounted to a substantial increase over the $6 million figure in the new legislation and also met one test of reasonableness—that of political realities—by matching the highest figure to emerge during the bill's legislative history (the Senate's figure). Six months later, at his regular monthly meeting with local government officials (Local Government Advisory Committee) on June 20, 1978, the governor said: "There has not been a state mandated program since January 1, 1976. . . . We are making significant progress. . . . Democracy is a messy system."

BIBLIOGRAPHY

Advisory Commission on Intergovernmental Relations, *State Mandating of Local Expenditures*, Report A-67 (Washington, D.C.: July 1978). See also ACIR Model Legislation on State Mandates.

Living with Mandates, A Guide for Elected Officials (Washington, D.C.: National Association of Counties Research, Inc., 1980).

CATHERINE LOVELL, et al., *Federal and State Mandating on Local Governments: An Exploration of Issues and Impacts* (Riverdale, CA: Graduate School of Administration, University of California, Riverside, June 1979).

CATHERINE LOVELL and CHARLES TOBIN, "The Mandate Issue," *Public Administration Review* 41,3 (May/June 1981):318-331.

JOSEPH F. ZIMMERMAN, "The Politics of State Mandates on Local Government," presented at the annual meeting of the Northeastern Political Science Association, Mt. Pocono, PA, November 11, 1977.

FOR DISCUSSION

1. Is the exclusion of government property from the property tax a state-mandated revenue loss when state property is involved?

2. How can it be determined what a local government would spend on a mandated activity were there no mandates?

3. On what basis could a service mandate be justified? Or a statewide requirement for compliance with generally accepted accounting principles? Are the reimbursement arguments identical?

4. Fiscal notes and reimbursement requirements raise the spectre of costly information requirements. Are the public and its representatives willing to pay a larger sum for a good decision rather than a smaller sum for a bad, indifferent, or high-risk decision? Will refined costing techniques and additional information supplant traditional decision-making techniques?

PROBLEM

Field Research Task.　　See Case no. 16.

16

Living with Mandates *

I. TYPES OF FEDERAL AND STATE MANDATES

REQUIREMENTS
　Program Mandates
　　Basic program
　　Program quality
　　Program quantity

　Procedural Mandates
　　Reporting
　　Performance
　　Fiscal
　　Personnel
　　Planning/evaluation
　　Record keeping

CONSTRAINT MANDATES
　Revenue base
　Revenue rate
　Expenditure limits

METHOD OF IMPOSITION
　Direct order
　Condition of aid

APPLICATION
　Specific (vertical)
　Crosscutting (horizontal)

Examples of Mandates

Program mandates specify something a jurisdiction or one or more of its departments is required to do. It must be an end product or objective of some service or function. Basic

*Reprinted from *Living with Mandates: A Guide for Elected Officials* (Washington, D.C.: National Association of Counties, 1980), Appendices, and based on the study of Catherine H. Lovell et al., *Federal and State Mandating on Local Governments: An Exploration of Issues and Impacts* (Riverside, Calif.: University of California, Riverside, Graduate School of Administration, 1979).

program mandates impose an action, responsibility, or goal but do not specify the quality of quantity of the program. For example, all jurisdictions must have a job-training program; and all participants must, to receive EDS funds, submit a plan for teenage job training. Program quality mandates specify the conditions and characteristics of a given unit of some product or service or of some entity or person to which this product or service is delivered. For example, lunches provided under a school lunch program must have sufficient and balanced nutrition, and each student receiving a lunch under a school nutrition program will receive the minimum recommended allowance of certain minerals and vitamins. Program quantity mandates specify the number of times a product or service must be produced or the number of people or objects to which the product or service is extended. For example, school lunch programs must be available to all children below the age of 13 in the school district, and jurisdictions with X percent of their students from low-income families qualify for the school nutrition program.

Procedural mandates regulate the way in which a jurisdiction or one of its agencies produces products or services. They are classified as reporting, performance, fiscal, personnel, planning and evaluation, and record keeping. *Reporting mandates* require a local jurisdiction to submit various types of reports, such as results of evaluation studies or documentation of eligibility. *Performance mandates* are nonfiscal mandates which are assumed to facilitate a goal (e.g., a drug abuse treatment center must have a career planning person). *Fiscal mandates* direct the manner in which fiscal resources must be organized, accounted for, or reported upon (e.g., audits or a specified accounting procedure). *Personnel mandates* specify procedures for recruitment, types of qualifications that can be required, or fringe benefits that must be provided, etc. *Planning and evaluation mandates* require that activities be coordinated with an overall plan, either of the agency or jurisdiction (e.g., programs for housing construction assistance must be consistent with local subdivision regulations).

Constraint mandates are requirements that limit the amount and type of local resources or limit the amount of money that can be spent. *Revenue base mandates* limit the kinds of fiscal resources that a jurisdiction can use to finance public service (e.g., user fees cannot be used to finance library expenses). *Revenue rate mandates* limit the amount of a particular revenue base (e.g., the property tax rate for municipal services cannot exceed the rate of $2 for every $100 of assessed valuation). *Expenditure limits mandates* limit how or what portion of locally generated resources are spent (e.g., no more than 10 percent of the budget for a program may be used for personnel).

II. GATHERING FISCAL IMPACT DATA ON MANDATES

Instructions to the Chief Administrative or Financial Officer for Forms I, II, and III

These forms were made as general as possible so that they could be used by jurisdictions of every variety. They may be modified to suit your jurisdiction by adding, omitting, or modifying questions. The time period for which data are to be collected is one year. Usually this will mean the fiscal year following the imposition of the mandate.

Before beginning to collect the data required on these forms, it is important that each mandate be identified properly by type.

The following data should be monitored:

Expenditure. Don't forget to include indirect expenditures if they are necessary in order to achieve compliance; for example, an increased workload for the accounting department due to a new financial reporting requirement in the health department.

Cost. Find out what expenditures were being made for any similar activity or activities before the mandate was imposed. This provides an estimate of *prior expenditure*. For example, if a mandate requires a $50,000 expenditure for program X, and your government was already spending $20,000 on a program similar to X, then the "prior costs" would actually be $20,000.

An attempt should be made to estimate expenditures if the mandate were to be withdrawn. This is the *present preferred cost*. For example, if a program costing $30,000 per year were continued at the same level after the mandate was withdrawn, the $30,000 would not be considered a cost which resulted from the mandate.

Compliance. Review reports, budgets, etc., to determine the degree to which your government has complied with the requirements of the mandate. Accurate reporting on the level of compliance is necessary in applying for proper reimbursement. In the case of condition-of-aid mandates, compliance may be monitored by the government supplying the grant.

Funding. Identify the source of funding (general fund, grant, etc.) in order to understand more clearly the financing of mandated activities.

Displacement. Determine what other projects or programs have been displaced or cut in order to pay for newly mandated ones. This will be a difficult task; nevertheless, it will enable you to include some of the more tangible effects of mandates in the final cost analysis.

Private sector. Note the effects of a new mandate on the private sector. New fees and/or requirements by your local government will show in part how much of a mandate's cost is being shifted and how much is being absorbed by your government.

Constraint mandates. Determine the amount of revenue loss due directly to the mandate. Also attempt to estimate how much revenue would increase if the mandate were dropped. This is the *present preferred revenue*.

Expense caps. Determine what reduc-tion in expense has been caused directly by the mandate; i.e., what was being spent com-pared to imposed limitations. Also find out how much this expenditure would rise if the limitations were removed. This is the *present preferred expenditure*.

Fiscal Impact Model

Form I: Program and Procedural Mandates

Expenditure Considerations

1.   What was the total expenditure on the program mandate for the first year after its imposition?

       a. direct labor
       b. supplies and other expendable inputs
       c. indirect labor
       d. indirect production
       e. general overhead
       f. building occupancy
       g. equipment depreciation

direct labor_____hrs.
direct labor expenditure $_____
total "other than direct labor" expenditure (total of b through g) $_____
grand total expenditure $_____

Cost Considerations

Prior Cost

2a. Did the mandate replace or partially replace a prior activity?

YES   **NO**   If not, then the prior cost of the mandate is equal to the expenditure on it (Question 1).

2b. Give the increase in expenditure due to the mandate. $_____

2c. If there was a decrease in expenditure due to the mandate, give the dollar amount of the decrease.
    $_____

3a. Have there been substantial expenditures due to disruption, delay, interference with another program or department, etc. as a result of meeting the mandate? (Note: List only those expenditures not included in Question 2.)

YES   **NO**

3b.   Give a complete list of types of expenditures and the amount spent on each.

                TYPE   **AMOUNT**

_____

_____

_____

Present Preferred Cost

4a. To the extent it is possible, determine the answer to the question: "If the mandate were discontinued, would the presently mandated activity be reduced?" Check below.

   YES   **NO**

4b. Circle the appropriate intervals of reduction of service:

   0-10%   11-25%   26-50%   51-75%   76-90%   91-100%

4c. How much would the jurisdiction continue to spend on this activity? $_____

Compliance Considerations

5a. In your opinion, how well is this mandate being performed? Check appropriate space:

   _____Not at all
   _____Minimally
   _____Substantially
   _____Completely

5b. What percent of complete compliance does the above represent:_____%

5c. Are the requirements specified by this mandate exceeded?

   YES   **NO**

5d. How much in excess? State the percent by which this mandate is exceeded_____%.

Funding Considerations

6. What are the sources of funding for the mandate? Check appropriately.

   General fund_____
   Special fund_____
   User fees_____
   Grant_____
   Other (specify)_____

7a. Is reimbursement by the mandating level of government complete, partial, or not at all?

   Complete_____   Partial_____   Not at all_____

7b. If partial, give the level of reimbursement._____%

7c. Specify the type of reimbursement provided by the mandating level (e.g., grant, shared tax)

   _____

   _____

   _____

   _____ _____   _____

   _____   _____

   _____

Displacement

8a. Does local financing of the mandated service diminish jurisdiction funds available for non-mandated services?

   YES   **NO**

8b. Were funds for other services cut in order to satisfy this mandate?

YES   **NO**

8c. By how much? Provide an expenditure figure, if possible. Expenditure cut $_____

8d. Were there cuts in services?

YES   **NO**

9a. If jurisdiction funds were spent on this mandate, was a local revenue source increased to offset the expenditure?

YES   **NO**

9b. What was the increase in revenues? Amount of increase $_____

Private Sector Considerations

10a. Were costs shifted to private citizens or firms as a result of complying with the mandate (e.g., cost of filling out forms, fees, permits)?

YES   **NO**

10b. List completely the types of costs shifted.

Shifted costs:

_____

_____

_____

Form II: Revenue Constraints

Lost Revenue

1. To the best of your ability, try to provide an estimate of the loss in revenue due to this constraint.

   Estimate of revenue loss $_____

Present Preferred Revenue

2a. If the mandate were lifted, would revenues rise?

   YES   NO

2b. By how much? $_____

Funding and Reimbursement

3a. Were other revenue sources tapped to make up for the loss (or potential loss) in revenue caused by this mandate?

   YES   NO

3b. Specify which revenue sources were tapped.

   _____

   _____

3c. Was the jurisdiction reimbursed by the mandating level of government for the loss, if any, in revenue, due to the mandate?

   YES   NO

3d. Give dollar amount of reimbursement.   Reimbursement $_____

Form III: Expenditure Caps

Reduction in Expenditure

1. List any services that were cut as a result of the mandate. Also list the amount by which they were cut and the reduction in expenditure on them. Be as specific as possible. If the reduction in expenditure is spread over the jurisdiction, specify this.

   Functional area where cut was made   **% of Functional Area Budget Cut**

   _____

   _____

   _____

   _____

Present Preferred Expenditure

2a. If the mandated expenditure cap were lifted, would expenditures rise?

   YES   NO

2b. By how much? $_____

Reimbursement Formula

The following reimbursement formula assumes that there is presently neither funding nor reimbursement by the mandating government. These can simply be subtracted from the amount of reimbursement calculated by the formula.

For program and procedural mandates, the most general form of the reimbursement formula is:

$$\text{Reimbursement} = \left\{ \begin{array}{l} \text{Prior Cost*} \\ \text{or} \\ \text{Expenditure} - \text{Present Preferred Cost} \end{array} \right\} - \begin{array}{l} \text{Reduction for} \\ \text{Overcompliance} \end{array}$$

For program and procedural mandates, the specific form of the reimbursement formula differs slightly depending upon whether it is calculated on the basis of prior cost or on the basis of present preferred cost. Both forms, however, are based upon the following two assumptions:

1. The mandating government wishes to reimburse *totally* for all prior cost (or present preferred cost) reported.
2. The mandating government does not wish to reimburse for *any* overcompliance of the mandate.

In words, the formula is:

$$\text{Reimbursement} = \left\{ \begin{array}{l} \text{prior cost} \\ \text{or} \\ \text{expenditure} - \begin{array}{l}\text{present}\\\text{preferred}\\\text{cost}\end{array} \end{array} \right\} - \left(\text{expenditure} - \left[\frac{\text{expenditure} \times 100\%}{100\% + (\text{overcompliance})\%} \right] \right)$$

Expressed in terms of the questions in Form I, the formula is:

$$\text{Reimbursement} = \left\{ \begin{array}{l} 2b. + 3b. \\ \text{or} \\ 1. - 4c. \end{array} \right\} - \left(1. - \left[\frac{1. \times 100\%}{100\% + (5d.)\%} \right] \right)$$

*The term "prior cost" may be confusing. It is defined as the amount by which the jurisdiction has increased its expenditure in order to comply with the mandate. "Present preferred cost," on the other hand, is defined as the amount *to which* the jurisdiction would reduce its expenditure if the mandate were removed.

For revenue constraint mandates, the most general form of the reimbursement formula is simply:

$$\text{Reimbursement} = \left\{ \begin{array}{l} \text{Lost Revenue} \\ \text{or} \\ \text{Present Preferred Revenue} \end{array} \right\}$$

We assume that the mandating government wishes to reimburse the local government totally for all lost revenue (or present preferred revenue). The specific form of the formula, expressed in terms of the questions on Form II is:

$$\text{Reimbursement} = \left\{ \begin{array}{l} 1. \\ \text{or} \\ 2b. \end{array} \right\}$$

CHAPTER FIVE

ANALYZING EXPENDITURES

How do we know how much we are spending? Is the sum trivial or significant? Too much or too little? Is it being spent well? How do we choose among competing claims upon limited resources? The classical formulation of the fundamental problem in expenditure analysis was developed by V. O. Key, Jr., who stated it in deceptively simple terms: "On what basis shall it be decided to allocate x dollars to activity A instead of activity B?"[1]

Allocation of funds has been based over the years on various criteria, including expediency, history, and serendipity. The most basic input measure, nominal dollars, is by itself almost wholly meaningless. This primitive measure not only relies solely upon quantitative units to which monetary values are assigned, but provides very little information for decision making. George Bernard Shaw, in reference to municipal expenditures, pointed out the problem with this approach more than three-quarters of a century ago. He wrote:

the balance sheet of a city's welfare cannot be stated in figures. Counters of a much more spiritual kind are needed, and some imagination and conscience to add them up, as well.[2]

More recently, the theme was repeated as follows:

the goal of the city is not to accumulate financial assets nor to maximize its income or profits . . . it is to provide services to people—a goal which cannot be measured by a city's accounting records alone.[3]

Budgeted sums have meaning only when they are expressed in terms of something else. Analytic relationships are required. Yet, there are still no purely "objective," technical standards or culturally derived

---

[1]V. O. Key, Jr., "The Lack of a Budgetary Theory," *American Political Science Review* 34 (December 1940), p. 1138.

[2]George Bernard Shaw, *The Common Sense of Municipal Trading* (Westminster: A. Constable & Co., Ltd., 1904) p. 169.

[3]U.S. Department of Housing and Urban Development, Office of Policy Development and Research, "Urban Fiscal Crisis: Fantasy or Fact? A Reply to the Touche Ross/First National Bank Study," Washington, D.C., March 1979, working paper, p. 1.

conventions that are universally accepted or wholly satisfactory.[4] One commonly used standard is expenditures expressed as a percentage of total budgeted expenditures (share of budget); this indicates only government priorities and omits any reference to total amounts or rate of change. Social priorities frequently are expressed as a percentage of the gross national product, despite the fact that decision makers do not have budgetary discretion over all the resources represented by the GNP, and what is really being expressed is the aggregated outcome of a multitude of component decisions. Standardization on a per capita basis is employed often, although the problem posed by identifying the appropriate population (e.g., direct user vs. beneficiary, daytime vs. nighttime residential) is only one of the several associated with this standard.[5] Spending can be expressed in terms of rate of growth, but this looks only to the internal history of the program, agency, or item and ignores changes in the larger government or society. One frequently adopted solution is to use a variety of measures that express a number of relationships. (That way, the analyst provides the information and leaves the judgment call to someone else.)

Budget analysis has been defined as "basically a comparison of the relative merits of alternative uses of funds."[6] With regard to "the allocation of expenditures among different purposes so as to achieve the greatest return,"[7] the most useful and best-known techniques are benefit–cost analysis and effectiveness-cost analysis. Both draw upon economic concepts to evaluate expenditure decisions, primarily capital investments. Benefit–cost analysis, founded upon formal welfare economics, has been defined as "nothing more than a logical attempt to weigh the pros and cons of a decision."[8] It assumes the validity of market-based measures and demands that a project's benefits and costs be measured in monetary terms. The goal is to maximize the ratio of benefits to costs.

Effectiveness-cost analysis may be employed when it is difficult to define or measure output or when the output is taken as a given. In effectiveness-cost analysis,

the task involves searching for the lowest cost means of attaining an explicit objective rather than evaluating both benefits and costs, and searching for that optimally designed project with the greatest surplus of benefits over costs.[9]

[4]Carol W. Lewis, "Interpreting Municipal Expenditures," in *Analyzing Urban-Service Distributions*, ed. by Richard C. Rich (Mass.: Lexington Books, 1982) pp. 203–17.

[5]George E. Peterson, "Finance," in *The Urban Predicament*, by William Gorham and Nathan Glazer (Washington, D.C.: The Urban Institute, 1976), p. 43.

[6]Verne B. Lewis, "Toward a Theory of Budgeting," *Public Administration Review* 12,1 (Winter 1952), p. 42.

[7]V. O. Key, Jr., *op. cit.*, p. 1137.

[8]Edward M. Gramlich, *Benefit-Cost Analysis of Government Programs* (Englewood Cliffs: Prentice–Hall, 1981), p. 3.

[9]Robert H. Haveman and Julius Margolis, eds., *Public Expenditures and Policy Analysis*, 2nd ed. (Chicago: Rand McNally, 1977), Introduction, p. 9.

The first two cases in this chapter illustrate the uses and limitations of benefit–cost analysis. Case no. 17, "Refining Gold under Pressure," is an evaluative case delineating the workings of political pressure. The context is intergovernmental; the locale is New York City. The case demonstrates the potential and limitations of "expertise" and suggests that more than economic feasibility is needed to justify budget decisions. (See related cases, nos. 2 and 6.) Decision makers act on a number of goals and incentives, and analysis either takes this into account or becomes "an argument in the political process rather than a guide."[10] Case no. 18 presents a relatively straightforward lease/buy decision in a military setting. It requires discounting and coming up with a specific, recommended alternative.

Analyzing personnel costs is the subject of cases 19 and 20. "Costing Out in the Public Sector" presents a comprehensive methodology for costing out a labor contract. Its follow-up, case no. 20, requires that the methodology be applied to selected costing problems in the contract for a local school system. Contracted net wage increase, average annual base salary, the roll-up factor, hourly rate, automatic step increases, costing additional holidays, the difference between expenditures and costs, and the pitfall of double counting are all topics covered by the model and its application.

Case no. 21 is a descriptive case, illustrating the political use and analytic meaning of the concept of inflation. It is the actual budget presentation of a New England town. "Now You See It, Now You Don't" introduces the consumer price index, producer price index, and the implicit price deflator. The first analytic problem is set in Des Moines and requires the use of the IPD to develop a presentation for the city council on the budgetary effects of price changes. The second asks that the CPI be used to calculate the effect of price change in New Orleans' budget and, in addition, asks how information on inflation can be incorporated into that city's zero-base budget.

The thrust of the chapter is to provide the reader with concrete applications of benefit–cost analysis as a major technique and personnel costs and inflation as two major problem areas in expenditure analysis. Related cases include nos. 2 and 6 on the limits of analysis in decision making, nos. 10 and 32 on the meaning of costs, and nos. 16 and 31 on the technique and problems of costing out government operations and programs.

●

---

[10]*Ibid.*, p. 10.

17

Refining Gold Under Pressure *

My intramural task force reported in September 1978 that the basic cost of refining gold was 99 cents per ounce for industry vs. $1.64 for the New York Assay Office (NYAO). This office—which is really a factory—was overtaken by time and events and now was located on Wall Street, amidst some of the most expensive real estate in New York City. Moreover, the office was not a mainline activity of the Treasury Department and thus was not getting adequate management attention. Much to everyone's surprise, since much of the NYAO equipment was not modern or efficient, our report showed that NYAO could become competitive with private industry if productivity were increased through improved methods while overhead and support costs were reduced. If the assay office could increase its annual output to 2.5 million ounces of gold and reduce refinery positions by about 20 percent by 1983, then NYAO would be cost competitive with commercial refineries. These were the recommendations of the Treasury Department to the Office of Management and Budget (OMB).

To assure that the results of this initial study would be valid under the procedures (firm bids, standard cost factors and costing techniques, and "winner-take-all" arrangements) established by the A-76 Circular, OMB put 1.3 million dollars in termination costs into the president's FY 1980 budget and requested a new study as follows:

*By John Garmat, Deputy Director of the Office of Budget and Program Analysis, U.S. Department of Treasury, and chairman of the Precious Metals Refining Evaluation Task Force. Based upon Precious Metals Refining Evaluation Task Force, "Follow-Up Comparison of In-House vs. Contractual Bullion Refining at the United States Assay Office in New York: A Cost-Benefit Comparison Based upon Decision Criteria Established by the Revised OMB Circular No. A-76" (Washington, D.C.: Department of Treasury, July 1979).

Refining gold and silver bullion—Gold and silver bullion are refined at the New York Assay Office. Preliminary determination indicates that these operations may be more effectively performed by the private sector. The 1980 Budget includes money to phase-out these operations; however, the final decision awaits additional study results.

The July 1979 cost–benefit analysis was undertaken on this authority and on the basis of OMB Director McIntyre's allowance letter of February 2, 1979. That letter states:

The Treasury Department should complete a final study on the desirability of terminating the New York Assay Office refining operations (per OMB Circular A-76). The result of this study will be used in reaching a final determination on the New York refining activities.

What happened as a result of the second OMB request was remarkable. There occurred a dramatic jump in productivity. By April 1979 NYAO was producing at an annual rate greater than the output projected for 1983 in the initial study. NYAO also decreased its staff below projected levels. As a result, the FY 1980 costs of production per ounce of gold refined would be slightly over $1.27, including capital costs and metal losses figured at the more realistic higher level but excluding the seven percent scheduled pay increase. By comparison, the contractor's price increased from 99 cents to $1.41 per ounce in the year between the informational quotations and the firm bids. Some of this difference was due to inflation and a small part due to the security requirement for escrow gold, a provision which had not been included in the informational quote.

At this point, the Cost Comparison Handbook that is used in the A-76 process permits a shortened analysis because additional factors that would be considered, such as termination costs, contract administration, etc., generally are favorable to a government operation. In this case, because of the high visibility and to assure that judgmental areas are minimized, the full analysis was conducted. The task force concluded that even if all judgmental issues were figured in terms most favorable to the contractor, the cost differential still justified retention of the in-house operation.

The numbers, while impressive, do not tell the whole story. An increase in output from adding an extra processing line and reducing the work force, combined with management improvements, had a pronounced impact on productivity. This is an example of what management and labor can do to achieve a common set of goals. It also suggests the implicit (and, in this case, explicit) threat in independent analysis, which may alter the costs and benefits associated with the operation under study.

The story also is an example of how standardized procedures protect the team conducting the cost–benefit analysis. The basic technical criterion—cost competitiveness with private industry—was not questioned. But technique, procedure, and expertise alone are no guarantee of insulation. The results of the study fortuitously corresponded to the political and institutional pressures brought to bear on those responsible for making the ultimate decision. The recommendation to continue gold refining at NYAO until 1984, when all unparted bullion should have been processed, happily represented an ideal solution to a difficult problem. The decision was made and was clearly articulated to the union and congressional interests: the refinery would be closed in 1984. In addition, since the remaining gold would be refined in less time and at a lower cost, the taxpayer also benefits. The union, in the meantime, was able to obtain a reprieve for its NYAO members. I feel that this is an example of the proper role of cost–benefit analysis decision making and legitimate, professional responses to political pressure.

FOLLOW-UP

Based on a February 4, 1981, memorandum of the Mint's director, Stella Hackel Sims, the actual 1980 cost was 3 percent under the estimate projected in the study. Part of the savings resulted from the partial hiring freeze. On balance, NYAO is still ahead of scheduled production volume.

FOR DISCUSSION

1. On the basis of what features of the study is this classified as a benefit-cost analysis?

2. A substitute for a market mechanism sometimes is needed in a government operation. The basic assumption of this A–76 study (according to guidelines of OMB Circular A–76) is that directly provided government services should be cost competitive with the private sector. Is this appropriate for all services, for instance, health or criminal justice? Give reasons.

3. This case illustrates that technique, procedure, and expertise do not guarantee insulation from political and institutional pressures. Is insulation of professional staff desirable, or even possible? Should the technical decision-making criteria, such as cost competitiveness, that underlie professional "objective" solutions be subjected to political review? For what purposes?

4. Benefit–cost analysis is only one of the many types of analytic techniques that have been introduced into public budgeting and financial decision making. What are the consequences of this increase in "expert" formation? Can expert analysis be a substitute for political judgment, or should it be? What is the appropriate role of such information in answering the question posed by V. O. Key, Jr.?

DECISION SUMMARY FOR IN-HOUSE OR CONTRACT PERFORMANCE BASED ON COST COMPARISON PER OMB CIRCULAR A-76

I. U.S. Department of the Treasury

Location Bureau of the Mint — U.S. Assay Office in New York

Function or Activity Gold refining

Currently Performed In-house

II. Contract Data:

Solicitation date 5/15/79   Solicitation No. BM 79-17

Number of bids 2   Closing date 6/17/79

Contract proposal is for 1 year with option for 4 additional year(s).

Cost comparison covered 5 years, from October 1, 1979, to September 30, 1984.

Proposed changeover date October 1, 1979

III. Total Adjusted Cost in In-house Perfor-
mance   (Line 33) $12,731,215

Total Adjusted Cost of Contracting-out
Performance   (Line 34)   20,203,305

Cost of In-house Performance under Cost
of Contracting-out Performance (Line 35)   ($7,472,090)

IV. Final Recommendation — Until existing stock of unparted bullion is exhausted,
                            continue to: Perform In-house ✔
                                          Contract Out

Prepared by: Approved by:

_____   _____

(Name)   (Date)   (Name)   (Date)

Deputy Director (Program Analysis)
Office of Budget and Program Analysis   Under Secretary
(Title)   (Telephone)   (Title)   (Telephone)

V. Action of Contracting Officer:
Perform In-house ✔   Bidders Notified _____
Contract Out _____   Contract No. _____
                                          Awarded To _____

                                                  JUN 28 1979
_____   _____
(Name)   (Date)

Chief, Procurement Division
(Title)   (Telephone)

TABLE 17.1. U.S. Department of the Treasury, Bureau of the Mint
Comparative Cost of In-House and Contracting-Out Performance of Gold Refining, June 15, 1979

(Enter Amounts Rounded to Nearest Dollar)

Line #	Cost Element	Remarks	First Year FY 1980	Second Year FY 1981	Third Year FY 1982	Fourth Year FY 1983	Fifth Year FY 1984	Total	Reference
In-House Performance									
1.	Direct Material	—	$ 131,336	$ 131,336	131,336	131,336	$ 131,336	$ 656,680	A-3
2.	Material Overhead	—	37,956	37,956	37,956	37,956	37,956	189,780	B-1
3.	Direct Labor	—	596,239	596,239	596,239	596,239	596,239	2,981,195	C-1
4.	Fringe Benefits on Direct Labor	—	153,041	153,041	153,041	153,041	153,041	765,205	D-1
5.	Operations Overhead	—	742,250	742,250	742,250	742,250	742,250	3,711,250	E-11
6.	Other Direct Costs	—	2,600	2,600	2,600	2,600	2,600	13,000	F-1
7.	General and Administrative Expense	—	280,246	280,246	280,246	280,246	280,246	1,401,230	G-1
8.	Inflation	—	Not Applic.	—¹	—¹	—¹	—¹	—¹	—
9.	Total		$ 1,943,668	$ 1,943,668	$ 1,943,668	$ 1,943,668	$ 1,943,668	$ 9,718,340	
Performance by Contracting-Out									
10.	Contract Price	—	$ 2,817,084	$ 2,817,084	$ 2,817,084	$ 2,817,084	$ 2,817,084	$ 14,085,420	H-1
11.	Transportation	4% of Contract Price	—	—	—	—	—	—	—
12.	Contract Administration	Assays, Handling, Security, 35 Avg. Positions	$ 112,683	$ 112,683	112,683	112,683	$ 112,683	$ 563,415	I-1
13.	Government-Furnished Property	—	—	—	—	—	—	—	—
14.	Standby Maintenance		—	—	—	—	—	—	—
15.	Other Costs		672,367	672,367	672,367	672,367	672,367	3,361,835	J-1
16.	General and Administrative Expense	—	133,459	133,459	133,459	133,459	133,459	667,295	K-1
17.	Total		$ 3,735,593	$ 3,735,593	$ 3,735,593	$ 3,735,593	$ 3,735,593	$ 18,677,965	

(continued)

TABLE 17.1. U.S. Department of the Treasury, Bureau of the Mint
Comparative Cost of In-House and Contracting-Out Performance of Gold Refining, June 15, 1979 — Contd.

Line #	Cost Element	Remarks	First Year FY 1980	Second Year FY 1981	Third Year FY 1982	Fourth Year FY 1983	Fifth Year FY 1984	Total	Reference
			(Enter Amounts Rounded to Nearest Dollar)						
Other Considerations									
Additions and (Deductions) to In-House Performance									
18.	Cost of Capital	Prorated to Reflect Refining Asset Only	$ 176,340	$ 176,340	$ 176,340	$ 176,340	$ 176,340	$ 881,700	L-1
19.	One-Time New-Start Costs	—						—	—
20.	Other Costs	Metal Loss	426,235	426,235	426,235	426,235	426,235	2,131,175	M-1
21.	Other Costs (Deduct)	—						—	—
22.	Total		$ 602,575	$ 602,575	$ 602,575	$ 602,575	$ 602,575	$ 3,012,875	
Additions and (Deductions) to Contracting-Out Performance									
23.	Cost of Capital on Gov't-Furnished Facilities	—						—	—
24.	Utilization of Government Capacity							—	—
25.	One-Time Conversion Costs	Severance Pay for 63 Avg. Positions	$ 220,442	$ 220,442	$ 220,442	$ 220,442	$ 220,442	$ 1,102,210	N-1
26.	Other Costs	—						—	—
27.	Federal Income Taxes	2% of Contract Price-Line 10	(56,342)	(56,342)	(56,342)	(56,342)	(56,342)	(281,710)	O-1
28.	Net Proceeds from Disposal of Assets (Annual Year)	Loss on Disposal of Refining Equipment	6,074	6,074	6,074	6,074	6,074	30,370	P-1

						Total
29. Other Costs (Deduct)	—	—	—	—	—	—
30. Total	$ 170,174	$ 170,174	$ 170,174	$ 170,174	$ 170,174	$ 850,870
Minimum Cost Differential						
31. New-Start	— (10% of In-House Personnel Costs)	—	—	—	—	—
32. Conversion	$ 134,894	$ 134,894	$ 134,894	$ 134,894	$ 134,894	$ 674,470 Q-1
Summary						
33. Adjusted Cost of In-House Performance (Line 9 ± Line 22 + 31)	$ 2,546,243	$ 2,546,243	$ 2,546,243	$ 2,546,243	$ 2,546,243	$12,731,215
34. Adjusted Cost of Contracting Out Performance (Line 17 ± Line 30 + 32)	$ 4,040,661	$ 4,040,661	$ 4,040,661	$ 4,040,661	$ 4,040,661	$20,203,305
35. Cost of In-House Over (Under) Cost of Contracting-Out Performance (Line 33 – Line 34)	$(1,494,418)	$ (1,494,418)	$(1,494,418)	$(1,494,418)	$(1,494,418)	$ (7,472,090)

¹Since contract price provided for cost inflationary factors, equally applicable to in-house and contracted refining, no inflationary increase is shown for years after 1980.

DEPARTMENT OF THE TREASURY
WASHINGTON. D.C. 20220

April 30, 1979

Dear Mr. Green:

This is in response to your request of April 10, 1979, asking for Treasury Department comments on a letter from Edward S. Karalis, National Vice President of the American Federation of Government Employees. The letter recommends that the Department make a change in the chairmanship of the New York Assay Office A-76 Task Force. Our review of the Task Force activities indicates that, for the reasons outlined below, such a change in personnel is unnecessary and not in the best interest of all parties concerned.

The A-76 Task Force was established to insure that the specifications for this study reflect the specialized knowledge of the Office of the Secretary and the Mint. Two members of the Mint are on the Task Force as well as four members from the Office of the Secretary representing specific functional areas. This broad representation insures that a balanced and objective study will be conducted and that the chairman or any other single member would have no undue influence on the study.

The study itself is being undertaken in strict conformance to the criteria and standards set forth by the Office of Management and Budget Circular No. A-76. This OMB Circular provides an extensive listing of objective criteria on which to base the judgment on conducting activities by contract or in-house. It is these objective standards against which the final decision will be made. The chairman of the Task Force has expressed his delight in the progress made by the New York Assay Office since the first study began. He is striving to assure that all views are considered and the study is balanced and objective. Further, given the broad representation on the Task Force and the criteria set forth in the Circular, we do not believe that the chairman, or any other member, could prejudice the outcome fo the study to conform to a preconceived result.

This conclusion is particularly true with respect to the charge that a particular refiner would be favored. In fact, consultation has been held with many potential bidders, including the New York Assay Office, to insure that the bid specifications are realistic and in the best interest of the government. The actual procurement documents will be issued by the Mint procurement staff, not the Task Force, and the results evaluated by the procurement staff. The Task Force chairman or other members will not have any role in receiving the bids. Moreover, the final determination with respect to the policy of whether or not to contract out refining operations will be made by Mint and Treasury policy officials -- not the chairman or members of the Task Force.

With respect to Mr. Karalis' statement that there is an intent to suppress information on the study, it should be noted that upon their request the AFGE has been supplied with copies of the Task Force minutes of the meeting of March 9. Minutes of subsequent meetings could similarly be available if requested in writing by the Union or other interested parties, or members of the Congress. In addition, on April 2, Mr. Blaylock, President of AFGE, was requested to designate a contact point with the Task Force to review the proposed specifications and to provide comments to insure that all concerns of the New York Assay Office work force would be fully taken into account. Clearly, the specifications will be critical in assuring a fair test. After a telephone follow-up of April 20, 1979, Mr. Scott Sullivan of the AFGE's General Counsel, indicated (on April 26, 1979) that the AFGE would like to review the proposed specifications. We provided a copy of the specifications to the AFGE on the same day.

Another of Mr. Karalis' requests is that the New York Assay Office Reorganization Plan be kept confidential. Many of the actions recommended in the proposal have already been carried out by the Mint. The Reorganization Plan would not be a topic for consideration by the Task Force, but would, of course, improve the Assay Office's competitive position in the bid evaluation process. Any additional improvement ideas offered by the Union would also help meet this goal. There would be no reason to pass on any details of the reorganization to those outside of the Mint; however, it is not possible to guarantee that the Plan itself can be kept confidential since the provisions of the Freedom of Information Act could apply to this administrative document.

It is currently expected that the Task Force will finish its major activity by April 30, 1979. At that time bid solicitations will be published in the Commerce Business Daily. The schedule calls for all bids, including that of the New York Assay Office to be opened on June 15, 1979.

The bids will be reviewed by Treasury policy officials and a final decision is expected by July 15, 1979. In order to meet this goal, the Task Force must complete its work on schedule. A copy of the approved project plan is attached for your information.

To change the chairman of the Task Force at this time would interrupt the work of the Task Force to no evident purpose, for the reasons outlined above. The Department's goal is to achieve a fair and objective study which will insure that the interests of the employees of the New York Assay Office and the public's interest are fully taken into account in establishing a cost effective means of refining gold.

We will be pleased to receive any suggestions you may have regarding this study and expect to inform you and other interested members of the Congress of the results of this study and provide all relevant supporting data as soon as the decision on the issue has been made.

Sincerely,

Gene E. Godley
Assistant Secretary
(Legislative Affairs)

The Honorable
Bill Green
U. S. House of Representatives
Washington, D. C.   20515

Attachment

THE CITY OF NEW YORK
OFFICE OF THE MAYOR
NEW YORK, N.Y. 10007

May 3, 1979

Honorable Michael Blumenthal
Secretary of the Treasury
U. S. Department of the Treasury
15th and Pennsylvania Avenue
Washington, D. C.   20220

Dear Mike:

I would like to express my opposition to the possible shutdown of the U. S. Assay Office in New York and the permanent
loss of approximately 175 jobs in New York City.

It is my understanding that the Department of the Treasury
Task Force recommended the conditional continuation of gold
refining activities at the Assay Office provided that the
Office was able to effectuate increases in productivity and
reductions in overhead and support costs. Notwithstanding
this recommendation, a second Treasury task force has been
commissioned to further review operations at the Assay office
and is expected to recommend the termination of operations at
this facility. Considering that the initial Task Force's
suggestions regarding management and productivity improvements
have been implemented ahead of the target date, it is difficult
to understand why the proposal to close the Office and needlessly
eliminate jobs vital to the economy of New York City is being
reviewed further at this time. In addition, I have been told
that the private sector's cost competitive edge can be misleading,
since it is based upon volume discounting and the doubtful assumption that costs will remain constant over a 6 or 7 year period.
Probable shutdown costs, including unemployment and welfare
benefits to dismissed workers, further support retaining the
facility.

Legitimate questions on closing the Assay Office have been raised
by Local 2856, American Federation of Government Employees. In
view of inadequate documentation to support a closing of this
facility, and the negative impact this action would have on
the workers and the New York City economy, it appears in the
best interest of all concerned to continue the gold refining
operations at the U. S. Assay Office in New York.

Sincerely,

Edward I. Koch
M A Y O R

EIK:ve

cc: President Jimmy Carter
     James T. McIntyre, Jr.
     Office of Management and Budget

AMERICAN FEDERATION OF GOVERNMENT EMPLOYEES
AFFILIATED WITH THE AFL-CIO

KENNETH T. BLAYLOCK   JOSEPH D. GLEASON   NICHOLAS J. NOLAN
NATIONAL PRESIDENT   EXECUTIVE VICE PRESIDENT   NATIONAL SEC -TREAS.

J F GRINER BUILDING

1325 MASSACHUSETTS AVE., N.W. ● WASHINGTON, D.C. 20005
Telephone: (202) 737-8700

IN REPLY PLEASE REFER TO:

8d/Assay Office

May 14, 1979

Dr. George Hunter
Chief of Assay Laboratories
United States Bureau of the Mint
501 13th Street, N.W.
Washington, D. C. 20220

Dear Dr. Hunter:

The Department of the Treasury will shortly finalize specifications relating to the refining of approximately 15 million
troy ounces of unparted Government bullion. These specifications
will be the basis for firm bids from the private sector for purposes of the A-76 cost comparison study now underway.

We have reviewed these specifications and would like to
offer the following comments.

Item IX: Notice of In-House Cost Analysis
for Award Purposes.

Will the Bureau of the Mint in-house cost
estimate be provided the AFGE local to
review prior to its being submitted? It
is of particular importance that the in-house
bid fully reflect the already achieved productivity improvements at the NYAO, as well
as those projected in the next 5 years. It
would also be important to take full advantage
of certain factors, such as security, transportation, insurance, etc., where the contractor's cost should be higher than the Government's
comparable special costs for this project if
done in-house.

Dr. George Hunter   May 14, 1979
Chief of Assay Laboratories

Item XI: Displaced Workers

The contractor shall report the jobs to be
filled to the Government contract officer
who shall inform the displaced federal personnel of such employment opportunities.
Such employees shall be given the first right
of refusal for jobs for which they are qualified. If more than one such employee is qualified and applies for a given job, preference
will be given on the basis of seniority as
calculated for reduction-in-force purposes.
Employees rejected by the contractor on the
basis of qualification or for other reasons
may request the government contract officer
to review such determinations for compliance
with the terms of the contract.

Item XII: Government Representation Facilities

NYAO employees displaced by this contract shall
be given preference for Assay Office postions
required in the administration of this contract.

        In conclusion, we appreciate the opportunity to review these
draft specifications, and hope that our comments will be given
careful consideration by the Precious Metals Evaluation Task
Force. We are confident, in light of the dramatic productivity
improvements at the NYAO, that the new A-76 cost comparison study
will clearly identify the many advantages associated with in-
house bullion refining.

                        Sincerely,

                        Kenneth T. Blaylock
                        National President

THE CITY OF NEW YORK
THE PRESIDENT OF THE COUNCIL
CITY HALL
NEW YORK, N. Y. 10007

CAROL BELLAMY
PRESIDENT

May 22, 1979

W. J. McDonald
Acting Assistant Secretary
Department of the Treasury
Washington, D.C. 20220

Dear Mr. McDonald: .

Thank you for your thoughtful reply to my letter to Secretary
Blumenthal concerning the New York Assay Office.

My staff counsel recently toured the Assay Office and was very
impressed with its operations, as well as with the report she
received (and which you confirmed in your letter) that the
increased efficiency standards mandated in the previous evaluation
of the Office had been met or exceeded.

I was also gratified by your assurances that the current evaluation
would be conducted in an objective and impartial manner. I would
hope that as part of the evaluation, consideration will be given
to the adverse impact the closing of the Assay Office's refining
operation (the loss of some 175 jobs) will have on the City of New
York. Can you advise me as to whether an "Urban Impact Statement"
is being prepared to address this issue?

In the meantime, I look forward to reviewing the materials you have
provided me and the final evaluation upon its completion. I will
be in touch with you if I have any further questions.

Thank you again for your attention.

Sincerely,

Carol Bellamy

CB/MM:hb

STATE OF NEW YORK
EXECUTIVE CHAMBER
ALBANY 12224

HUGH L. CAREY
GOVERNOR

June 12, 1979

Dear Secretary Blumenthal:

I am writing in support of the continued operation of the New York Assay Office in New York City.

I am advised that a Department of Treasury Task Force has recommended retention of the facility provided productivity is increased and costs decreased. It is my understanding that the Assay Office has achieved commendable headway in meeting these standards.

As you know, New York State and New York City are cooperating in an effort to firm up the City's economy and increase opportunities for business development, and I strongly affirm that this is no time for the Federal government to cut jobs and the economic benefits the City accrues from them.

I urge you to give careful consideration to retention of the New York Assay Office in New York City, especially in light of the improved production and management measures which have been implemented at the facility.

Sincerely,

Hugh L. Carey

Honorable W. Michael Blumenthal
Secretary of the Treasury
15th Street and Pennsylvania Avenue
Washington, D. C. 20220

Department of the *TREASURY* NEWS

WASHINGTON, D.C. 20220   **TELEPHONE 566-2041**

FOR IMMEDIATE RELEASE   Contact: Al Hattal
June 21, 1979   (202) 566-8381

NEW YORK ASSAY OFFICE TO REMAIN OPEN

The Treasury Department announced today that it had
completed a reorganization of the New York Assay Office
and has determined that the facility will continue in
operation until the remaining unrefined bullion is processed,
which it is estimated will require four or five years. The
Assay Office is the only Federal facility that still refines
gold and silver bullion.

Enhanced security, accountability and staffing procedures have been implemented. "A spirit of cooperation with
the labor force, union officials, largely through the
efforts of the Superintendent of the New York Assay Office,
has been fostered" stated Robert Carswell, Deputy Secretary
of the Treasury. "This has resulted in an extraordinary
effort on the part of the employees to reduce costs and
thereby save the refining operation."

An updated cost comparison for refining the remaining
16 million ounces of unparted gold bullion at the New York
Assay Office has been completed. The Assay Office costs
are considerably lower than the best bid received from the
private sector. Since the beginning of the fiscal year,
substantial progress has been made in reducing costs and
increasing productivity. The output of refined gold has
increased by more than 25 percent since October of 1978.
At the same time the work force has decreased from more than
190 employees to 165 employees by attrition.

The Treasury Department estimates that the increase
in productivity will result in a savings of about $300,000
in fiscal year 1979 and $400,000 in fiscal year 1980. It
is estimated that the remaining unrefined gold bullion will
be refined in approximately five years and that the refinery
will close when the job has been completed. The Treasury
Department will carefully monitor production costs and
staffing during the remaining years of operation in order to
make certain that the high productivity is maintained.

The Assay Office, situated in Lower Manhattan, was
established in 1854.

AMERICAN FEDERATION OF GOVERNMENT EMPLOYEES
AFFILIATED WITH THE AFL-CIO

KENNETH T. BLAYLOCK
NATIONAL PRESIDENT

JOSEPH D. GLEASON
EXECUTIVE VICE PRESIDENT

NICHOLAS J. NOLAN
NATIONAL SEC. TREAS.

1325 MASSACHUSETTS AVE., N.W. ● WASHINGTON, D.C. 20005
Telephone: (202) 737-8700

J F GRINER BUILDING

IN REPLY PLEASE REFER TO:
8h/L-2856

June 29, 1979

Mr. John Garmat, Deputy Director
Office of Budget and Program Analysis
U. S. Department of the Treasury
15th & Pennsylvania Avenue, N.W.
Washington, D. C. 20220

Dear Mr. Garmat:

This is to express my appreciation for the depth of
your A-76 study on the New York Assay Office and for the
cooperation the Department of Treasury has exhibited with
AFGE in our mutual striving for the most efficient and
least costly gold refining operation available to the U. S.
taxpayer.

Naturally, we are pleased that in-house operation has
proved to be the better choice. Nevertheless, had the
decision been to contract-out, we still would have appre-
ciated the work that went into the study and cost comparison.

Sincerely,

James J. McGuinn,

James R. Rosa *Acting*
General Counsel

MHJ/adb

cc: P/L-2856
Dr. George Hunter

TO DO FOR ALL THAT WHICH NONE CAN DO FOR ONESELF

18

*Fort Saxon's Word Processing System Request**

In January Colonel William Cullen, the Adjutant General (AG) at Fort Saxon, met with his deputy, Major Paul Martin, and CW3 Jerry Anderson to discuss personnel problems in the Separation Transfer Section. Several civilian workers in the section had complained about the quality of management. Anderson, the head of the section, said he was convinced that the only problem was that the section had too many civilians working in it. Sixteen civilian employees and the noncommissioned officer-in-charge (NCOIC), SFC Thomas James, worked within the section. Civilian personnel regulations kept Anderson from shifting employees from one function to another because of their job descriptions. He told Colonel Cullen that if military personnel replaced half of the civilians, the organizational continuity and corporate memory of the civilians would be maintained while job flexibility would be gained with the military personnel.

After Anderson departed, Colonel Cullen told Major Martin that Anderson's suggestion only provided a short-term solution. He said the problem could be traced to the supply and demand for services. The number of Army personnel being separated from the service at Fort Saxon had declined by one-fourth over the past seven years while the

Separation Transfer Section's staff had been reduced by one-half. Nonetheless, the section had been functioning effectively. All of the Army's separation processing time standards were being met. However, Colonel Cullen told Major Martin that Anderson met the time standards by pressuring the civilian employees, which drove them to lodge formal complaints. A pending reduction of two civilian positions in the section was sure to compound the pressure and increase the complaints.

The Army separation workload at Fort Saxon was forecasted to remain constant for the next few years. If it did, and if trends continued, the number of employees authorized for the section would probably be reduced even further. Colonel Cullen told Major Martin that the only way to relieve the workload pressure and increase efficiency was to automate part of the paperwork processing. Fort Jackson, S.C., and Fort Dix, N.J., had acquired microprocessor-based word processing (WP) systems that reportedly reduced both the time and costs of processing separation documents.

Cullen directed Anderson to study the WP operations at Jackson and Dix. CW3 Mike Sweedon, a computer specialist from the Standard Installation Division Personnel System (SIDPERS) Section, within the Adjutant General Division, was to assist Anderson in his research.

CW3 Anderson and Sweedon identified four areas that would be included in their proposal to Colonel Cullen: processing separation documentation, postal locator services, personnel orders preparation, and centralized typing. Fort Jackson had already purchased a software package, which included all of these functions except centralized typing, from Digital Equipment Corporation (DEC) for $60,000. Since Fort Saxon would not have to

*This case was prepared by Captain John M. Hardesty, United States Army, and Kenneth J. Euske and William J. Haga, Naval Postgraduate School. The case is intended as a basis for class discussion rather than to illustrate effective or ineffective handling of an administrative situation. Names and certain facts have been changed to avoid the disclosure of confidential information while not materially lessening the value of the case for educational purposes. Copyright © 1980 by the NPS Casewriters Institute. Distributed by the Intercollegiate Clearing House, Soldier's Field, Boston, MA 02163. All rights reserved to the contributors. Printed in the USA.

absorb any of these developmental costs, Anderson told Sweedon that additional cost savings would be realized if these areas were included in the proposal.

The preliminary work indicated that a WP Center would be established in Wright Hall, which housed most of the AG sections. DEC was selected to provide the equipment (Table 18.1) for the separation documentation preparation, orders preparation, and postal locator functions because of Fort Jackson's success with DEC equipment. In addition, the hardware and software would allow expansion up to 63 simultaneous users. Anderson contended that the large storage capacity requested was justified in light of the fact that other staff agencies on Fort Saxon had expressed interest in tying-in to the Word Processing Center. Dictaphone equipment (Table 18.2) was selected for the centralized typing function because a Fort Saxon Tenant Command, which utilized Dictaphone equipment, received excellent service from the vendor. Both the DEC and Dictaphone equipment had an expected economic life of five years. The WP Center would be staffed with personnel drawn from the various AG sections. Additional WP Center start-up costs are shown in Table 18.3.

The AG Division at Fort Saxon already

TABLE 18.1   Fort Saxon's Word Processing System Request

Description	Quantity and Location	*Annual Maintenance*[2]	*Annual Lease Payment*	*Total Purchase Price*
Digital Equipment Corporation Equipment				
Shared Logic[1]				
Word Processor	1 WP Center	7,548.00	46,207.32	108,517.05
67MP Disk Drives	1 WP Center	1,680.00	7,524.00	17,670.00
Multiplexer	1 WP Center	552.00	1,524.60	3,580.50
CRT Terminal	3 WP Center			
w/keyboard	4 Sep. Transfer			
	2 Postal Locator			
	2 Trainee Personnel			
	1 One-Stop Processing	2,448.00	10,454.40	24,552.00
Remote Communication				
Cable	10	-0-	522.72	1,227.60
100' Communication				
Cable	5	-0-	237.60	558.00
High Speed Printer	2 Sep. Transfer			
	1 Postal Locator	1,980.00	4,478.76	9,402.30
Medium Speed Printer	2 WP Center	2,640.00	2,985.84	7,012.20
Letter Quality Printer	4 WP Center	2,256.00	6,328.32	14,861.40
Word Processing Station	4 WP Center	5,010.00	16,624.32	39,041.40
Sorter RSTS	1 WP Center	-0-	146.52	344.10
Datatrieve 9 Track Tape	1 WP Center	-0-	1,782.00	4,185.00
Document Transmission				
Option	1 WP Center	-0-	990.00	2,325.00
TOTALS		$24,114.00	$99,806.40	$233,276.55

[1]Includes processor, 256 KB Memory, Cabinet, expansion box, bookplane, 67 MB disk and controller, magtape drive and controller, 16 line multiplexer, Operating System Software.
[2]Annual maintenance fee applies to equipment that is either leased or purchased.

TABLE 18.2. Fort Saxon's Word Processing System Request

		Dictaphone Equipment	
Description	Quantity[1]	Annual Lease Payment[2]	Total Purchase Price
Thought Tank Machines	3	2,489.76	5,850.00
Transcription Terminals	5	703.20	1,625.00
Phone In Adapter	1	164.40	395.00
ADM with DCK Interface	3	1,085.40	2,550.00
Cabinet	1	193.80	450.00
Dictameter Panels	3	360.00	825.00
Blank Meter Panels	1	3.84	10.00
Secretarial Panels	5	227.40	500.00
Blank Secretarial Panels	3	11.40	30.00
EGM Panel	1	140.64	320.00
Auto. Transfer Panel	1	81.00	175.00
Auto. Throughput Director Panel	1	76.08	175.00
Transcription Priority	3	107.64	225.00
Phone In Adapter Director Panel	1	28.92	75.00
Standard Cassette Trans. Unit	1	249.48	589.00
Master Mind Basic Unit	1	4,191.24	9,995.00
Report Printer	1	420.24	995.00
193 Modification	3	57.96	150.00
TDM/DDM Modification	3	115.92	300.00
Printer Paper	1	19.32	50.00
Mini Diskettes	1	25.08	65.00
Mini Diskettes Archive	1	25.08	65.00
		$10,777.92	$25,414.00

[1]All dictaphone equipment would be utilized in the WP Center.
[2]Dictaphone equipment lease includes maintenance. If purchased, annual maintenance fee would be $1,206 annually.

leased a variety of WP equipment (Table 18.4). Most of this WP hardware would be redundant with the proposed system. Additionally, a lack of standardization among the present WP devices prevented operational and storage compatibility with the proposed system, justifying termination of these leases.

TABLE 18.3. Fort Saxon's Word Processing System Request

Additional WP Center Start-Up Costs[1]	
Facility Modification	$26,000
Telephone Installation	9,600
Office Furniture	21,538

[1]These expenses would be paid for in a single payment out of the Adjutant General Division's operating budget.

THE SEPARATION TRANSFER FUNCTION

Under the existing system, the Separation Transfer Section prepared separation documents for 10,500 people each year who were discharged from the army via Ft. Saxon. The procedure for processing a routine separation packet is illustrated in Exhibit 18.1 and the civilian personnel pay-rate table is presented

TABLE 18.4. Fort Saxon's Word Processing System Request

		Present System WP Equipment		
Manufacturer's Model Number	*Serial Number*	*Owned or[1,2] Leased*	*Monthly Rental Cost*	*Proposed Distribution*
AB Dick Magna I — Model 2700	629505	Leased	299.90	Return to Vendor
AB Dick Magna I — Model 2700	835056	Leased	478.90	Return to Vendor
IBM Mag Card I — Model 6610	9669402	Leased	164.90	Return to Vendor
IBM Mag Card I — Model 6610	9669396	Leased	164.90	Return to Vendor
IBM Mag Card II — Model 6616	0019347	Leased	266.75	Return to Vendor
IBM Mag Card I — Model 6610	9646326	Leased	164.90	Return to Vendor
IBM Mag Tape IV — Model 1021	085008	Leased	205.00	Return to Vendor
IBM Mag Tape II — Model 1011	106215	Leased	205.00	Return to Vendor
IBM Mag Tape II — Model 1011	096739	Leased	205.00	Return to Vendor
IBM Mag Tape II — Model 1011	0104532	Leased	205.00	Return to Vendor
IBM Mag Tape II — Model 1011	4694653	Leased	205.00	Return to Vendor
IBM Mag Tape IV — Model 1021	0110576	Owned	56.26 (monthly maintenance)	Transfer to another post activity
IBM Mag Tape IV — Model 1021	0083128	Owned	56.26 (monthly maintenance)	Transfer to another post activity
IBM Card Reader — Model 1056	10379	Leased	96.00	Return to Vendor
IBM Card Reader — Model 1056	10940	Leased	96.00	Return to Vendor
IBM Card Reader — Model 1056	15936	Leased	96.00	Return to Vendor
IBM Card Reader — Model 1056	12613	Leased	96.00	Return to Vendor
4 each Junction Box		Leased	@57.00 each	Return to Vendor
Monthly Lease	$3289.77 \times 12 = 39,477.24$			

[1]Maintenance Cost is included in the rental charge.
[2]Equipment had renewable option at current rental price.

EXHIBIT 18.1. Fort Saxon's Word Processing System Request, Separation Procedure.

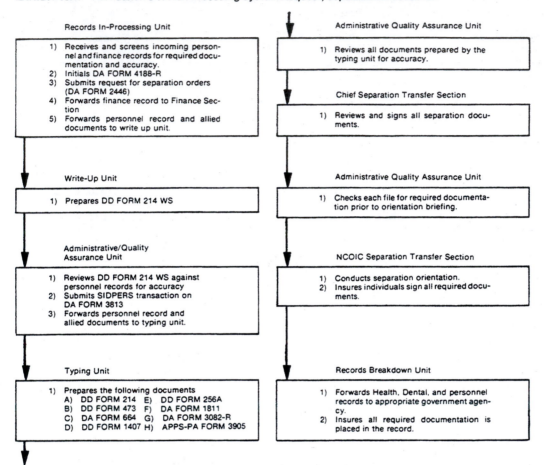

in Table 18.5. The average time to process a separation manually was five days, because of backlogs and corrections. Under the WP system proposal, two GS–4, step one, positions would be eliminated and the processing time would be reduced to one day. The proposed system would use WP equipment (Table 18.1) for the labor-intensive task of filling out forms.

Instead of constantly reorganizing, reformatting, and retyping information, variable data would be entered only once on a keyboard, then displayed on a cathode ray tube (CRT) terminal. For each separation being processed, the CRT would display forty questions requiring operator responses. The responses would create a data file for each person being separated. Once this information was entered, finished forms would be printed on high-speed printers.

THE POSTAL LOCATOR FUNCTIONS

The Adjutant General Division, Postal Locator Section, maintained a file on 52,000

TABLE 18.5. Fort Saxon's Word Processing System Request

	[STEP]	1	2	3	4	5	6
		Standard Civilian Rate Table[1]					
GS-1	Annual	7210	7450	7690	7930	8170	8410
GS-2		8128	8399	8670	8902	9002	9267
GS-3		8952	9250	9548	9846	10144	10442
GS-4		10049	10384	10719	11054	11389	11724
GS-5		11243	11618	11993	12368	12743	13118
GS-6		12531	12949	13367	13785	14203	14621

7	8	9	10
8630	8890	8902	9126
9532	9797	10062	10327
10740	11038	11336	11634
12059	12394	12729	13064
13493	13868	14243	14618
15039	15457	15875	16293

[1]Does not include fringe benefits, which constitute an average additional cost of 9%.

assigned or recently departed personnel. The file was utilized by postal locator personnel to accomplish mail redirects and handle address inquiries. Locator information was maintained on DA form 3955 in 21 visible index stands of 35 panels each. Daily additions of locator cards required constant shifting of the cards between the panels. All the cards had to be edited on a monthly basis to remove officially inactive cards. In order to redirect the mail it had to be sorted into alphabetical sequence and then broken down into groups that corresponded to one of the 21 file stands. The mail was then readdressed by retrieving the correct locator card and writing the forwarding address on the pieces of mail.

Under the manual system, locator inquiries could be handled only during normal duty hours (7:30 through 4:30, Monday through Friday). At all other times the One-Stop In and Out Processing Section provided locator information from the SIDPERS data base for the 20,000 currently assigned people at Ft. Saxon.

Under the proposed system, the 52,000 records would be stored in the WP system on disk drives providing instant access on the CRT terminals. (Table 18.1 shows postal locator equipment requirements.) The CRT terminal would provide keyboard access to all locator records. File updates would occur by extracting arrival and departure listings from the SIDPERS magnetic tape. The system would automatically purge obsolete locator records after Army retention requirements had been met. Address labels for redirecting mail would be provided from the locator data base on a high-speed printer. An additional CRT terminal would be placed in the One-Stop In and Out Processing Section to handle after-duty-hours locator inquiries.

Under this proposal, CW3 Anderson and Sweedon estimated that two enlisted E-4 positions from the Postal Locator Section could be eliminated. (For Military Pay Chart, see Table 18.6.) Mail readdressing and locator inquiry times would be reduced by one-half. Additionally, if the new system pro-

TABLE 18.6. Fort Saxon's Word Processing System Request

Composite Standard Military Rate Table[1]			
E-9	23,612	O-6	43,494
E-8	20,260	O-5	35,543
E-7	17,304	O-4	29,489
E-6	14,562	O-3	24,161
E-5	12,279	O-2	18,591
E-4	10,443	O-1	13,777
E-3	9,300	CW-4	27,959
E-2	8,435	CW-3	22,495
E-1	7,499	CW-2	19,447
		CW-1	16,510

[1]Includes cost of fringe benefits.

posal were approved, Ft. Saxon would not have to purchase 21 visible index stands because a forthcoming edition of DA form 3955 would be a different size. The decision to purchase the stands would not be made until a decision was made regarding the acquisition of a word processing system. The new stands would cost a total of $8,000.

PREPARATION OF MILITARY PERSONNEL ORDERS

Under the existing system, 1200 orders per week were processed on IBM magnetic card equipment (Table 18.4) at two locations: Trainee Personnel Section and Administrative Services Section. Information required in the preparation of orders was contained on DA form 2446, Request for Orders; APPA-AG form 2017, Assignment Control Card; and other documents. Order clerks often would have to produce orders quickly, increasing the chance of error. Most errors were made in the standard name line. (The army standard name line consists of name, grade, SSN, unit identification code, and unit of assignment.) Amendment orders would then have to be issued to correct erroneous orders.

Under Anderson and Sweedon's proposal, the SIDPERS assignment instruction file received from Washington would be loaded into the WP system so that those items required for orders preparation would not have to be included on the orders request form. A handwritten orders request form, requiring only essential data, would be forwarded from the Redeployment and Trainee Personnel Sections to the WP Center. The system would be programmed so that the CRT Terminals at the WP Center would lead the operators through a series of interactive questions which would require the operator to enter the items contained on the handwritten order request. The system would pull the order format from the disk file, format the keyed information, and print out a military order.

Anderson and Sweedon estimated that the proposal would reduce paper costs by $10,000 on an annual basis, eliminate two enlisted E-4 order clerks at Trainee Personnel Section, and two enlisted E-3 positions at the Redeployment Section.

THE CENTRALIZED TYPING FUNCTION

Under the current system, each of the ten AG sections had its own secretary in addition to other clerks who did routine typing. All section typing requirements were performed on site.

Under the proposed system, users would each have a detailed manual for document origination. A document originator would choose a specific correspondence format and then telephonically call in variable input following the user's manual. This information would be processed through the computer's Master Mind Basic Unit and recorded on a Thought Tank Machine (Table 18.2). The typist would then retrieve this information and, using an ear phone Transcription Terminal, type the data on a Word Processing

Station (Table 18.1). The Word Processing Station consists of a CRT, keyboard and limited storage device which connects to the Shared Logic Word Processor and Master Mind Basic Unit. Output would be provided on the report printer (Table 18.2) or letter quality printer (Table 18.1).

WP SURVEY

In order to meet Army requirements for a WP system request, CW3 Anderson and Sweedon conducted a typing survey. The intent of this survey was to determine the number of personnel who would be required to run the WP system. In addition to the personnel reductions previously discussed, the men identified one enlisted E-3 position from the Personnel Actions Section for elimination, and one enlisted E-4 position from the Personnel Management Section. In addition, overtime costs would be reduced by $4,000 on an annual basis.

SUMMARY

Anderson told Sweedon that the system they were about to propose to Colonel Cullen would: (1) improve overall operations because of faster access to files; (2) provide improved output control; (3) add the capability to compile recurring statistical reports; and (4) reduce costs. Anderson and Sweedon agreed that the orders preparation, postal locator, and personnel transfer functions would be easy to sell to Colonel Cullen because these functions were already automated at Ft. Jackson. They did not know how the centralized typing function and associated dictaphone equipment would be received.

BIBLIOGRAPHY

HAROLD BIERMAN and SEYMOUR SMIDT, *The Capital Budgeting Decision*, 2nd ed. (New York: Macmillan Press, 1966).

EDWARD M. GRAMLICH, *Benefit–Cost Analysis of Government Programs* (Englewood Cliffs: Prentice-Hall, 1981).

ROBERT H. HAVEMAN and JULIUS MARGOLIS, eds., *Public Expenditure Analysis*, 2nd ed. (Chicago: Rand McNally, 1977).

CHARLES T. HORNGREN, *Cost Accounting: A Managerial Emphasis*, 4th ed. (Englewood Cliffs: Prentice-Hall, 1977).

FREMONT J. LYDEN and ERNEST G. MILLER, *Public Budgeting: Program Planning and Evaluation*, 4th ed. (Englewood Cliffs: Prentice-Hall, 1982).

LEONARD MEREWITZ and STEPHEN H. SOSNICK, *The Budget's New Clothes, A Critique of Planning–Programming–Budgeting and Benefit–Cost Analysis* (Chicago: Rand McNally, Markham series, 1971).

PETER G. SASSONE and WILLIAM A. SCHAFFER, *Cost–Benefit Analysis: A Handbook* (New York: Academic Press, 1978).

PROBLEM

Evaluate the potential savings of the WP System. Most DOD capital investment decisions require the use of a 10 percent discount rate.

FOR DISCUSSION

1. What criteria were used to choose the suppliers? What other criteria would you propose?
2. Explain the concept of "cost savings" used to develop the proposal so that it conforms to Fort Jackson's software package. (See "Asphalt Paradox," case no. 7.)

19

Costing Out in the Public Sector*

INTRODUCTION

During the collective bargaining process, one of the most useful pieces of information the parties can possess is the effect of present demands on future costs of operation. Not only does it aid each party during negotiations but also it helps to prepare for future management of the workplace. The process by which costs for a future contract may be computed, is commonly referred to as "costing out."

This describes a method by which either party may cost out demands . . . This method of costing-out entails calculating the average compensation costs for the unit and determining the true value of increased demands made during negotiations.

CALCULATING COMPENSATION COSTS

During bargaining one of the most important statistics that may be used is the bargaining unit's average compensation, or the weighted average compensation. This is the employer's average expense for each person on the payroll. When a settlement proposal is offered, the average compensation figure will help in reaching a decision regarding the proposal.

In order to compute the average com-

*Adapted with permission from the *Midwest Monitor* (May/June 1980): 1–8. Edited by Richard S. Rubin, the *Midwest Monitor* is published by the Midwest Center for Public Sector Labor Relations (School of Public and Environmental Affairs, Indiana University, Bloomington) on behalf of the Midwest Public Employment Labor Relations Committee.

pensation costs, the following information is necessary:

salary scales and benefit programs
the distribution of employees in the unit according to pay steps, shifts, and length of service
each employee's coverage status for each of the benefits

These figures need not be a year's compilation; rather they may be chosen from a fixed point in time. The time should be as close to the beginning of collective bargaining as possible.

If these three figures are known, almost all costs of compensation and increases in compensation can be computed. The only exception is overtime costs. Because these may vary from week to week, overtime costs generally cannot be computed with any degree of certainty.

The first step in computing compensation costs is to develop the *base* or *existing* compensation figure. The base compensation figure varies from unit to unit; thus a $500 increase means something different to a unit whose base compensation is $20,000 and something else to a unit whose base compensation is $10,000. The base compensation figure is essential in determining the percentage value of a requested increase in compensation. For the unit with a base compensation of $20,000, a $500 increase represents a 2-1/2% increase, while for the unit with a base compensation of $10,000, $500 represents a 5% increase.

A sample firefighter bargaining unit will be used to illustrate the process for computing the base compensation figure and for costing out a contract settlement.

1.   SAMPLE BARGAINING UNIT

(a)   Employment and Salaries

Classification	Number of Firefighters	Salary
Probationary		
Step 1	5	$10,000
Step 2	10	11,100
Private	65	12,100
Lieutenant	15	13,500
Captain	5	14,500
	100	

(b)   Longevity Payments

Longevity Step	Number of Firefighters	Longevity Pay
Step 1	20 Privates	$ 500
Step 2	10 Privates	1,000
Step 2	15 Lieutenants	1,000
Step 2	5 Captains	1,000

(c)   Hours of Work

The scheduled hours consist of one 24-hour shift every three days (one on; two off), or an average of 56 hours per week and a total of 2,912 hours per year.

(d)   Overtime Premium

All overtime hours are paid at the rate of time-and-one-half. The sample bargaining unit worked a total of 5,000 overtime hours during the preceding year.

(e)   Shift Differential

The shift differential is 10 percent for all hours between 4 p.m. and 8 a.m. However, 10 members of the unit work exclusively on the day shift, from 8 a.m. to 4 p.m. They are 1 Captain, 3 Lieutenants, 3 Privates at Longevity Step 2, and 3 Privates at Step 1.

(f)   Vacations

15 employees — (probationers) 5 shifts
35 employees — (privates) 10 shifts
50 employees — (all others) 15 shifts

(g)   Holidays

Each firefighter is entitled to 10 paid holidays, and receives 8 hours pay for each holiday.

(h)   Clothing Allowance

$150 per employee per year.

(i)   Hospitalization

Type of Coverage	Number of Firefighters	Employer's Monthly Payment
Single Coverage	15	$20.00
Family Coverage	85	47.00

(j)   Pensions

The employer contributes an amount equal to six percent of the payroll (including basic salaries, longevity, overtime, and shift differentials).

2. AVERAGE ANNUAL BASE SALARY

(1) Classification	(2) Number of Fire- fighters	(3) Salary	(4) Weighted Salaries (2) × (3)
Probationary			
Step 1	5	$10,100	$ 50,500
Step 2	10	11,100	111,000
Private	65	12,100	786,500
Lieutenant	15	13,500	202,500
Captain	5	14,500	72,500
	100		$1,223,000

Average Annual Base Salary =
$1,223,000 ÷ 100; or $12,230 per year

3. LONGEVITY PAY

(1) Longevity Step	(2) Number of Fire- fighters	(3) Longevity Pay	(4) Total Lon- gevity Pay (2) × (3)
Step 1	20	$ 500	$10,000
Step 2	30	1,000	30,000
			$40,000

Average Annual Longevity Pay =
$40,000 ÷ 100;* or $400 per year

*Since the unit is trying to determine its average base
compensation — that is, all the salary and fringe benefit items its members receive collectively — the total
cost of longevity pay must be averaged over the entire unit of 100.

4. OVERTIME

Overtime work for the Sample Bargaining Unit is paid for at the rate of time-and-one-half.
This means that part of the total overtime costs is an amount paid at straight-time rates
and part is a premium payment.

	(1) Annual Cost	(2) Number of Firefighters	(3) Average Annual Cost (1) ÷ (2)
Straight-time cost ($4.337 × 5,000 overtime hours)*	$21,685.00	100	$216.85
Half-time premium cost (½ × $21,685.00)	10,842.50	100	108.43
Total Overtime Cost	$32,527.50		$325.28

*Based on preceding year's total overtime hours.

COMPUTING BASE COMPENSATION

With the information in the table it is possible to compute a base compensation figure. Given the distribution of employees according to each classification and each of their salaries, one can obtain the *weighted salary* for each classification. The weighted salary is then divided by the total number of employees, and the result is the *average annual base salary*.

This method will also produce an average annual cost for longevity pay. The combined average salary cost and average longev-ity cost amount to $12,630 per year. On an hourly basis, this comes to $4.337 (12,630 ÷ 2912 hours). This hourly rate is needed to compute the cost of some fringe benefits. It is now possible to calculate the cost of overtime, shift differential, vacations, paid holidays, insurance, and pensions. (In this example, overtime, shift differential, vacations, paid holidays, and pensions are all computed using an hourly pay rate which includes both salary and longevity pay. This is an important factor when determining the effect of salary increase on these benefits.)

---

5. SHIFT DIFFERENTIAL

The Sample Bargaining Unit receives a shift differential of 10 percent for all hours worked between 4 p.m. and 8 a.m. But 10 members of the unit who work in headquarters work hours that are not subject to the differential. This leaves 90 employees who receive the differential.

Since the differential is paid for hours worked between 4 p.m. and 8 a.m., it is applicable to only two-thirds of the normal 24-hour shift. It, therefore, only costs the employer two-thirds of 10 percent for each 24 hours. That is the reason for column (5) in the following calculation. Each employee receives the differential for only two-thirds of his 24-hour tour.

(1) Classification	(2) No. on Shift Pay	(3) Salary	(4) 10% of Col. (3)	(5) .667 of Col. (4)	(6) Total Cost (2) × (5)
Probationary					
Step 1	5	$10,100	$1,010	$ 674	$ 3,370
Step 2	10	11,100	1,110	740	7,400
Private					
Longevity-0	35	12,100	1,210	807	28,245
Longevity-1	17	12,600*	1,260	840	14,280
Longevity-2	7	13,100*	1,320	880	6,160
Lieutenant	12	14,500*	1,450	967	11,604
Captain	4	15,500*	1,550	1,034	4,136
	90				$75,195

Average Annual Cost of Shift Differential = $75,195 ÷ 100, or $751.95 per year**

*Base salary plus longevity pay ($500 for Step 1 and $1,000 for Step 2).
**Since the unit is trying to determine its average base compensation—that is, all the salary and fringe benefit items its members receive collectively—the total cost of the shift differential must be averaged over the entire unit of 100.

6. VACATIONS

Vacation costs for the unit are influenced by (a) the amount of vacations received by the employees with differing lengths of service, and (b) the pay scales of those employees.

(1) Classification	(2) Number of Firefighters	(3) Hourly Rate*	(4) Hours of Vacation**	(5) Total Vacation Hours (2) × (4)	(6) Total Vacation Costs (3) × (5)
Probationary					
Step 1	5	$3.468	120	600	$ 2,080.80
Step 2	10	3.812	120	1,200	4,574.40
Private					
Longevity-0	35	4.155	240	8,400	34,902.00
Longevity-1	20	4.327	360	7,200	31,154.40
Longevity-2	10	4.499	360	3,600	16,196.40
Lieutenant	15	4.979	360	5,400	26,886.60
Captain	5	5.323	360	1,800	9,581.40
	100			28,200	$125,376.00

Average Annual Vacation Cost = $125,376 ÷ 100; or $1,253.76 per year

*Derived from annual salaries (including longevity pay), divided by 2,912 hours (56 hours × 52 weeks). The 10 firefighters who do not receive shift differential would be on a regular 40-hour week and would, therefore, have a different hourly rate and vacation entitlement. The impact on cost, however, would be minimal. It has, therefore, been disregarded in this computation.

**Since each firefighter works a 24-hour-shift, the hours of vacation are arrived at by multiplying the number of work shifts of vacation entitlement by 24 hours. For example, the figure of 120 hours is obtained by multiplying 5 shifts of vacation × 24 hours (one work shift).

7. PAID HOLIDAYS

Unlike vacations, the number of holidays received by an employee is not typically tied to length of service. Where the level of benefits is uniform, as it is with paid holidays, the calculation to determine its average cost is less complex.

In the Sample Bargaining Unit, each firefighter receives 8 hours of pay for each of his 10 paid holidays, or a total of 80 hours of holiday pay:

Average Annual Cost of Paid Holidays = $346.96 (80 hours × $4.337 average straight-time hourly rate derived from average salary cost plus average longevity cost.

8. HOSPITALIZATION INSURANCE			
(1)	*(2)*	*(3)*	*(4)*
		Yearly	*Total*
	Number	*Premium*	*Cost to*
Type of	*of Fire-*	*Cost to*	*Employer*
Coverage	*fighters*	*Employer*	*(2) × (3)*
Single	15	$240	$ 3,600
Family	85	564	47,940
	100		$51,540

Average Annual Cost of Hospitalization Insurance = $51,540 ÷ 100; or $515.40 per year

---

9. OTHER FRINGE BENEFITS

(1) Pensions cost the employer six percent of payroll. The payroll amounts to $1,370,723 (salary cost of $1,223,000; longevity cost of $40,000; overtime cost of $32,528; and shift differential cost of $75,195). Six percent of this total is $82,243, which, when divided by 100, yields $822.43 as the average cost of pensions per firefighter, per year.

(2) The yearly cost of the clothing allowance is $150 per firefighter.

The nine figures may then be grouped together to provide a total figure for annual compensation:

Base salary	$12,230.00
Longevity pay	400.00
Overtime	325.28
Shift differential	751.95
Vacations	1,253.76
Holidays	346.96
Hospitalization	515.40
Clothing allowance	150.00
Pension	822.43
Total	$16,795.78

COMPUTING THE COSTS OF INCREASES

Once the *base compensation costs* have been determined, *increases* in those costs can be computed. Computing these new costs is commonly referred to as "costing out."

Assume that the Sample Bargaining Unit negotiates a settlement which contains the following changes:

five percent increase in base salaries
two additional vacation days for all employees at the second step of longevity

an improvement in the benefits provided by the hospitalization program, which amounts to an additional $4.00 a month per family coverage and $2.50 for single coverage

The objective in costing out this increase is to obtain the *average cost* (per firefighter) of the increase per year.

To compute the average annual increase, the base salary ($12,230.00) is multiplied by the percent increase (5%). This results in an increase of $611.50. There is no increase in longevity pay for this example. Had the longevity pay been tied to the base salary on a percentage basis there then would have been an increase in that amount also. As a result, the increase in the unit's *average annual salary* (base salary and longevity payments) is not 5% but 4.8%. This is determined by dividing the increase ($611.50) by the base salary plus longevity payments ($12,630).

Computing the cost of an increase is important because of the impact on the cost of fringe benefits. This impact on benefits is often referred to as the *roll-up*. As salary increases, so does the cost of fringe benefits, such as vacations, holidays, and overtime premiums. The cost of the benefits increases even if the level of benefits does not go up. In the example on longevity pay, the roll-up did not come into play because the longevity pay was a fixed amount. Other types of benefits which are often exempt from the roll-up are shift differentials, clothing allowances, and most group insurance plans. Any of these examples might be affected by the roll up if their cost is tied to the base salary amount.

Using the Sample Bargaining Unit, what items will not be affected? It has already been determined that there will be no change in longevity pay because it is a fixed dollar amount. The hours of work are not affected, nor the clothing allowance.

The remaining items in the budget will be affected in some manner. The next step is to identify in what manner they are changed. There are some items whose cost will be changed because of the roll-up effect. In the sample bargaining unit, those items include:

overtime premiums
shift differentials
holidays
pensions

These benefits are tied to the original average annual salary (base salary plus longevity). The 4.8% increase in the average annual salary will increase the cost of these benefits.

(1)	(2)	(3)	(4)
Fringe Benefit	Base Average Annual Cost*	Increased Roll-up Factor	Cost (2) x (3)
Overtime	$325.29	0.048	$ 15.61
Shift differential	751.95	0.048	36.09
Holidays	346.96	0.048	16.65
Pensions	822.43	0.048	39.48
			$107.83

*See previous boxes for derivation of these costs.

Once it has been determined which items have been changed by the roll-up effect, the next step is to identify which items are changed by an increase in benefits. Items may be changed either by the roll-up effect or an increase in benefits, or both. In the sample bargaining unit, the hospitalization benefit costs are changed because of an increase in benefits. The cost is a fixed dollar amount and thus is not subject to an increase in benefits on account of the roll-up. Costing out this benefit for the new contract entails multiplying the cost of the new program by the employees receiving the benefits:

(1)	(2)	(3)	(4)
Type of Coverage	Number Covered	Annual Cost of Improvement	Total New Cost (2) × (3)
Single	15	$30	$ 450
Family	85	48	4,080
			$4,530

The unit's average hospitalization cost will be increased by $45.30 per year ($4,530 ÷ 100 employees).

Finally, one item is affected by both the roll-up and an increase in benefits. This is the vacation program. All vacation days will be increased by the cost increase in base salaries plus an increase of two shifts (48 hours) for all employees at the second step of longevity. The first step is to compute the cost of the two additional shifts prior to the 4.8% salary increase.

The added cost of the vacation benefit has two aspects: the $7,021.92 that represents the increase in benefits and the $6,355.10 which is a result of the increase in wages. When the two are totalled and divided by the number of firefighters in the unit, the total average cost of the new vacation benefit is $133.77 ($13,377.02 ÷ 100 employees).

Had the vacation improvement been granted across-the-board, to everyone in the unit, the calculation would have been different—and considerably easier. If the entire unit were to receive an additional 48 hours of vacation, the total additional hours would be 4,800 (48 hours × 100 employees). These hours would then be multiplied by the unit's old average straight-time rate ($4.337), in order to arrive at the cost of the additional vacation improvement, which would have

(1) Number of Firefighters	(2) Hours of In- creased Vacation	(3) Total Hours (1) × (2)	(4) Existing Hourly Rates*	(5) Cost of Improvement (3) × (4)
10 Privates	48	480	$4.499	$2,159.52
15 Lieutenants	48	720	4.979	3,584.88
5 Captains	48	240	5.323	$1,277.52
				$7,021.92

*See the vacation box for derivation of hourly rates.

With no increase in salaries the increase in vacation days would cost $7,021.92. The next step is to compute the total cost of the 4.8* increase.

(1) Classification	(2) Existing Vacation Costs*	(3) Increase in Cost**	(4) Adjusted Base Costs (2) + (3)	(5) Roll-up Factor	(6) Increased Cost from Roll-up (4) × (5)
Probationary					
Step 1	$ 2,080.80	—	$ 2,080.80	0.048	$ 99.88
Step 2	4,574.40	—	4,574.40	0.048	219.57
Private					
Longevity-0	34,902.00	—	34,902.00	0.048	1,675.30
Longevity-1	31,154.40	—	31,154.40	0.048	1,495.41
Longevity-2	16,196.40	$2,159.52	18,355.92	0.048	881.08
Lieutenant	26,886.60	3,584.88	30,471.48	0.048	1,462.63
Captain	9,581.40	1,277.52	10,858.92	0.048	521.23
	$125,376.00	$7,021.92	$132,397.92	0.048	$6,355.10

*The base (or existing) vacation costs are from the vacation box and derived from average annual salary (base salary plus longevity).
**From data in preceding table.

---

come to $20,817.60 (4,800 hours × $4.337). And, in that case, the total cost of vacations — that is, the across-the-board improvement plus the impact of the 4.8 percent average annual salary increase — would have been computed as follows:

(a) roll-up of old vacation costs

($125,376 × 0.048)   = $ 6,018.05

(b) cost of vacation improvement

= 20,817.60

(c) roll-up cost of improvement

($20,817.60 × 0.048)   =   999.24

These pieces total $27,834.89. When spread over the entire Sample Bargaining

Unit, the increase in the average cost of vacations would have been $278.35 per year ($27,834.89 ÷ 100 employees).

The latter method of calculation does not apply only to vacations. It applies to any situation where a salary-related fringe benefit is to be improved equally for every member of the unit. An additional paid holiday is another good example.

THE TOTAL INCREASE IN THE AVERAGE COST OF COMPENSATION

At this point, the increase in the costs of all the items of compensation which will change because of the Sample Bargaining Unit's newly negotiated package have been calculated. All that is left is to combine these individual pieces in order to arrive at the total increase in the unit's average cost of compensation.

Increase in Average Annual Cost of Compensation For Sample Bargaining Unit

Base salary	$611.50
Longevity pay	—
Overtime	15.61
Shift differential	36.09
Vacations	133.77
Holidays	16.65
Hospitalization	45.30
Clothing allowance	—
Pensions	39.48

Total Increase in Average Annual Cost of Annual Compensation = $898.40

There remains one final computation that is really the most significant—the percent increase that all of these figures represent. The unit's average base compensation per year was $16,796. The total dollar increase amounts to $898. The percent increase, therefore, is 5.3 percent ($898 ÷ $16,796), and that is the amount by which the unit's package increased the employer's average yearly cost per firefighter.

COMPUTING THE HOURLY COST OF COMPENSATION

The increase in the cost of compensation per hour will be the same. The approach to the computation, however, is different from that which was used in connection with the cost per year. In the case of the hourly computation, the goal is to obtain the cost per hour of work. This requires that a distinction be drawn between hours worked and hours paid for. The difference between the two is leave time.

In the Sample Bargaining Unit, for example, the employee receives an annual salary which covers 2,912 regularly scheduled hours (56 hours per week times 52). In addition, each works an average of 50 hours of overtime per year. The sum of these two—regularly scheduled hours and overtime hours, or 2,962—is the number of hours paid for.

But they do not represent hours worked, because some of those hours are paid leave time. The Sample Bargaining Unit, for example, receives paid leave time in the form of vacations and holidays. The number of hours actually worked by each employee is 2,600 (2,962 hours paid for minus 362 hours of paid leave).

Each firefighter receives 80 hours in paid holidays per year. The average number of hours of vacation per year was derived as follows:

15 firefighters × 120 hours (five 24-hour shifts)	=	1,800 hours
35 firefighters × 240 hours (ten 24-hour shifts)	=	8,400 hours
50 firefighters × 360 hours (fifteen 24-hour shifts)	=	18,000 hours
Total		28,200 hours

This averages out to 282 hours of vacation per firefighter (28,200 ÷ 100) which, together with 80 holiday hours, totals 362 paid leave hours.

The paid leave hours are hours paid for above and beyond hours worked. Thus, in order to obtain the hourly cost that they represent, the annual dollar cost of these benefits is divided by the annual hours worked.

So it is with all fringe benefits, not only paid leave. In exchange for those benefits the employer receives hours of work (the straight-time hours and the overtime hours). Consequently, the hourly cost of any fringe benefit will be obtained by dividing the annual cost of the benefit by the annual number of hours worked.

In some instances that cost is converted into money that ends up in the employee's pocket, as it does in the case of such fringe benefits as shift differentials, overtime premiums, and clothing allowances. In other instances—such as hospitalization and pensions—the employee is provided with benefits in the form of insurance programs. And in the case of paid leave time—holidays, vacations, sick leave, etc.—the return to the employee is in terms of fewer hours of work.

The average annual cost of the fringe benefits of the Sample Bargaining Unit were developed earlier in connection with the computations of the unit's average annual base compensation.

In order to convert the costs of these fringe benefits into an average hourly amount, they are divided by 2,600—the average hours worked during the year by each employee in the unit. As can be seen, the hourly cost of all fringe benefits amounts to $1.518.

In addition to the fringe benefit costs, compensation includes the base pay. For our Sample Bargaining Unit this is $12,630 per year (average salary plus average cost of longevity payments). On a straight-time hourly basis, this comes to $4.337 ($12,630 ÷ 2,912 hours). Even with the straight-time portion for the year's overtime included ($216.85), the average straight-time hourly rate of pay will still remain at $4.337 ($12,846.45 ÷ 2,962 hours).

A recapitulation of these salary and fringe benefit cost data produces both the average annual base compensation figure for the Sample Bargaining Unit and the average hourly figure:

(1) Cost Fringe Benefit	(2) Average Annual Cost	(3) Average Hours Worked	(4) Average Hourly (2) ÷ (3)
Overtime Premium*	$ 108.43	2,600	$0.042
Shift differential	751.95	2,600	0.289
Vacations	1,253.76	2,600	0.482
Holidays	346.96	2,600	0.133
Hospitalization	515.40	2,600	0.198
Clothing allowance	150.00	2,600	0.058
Pensions	822.43	2,600	0.316
Total	$3,948.93		$1.518

*Includes only the premium portion of the pay for overtime work.

	Yearly	Hourly
Earnings at Straight-time	$12,846.85 ÷ 2,962	= $4.337
Fringe Benefits	3,948.93 ÷ 2,600	= 1.519
Total Compensation	$16,795.78	$5.856

Essentially the same process is followed if the increase in compensation is to be measured on an hourly (instead of an annual) basis.

The five percent pay increase received by the Sample Bargaining Unit would be worth 21 cents ($12,230 × 0.05 = $611.50; $611.50 ÷ 2,912 = $0.21). The annual increase in the unit's fringe benefit costs per firefighter—$276.49 for all items combined (overtime—premium only, shift differential, vacation, holidays, hospitalization, pensions, and clothing allowance)—works out to 10.6 cents per hour ($276.49 ÷ 2600 hours).

Together, these represent a gain in average compensations of 31.6 cents per hour, or 5.4 percent ($0.316 ÷ $5.856). This is one-tenth of a percentage point off from the amount of increase (5.3 percent) reflected by the annual data—a difference due to rounding decimals during the computation process.

CONCLUSION

If the data that were used for the Sample Bargaining Unit in our discussion are available for an actual unit, almost all demands can be evaluated in terms of future costs. Costing out demands requires careful documentation and thorough record keeping. But in return, either of the parties will have the ability to see what effect the increases will have on the budget. Costing out prepares the parties for realistic negotiations; offers and demands are supported by the facts obtained through costing out. Finally, because costing out is a clearly defined method, it reduces the discrepancies and disagreements over budget items. Although it will not provide answers to every question that arises, it will provide important, pertinent information for the parties' use during collective bargaining.

20

*Local 1984's Contract**

The town of Chelmsville is a relatively small community, with a population of about 18,000. The seven schools in Chelmsville—the high school, junior high school, and five elementary schools—together accommodate 3,639 students. The total education budget for 1979-80 amounted to $7,977,672, or a per-pupil expenditure of $2,020. The 1980-81

*By Lisa Weinberg, graduate of the Master of Public Affairs Program, and Carol W. Lewis, The University of Connecticut. The cooperation of Connecticut Council #4, AFSCME, AFL–CIO in providing background information for the preparation of this case is appreciatively acknowledged. The data set and community are composites derived from actual circumstances and adjusted for the purposes of this case.

and 1981-82 projected school budgets are $7,977,672 and $9,146,378, respectively. Because the Chelmsville Board of Education is currently in the process of conforming to the fiscal year used by general governments statewide, the 1980-81 budget only covers the 10-month transition period (September 1980 through June 1981).

In the spring of 1980, the Chelmsville Board of Education negotiated a new three-year labor agreement with Local 1984, the bargaining unit of maintenance and custodial workers. (The bargaining unit's composition is shown in Table 20.1.) The new contract became effective on September 1, 1980, but, even after it had been in effect for many months, its ultimate costs to the community

TABLE 20.1   Local 1984 Bargaining Unit, 1979–80

Classification	Number of Employees	Salary
Maintenance, General		
Step 3	2	$ 9,984.00
Step 4*	1	10,275.20
Maintenance, Carpenter		
Step 4*	2	10,587.20
Maintenance, Swim Pool (Day)		
Step 4*	2	10,420.80
Maintenance, Swim Pool (Night)		
Step 4*	1	10,337.60
Custodial, First Shift		
Step 2	1	9,318.40
Step 3*	1	9,630.40
Custodial, Second & Third Shifts**		
Step 1	4	9,110.40
Step 2	6	9,422.40
Step 3*	14	9,692.80
Group Leaders		
High School	1	10,795.20
Junior High	1	10,504.00
Elementary School	5	10,400.00

*Denotes maximum step in classification.
**There was some turnover during the summer of 1980 among custodial workers on the second and third shifts. Four custodians, two each then on Step 2 and Step 3, left the school system; they were replaced by four new employees. The 1980–81 structure is, therefore: four employees in Step 1, four in Step 2, and 16 in Step 3.

still were not known. Mr. Watson, who has so many financial and administrative responsibilities in the school system that he describes himself as the "business manager" for the Board of Education, had recently indicated that he himself still "had no idea" how much the new contract would cost the town. Because he felt he had neither the time nor training to cost-out the entire contract, the only information he had added to the bargaining process was that the new contract represented an annual nine percent general wage increase in the first year.

Several features of the new contract suggest that these costs could be considerable for the small town. For example, the new contract provides for the 13 paid holidays also allowed under the prior contract. In addition, both contracts granted employees one paid day in celebration of their birthday. Under the old contract, however, this "birthday provision" came with the qualifier that the day be subtracted from the employee's personal leave allowance (three days per year). The new contract contains no such qualification and thereby increases the number of hours paid for but not worked.

While the change does not increase educational expenditures independent of wage increases, the change does represent an additional cost. It would have been possible during the labor negotiations to determine that increased cost to the school system. Someone at least could have asked what the increase in the average annual cost of paid holidays would be in the initial year of the new contract. Of course, this would have meant calculating the net wage increase in terms of average base salary. The calculation is somewhat complicated by the automatic promotion provision, which itself adds costs to the contract. According to the promotion provision, an employee moves up one increment or step within the general classification on the salary schedule each year.

Both contracts recognize that the inspection of all school buildings within the jurisdiction of the Board of Education is a daily responsibility. Accordingly, an inspection is to be conducted by one employee in each school on each weekday and on Saturdays and Sundays. While the high school requires one and one-half hours for each inspection, inspection in all other schools demands only one hour a day. The contract provides that the employee conducting the inspection is to be compensated by a reduction in working hours during the regular work week at a rate of one and one-half hours for each weekend hour worked. As far as hours of work are concerned, the annual total of 2,080 scheduled hours consist, by contract, of eight hour days, five working days a week, Monday through Friday, for all 52 weeks.

Like holiday costs, inspection costs could not simply have been added to other budgeted expenditures nor would they have altered expenditure projections. Since the average base salary is calculated in terms of an employee's scheduled hours of work on an an-nual basis, hours paid for but not worked already are accounted for in the base salary. Although the inspection provision does not constitute an additional benefit in the new contract, inspection costs rise as wages rise. No one asked, prior to settlement, just how much those weekend inspections cost the educational system in Chelmsville.

Even considering only selected costing issues that are tied directly to wage and salary changes, there remain—unasked and unanswered—significant questions about the cost impacts of the new contract between the Board of Education and Local 1984:

1. What is the net wage increase from 1979–80 to 1980–81? Express it in terms of the average annual base salary for 1980–81. What is the initial-year's roll-up factor? Note that the model (case 19) requires costing using last year as base, NOT from what the prior contract would have cost were it still in effect. Therefore, the roll-up factor is calculated by including costs associated with initial-year step increases.

2. What is the increase in the average annual cost of paid holidays (for first year of new contract only)? Exclude personal leave allowance but consider the effect of the "birthday" provision.

3. What is the initial-year, 12-month annual cost of weekend building inspections, based on the average hourly rate? How many hours are compensated but not worked? (Use a 12-month contract year rather than prorating for the 10-month fiscal period.)

21

*A Brief Look at Arlington's Budget**

This is about the budget of the Town of Arlington and about the impact that inflation has had on that budget. As a resident of Arlington, you know that your tax rate has gone up a great deal in the last ten years in order to pay for increased town expenses. As the material in the following pages will show, these increases in expenses are due almost entirely to inflation. This is the most important fact to keep in mind when discussing Arlington's finances: although per capita town spending (the amount of money spent per person) has risen 68.8% since 1971, inflation accounts for 100% of this increase.

The Bureau of Labor Statistics, a division of the U.S. Department of Labor, has been keeping track of the effects of inflation since 1967. (See Exhibit 21.1.) All discussions of "what the dollar is worth" are based on the assumption that in 1967 one dollar was worth 100 cents. In 1971, the year that this report begins to look at Arlington's finances, the dollar was worth 82 cents. As you know, the dollar has continued to decline in value every year. Today, it is worth less than 50 cents. So, even though Arlington has appropriated more and more money to pay for its expenses, every town department has less "real" money to spend than it had ten years ago.

BUDGET HIGHLIGHTS

Here are some additional important facts about Arlington's budget:

*Reprinted by permission from "A Brief Look at Arlington's Budget," Arlington, Massachusetts, Selectmen's Committee for Service Priorities Budget Task Force (chaired by Allan Tosti) and the Department of Urban Studies and Planning of the Massachusetts Institute of Technology, June 1980.

Arlington's tax base has "increased" in value by about 4% during the last ten years. However, after inflation has been taken into account, Arlington's tax base has decreased by about 44%.

Arlington's appropriations for town departments, for the Metropolitan District Commission, for the MBTA, for the county, and for Minuteman Regional have increased by about 14.7 million dollars. However, after inflation has been taken into account, these appropriations have actually decreased by 7.6%.

Arlington's tax rate has risen from $51.80 per $1000 of assessed value to $81.00 per $1000 of assessed value. However, after inflation has been taken into account, Arlington's taxes have actually decreased by 14%.

EXHIBIT 21.1 The Impact of Inflation on Town Appropriations 1970-1980

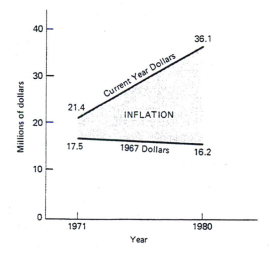

Arlington has increased spending for its public schools by $6,259,543 since 1971. However, after inflation is taken into account, Arlington's public school budget has actually decreased by 8.1% (or $614,426).

Arlington's per-pupil spending in 1978 (the most recent year for which information is available) was $1,812. The Massachusetts average was $1,598.

Arlington's tax rate is 17th among Massachusetts communities with populations greater than 50,000. Five communities of a comparable size have a lower tax rate.

In 1971, state charges for mandated programs, such as the MBTA, exceeded state aid. Today, state aid for such programs exceeds state charges. After inflation has been taken into account, state aid has increased by almost 17%.

We hope that this will help you understand more clearly the trends in Arlington's finances over the last ten years. The figures used in this report are appropriations—the amounts of money set aside by Town Meetings for spe-cific uses. Although the figures given are not the actual dollar amounts spent, they are very close to the actual amounts. These figures will help you make comparisons between 1971 and 1980.

CHANGES IN TOWN SPENDING 1971–1980

The following tables show the changes in appropriations over the past ten years. They show the percentage of the total budget appropriated to each department and the impact of inflation on appropriations. The figures indicate that while both appropriations and per capita spending have increased in dollar amounts over the last ten years, once inflation is taken into account they have actually decreased by 7.6%.

From 1971 to 1980 appropriations for the various purposes listed on the tables have increased by $14,716,061. Discounting inflation, spending has actually decreased $1,341,308 or 7.6%.

In terms of per capita spending, or

TABLE 21.1   Town Appropriations 1971

Budget Category	1971 Appropriations	Percent of Total	Appropriations in 1967 Dollars
General Government	$ 541,695	2.5%	$ 444,731
Planning & Community Development	127,379	0.7	104,578
Properties & Natural Resources	590,226	2.8	484,576
Public Works	2,439,100	11.4	2,002,501
Community Safety	2,808,966	13.0	2,306,161
Education	9,206,885	43.5	7,558,852
Minuteman Regional	0	0	0
Human Resources	648,864	3.0	532,717
Library	478,056	2.2	392,483
M.B.T.A.	979,495	4.6	804,165
M.D.C.	934,286	4.3	767,048
County	1,100,046	5.0	903,137
Insurance & Pensions	1,512,797	7.0	1,242,008
	$21,367,795	100.0*	$17,542,959

spending per each Arlington resident, the amount of spending has increased. In 1971 it was $427.35 per person and today it is $721.67. After correction for inflation, however, the actual per person spending in Arlington over the last ten years has decreased by 7.6%. In 1967 dollars in 1971 it was $350.85 per capita and in 1980 it is $324.03 per capita. Spending in 1967 dollars has decreased by $26.82 per person.

TABLE 21.2 Town Appropriations 1980

Budget Category	1980 Appropriations	Percent of Total	Appropriations in 1967 Dollars
General Government	$ 951,210	2.6%	$ 427,093
Planning & Community Development	122,053	0.3	54,801
Properties & Natural Resources	833,709	2.3	374,335
Public Works	2,988,363	8.2	1,341,770
Community Safety	4,977,157	14.0	2,234,743
Education	15,466,428	43.0	6,944,436
Minuteman Regional	886,533	2.4	398,053
Human Resources	832,458	2.3	373,773
Library	680,124	1.9	305,375
M.B.T.A.	1,796,547	5.0	806,649
M.D.C.	1,064,232	3.0	477,840
County	682,144	1.8	306,282
Insurance & Pensions	4,802,898	13.2	2,156,501
	$36,083,856	100.0%	$16,201,651

TABLE 21.3 Changes in Department Per Capita Expenditures

Budget Category	1971 Per Capita	1980 Per Capita	Percent Change
General Government	$ 8.89	$ 8.54	− 3.9%
Planning & Community Development	2.09	1.09	− 47.5
Properties & Natural Resources	9.69	7.48	− 22.8
Public Works	40.05	26.83	− 32.9
Community Safety	46.12	44.69	− 3.0
Education	151.20	138.94	− 8.1
Minuteman Regional	—	7.96	—
Human Resources	10.65	7.47	− 29.8
Library	7.84	6.10	− 22.1
M.B.T.A.	16.08	16.13	+ 0.3
M.D.C.	15.34	9.55	− 37.7
County	18.06	6.12	− 66.0
Insurance & Pensions	24.84	43.13	+ 73.6
TOTAL	$350.85	$324.03	− 7.6%

The following table shows Arlington tax rates from 1971 to 1980. The second column gives the rates in 1967 dollars. Although the town reevaluated property at 100% market value in 1969, the present assessment is about 45% of market value.

TABLE 21.4   Town Taxes

Year	Tax Rate	Tax Rate in 1967 Dollars
1971	$51.80	$42.52
1972	56.80	45.26
1973	56.80	40.10
1974	28.20	20.16
FY 1975	67.20	41.39
FY 1976	67.20	39.24
FY 1977	74.80	40.99
FY 1978	78.00	39.62
FY 1979	84.60	38.66
FY 1980	81.00	36.36

Of the 22 communities in Massachusetts with populations of 50,000 or more, 16 of the communities have a higher tax rate than the Town of Arlington and just five have a tax rate lower than Arlington's. In 1967 dollars, Arlington residents are paying 14.4% less in taxes than they did in 1971.

TABLE 21.5   Tax Base

Year	Assessed Value	Change in Assessed Value	Percent Change in Assessed Value
1970	$334,352,700		
1971	337,440,550	+ $3,087,850	.92%
1972	339,254,750	+ 1,814,150	.54
1973-74	341,760,750	+ 2,506,050	.74
1975	345,925,600	+ 4,164,850	1.22
1976	346,665,200	+ 739,600	.21
1977	346,704,200	+ 39,000	.01
1978	346,964,250	+ 60,050	.02
1979	347,188,700	+ 224,450	.06
1980	348,141,750	+ 953,050	.27

Total Increase in Tax Base: 1970 – 1980 = 4.12%
Average Annual Increase in Tax Base: 0.40%

In 1967 dollars, state aid to Arlington for mandated programs has increased 79.5% since 1971. The state now requires Arlington to conduct many programs the town was not required to conduct in 1971.

EXHIBIT 21.2 State Aid and State Charges 1971–1980

FOR DISCUSSION[1]

The data presented in the Arlington exhibit portray the effect of inflation on a variety of budgetary concerns facing municipal decision makers. Inflation, in fact, can be seen as a fiscal scapegoat in this instance. Are there factors that play an equally important role in explaining the decline of a community's purchasing power and ability to provide an acceptable level of services?

The measure used to track inflation can be an important determinant in "explaining" the actual impact of inflation on any budget. How important is it to understand the biases contained in indexes designed to measure in-

[1]Note: These questions are the editor's addition to the case and are not part of the Arlington presentation.

flation? In the Arlington example is it clear what index is employed to track inflation? If not, what are the implications?

Changes in service level or quality, as well as changes in intergovernmental revenue patterns, affect expenditures. The relationship of inflation to these variables is more difficult to measure. Do these factors play a role in the Arlington exhibit?

To local public officials translating expenditures into dollars on the tax rate is an issue of considerable importance to the community and to the officials' own political futures. From the type of data presented in the Arlington case, what effect has inflation had on the tax rate and what potential effect does the data have on community perceptions of Arlington's tax rate?

22

*Now You See It, Now You Don't**

THE IMPLICIT PRICE DEFLATOR

The *Gross National Product* (GNP) is the market value of all final goods and services produced by labor and property supplied by residents of the United States in a given period of time. The GNP consists of purchases of final goods and services by individual consumers and by government, of gross private domestic investment, and of net exports. The *Implicit Price Deflator* (IPD) is the price index for the GNP.

The IPD is the ratio of GNP in current dollar prices (the dollar value of a good or service at the time the good or service was sold) to GNP in constant dollar prices (dollar value adjusted for changes by a price index, such as the IPD). Simply, the IPD is an index which shows the effect of price changes by placing current expenditures in constant dollars. The IPD is divided into a number of categories. In state and local government budgets the applic-

*Francis J. Leazes, Jr., doctoral candidate, Department of Political Science, and Carol W. Lewis, The University of Connecticut.

able IPD category is the Implicit Price Deflator for State and Local Government Purchases of Goods and Services. The complete IPD as well as its subcategories are available in a monthly publication of the Department of Commerce's Bureau of Economic Analysis, called the *Survey of Current Business*.

Because it is a measure of the GNP, the Implicit Price Deflator is best used for aggregate data and generally is considered the best single indicator of broad price movements in the economy. The various subcategories indicate price movement for the sectors included in the category. Consequently, using the IPD for State and Local Government Purchase of Goods and Services demonstrates the change in the purchasing power of the dollar spent by government. Because the IPD measures change both in prices and in consumption, the index can decline as consumer patterns shift from higher priced items or articles with rapidly rising prices to items with lower prices or articles whose prices rise less rapidly. Consequently, the IPD has been criticized as a measure which may understate inflation.

HOW TO USE THE IPD

Any price deflator can be determined by following three steps.

Step 1: Create a price ratio by dividing current dollar prices by a corresponding base year price for the same expenditure.

$$\frac{\text{current dollar price}}{\text{base year price}} = \text{price ratio}$$

Step 2: Divide the price ratio obtained in Step 1 into the current dollar expenditure, yielding a deflated expenditure, i.e., an expenditure in constant dollars.

$$\frac{\text{current dollar expenditure}}{\text{price ratio}} = \frac{\text{constant dollar}}{\text{expenditure}}$$

Step 3: Create a price deflator by dividing current dollar expenditures by the constant dollar expenditures.

$$\frac{\text{current dollar expenditure}}{\text{constant dollar expenditure}} = \text{price deflator}$$

The Implicit Price Deflator for State and Local Government Purchases of Goods and Services is derived in this manner. Few analysts have the luxury of time to create their own localized price deflators; therefore the IPD provided in the *Survey of Current Business* is the best alternative.

Using the IPD is relatively easy and is summarized in the following formula: Select a base year IPD. Divide current dollar expenditures by the current IPD and multiply the resulting divident by the base year IPD.

$$\frac{\text{current dollar expenditure}}{\left(\dfrac{\text{current IPD}}{100}\right)} \times \frac{\text{base year IPD}}{100} = \frac{\text{current expenditures in base year dollars}}{}$$

In Table 22.1 the IPD is applied to New Orleans expenditures in 1980 and 1981. The 1965 IPD was used as a base year price deflator. Consequently, the equation by which to arrive at 1980 expenditures in 1965 dollars is:

$$\frac{\text{1980 current dollar prices}}{\left(\dfrac{\text{1980 IPD}}{100}\right)} \times \frac{\text{1965 IPD}}{100} = \frac{\text{1980 expenditures in 1965 dollars}}{}$$

Therefore,

$$\frac{\$270{,}761}{\left(\dfrac{184.7}{100}\right)} \times \frac{123.2}{100} = \$180{,}605$$

A more recent base year IPD can be used if an analysis of long term trends is not considered important. Table 22.1 shows the results obtained when the 1972 and 1975 IPD for State and Local Government Purchases of Goods and Services is applied.

TABLE 22.1 New Orleans: General Expenditures (in thousands of dollars)

Expenditures	1980	1981
Current dollars	$270,761	$281,466
1965 constant dollars	180,605	178,286
1972 constant dollars	268,562	256,113
1975 constant dollars	190,280	187,839

Source: City of New Orleans, *Operating Budget for Calendar and Fiscal Years 1980 and 1981.*

PRICE INDEXES

The Producer Price Index (formerly the Wholesale Price Index) and the Consumer Price Index can be used for aggregate expenditures, as well as for detailed budgetary items. The Producer Price Index (PPI) is a set of measures of average change in prices recorded in all stages of processing by producers of commodities. The PPI for Finished Goods (the most commonly cited PPI) measures price changes of goods that are completely processed and ready for sale to consumers. The Index is a useful tool for analyzing price trends. Published by the Bureau of Labor Statistics in its monthly publication, *Producer Prices and Price Index*, the PPI for Finished Goods is used by industry analysts as a long-term indicator of price movement and inflationary trends, especially when the CPI is being distorted by rising or falling interest rates and housing prices. But like all measures, the PPI has weaknesses. The PPI is mostly criticized for its reliance on book prices and for ignoring producer discounts in the development of the index.

The Consumer Price Index (CPI) is an index of price changes occurring in a fixed "market basket" of goods and services customarily purchased by urban consumers. The CPI consists of two series. The first and oldest (CPI-W) is derived from prices paid by urban wage and salary workers. The second series (CPI-U), initiated in 1978, is based on prices paid by all urban consumers. It was begun to determine if goods and services bought by one group of consumers rise in price more quickly than the same goods and services bought by another group. Like the PPI, the Consumer Price Index appears in a Bureau of Labor Statistics monthly publication, *Consumer Prices and Price Index*. This same publication contains regional CPI's and CPI's for selected cities throughout the country.

In many ways the CPI-W is a more significant index than either the PPI or CPI-U (despite its broader population base), because the CPI-W is widely used, is employed for a variety of purposes, and, consequently, is a better-known index. Currently, the CPI-W is used as the escalator for Social Security payments and federal retirement benefits. (As a consequence, for each percentage point increase in the CPI-W, a several billion dollar increase in federal outlays can be expected.) The CPI-W is also the index most frequently employed by labor unions in bargaining for wage and benefit increases.

Recently, the CPI has come under criticism for the overweighting of housing costs in the development of the index. Housing represents approximately one-quarter of the overall index and literally treats home purchases and upkeep as just another consumer purchase, overstating the rate of inflation as interest rates and housing prices rise and understating the rate of inflation as housing prices and interest rates decline. The Bureau of Labor Statistics plans to shift the emphasis on housing from the cost of ownership to a rental equivalent beginning in 1983. The CPI will take on added significance with the coming of income tax indexation since tax brackets, personal exemptions, and zero-bracket rates will be altered by average increases in the CPI.

HOW TO USE THE CPI AND THE PPI

The CPI and the PPI are used in the same manner as the IPD. A major difference is that the IPD provides an index for various sectors of the economy while the two price indexes measure price movements for individual commodities. What follow are the formula for calculating expenditures in constant dollars using these two indexes and an illustration of the uses of each index.

$$\frac{\text{current dollar expenditures}}{\left(\dfrac{\text{current CPI or PPI}}{100}\right)} \times \frac{\text{base year CPI or PPI}}{100} = \begin{array}{l}\text{expenditures} \\ \text{in base year} \\ \text{dollars}\end{array}$$

New Orleans uses a zero-base budgeting procedure which facilitates an analysis of the impact of inflation on individual municipal programs. Appendix I is a decision-unit budget summary for the Equipment Maintenance Division (EMD) of New Orleans. One of the EMD's responsibilities is to provide fuel for the city fleet (police, fire, sanitation, and others). The fuel-supply program goal was to reduce fuel consumption in 1981 to 73 percent of the fleet's 1980 consumption. Table 22.2 describes the results from using the appropriate commodity categories of the PPI (Refined Petroleum—Gasoline) and the CPI (Gasoline: Regular—Premium). Exhibit 22.1 summarizes the major features of the IPD, the PPI, and the CPI.

TABLE 22.2   New Orleans: EMD Fuel Expenditures

Fuel Expenditure	1980	1981
Current dollars	$1,641,135	$1,787,606
1972 PPI	263,989	249,394
1973 CPI	472,240	459,363
1979 PPI	1,025,583	968,884
1979 CPI	1,224,114	1,190,735

Source: City of New Orleans, *Operating Budget for Calendar and Fiscal Years 1980 and 1981.*

The popular conception of inflation derives from the CPI. However, the selection of an index as an aid in budget analysis should not rest solely on the popularity of the index. A matrix of budgetary needs, purposes, audience, and time availability may make it more useful to rely on the PPI or the IPD. Indexes are not "neutral." The selection of a particular base year index will produce outcomes different from another year's. Remember, the analyst's choice affects the results.

PROBLEM 1: THE IPD IN ACTION IN DES MOINES, IOWA

Des Moines has experienced a continual increase in expenditures. Table 22.3 provides a summary of the city's population and expenditures.

TABLE 22.3   Des Moines: Expenditures and Population, 1965–1979

Year	General Expenditures	Population
1965	$18,503,000	208,982
1970	37,520,000	200,587
1972	43,006,000	201,404
1975	64,583,000	199,145
1979	80,940,000	193,772

Source: U.S. Department of Commerce, Bureau of the Census, *City Government Finances,* 1965, 1970, 1972, 1975, 1979.

To allow for the effects of price changes on the Des Moines city budget over a prolonged period, the Implicit Price Deflator is the best available index. The IPD for State and Local Government Purchases of Goods and Services for the following years were:

1965	123.2
1970	165.1
1972	183.2
1979	177.1

EXHIBIT 22.1   Summary of the Major Features of the IPD, the PPI, and the CPI

IPD	CPI	PPI
Measures broad price movement	Measures changes in "market basket"	Measures long-term price movements
Used to deflate state and local government purchases	Used in labor negotiations and escalator clauses	Used as an indicator of speculative pressures
Better suited for aggregate data by sector	Can be used for item-of-detail and aggregate data	Can be used for item-of-detail and aggregate data
Does not provide localized index	Overemphasis on housing in the index	Relies on book prices/ignores producer discounts

Using 1965 as the base year, develop a presentation for the Des Moines City Council which shows the effects of price changes on the FY 1979 budget. The presentation should include tables and graphs, as well as a brief written summary explaining your findings. Explain the choice and meaning of the IPD. Compare your findings with those evident in the Arlington exhibit.

For Discussion (Problem 1)

1. The selection of a base year will affect the results obtained. The effect of price change on expenditures can be exagerated or diminished depending on the base year indicator.

2. In what ways do methodologies employed to deflate prices, such as indexes, affect budgetary outcomes? In particular, would the type of data obtained from Des Moines encourage or discourage spending? What effect on the tax rate could the availability of this type of information have?

3. Are there circumstances under which accounting for inflation may not be appropriate? Who benefits the most and who the least from having this data available to them?

PROBLEM 2: THE CPI AND A MUNICIPAL INVENTORY NEW ORLEANS, LOUISIANA

The New Orleans Equipment Maintenance Division is responsible for keeping the city motor vehicle fleet operational. The program objective in the FY 1981 budget is "to achieve an overall cost effectiveness which is optimum." The budget document defines optimum as "repair when the cost of repair is 20 percent less (or lower) than the value of a vehicle."

For 1980, expenditures for repair supplies were budgeted at $1,231,619.00. In 1981, expenditures were budgeted at $1,118,747.00, a 9 percent cut in current dollars. The CPI for car maintenance and repair can be used to calculate the change in current dollars. The following figures are the CPI for urban wage earners, clerical workers for car maintenance and repair:

1972	135.2
1979	244.4
1980	270.0
1981	290.7

Using 1972 as your base year, calculate the effect of price change on car repairs for the New Orleans fleet for 1980 and 1981. Repeat the operation using 1979 as the base year. Summarize your findings for the division head. Using Appendix I as your model, design a zero-based budget (ZBB) decision unit that incorporates information about inflation. In designing the decision unit keep in mind the basic premises of ZBB.

For Discussion (Problem 2)

1. Can you infer from this type of data alone that a city is buying more or less? Would either inference be valid? Variables other than price change may affect purchasing. Such factors as bulk purchasing, entrepreneurial purchasing agents, timely billing and payment schedules, and supplier discounts affect purchasing power as well.

2. Based on what is observed in these problems and cases (Arlington, Des Moines, and New Orleans), to whose advantage is it to use the CPI, PPI, and IPD? This question should be answered in relation to the following participants: labor unions, elected officials, public administrators, and the general public.

DECISION UNIT BUDGET SUMMARY

CAO   EMD-Fuel Supply   2298

CLASSIFICATION OF EXPENDITURE	ADOPTED BUDGET 1980	ADOPTED BUDGET 1981	SOURCE OF FUNDING	ADOPTED BUDGET 1981
PERSONAL SERVICES	$ -0-	$ -0-	GENERAL FUND-DIRECT	$1,787,606
CONTRACTUAL SERVICES	-0-	-0-	REVENUE SHARING	
SUPPLIES AND MATERIALS	1,641,135	1,787,606	DOWNTOWN DEVELOP. DIST.	
EQUIPMENT AND PROPERTY	-0-	-0-	COMMUNITY DEVELOPMENT	
OTHER CHARGES	-0-	-0-	WELFARE	
TOTAL EXPENDITURES	$1,641,135	$1,787,606	MANPOWER	
			LEAA	
BUDGETED POSITIONS	0	0	FEDERAL GRANTS	
CETA POSITIONS	0	0	STATE GRANTS	
			INTERGOVERMENTAL	
			TOTAL	$1,787,606

(A) PROGRAM OBJECTIVES WITH METHODS OF DELIVERY; (B) SIGNIFICANT CHANGES FROM CURRENT YEAR SERVICE LEVELS

(A)   The program objective is to provide quantities of fuel and lubricants for the fleet (this includes some fuel supplies to the Police Department).

(B)   This level provides fuel and lubricants sufficient to satisfy 75% of the fleet's present consumption.

CITY OF NEW ORLEANS, LA.   ZBB NO. 12

CHAPTER SIX

PERFORMANCE MEASUREMENT AND BUDGETING

In a national financial management needs assessment, over 2,000 local officials identified performance budgeting as one of their highest priorities.[1] In its broadest sense, measuring performance involves

any systemic attempt to learn how responsive a . . . government's services are to the needs of the community, and to the community's ability to pay . . . . Performance measurement is a government's way of determining whether it is providing a quality product at a reasonable cost.[2]

Harry Hatry authoritatively defines performance measurement as "the systematic assessment of how well services are being delivered to a community—both how efficiently and how effectively."[3]

A practical application of performance measurement demands a *systematic* approach to the key concepts of "efficiency" and "effectiveness." Efficiency usually refers to the "relation of the amount of input required to the amount of output produced."[4] Put another way, efficiency is the "ratio of the quantity of service produced . . . to the cost, in dollars of labor, required to produce it."[5] Effectiveness, on the other hand, involves the purposes (goals, objectives) of public programs and services and whether they are being met. Effectiveness considers service impacts, delivery attributes or quality, community needs, and government's responsiveness to these needs. Some formulations incorporate unarticulated needs and community demands within the concept of effectiveness.

---

[1]*National Conference on the Financial Management Needs of Local Government: Final Conference Report* (Washington, D.C.: U.S. Department of Housing and Urban Development, Office of Policy Development and Research, June 1978).

[2]Paul D. Epstein, *Using Performance Measurement in Local Government: A Guide to Improving Decisions, Performance, and Accountability* (Washington, D.C.: U.S. Department of Housing and Urban Development, 1981 draft), Chapter 1. Forthcoming under same title from Van Nostrand and Reinhold.

[3]Harry Hatry, "Performance Measurement Principles and Techniques"; paper prepared for presentation at four HUD-sponsored workshops, Measuring and Improving Local Government Services (Washington, D.C.: State and Local Government Research Program, The Urban Institute, 1979).

[4]*Ibid.*, p. 1.

[5]Epstein, "Using Performance Measurement," Chapter 2.

●

It has been suggested that the distinction between the two concepts lies in the answers to two questions:

"What are we getting for our tax dollars?" (efficiency)
"What good is it doing?" (effectiveness)[6]

There are many technical problems associated with performance measurement and improvement programs. These efforts have evolved differently in different communities in response to different local conditions, which affect measurement purposes and measurement techniques. While there are no universally accepted standards for different types of measures, the most useful tend to be systematic, dynamic, tailored to local conditions, practical, and public. They are aids to decision making rather than the sources of decisions; they are useful insofar as performance is measured and, ultimately, improved.

This suggests that the single most important consideration for choosing performance measures is their usefulness for decision making. Do they provide useful, meaningful information for decision makers? Generally, it is not considered appropriate to phrase questions about performance measures in terms of "good versus bad." It is more appropriate, especially for practical applications, to accept any indicator and sets of measures that a government can use to its benefit.

Alternatively, the full set of measures can be evaluated in terms of its congruence with theoretically derived criteria, established specifically for selecting a set of measures for a service. One such set includes the following criteria:

1. validity/accuracy (measurement and data collection procedures)
2. comprehensibility for decision makers
3. timeliness
4. minimization of perverse behavior (incentives, disincentives, counterproductive behavior)
5. uniqueness (multiple vs. overlap, duplicative measures)
6. cost of collection (and analysis)
7. controllability (Is what is being measured subject to the jurisdiction's manipulation? This is important both for accountability and when individual's efforts are being measured.)
8. comprehensiveness of the set of measures.[7]

Effectiveness and quality measures are performance measures.[8] Because they are derived necessarily from statements of program goals and service objectives, clear and empirically verifiable statements are

[6]*Ibid.*

[7]Hatry, "Performance Measurement Principles."

[8]Harry Hatry et al., *How Effective Are Your Community Services? Procedures for Monitoring the Effectiveness of Municipal Services* (Washington, D.C.: The Urban Institute and the International City Management Association, 1977).

the key to useful measures of this type. They must be developed to suit each community and in terms of each community's goals. They are best evaluated as an interrelated set rather than individually inasmuch as the set represents "quality controls" for efficiency measures.

There are different ways of choosing objectives and these affect the type of performance measures. Overall, it is still quite common to use historical data in conjunction with expert staff judgment. This seems reasonable enough, so long as the approach is not confused with ideal standards. The main advantage to the "historical approach" is that it is based upon the organization's existing ability to deliver services. The main disadvantage is that this may entail perpetuating existing inefficiencies or patterns of ineffectiveness. It does allow for adjusting for local circumstances ("environmental factors").[9] Expert staff judgment need not be local, however. Some professional organizations have developed service norms; accreditation standards exist for some agencies and services; and some standards, such as residential care levels or pupil–teacher ratios, may be mandated by law.

Efficiency and productivity measures relate the amount of resources (input) to the amount of product produced (output). Productivity is the ratio of output to input, whereas the ratio of input to output is an efficiency (or unit cost) measure. Many of the more reliable targets expressed as efficiency ratios rely upon engineered work standards (e.g., time and motion studies) but these are not available for all services. Efficiency ratios like these relate actual unit cost to an ideal work standard expressed in time per unit for a given activity.

A more sophisticated—and more costly—approach uses composite productivity indices. Furthermore, some measures indicate potential rather than actual performance. Resource utilization measures cover equipment downtime, unused capacity, losses, and personnel lost time instead of productive time.

The technique most often is assessed in terms of cost, but this is only one of several criteria. According to Hatry,

ultimately, the cost of performance measurement has to be justified by its value in improving decision-making, reducing or avoiding service costs, improving service effectiveness, or improving service management.[10]

And, in line with the preceding chapter, the same author has suggested that benefit–cost ratios present such a significant valuation problem for local jurisdictions that they are not suitable for use in routine performance measurement.[11]

The two cases that follow examine some of the major themes and problems associated with developing and implementing performance

[9]Epstein, "Using Performance Measurement," Chapter 7.

[10]Hatry, "Performance Measurement Principles," p. 1.

[11]*Ibid.*, pp. 16–17.

measurement in municipal government. The first describes the attempt in the City of St. Petersburg to measure municipal services and implement an effective system of measurement and evaluation. For purposes of the discussion questions, this evaluative case divides the case into two stages: a seven-year period during which the comprehensive system was initiated and a subsequent, shorter period during which substantive and substantial changes were introduced.

Case no. 24, "Dayton, Ohio's Program Strategies," describes the circumstances in this professionally managed municipality. It concludes with three short decisions, each detailing an actual application. Two of these are evaluative; a third examines the distinction between efficiency and effectiveness and requires that a decision be made and justified.

Both cases integrate the development and implementation issues with larger concerns about strategic planning and management improvement. Both cases touch upon the appropriate role of citizen surveys in making service decisions. A related case, which explicitly considers performance budgeting in terms of budget reform, is no. 33, "A Council Member Looks at Performance Measurement."

23

*The City of St. Petersburg Measures Its Services** *

THE PROBLEM AND THE CONTEXT

The city of St. Petersburg, like many units of local government across the county, has been faced with the problems of increasing costs of services and increasing demands for more and better services without a comparable expansion of revenues.

The city is located on the west coast of Florida with a population of 237,000. It employs the council–city manager form of government. It has 21 departments with an annual budget of $136 million for the fiscal year ending September 30, 1982, and a total of 2,887 full-time and 680 part-time employees.

The administrative problems of the city can be better understood in light of its social, economic, and geographical characteristics. The city is located on a peninsula; because it is surrounded by water and other cities, there is almost no room for expansion. The economic base of the city is derived mainly from service industry (tourism) and the expenditures of senior citizens, who constitute over one-third of the population.

As a result of such environmental conditions, the city manager (Alan N. Harvey) describes the economy as "static" or "no growth." He concedes that there is "no room to change the city's economic base to any appreciable

degree." The city manager believes that the current economic strategy of the city has to be basically supporting what is in existence and taking advantage of the city's esthetics: good weather, sunshine, and the sea.

The static economic base creates serious difficulties in managing the city, particularly under conditions of citizen pressures for more and better service in an era of high inflation. In fact, the citizens, as well as the *St. Petersburg Times*, the only major morning paper in the city, have always been watchful of and involved in the management of municipal services.

The Solution

Under conditions of fast-increasing costs of services, unmatched by the growth of available resources, the city administration viewed productivity improvement as a possible solution to the city's problem. A contributing factor to the selection of this approach is the city's tradition of professional management. By 1973, measures of effectiveness had been developed in some functional areas of service and the city administration had completed a goals study. Attempts to adopt planning, programming, and budgeting techniques relied on data that did require gathering.

In a report entitled "City-Wide Effectiveness/Productivity Measurement System," a group of consultants concluded on January 10, 1973: "What is needed now is to design effectiveness indicators that will quantitatively and qualitatively measure the effectiveness and productivity of municipal services . . . ." The city management agreed and, in 1973, began efforts to initiate a new comprehensive productivity measurement system.

*By Jamil E. Jreisat, University of South Florida. The author, who is responsible for any failure or shortcoming of this case, is grateful for the cooperation and help of many individuals in St. Petersburg, particularly Alan Harvey (City Manager), Rick Smith (Assistant Chief of Police), and Gerry Mason (The Budget Office).

The Participants

All departments in the government of the city participated in the effectiveness/productivity measurement system. Initially, the service areas were identified and grouped by functional objectives.

In a two-phase effort, carried out jointly with the Urban Institute and International City Management Association, St. Petersburg embarked on the development of productivity measures with the objective of transfer and dissemination to all units of local government. The task plan for the installation of the new system required eighteen months, beginning January 1973.

The development of the new productivity measurement was supported by the National Commission on Productivity, the National Science Foundation, and the Department of Housing and Urban Development through funding and other technical assistance.

An important element in the new measurement system was citizens input and evaluation of municipal services. As a result, a multiservice citizen survey was inaugurated by the city management in 1973 and has been repeated annually or biannually since then.

THE PROCESS OF MEASUREMENT DEVELOPMENT

Measurement of productivity (or any other major organizational activity) is a systematic process that utilizes various techniques of data collection, coordination, and analysis. Measurement procedures are essentially based on pragmatic grounds and are designed to serve established and defined objectives. Also, a sound measurement system endeavors to coordinate the operational and the conceptual and to bridge the gap between them.

There are many stages in the development of a measurement system. In St. Petersburg, the following major steps were the most pronounced in the total process:

1. Conceptualization
2. The development of indicators
3. Setting the anticipated activity level
4. Collection of data
5. Examination, coordination, and publication of data
6. Conducting the multiservice citizen survey

1. The conceptualization of the measurement system. This conceptualization guides all subsequent phases of the process, from the general purpose statement to the most specific application of measurement techniques. What is it the city of St. Petersburg wants to measure? The answer to this question is important in that it is inseparable from the need to establish the purpose of the measurement efforts and the means to coordinate the various indicators and constructs utilized in the process.

The city had a choice of many types of measurement serving different objectives. *Input measures* are the most familiar; they have been widely used by public organizations to identify dollar costs of activities or man-hour (month) needs and are integrated with the budget process.

With the advent of program budgeting (performance budgeting), and planning–programming budgeting, *output measures* began to take priority. Under such emphasis, the focus shifted to results such as the number of housing units inspected, gallons of sewage processed, miles of streets resurfaced, and so forth.

Effectiveness measures, however, are different from input and output measures in that they relate accomplishments to objectives. They attempt to assess to what degree a program or organization's purpose is being achieved without neglecting the quality of service. Effectiveness measures, for example, are concerned with the number of citizens' complaints received in a municipal service and the number resolved.

Another important measure is *efficiency*, which usually posits outputs (results) against inputs (costs) in order to determine how economically the city is able to produce and deliver its services. The input must include all resources used in producing the service, such as manpower, capital, technology, machinery, land, etc. Efficiency is expressed in terms of the ratio between input and output.

Productivity is a form of efficiency measurement. It is a more simplified and concrete aspect of efficiency that compares output to a factor of production or other small measureable unit of input. In a municipal housing program, for example, productivity measures are reported as total inspections per man-day or construction permits issued per man-month.

The above summarizes the more prominent performance measures or options available to the city of St. Petersburg in 1973. Of course, other variations and combinations are possible and some of them have been tried, although randomly and unsystematically, by the city.

From all indications we can gather, St. Petersburg adopted a full-blown scheme offered to it by a group of consultants. The management of the city accepted the new measurement system without an adequate internal examination of its elements and advantages in relation to the city's needs and technical capabilities. The consultants recommended a citywide effectiveness/productivity measurement system with a stipulation that any developed measurement procedures be compatible with the budget system in order to provide improved information on a regular basis. This recommendation was based on a false assumption—that the city management employed a planning, programming, and budgeting system.

The proposed measurement project emphasized the importance of effectiveness (fulfilling policy mandates) and citizen input in evaluating municipal services. This qualitative dimension was seen as justified by experience, which had demonstrated that the number of tons of garbage collected per dollar of man had in no way indicated how clean the streets were. Consequently, the city adopted a system of measurement with three groups of indicators. These groups are designed to measure the actual *workload* experienced in providing a public service, the *effectiveness* of the service provided, and the *productivity* of the organization delivering the service. (See Table 23.1 for illustration.)

1. Workload indicators show the activities of a particular program during a period of time, such as the number of building permits issued in a month.

2. Effectiveness indicators measure the impact and quality of a service being delivered to the public. A central concern of the city in measuring effectiveness is the public and its expectations, desires, and satisfaction. Therefore, a multiservice citizen survey was initiated in 1973 and repeated several times. Consequently, effectiveness (including citizen sentiment) may not reflect an objective increase in productivity figures or workload, whether designated through specific legislative commitments or through definitions of administrative targets.

3. Productivity indicators quantify output in relation to the input of a program. Therefore, it is commonly defined as a ratio or a relationship between them. The most emphasized productivity measures in St. Petersburg, however, are those dealing with real output per man-hour or other units of production without establishing actual costs. The lack of data on cost factors proved to be a serious limitation.

2. The development of indicators. The city manager created a specialized department called the Management Improvement Department (MID) within the Office of Management and Budgeting to coordinate and supervise the implementation of the measurement system. One year later (1974), MID split from the Management and Budget Office, becoming autonomous but with an open access to the city manager.

The responsibility for the development of indicators was shared between operating units and MID staffers. The director of MID described the effort as "an attempt to portray the total picture of an operation." Line agencies developed indicators representing their operations and submitted them to MID. Line agencies were allowed to develop other indicators for their own purposes; those appearing in the monthly report, however, were mainly determined by the MID staff. Indicators were developed to measure workloads, productivity, and effectiveness of each operational program. Some programs suggested about 66 indicators to represent their activities. The final range for each individual program, however, was kept between 7 and 29; the total number of indicators appearing in the monthly report reached 279.

The reduction of the number of indicators submitted by some line departments by the MID staff was not totally acceptable. Some administrators of programs felt that the selection made from their lists of indicators was arbitrary. These perceptions were early signals of a gradual decline in cooperation between line agencies and MID. As far as can be determined, the efforts to develop or select an appropriate set of indicators for collecting performance information were not guided by agreed-upon specific and objective criteria. Each selection was highly judgmental and subjective, and, despite ostensible agreement, many staff members were, in fact, skeptical.

In order to enhance the confidence of operational units of the city as well as its central staff in the selection of measures of performance, the process must enforce realistic and trusted criteria. One such criterion is a validity test of the measures to determine the degree of their accuracy. Other important factors in the selection are controllability and measurability of the indicators, and, at the same time, a reasonable degree of simplicity to ensure understanding of these measures by city staff, council members, and citizens.

While city officials expressed awareness of such criteria, they were unable successfully to translate concepts into operational techniques.

For reporting purposes, the operations of the city government were divided into five major functional objectives, similar to those used for budget classification. Each major functional objective was, in turn, broken down into operating programs, as follows:

1. *Maintaining Satisfactory Environmental Living Conditions*:
   Community Development
   Water Supply
   Wastewater
   Solid Waste
   Environmental quality assurance

2. *Providing for Ease of Movement*:
   Vehicular movement
   Personal movement
   Public transportation
   Air and water transport

3. *Providing for Community Enrichment*:
   Participating recreation
   Cultural opportunities

4. *Protecting People's Rights and Property*:
   Protection from criminal attack
   Protection from fire
   Protection from civil wrongs

5. *Health Care*:
   Paramedic rescue service

Each functional category, as well as each line operation, was described in a brief statement delineating its goals. The specification of goals is an essential element in deciding which measures to use and in developing indicators to portray each operation. For example, the goals of community development were stated as "to assure the optional use of land, maintain compliance to standards for construction, and the quality redevelopment of blighted areas." Table 23.1 illustrates each type of indicator used for measuring the services of community development.

TABLE 23.1 Indicators Illustrating the Measurement of Services by a St. Petersburg Agency

Agency/Program	Ref NR	Measure/Indicator	Report Frequency	
Community	F001	Building Permit Valuation — X $M	Monthly	(W)
Development	F002	No. of Bldg Permits issued	"	(W)
	F003	No. of Living Units in Permits Issued	"	(W)
	F004	No. of Living Units C.O. ED	"	(W)
	F005	Add or Remod Permits Issued	"	(W)
	F006	New Com Bldg Permits Issued	"	(W)
	F007	New Res Bldg Permits Issued	"	(W)
	F009	No. of Demolition Permits Issued	"	(W)
	F010	Electrical Permits Issued	"	(W)
	F011	Plumbing Permits Issued	"	(W)
	F012	No. of Inspections — Building	"	(W)
	F013	No. of Inspections — Electrical	"	(W)
	F014	No. of Inspections — Plumbing	"	(W)
	F015	No. of Inspections — Housing	"	(W)
	F016	No. of Inspections — Total	"	(W)
	F017	Total Inspections per Man-Day	"	(P)
	F018	Construction Permits Issued per Man-Mo	"	(P)
	F035	Housing Complaints Received	"	(E)
	F036	Housing Complaints Resolved	"	(E)
	F037	Substd Housing Code Viol Issued	"	(W)
	F038	Substd Housing Code Viol Eliminated	"	(W)
	F039	% of Substd Violations Eliminated	"	(E)

Source: Management Statistical Journal of St. Petersburg (May 1978).

(W) = Workload indicator
(P) = Productivity indicator
(E) = Effectiveness indicator

3. Setting the anticipated activity levels (AALs). Performance data on the established indicators are reported by departments in order to be compared with targets referred to as anticipated activity levels (AALs), which serve as the basis for measurement. The process of establishing AALs is described by the city's Office of Budget and Management as essentially using the same technique followed in the budget preparation. Namely, the Budget Office sets the ground rules for departments in the preparation of AALs. After submittal by the departments, the Budget Office seeks the approval of the city manager.

It is assumed that the departments, by virtue of their stated AALs, will have established standards or performance levels of work to be achieved in a given time span, in many instances, monthly, and always on a yearly basis. According to the City Management Statistical Journal (78–79), AALs are normally established by (1) the historical method based on past performance, (2) the synthesis method using a combination of observation and analysis for projecting AAL, and (3) the historical/synthesis method which combines historical trends and the tools of management planning in calculating anticipated demands of service.

The city management claims that departmental indicators attempt to measure workload, productivity, and effectiveness against a forecasted level of performance. Continual review by top management insures that these performance levels are in accord with city goals and objectives. The AAL for a particular service may indicate a desired maximum, whereas in other cases it may designate a desired minimum.

4. *Collection of data*. This is the responsibility of each line department in accordance with established indicators. As pointed out earlier, the indicators of each municipal operation were grouped into categories of workload, productivity, and effectiveness.

On the surface data collection, as a step in the process, is a straightforward and uncomplicated activity, particularly because indicators and functions have been determined in advance. Nevertheless, the reliability of the data collected here was frequently questioned. Some employees questioned the utility of the whole process of data gathering. They intimated that line departments did not take this responsibility seriously and may have simply forwarded nonacturial (or made-up) data. Others charged that data were doctored to eliminate "flammable information", i.e., data which were negative or potentially embarrassing.

In the absence of a mechanism for verification through spot checking or some sort of audit comparing claims against real performance, it would be very difficult to establish a degree of confidence in data collected. The dilemma was further aggravated in this case by the absence of clear links between the data collected and their operational use. In other words, programs did not utilize published data for analysis, evaluation, or change in their management.

5. *Examination, coordination, and publication of data*. At the initial stage in the development of the measurement system, line agencies submitted their monthly data to the Management Improvement Department. MID staff gathered and compared results in the reports with previous months to establish trends or unusual positive or negative results of operations. If unusual results were indicated, "exception reports" would be requested from line agencies to explain them.

Reports from all line departments were reproduced in a standardized format (see Table 23.2) indicating the actual monthly result for each indicator and the anticipated activity level of the indicator. The same indicator was tabulated to show results of actual levels and AALs for the fiscal year to date. Moreover, comparative data were presented to point out percentages of actual results to AALs and to previous months and years.

6. *Multiservice citizen survey*. As we pointed out above, measures of the effectiveness of service by the city of St. Petersburg cannot be isolated from public expectations, desires, and satisfaction. Therefore, multiservice citizen surveys were administered almost annually from 1973 (seven times by the end of 1981), "to provide an insight into perceptions and impressions of the citizenry as consumers of municipal services," according to survey reports. Such survey data, the city administrators believed, would be used to temper the more traditional techniques of information that provide most of the data base upon which policy and program determination, direction, and application were founded.

Through citizen surveys, the city hoped to quantify subjective attitudes or feelings toward the city and its services so that differences in service could be noted and "remedial" or "replicative" action taken. According to the survey report, 1978, "The rationale supporting such surveys is that although individual opinions or perceptions can be challenged as prejudiced or personally biased, group impressions of carefully selected samples ag-

TABLE 23.2   Format of Monthly Reporting of Measurement Data on St. Petersburg's Municipal Services

Building Standards Regulation

Activity Measure	Month		Fiscal YTD	
	AAL*	Actual	AAL*	Actual
Building Permit Valuation ($)	2.5M	2.45M	2.5M	2.45M
No. of Bldg. Permits Issued	650	677	650	677
No. of Living Units in Permits Issued	15	8	15	8

	Comparative Data (Percent)				
	This Month Actual	% Met This Month	This Month	This Month	This YTD
	AAL	Last Month	Same Month Last Year	Last Month	Last YTD
Building Permit Valuation ($)	98	208	11	86	11
No. of Bldg. Permits Issued	104	124	90	124	90
No. of Living Units in Permits Issued	53	883	1	89	1

Source: City of St. Petersburg Public Service Evaluation Reports

*AAL = Anticipated Activity Level

gregated into statistical significance represent an accurate assessment of the feelings of the population as a whole."

The interviewing was performed by Suncoast Opinion Surveys, a St. Petersburg polling firm. The sample reached 500 households and in-the-house interviewing techniques were used to provide the increased reliability of face-to-face interviews.

In several instances, citizens were asked to rate municipal services as excellent, good, fair, poor, or don't know. Table 23.3 is a tabulation of the findings for selected operations.

TABLE 23.3.   Selected Responses by Citizens

Service	Percent of Citizens Who Rated the Services Excellent or Good					
	1974	1975	1976	1977	1978	1981
Water	87	81	90	88	87	83
Garbage Collection	74	81	83	84	82	85
Municipal Transit	60	73	72	74	57	61
Park Maintenance	65	76	70	72	69	67
Police	66	72	77	77	73	70
Fire	66	77	77	75	77	72

Source: Citizen surveys for 1974–81.

LOFTY GOALS AND DIFFICULT IMPLEMENTATION

In 1975, this author examined the measurement system in St. Petersburg after it was in operation for about one year. The following conclusions and problems facing the newly developed system of productivity measurement were among those reported:

1. There was no agreement within city government that the measurement indicators were the most indicative of performance. In fact, staff members of certain line agencies charged that the selection of indicators was influenced by political considerations. The involvement of line agencies in the whole process of measurement was mainly reduced to (a) submitting proposals for the development of indicators, (b) supplying monthly data, and (c) submitting exception reports as needed. The first and last obligations were infrequently required. The second one became a casual routine action.

2. There was no measurement of input or cost of city service to determine the ratio of cost to benefit. In the absence of resource measurement, most output indicators became workload indicators similar to those utilized regularly by the budget staff. In addition, the separation of the measurement system from the budget reduced its value as a management tool for planning and evaluation of effectiveness and productivity of services.

3. Many departments were gathering and reporting work program statistics before the inauguration of the measurement system to justify staffing requirements or desired capital expenditures. Several of those departments continued to use their own systems of data collection in the same manner as before. The Police Department, for example, employed its own reporting system in addition to the "uniform crime report," a federal requirement. The Budget Department sought its own data from operating programs to assist in analyzing budget requests and to compare workloads and workforce.

This condition helped to further undermine the significance of the monthly report of measurement as a tool of management. Seven senior officials of the city, including the city manager, the budget director, and the director of MID, agreed that the monthly reports of outputs by various programs had not been widely or systematically utilized for planned action to improve the quality or the quantity of output in the departments.

4. The Multiservice citizen surveys conducted for the city provide useful demographic data, such as area of residence, age, sex, race, income, education, etc. The monthly evaluation reports, however, did not deal with the distribution of urban public services among different population groups within the city, making analysis and comparison difficult. It is noteworthy here to indicate that some departments, i.e., police and sanitation, gathered and analyzed their own data on the use of their services as a separate activity from the requirements of the monthly reports.

5. The schism between the Budget Office and the MID proved to be unjustifiable from an organizational, as well as a functional, perspective. The decision was a consequence of weak managerial processes for conflict resolution within city government and misconception of the relationship between management improvement operations and the budget. In fact, for these reasons, along with the pressures of budget cuts and the appointment of a new city manager and budget director, the MID was abolished in September 1981. Most of MID's activities, particularly in the area of man-

agement improvement, were transferred to Program Evaluation Division in the Budget and Management Department.

The city of St. Petersburg adopted a new charter in July 1975, in which the council was directed to have management of the city evaluated periodically by an independent consulting organization. The first such report was submitted in May 1976, by McKinsey and Company, and entitled "An Assessment of Management Effectiveness in the City of St. Petersburg." The following are among its findings ((pp. 2–13):

> A number of advanced concepts of reporting had been introduced, but the application of those concepts had not to date (1976) exploited their full potential. The ultimate user of many reports was not defined. For example, it is not clear whether many of the more costly and time-consuming reports are intended to be management reports or whether they are simply evidence, for external consumption, that something is being accomplished.
> The reporting burden on operating departments was quite heavy.
> Operating managers received little if any feedback on their reporting . . . .
> As a result, many were quite cynical about the proliferating reporting burdens placed on them.
> The monthly report (the Public Service Evaluation Report) was not used by managers, nor was it representative of the key factors in their operations.

These findings by outside consultants to the city confirm this author's own assessment of the measurement system.

In March 1980, Alan Harvey became the city manager, replacing retiring Raymond Harbaugh, during whose tenure the productivity measurement system was introduced. Harvey is a different city manager from his predecessor in many ways. The new manager is younger, more involved, more enthusiastic, and deeply aware of the financial challenges facing city governments.

For Alan Harvey, the negative aspects of the measurement system were too apparent and too compelling to be ignored. "It ceased to perform or to be of assistance to departments. It is not addressing the kinds of problems originally designed for, nor providing departments with necessary information," he noted. Harvey acknowledged the generation of massive data but, in most cases, the information was not what departments were looking for. Therefore, it is not surprising that the new city manager ordered that most activities of data gathering under the productivity measurement system be examined and modified.

REDESIGN THE SYSTEM TO FOCUS ON PROGRAMS

The effective management of the city is highly dependent on the ability to collect, analyze, and utilize information. At the same time, management must guard against the accumulation of useless data and filing of costly reports inspired by "data dazzle" rather than management needs. For the city manager, data must contribute to programmatic analysis.

"My approach," said Harvey, "is first to define programs, then to go ahead and determine how we are going to measure the productivity of the programs." Most measurements do not adequately measure program results and productivity. The tendency is to have workload or one-activity measures. "What I want to do," said Harvey, "is to have some modification starting this year (1981), because the available data system is not sophisticated enough to capture some of the data needed."

The core concepts of the change being gradually introduced by the city management may be summarized in the following:

The operations of the city will be

grouped into budget programs focusing on services rather than organization.

A program is the delivery of a service (or a group of similar services) or product to the consumer (public). Therefore a program has a measurable activity, results, or a work product.

Costs are allocated to programs in order to arrive at a true picture of resources used. This allocation includes shared overhead or administrative costs which will be prorated to programs.

Programs are viewed as discrete units distinguishable from each other conceptually and analytically.

Three basic types of measures, as stated by the 1982 budget document, are used to assess whether goals are being achieved: workload statistics, measures of efficiency (productivity), and measures of effectiveness. Applicable measures for which data are currently available are included in the 1982 program budget. However, "additional refinements" of these measures are in progress, according to the city manager.

The program approach, therefore, is the new mode of analysis and measurement in St. Petersburg. The expected benefits of the new design as presented by the city manager include:

1. a more systematic approach to management of services
2. an easier way to introduce a modified version of zero-base-budgeting techniques and facilitate greater flexibility in allocation of resources
3. better review of city activities by the council, mayor, and citizens
4. facilitation of long-range planning of policies and programs
5. greater departmental involvement in setting goals, developing plans, devising measurement techniques, and collecting data
6. use of more relevant data gathered in more efficient methods.

In terms of implementation, we find the 1983 budget achieving some refinements of the new design while encountering some difficulties in specific areas, requiring further revisions. One such difficulty is the inability to depart from organizational lines in formulating program structures. The city manager describes it this way: "Because we do not have the automatic capacity to collect and collate data at the level of detail I want, our budget shows programs approached and limited to departments without crossing departmental lines." The city management is hoping to reach a stage of development where the focus will be on services, irrespective of organizational structure. Another constraint faced in preparing the 1983 budget is the development and use of valid and manageable measures or service rendered by each program. This process is still in progress. "In my opinion," said the City Manager, "it is better to have two to five good and solid measures rather than numerous poor ones." At this stage departments are checking the measures in use to determine their appropriateness.

Beyond these two constraints, the 1983 budget represents a basic departure from previous practices in several ways:

1. Departments are instructed to identify programs and decision packages within their domain, including suggestions for adding to, substituting for, revising, or deleting from the existing program. This is done with consideration to community needs and using citizen input data where appropriate. The suggestions have to be specific and explained in order to allow action by the city council.
2. Departments should establish the relative priority of the remaining programs in terms of importance. (See Appendix I.)
3. Budget estimates should be presented in three cases: worst, most likely, and best case.

For example, the Police Department (PD) identified a list of ten programs of services it performs. Each program could be presented at base level in order of its importance to the department. Under the "worst case" category the most essential programs would be maintained at 89% of current budget ($16,567,300). At this level, five programs, such as public information and neighborhood crime watch, would not exist.

Under the "most likely case" category each of the ten programs would be retained up to current level at 100% of current budget. The "best case" category would include two enhancements, bringing the budget to 102% level. (See Memorandum, Appendix II.)

The program budget as implemented by the city allocates resources in a manner that facilitates measurement of progress toward meeting stated goals. Also, it allows evaluation of allocations in terms of program effectiveness. Through a small group process departments themselves have developed criteria for defining service level and breaking it down into discrete decision packages. This process has made departments prone to look at options and alternatives. For the first time, says the city manager, departments face the question: "Are there some discrete levels of activity that we could possibly do without—under certain circumstances?" Other improvements introduced with the new design include a restoration of greater integration between the budget process and the measurement of city services after a period of organizational and functional separation. Within the departments, as well as at the central level of city management, a meaningful interface of budget estimates and performance measurement is attempted.

The role of the city council is not escaping some subtle and significant change resulting from these revisions. The council is fully involved by reviewing and approving the priority system of programs that recognizes the essential, the important, and the less important. The council has a greater involvement and responsibility in the decision process. The city, therefore, may be in a better position to face fiscal stress and avoid periods of indecision where and when reduction of expenditures may be necessary. St. Petersburg has had a tradition of professional management and inactive interest groups and municipal unions; but even in a less politicized city the new design would improve the capability of a city's management to face worsening financial conditions and make retrenchment decisions.

Finally, the management of the city of St. Petersburg and its decision processes are constantly revised and improved in order to achieve higher levels of rationality and objectivity. However, as Alan Harvey concedes, "you have to accommodate your professional direction and experience to reality and make adjustments accordingly."

BIBLIOGRAPHY

F. J. LYDEN and E. G. MILLER, *Public Budgeting: Program Planning and Implementation*, 4th ed. (Prentice-Hall, Englewood Cliffs, N.J.), 1982.

HARRY HATRY, "Performance Measurement Principles and Techniques," *Public Productivity Review* (December 1980), 312-39.

The Urban Institute, *Measuring the Effectiveness of Basic Municipal Services* (Washington, D.C., 1974).

_____, *Monetary Incentives and Work Standards in Five Cities* (Washington, D.C., 1977).

FOR DISCUSSION

The above case presented the city of St. Petersburg in its attempt to measure municipal services. The city's struggle to implement an effective system of measurement and evaluation illustrates numerous administrative issues.

Stage 1

By studying the case, the students may analyze the decisions that were made—with varying degrees of success—as the city tried to reach its proclaimed goals. For the purpose of discussion, the case may be viewed as consisting of two stages of development representing different managerial orientations.

The first stage extended over the period between 1973 and 1980, during which the comprehensive system of measurement was initiated. It is clear from the unfolding of events that the efforts during this period fell short of their targets. In order to develop his/her evaluative skills, the student should be able to answer specific questions about this period, such as the following:

1. Do you believe there was a thorough understanding of the measurement system prior to implementation so that participants knew what to expect and what was expected of them? If not, how can such understanding be ensured?
2. The active support of the city manager was required to ensure success of the change proposed. Do you believe such leadership was forthcoming during the first stage?
3. What were the organizational problems that occurred during the implementation of the measurement system, and how were they faced by management? Can you suggest alternative responses?
4. Assume you were the city manager of St. Petersburg between 1973 and 1980; what managerial decisions would you alter?
5. There is a consensus that the productivity measurement system in operation by 1974 failed to achieve its goals. The student should be able to discuss some of the reasons for this failure of policy and

techniques and recommend alternative approaches.

Stage 2

The second stage of the case extended from 1980 to the present. During this time substantive changes were introduced, among them, altering the focus of the system, the quantity and quality of data collected, the role of municipal departments, and the role of the city manager. Students should discuss the following questions:

1. In your opinion, what were the most important changes made in order to adapt the previous practices of measurement to serve programmatic designs?
2. Review the relationship between measurement of services and the budget process during the preparation and authorization stages in terms of organization and process, comparing the first and second periods.
3. Needless to say, the city manager and the employees face an increasingly complex environment. They are concerned with shrinking revenue and the increasing demand for services. Which measurement design offers greater flexibility of managerial decisions about retrenchment — the comprehensive one, as implemented in the first period, or the program-oriented one, as implemented in the second period? In what ways is one better than the other?

General Instructions

The program and decision packages have been grouped by department. The first page of each department's grouping is a summary page listing the base level program and decision packages in declining priority, i.e., the highest priority program is listed first, and the program of lesser priority (not necessarily of importance) is listed last.

There are three horizontal, colored (red, green, and blue) lines on this page that denote the department's recommendations for worst case (red); most probable (green), and best case (blue) options. For example, the programs (base level and decision packages) that fall above the red line are the department's recommendations for their "worst case" budget.[1] Similarly, all those programs listed above the green line are its recommended "most probable" budget, and those above the blue line a "best case" budget.

Assignment

To prepare yourself to use our time most expeditiously, please follow the described steps. To be most helpful and maximize the benefit of the workshop, the worksheets should be completed *before the workshop*.

Step 1: Analyze each program carefully and thoroughly.

Step 2: Carefully considering *only those programs listed above the red line*, list in the space provided those programs you think should be changed in some way. "Change" is defined as meaning you: Don't think programs belong there; other programs should be added; other programs should be substituted, the program should be revised; or some other problem exists. Be sure to be specific and note what change you would recommend for the council's consideration. These will be discussed at the workshop where conclusions will be based on the consensus of the council.

Step 3: You will now be asked to make a judgment of the relative priority of the remaining programs. Your task now is to evaluate the remaining programs, i.e., those listed below the red line (worst case), and list them in one of the following three categories:

ESSENTIAL   These programs are critical to the city and its service program. They represent activities that are strongly related to the city's basic responsibilities or are so important as to be almost indistinguishable from basic service. These should be cut only as à last resort.

IMPORTANT   These programs add quality to the city's service program. They provide depth or breadth to our existing base-level program or are activities in their own right that supplement or add dimension to other higher priority programs. They could be cut, but only in the event of major reductions.

OF LESSER IMPORTANCE   These activities are, by their nature, nice-to-have services. They may or may not be directly involved with a base-level service. The activity represents a significant quality dimension to the service program. Loss of these programs would be difficult but could be accommodated within manageable proportions.

The colors mentioned here are not shown in this sample but appeared in the original source.

•

Step 4: On the worksheet, using the categories defined in Step 3, classify the programs or decision packages below the red line into one of the three categories:

ESSENTIAL—

IMPORTANT—

OF LESSER IMPORTANCE—

Step 5: Your listing will be consolidated at the workshop and a council consensus of the priority developed.

APPENDIX II
MEMORANDUM

TO: Neal L. Heintz, Director, Budget & Management

FROM: S. F. Lynn, Chief of Police

DATE: January 27, 1982

SUBJECT: Summary of Program Budget

     The attached information includes a list of ten program which I have identified for the Police Department. Each program is presented at base level through current level in order of its importance to the department.

     For your convenience, the worst case, most likely case, and best case for this department are summarized below.

A.   Worst Case
1.   Patrol Operations is maintained at its current strength of 256 officers, 29 sergeants, and 5 lieutenants. This staffing will provide the entire City with police protection including a fourth relief to provide coverage during periods of peak activity. In addition, foot patrols can be deployed two of the three shifts and K–9 officers will be available 24 hours a day. Officers in the Field Training Officer Program will have the time to fully train new officers. The Traffic Section will continue to handle approximately 65% – 75% of all reported accidents, allowing Patrol officers to handle calls for service and perform directed patrol.
2.   Investigations—Includes Narcotics, Vice, Intelligence, Youth Services, S.O.S., Homicide, Rape, Robbery, Assault, Larceny, Worthless checks, Burglary, Auto Theft.
    a.   Narcotics Section—allows for a minimal number of protracted investigations, which will limit the number of seizures of drugs and property.
    b.   Vice—reduces the number of protracted investigations involving vice-related crimes.
    c.   Intelligence—There will be no proactive investigations, only tactical investigations.

d. Youth Services — will provide initial and follow-up investigations for crimes committed against or by children. Also provides for a School Liaison Officer Program for the schools.

e. S.O.S. — will provide for the covert coverage of crime pattern abuse.

f. Homicide/Rape/Robbery/Assault — The Robbery/Homicide Squad will become one unit, and only simple batteries will be investigated. Limited investigation of purse snatch, muggings and felonious assaults. Throwing deadly missiles investigations are eliminated.

g. Larceny — Shoplifting will be investigated; however, arson and bomb investigations will be eliminated. Number of case assignments is 40%.

h. Worthless Checks — will provide follow-up investigation on forgeries and felony worthless checks, but will eliminate misdemeanor worthless checks under $50.00. Eliminates Saturday coverage.

i. Burglary — will provide follow-up for burglaries; however, case assignment is at 30%. Eliminates night and week-end coverage.

j. Auto Theft — will investigate thefts of mopeds, auto accessories, license tags, and autos. Eliminates week-end and night shift.

3. Records/Police Information — The front desk will be manned 24 hours a day; however, patrol officers will be required to fill in during illness, vacation, and holidays. The Sheriff's Office must furnish a deputy for bonding services. Service to the public will be considerably reduced.

4. Emergency Complaint Writers — The number of complaint writer positions would remain at current strength allowing for the processing of administrative and non-emergency calls. The sergeants would be eliminated from the Communication Center resulting in less supervision and reduction of criminal law expertise. CAD is also eliminated.

5. Fire/EMS Dispatching — provides for the current operation of this program.

6. Public Information — program does not exist at this level.

7. Neighborhood Crime Watch — program does not exist at this level.

8. Crime Awareness Speeches — program does not exist at this level.

9. Bicycle Licensing — program does not exist at this level.

10. Off-Duty — program does not exist at this level.

B. Most Likely Case — This case would bring each of our ten programs up to current level.

C. Best Case — There are two enhancements which this department would like if the Best Case is approved.

1. To add a sergeant's position to supervise the SOS Squad. There have been 12 officer positions approved; however, the squad needs a sergeant to supervise the squad, take care of administrative functions and make the squad more effective through organization and planning.

2. Institute a Selective Enforcement Unit consisting of ten police officers and one sergeant. This unit will be utilized for several different functions including a Selective Enforcement Unit, Crime Prevention Unit, Crime Deterrent Unit, and a Selective Foot Patrol Unit. This unit will maintain the flexibility to act in whatever function is needed according to the situation.

This summarizes the worst, most likely, and best case situations. If you have additional questions, please contact me.

24

*Dayton, Ohio's Program Strategies**

In the 1960s and early 1970s, the city of Dayton adopted several "modern management" techniques, such as program budgeting, management-by-objectives (MBO), and citizen surveys. In 1974, these were combined into a decision-making framework called "program strategies." As it evolved, Dayton's program strategies framework now includes: a strategic planning process; a five-year program budgeting structure; special client surveys, as well as regular general citizen surveys, MBO and audits of the MBO programs, and special program evaluations; and a performance-based merit pay plan for executive level, senior, and middle managers.

The purpose of the program strategies framework is to provide the city commission with a practical means to articulate as well as control public policy issues. Further, it is designed to insure the translation of policies and strategies into programs, and programs into desired outcomes. As shown in Exhibit 24.1, program strategies assume a continuum of decisions, actions, and measurable results operating within three strategic dimensions. As summarized below, each dimension has its own set of key questions and its own planning and measurement format:

Dimension	Question	Planning and Measurement Format
Policy	What ought to be?	Policy goals and strategies
Situation	What was? What is?	Effectiveness measures, in terms of community conditions and perceptions
Approach	How to? How much? Which?	Tactical plans; resource allocation; and program, management, and personal objectives

The program strategies process assumes that the purpose of all public policy is to control or alter certain community conditions through the delivery of municipal services. Though I will describe the dimensions individually, remember they are intended to work together as a continuum (hence the circle format of Exhibit 24.1), with the results of each dimension affecting the actions in all three. The three brief cases at the end of this example demonstrate, to some extent, how the dimensions affect each other.

THE POLICY DIMENSION

For a body of public policy to be more than an expression of lofty goals, it must be internally consistent, measurable over time, and reasonably achievable. In the Dayton decision-making process, the apex of the policy hierarchy consists of our grand strategies (see Exhibit 24.1), which are annually reviewed by the city commission at the commencement of the budget preparation cycle. Each of these four policy goals have a set of measurable objectives. For example, the goal of "economic vitality" is delineated by eight objectives such

*Adapted from Paul R. Woodie, Assistant City Manager. Reprinted from Paul D. Epstein, *Using Performance Measurement in Local Government: A Guide to Improving Decisions, Performance, and Accountability* (Washington, D.C.: U.S. Department of Housing and Urban Development, 1981 draft). Forthcoming under same title from Van Nostrand Reinhold.

EXHIBIT 24.1. Program Strategies, Dayton, Ohio.

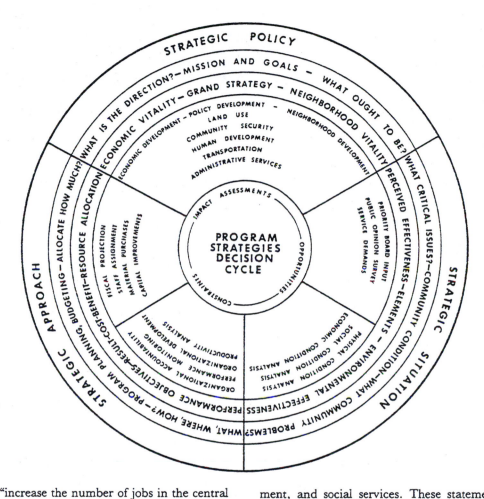

as "increase the number of jobs in the central business district." Progress toward each objective is annually appraised using verifiable indicators (how many jobs this year compared to last). All other strategic, departmental objectives, and major legislative actions, are subordinate to these policy goals and tested against the set of objectives.

Just below these grant strategies are the three- to five-year action plans called "strategy statements." Strategy statements have been formally adopted for several issues, including transportation, land use, economic development, and social services. These statements are usually fashioned by a task force of citizens, policy analysts, and program operators. Each action plan includes documentation of current community trends, a set of strategy objectives, program priorities, and demographic targets. Most importantly, each statement must contain an impact assessment on each policy goal. For example, the transportation strategy describes a plan not only for the efficient movement of people and goods, but also for enhancing economic vitality and neighborhood vitality. The consequence of this process resulted in the abandonment of public easement within neighborhoods in order to positively affect the perception of neighborhood integrity.

Without the hinge provided by the strategy statements, the policy goals would be merely rhetorical, and the program objectives might be nothing more than bean counting.

The Policy Dimension of Dayton's Program Strategies

I. Grand Strategies

Policy Goals For: Economic Vitality
Neighborhood Vitality
Dayton's Unique
    Character
Regional Leadership

II. Strategy Statements

3-to 5-Year
Action Plans For: Economic Develop-
    ment
Neighborhood
    Development
Human Development
Land Use
Transportation
Community Services

THE SITUATION

In a political environment the urgency of a given policy or strategy is dependent upon either the perception or reality of a community condition trend. Perception and reality are equally important to an elected official. For example, while downtown might statistically be the safest place to be in the city, there may well be a general feeling of insecurity on the part of both merchants and potential customers. To ignore one fact or the other might result in an irrational action by the elected officials. The city manager could well convince the city commission that no problem exists and, therefore, no action is necessary. Or the elected officials, under pressure from

merchants, might order the deployment of additional police downtown resulting in a reduction of police protection elsewhere or a large increase in the police budget. Both solutions are incorrect. If, indeed, the sense of security downtown is low, the feeling will inevitably translate itself into loss of trade and loss of tax base. The mandate of our economic vitality goal would be adversely affected. However, putting extra police where there is no real crime problem is costly and inefficient. This problem did arise in Dayton. Our response is described in the first brief case at the end of this example.

That is but one example of the importance of combining verifiable "facts" about community conditions with public perceptions. This process results in "community condition statements," which exist for every major service, strategy, or new program. The statements are designed to provide decision-makers with basic information about trends, perceptions, and demographics. As a part of this effort, the city has commissioned an annual public opinion survey since the early 70's. This survey provides essential information about ongoing effectiveness of basic municipal services. In addition special surveys are conducted periodically to appraise opinions and attitudes which affect human choice (e.g., locational decisions of businesses), as well as special "client" surveys of the users of specific programs.

There is an important fact that should be remembered when using opinion surveys. Surveys are only useful in establishing a trend line. Analyzing a single survey, and proclaiming that 65% of the general public believe streets are clean, and that they should be, will only raise the question about the other 35%. Or ranking satisfaction of one service over another may only mean that one is more popular than the other. (No one thinks the level of housing inspection is satisfactory.) What *is* important in determining program effectiveness is a comparison of one year to the next.

The importance of trends can be extended generally to all measures of community conditions. Rarely is a condition found through periodic measurement that is so hazardous to public health and safety that immediate, "all-out" action against the problem must take precedence over other city business. Generally, new programs, or changes to existing programs, to improve conditions can be considered in the context of overall community strategies during the normal planning and budgeting cycles. Policy and program effectiveness are determined by the *trends* of measured community conditions. Are they better this year than last? Are they worse? Are we winning or losing the game to reach our policy objectives?

THE APPROACH

Within the policy goals and strategies and in response to changing community conditions, programs are devised, modified, and abandoned; tactical plans are established; resources are allocated; and individual performance contracts are drawn. Objectives are seen as a means toward an end. Resources are generally the fuel.

As part of Dayton's longstanding management-by-objectives program, every program within the city or funded by the city has a set of annual objectives and corresponding performance measures. Overall, the MBO program involves a mix of both effectiveness measures and efficiency measures. The objectives are prepared by the departments in response to a budget message, which includes the policy goals, strategies, and condition statements. After a determination by the policy analyst that the objectives are responsive, they are reviewed by the various neighborhood councils and appropriate task forces and submitted to the city commission as part of the program strategies document. Here is a sample of these program objectives and performance measures:

Objective: To increase by 3% the level of perceived security among residents.
Performance measure: Percentage of public-

opinion survey respondents who classify neighborhoods as "safe."

Objective: To limit the number of valid citizen complaints pertaining to waste collection.
Performance Measures: (a) valid complaints per 1,000 housing units served; (b) total number of valid complaints.

Objective: Complete 95% of hazardous street and alley repairs within one work day.
Performance Measures: (a) number of hazardous street and alley repairs; (b) number completed within one work day; (c) percentage completed within one work day; (d) percentage completed within three workdays.

Departments report performance against most objectives quarterly. (See Exhibit 24.2.)

In addition to organizational objectives, for the past several years the city has had an incentive pay plan for management employees that centers around a set of personal and professional achievement objectives. The incentive pay plan was started with "executive level" managers (e.g., the city manager and department directors) and has recently been extended down to middle managers at the program level. The plan allows the city commission to apply the limited funds available for managerial raises differentially to reflect individual performance. It gives managers an extra incentive to achieve the city's objectives.

The Office of Management and Budget coordinates the MBO program and annually conducts a number of "MBO audits" and special evaluation studies of service agencies to verify reported performance and identify potential operating improvements.

CONCLUSION

Program objectives, even when measured, ought not to become the end product. Programs are means, not ends. The salient ques-

EXHIBIT 24.2 1981 Quarterly Performance Review

GROUP ADMINISTRATIVE SERVICES	RESPONSIBLE AGENCY	QUARTER

OBJECTIVES	PERFORMANCE CRITERIA	UNITS		
		Qtr.	Y.T.D.	81 Est.
ASSISTANT CITY MANAGER FOR ADMINISTRATIVE SERVICES				
1. *Satisfactorily complete all 1981 Program Strategies and strategic planning issues assigned to Administrative Services Group.	1. Percent of assignments satisfactorily completed	20% (1 of 5)	20% (1 of 5)	100%
2. *To assist Directors in the Group in achieving at least 90% of the 1981 high priority departmental objectives.	2a. Number of High Priority Objectives b. Percent of High Priority Objectives completed			45 90%
3. *To achieve the 1981 Affirmative Action objectives for non-competitive positions for the Administrative Services Group.	3. Dates reports of Affirmative Action Monitoring Committee submitted	–	–	6/81
AVIATION DEPARTMENT				
AIRPORT				
Administration				
1. *To maintain self-supporting status of Dayton International Airport (D.I.A.) by having a break-even or better financial operation in 1981.	1a. 1981 D.I.A. revenues b. 1981 D.I.A. expenses c. 1981 D.I.A. revenues minus expenses	1.7 1.5 .2	3.3 3.1 .2	$7.8 mil $7.8 mil -0-
2. *To maintain the self-supporting status of Dayton General Airport South (D.G.A.S.) by insuring that expenses do not exceed revenues by more than $42,000 in 1981.	2a. 1981 D.G.A.S. revenues b. 1981 D.G.A.S. expenses c. 1981 D.G.A.S. revenues minus expenses	10,158 14,691 (4,533)	26,815 61,284 (34,469)	$263,000 $305,000 ($42,000)
3. *To plan and have under construction by 12/31/81 at least 75% of 1981 Capital Improvement Projects.	3. Percent of capital improvement Projects completed or under construction by 12/31/81	7%	33%	75%
4. *To insure actual Dayton International Airport revenues for 1981 are at least 97.5% of forecasted revenues.	4a. Actual revenues b. Percent of forecast	1.7 89.5	3.3 86.5	97.5%
Operations				
6. *To maintain compliance with all present FAA certification requirements under Part 139, "Certification of Airports".	6a. Number of findings by FAA b. Number of warnings	0 0	0 0	-0- -0-
7. *To avoid closing the Dayton International Airport due to maintenance or related problems in 1981.	7. Number of times Airport closed	0	0	-0-
10. *To insure the number of hours in unscheduled down time on the HVAC does not exceed 1980 hours by insuring the use of the preventive maintenance program.	10a. Number of hours in unscheduled down time in 1980 b. Number of hours in unscheduled down time in 1981	26 70	218 220	785
Safety				
11. *To plan and direct the Security Program for the D.I.A. under FAA security regulations Part 107, and insure no findings or fines levied against the City.	11a. Number of findings or fines levied b. Number of warnings issued	0 0	0 0	-0- -0-
12. *To maintain compliance with the appropriate sections of FAA Certification Part 139 relating to Crash Fire Rescue (CFR).	12a. Number of notice to Airmen (NOTAM) issued under Part 139 b. Number of unannounced test runs c. Time of first vehicle in seconds d. Time of second vehicle in seconds e. Time of third vehicle in seconds	0 1 90 120 120	0 2 125 172 172	-0- 4 180 240 270
13. *To maintain response time and clear time on calls by the security station to 4 minutes or less on response time and 15 minutes or less on clear time.	13a. Average response time quarterly in minutes b. Average clear time quarterly in minutes	3.5 10.9	3.4 9.6	4 15
*HIGH PRIORITY OBJECTIVES				

tions in any performance measurement system are: Why are we measuring this? Where have we been? and Where are we going? Unless we can answer the latter, we might as well be counting beans.

THREE DAYTON DECISION CASES

1. Perception vs. Reality

As mentioned previously, in Dayton the statistical reality of low crime rates downtown was in direct conflict with citizens' perceptions of insecurity, as measured by citizen surveys. The situation of people feeling unsafe downtown threatened the policy goal of achieving economic vitality. But moving more police downtown, where there was little crime, would either significantly increase costs or leave other areas underprotected.

The proper approach was to define the problem as one of perception. Our response was to devise an action program whose singular purpose was to alter feelings of safety. It had two thrusts:

> Since the image of downtown was fostered by the media, we countered with a media campaign and a presentation to editorial boards.
> Since the perception of safety could be raised by a "police presence," we established a civilian force of uniformed parking control officers with walkie-talkies. The cost was half that of police officers and was self-supporting through increased collections of parking fines.

In order to measure our program's success, we conducted an opinion survey of downtown merchants, downtown customers, and the general public prior to implementation to gauge the intensity of feelings of safety. After a year of experimentation, we commissioned another survey. Surprising to me, there was a rather dramatic increase in the feeling of safety. If there had not been, we were prepared to drop the program entirely.

2. Efficiency vs. Effectiveness

In 1974, in response to low citizen satisfaction with the cleanliness of alleys, the city commission included in the five-year service plan a monthly alley cleaning program. Since this was a new program, we were able to employ the latest technology and the most efficient application of manpower. Nevertheless, the general perception of cleanliness continued to decline. An evaluation suggested some minor adjustments and recommended a differential service in each neighborhood depending on the perception of cleanliness. Unfortunately, even this did not alter general feelings. As a result, at the end of the fourth year a decision had to be made. What action would you recommend, and why?

3. The Objective Should Follow the Policy

Since the late 60's the city had established a program objective to demolish 200 nuisance structures per year. After fine-tuning the program in the mid-70's, we were able to efficiently meet the production requirement. Nevertheless, the commission and the neighborhoods were concerned. After drawing a "condition statement," two facts emerged. First, the inventory of nuisance structures was growing at the rate of 300 per year. The city commission had unwittingly adopted an objective to get farther and farther behind the problem. Second, while demolition increased the sense of security in certain neighborhoods, it reduced the feeling of neighborhood prosperity in others, so the contribution to the neighborhood vitality policy goal was, at best, mixed. What was called for was a differential approach, using demolition as one means, and sufficient resources to deal, in a variety of ways, with 300 nuisance structures.

CHAPTER SEVEN

RISK MANAGEMENT

Risk management is only one component of a set of general concerns that constitute the diverse and complex area of *financial management*. The latter is a potpourri of relatively technical, largely administrative, and increasingly sophisticated responsibilities associated with managing a jurisdiction's financial resources and assessing its overall financial condition and direction. Financial management is recognized as a cornerstone of efficient and effective management, a pillar of sound budgeting, and a source of potential savings, earnings, and legal and financial liabilities. Specifically, it most often refers to: risk, cash, debt, and pension management; tax administation; purchasing, inventory, and leasing functions; and fiscal analysis and forecasting. Data processing, grants management, and contract negotiating (including labor contracts) may fall under the classification as well.

Some of these areas are covered by cases in other chapters of this casebook. Case no. 8 deals with tax choice, no. 14 with grants management, no. 18 with a lease/buy decision, and nos. 19 and 20 with labor contracts. The cases in the next three chapters examine risk, debt, and cash management concerns, plus evaluating and forecasting financial conditions.

Risk management has been defined as "preventing and reducing a jurisdiction's exposure to the risks of accidental loss of its assets."[1] Especially important in light of changes in the concepts of "sovereign immunity," preventative health, and labor safety and compensation, the discussion of risk management is introduced by an excerpt from the International City Management Association's study of current practices (introduction to case no. 25). A glossary of terms is appended to the case.

Following this excerpt are three evaluative cases drawn from the experiences of local governments. Case no. 25, "Kirksville's Risk Management Program," probes the issue of insurance in a small community and acquaints the case reader with coinsurance, agreed amount endorsements, and updating policy coverage. The case on an occupation health program, no. 26, describes the implementation of a larger county jurisdiction's program "to reduce the rate of sick leave usage

---

[1] Edward A. Lehan, "Ease Budget Strains by Managing Risk," *Financial Management Digest* (7), p. 1.

through the provision of health care services." Case no. 27 is based upon Westchester County's effort to "cut losses" and traces the development of an Office of Risk Management, insurance and indemnification requirements, a monitoring system, and a countywide safety program. All three focus upon the importance of protecting assets by minimizing loss as an ongoing management concern.

25

Kirksville's Risk Management Program *

INTRODUCTION

Every local government is faced with the task of protecting itself from various types of loss: loss resulting from damage to a vehicle fleet, loss caused by negligence of a public employee, and loss occurring through on-the-job injury. Because of the diverse nature of local government operations, the possibility of and exposure to loss are almost infinite. A typical local government provides services as varied as housing, health care, education, transportation, public safety, sanitation, recreation, and criminal justice. And the physical assets of a local government may range from an airport to a zoo. Taking action to protect the government from these exposures is the function of risk management.

Over the years local governments have typically protected themselves by purchasing insurance. However, their ability to do this changed drastically during the 1970's. This was due to legal, social, and economic developments which profoundly affected the availability and cost of public sector insurance. The most dramatic development was the elimination by the courts of the common law—"doctrine of sovereign immunity." Sovereign immunity protected governmental entities from third-party liability suits, e.g., a person injured in a traffic accident suing a city for not posting a stop sign at a hazardous intersection. The elimination of sovereign immunity

meant that citizens who considered themselves wronged by the actions of the government could now sue the government for damages.

During the 1970's individuals or groups of citizens suing the government became a common occurrence. Suits ranged from individuals seeking damages for civil rights violations to citizens seeking relief from airport noise pollution. As these suits proliferated and as the courts became more liberal in their awards, commercial insurers came to view local governments as a poor risk. The market for public sector insurance contracted, premiums soared, and many kinds of coverage disappeared.

In response to these pressures local governments began to reassess their methods of financing and controlling exposures. With this reassessment came a renewed interest in risk management and a greater role for risk management in governmental operations.

What Is Risk Management?

Risk management is a planned approach to protecting a local government from accidental loss. Risk management focuses on controlling the risk of loss in the following areas:

1. Loss of property, which includes both real property (e.g., bridges, buildings), and personal property (e.g., cash, inventories, equipment, vehicles).
2. Loss through liability suits which could result from either:
    a. *contractual liability* incurred through lease agreements, construction contracts, purchase agreements, and/or service agreements
    b. *tort liability* incurred through medical malpractice, workers' compensation claims, false arrest, and/or libel suits

*Adapted by permission from Paula R. Valente (in cooperation with the Public Risk and Insurance Management Association), *Current Approaches to Risk Management: A Directory of Practices,* Management Information Service Special Report No. 7 (Washington, D.C.: International City Management Association, November 1980), pp. v, vi, 11–13, 45. For annotated bibliography, see pp. 47–48. Reprinted with permission from the International City Management Association.

3. Loss through employee illness, injury, or work stoppage.

What Is a Risk Management Program?

A risk management program comprises five basic elements: identification, evaluation, control, funding, and administration of risks. Risk control and risk funding are the centerpieces of the risk management functions, so more emphasis is given to them.

I. *Risk Identification* is a systematic process of identifying all of a municipality's resources that are subject to accidental loss.

II. *Risk Evaluation* involves efforts to measure the loss potential of each identified risk, that is, how frequently the loss is likely to occur and how severe it might be.

III. *Risk Control* involves efforts to avoid or reduce risk.

    1. *Avoidance of Risk*: With this method a municipality simply decides to forego a program or service because the risks involved are too great.

    2. *Reduction of Risk*: This method focuses on eliminating or preventing losses by reducing incidences of personal injury and liability claims. Safety management is an integral part of this method and includes such activities as:

        a. Personnel safety programs—to develop safety standards and procedures to meet federal, state, and local occupational health and safety laws.

        b. Motor vehicle safety programs—to train employees in safe driving techniques and to establish preventive maintenance procedures.

        c. Property conservation programs—to protect property from loss due to fire and natural disaster.

        d. Environmental protection programs—to control the disposal of solid, toxic, liquid, and gaseous wastes.

        e. Emergency preparedness programs—to develop contingency plans to handle potential disasters, either man-made (e.g., train derailments, bomb threats, airplane crashes) or natural (e.g., floods, hurricanes, ice storms).

IV. *Risk Funding* involves establishing the capacity to pay for losses. This can be done either by transferring the risk or retaining the risk.

    1. *Transfer of Risk*: Through this method a municipality funds its risk by purchasing commercial insurance to cover its losses. Risk can also be transferred through inclusion of an indemnity clause in contracts with other entities.

    2. *Retention of Risk*: With this method a municipality funds its risks by assuming responsibility to pay for a portion or all of the potential loss. Retention takes several different forms:

        a. Pure retention—a noninsurance technique in which the municipality pays for any losses incurred out of its current operating budget or from funded reserves.

        b. Retention through deductibles—the assumption of a small portion of the loss (e.g., the first $1,000 of a loss), with the remainder of the loss absorbed by insurance coverage.

        c. Retention with catastrophic insurance coverage—the municipality, through a self-insurance program, assumes of a sizable portion of its incurred losses (e.g., the first $500,000), and purchases commercial catastrophic insurance to cover losses exceeding that level.

d. Retention through pooling with other jurisdictions—a group of local governments pool resources to provide mutual protection from common risks. A typical pool consists of:

- A level of individual self-retention—each entity in the pool assumes a portion of the risk by covering a specified first-dollar portion of the loss.

- A level of collective retention—losses above the self-retention threshold and up to a maximum predetermined amount (e.g., $500,000) are paid for out of reserves which have previously been pooled.

- A level of catastrophic insurance coverage—losses exceeding the upper limit of the pool's collective retention are handled through the purchase of excess insurance coverage.

Pools are becoming more and more common. They are now legal in nineteen states, and it is likely the number will grow as their benefits become more widely known. Some of the benefits pools claim to offer to their members are significantly reduced costs, a broader range of coverage, better catastrophic coverage, and improved loss prevention and control procedures.

V. *Risk Administration* focuses on the development of the administrative capacity needed to carry out the risk management function. An integral part of this task is establishing the lines of authority for the program and defining a program philosophy and goals.

KIRKSVILLE'S PROGRAM

Kirksville, Missouri, is one of many communities where the amount of city funds expended for insurance premiums, deductibles, and employee benefits is second only to salaries as the largest fixed cost; but, like most small communities (population: 15,443), Kirksville cannot justify a full-time risk manager. Generally, the person most likely to perform some or all of the risk management functions has other duties and responsibilities that overshadow risk management. It is all too easy to assume that insurance will take care of itself while dealing with the more pressing issues of personnel, finance, budgeting, record-keeping, and other daily administrative activities.

Because of the increased exposure due to the loss of sovereign immunity and the additional role cities play in providing leisure-time activities, code enforcement, workers compensation claims, and other potential loss areas, the old method of letting insurance take care of itself simply will not work. The simultaneous challenges of increased expectations for expanded services, spiraling inflation, and community pressure to reduce expenditures have forced cities to seriously evaluate how to use insurance dollars more effectively. Kirksville is currently in the process of correcting the heretofore self-perpetuating deficiencies through the establishment of risk management policies and methods to assure that its insurance program will be appropriately monitored and implemented.

Determining Problem Areas

The problems and solutions found in Kirksville may have some applicability in other small communities. After extensive research and evaluation of our program, four areas surfaced as the most serious obstacles to the successful implementation of a risk management program using existing staff and resources.

The first problem that had to be addressed was to develop a clear-cut policy on what to insure and for how much. It was fruitless to attack the problem of risk exposure until it was determined to what extent risk could be assumed and where the various exposures existed. A thorough inventory of existing property, buildings, and vehicles and detailed loss records were mandatory to make the best decisions regarding needed changes in risk coverage. This was a time-consuming task and one that proved frustrating because of the unavailability of information. Much of the data collection was performed by persons most associated with the area; for example, the central garage personnel knew more about the history, status, use, assignment, and number of vehicles in the fleet than existed in city hall files. For the bulk of this data gathering, Kirksville utilized a management intern from the local university, who proved invaluable to the city.

Once the information had been gathered, the person most responsible for risk management needed to review the data and formulate some recommendations for the city council. Some of the policy considerations included

1. Whether to insure vehicles over a certain age for damages.
2. What level of deductible should the city assume for property and liability insurance.
3. What types of blanket coverage could be utilized.

After these decisions were made, the individual policies were recorded. This record served as the foundation for a risk management manual. The manual outlined all of the major provisions of the policy and was reviewed with the entire management staff. Kirksville is currently reviewing the rough data and refining its manual.

The second problem dovetailed with the first. After researching and documenting the current inventory of property and vehicles, the inventory data were compared with current insurance policies. We found we had too many agents and policies and too much decentralization of knowledge. As of the first part of 1979, the city had twenty-five separate policies with eighteen companies and thirteen different agents. Moreover, it was found, many facilities were not insured: a fire station, the waste-water treatment plant, and the airport T-hangars.

A simple grouping by policy type, i.e., fire, boiler and machinery, inland marine, general liability, or public officials liability, exposed much duplicate coverage or no coverage at all. Reading policies to determine the exceptions and levels of coverage led to issues that needed clarification by city policy, for example: Does the general liability policy exclude product liability? —a possible problem if the city operates a utility.

Competitive bidding has been the prescription for many insurance ills in recent years. It is true that competitive rates are desirable, but there are hidden dangers to placing insurance out for bid. The first is the design of the bid specifications. There are boilerplate specifications for certain types of coverage available, which may or may not reflect the desires of the city. Many communities use a selection board for development of specifications and placement; this is an excellent idea if qualified persons, other than current or future agents, sit on the board.

The recent trend has been not to select agents or individual policies but, through prequalification review, to use agents/brokers or large brokerage firms. This solution could cause considerable problems in a small community when the prevalent feeling is to "keep the business in town." The key area to review is that of services. If a local agent has provided excellent service in the past and can present a competitive bid proposal, his/her past service should be given prime consideration.

One final pitfall of bidding coverage is that of duplicate bids from different agents using the same insurance company. The best way to combat this is to ask for an "agent of record" for any companies that may bid on the package. Kirksville, for instance, experienced this problem with three agents using the same low-bid company.

The third area most likely to become a problem in a small community is failing to update policy coverage amounts at the time of renewal. This oversight can occur whether a risk management manual is in effect or not; an update is simply a part of good risk management. Most property insurance policies contain two important pieces of information on the face of the document. The first is the property covered, the amount of coverage, and on what the coverage is based (either replacement cost or actual cash value). The second item is the coinsurance clause. Both of these items can cause an unpleasant surprise at the time of a loss.

The past practice has been to have an independent appraiser establish the actual cash value of an existing structure prior to the award or renewal of the policy. Although an appraisal is a good idea, its cost can be prohibitive for a small·community. One less expensive method is for city staff to use a "costimator"—an annual booklet published by some insurance companies that provides a per-square-foot cost estimate based on utilization and construction material. Requesting the "agreed amount endorsement," the figure derived from the "costimator," when awarding or renewing a policy, can be helpful because the insurer is, in effect, agreeing that the value stated in the policy is an acceptable one.

The mistake of not updating a policy's face value and not having an agreed amount endorsement can cause serious problems when a loss occurs. The coinsurance penalty, very simply stated, is the insured agreeing to ab-sorb a portion of a loss, generally 10–20 percent, based upon the current value of the structure at the time of loss. For example, Kirksville had for many years insured its city hall for $110,000. Based upon costimator calculations, the building and contents were worth $775,000. Such underinsurance could have caused a serious financial loss. If a $50,000 loss had occurred, the city could only have recovered $8,871. The formula for reimbursement is as follows:

$$\frac{\$110,000 \text{ (coverage)}}{80\% \text{ (coinsurance) x \$775,000 (value) x \$50,000 (loss)}} = \$8,871$$

Under the recently awarded insurance, using agreed amount endorsements, the entire loss can be recovered.

The final challenge for the small community is one of ongoing review of the loss-control efforts. At the heart of risk management is the concept that, like any management, it is a day-to-day operation.

A good reporting system, coupled with safety efforts and accident review, can make a community a more attractive client to an insurance company. In fact, even though most premiums are calculated by standard rates, the companies can use such fudge factors as experience, longevity, safety programs, and other catch phrases that allow them to adjust rates.

Kirksville has recently established two committees, the Accident Review Committee, composed of five department heads, and the Safety Committee, a spin-off responsibility of the Employees Council. The Accident Review Committee reviews each property or personal injury; makes recommendations to reduce the likelihood of recurrence; determines if the accident was preventable; and, through the appropriate department head, recommends discipline based upon approved guidelines. The Safety Committee brings potentially dangerous situations to the attention of management. Most insurance companies will provide a safety engineer to help educate employees and establish a safety program.

All recommendations from both committees are brought before the city manager periodically for review in light of fiscal constraints for improvements and severe employee disciplinary actions. To date, a thirty percent reduction in the number of accidents as compared with last year has been experienced.

Results

Risk management for small communities is unique in some ways, but many of the methods for larger communities can be applied. The four most important considerations to address are:

1. The establishment of a clear-cut policy from management concerning insurance and safety management.
2. The reduction of excessive numbers of policies and agents to take advantage of blanket rates and policies.
3. The need to review annually policy amounts and coinsurance clauses to keep penalties to a minimum.
4. The establishment of a good reporting system and loss-control efforts.

Many other aspects of good risk management, such as retention funds, self-insurance, umbrella policies and pooling are certainly important. Nevertheless, they are a group of secondary decisions that should be made once a risk management program is undertaken in earnest. The city of Kirksville will be evaluating these areas once the current program is comfortably in place.

GLOSSARY

Catastrophic insurance coverage Also referred to as excess insurance; insurance coverage for large losses (e.g., over $500,000) and usually up to a specified limit.

Contractual liability The obligation assumed by contract to pay for losses for which another is legally liable.

Deductible A clause in an insurance policy which specifies how much loss the individual (or municipality) must assume before insurance coverage becomes effective. (See First-dollar health insurance coverage.)

Exposure base The financial, physical, and natural resources for which a government is responsible and which are exposed to the risk of accidental loss.

First-dollar health insurance coverage A health insurance policy which contains no deductible and which provides that insurance coverage will start when the first dollar of medical expense is incurred.

Indemnity Compensation for injuries or losses sustained.

Liability The responsibility incurred for the consequences of one's actions, usually actions which create a loss or injury to someone else.

Liability exposure Governmental actions or duties which could result in loss or injury to others and for which the government is held legally liable.

Loss control Reducing or eliminating risks through improvement in security procedures, personnel safety practices, environmental protection, fire prevention, motor vehicle safety, and emergency planning.

Municipal liability Responsibility incurred by local governments for injuries or losses arising from governmental actions.

Pooling A contractual agreement among local governments to share their resources to provide mutual protection against common risks.

Premium The amount paid for an insurance policy.

Risk management A planned approach to protecting a municipality's assets from accidental loss.

Self-insurance (i.e., Retention) A municipality assumes responsibility to pay for a portion or all of incurred losses.

Sovereign immunity Freedom from prosecution granted to governments for losses or injuries caused by governmental actions performed within the scope of their authority.

Tort liability The legal responsibility incurred for a wrongful or negligent act which results in loss or injury to another person (e.g., medical malpractice, false arrests, libel).

Umbrella liability insurance policy An insurance policy that fills the gaps in liability protection associated with basic insurance coverage or self-insurance.

Underwriting The process by which insurance companies accept or reject risks (i.e., prospective insureds).

26

Jefferson County, Alabama's Occupational Health Program *

In 1978 Jefferson County, Alabama (population: 1.4 million), expanded its occupational health program. One health center was already in place serving county hospital employees when two new centers were opened in 1978. The new health centers would serve Public Works Department employees.

The expanded program was implemented to provide better, more immediate care for employees injured on the job; to lessen the work time lost as a result of these injuries; to reduce production costs; and to reduce the rate of sick leave usage through the provision of preventive health care services. The program utilizes on-site health centers to provide on-the-job injury screening, pre-employment physicals, documentation and follow-up of workers' compensation claims, annual physicals, health evaluations, and a clinic to handle minor health complaints (e.g., colds, headaches, sore throats).

The Public Works Department was chosen to participate in the expanded program because its employees are exposed to the greatest risk of on-the-job injury and illness. Also, a large portion of the county's 4,000 employees work within the department (between 28 and 33 percent, depending on the season of the year). When the program was implemented, the average lost time per incident of injury for the Public Works Department was 29 percent *above* that of other county departments.

No codified procedures existed for responding to worker injuries. An analysis of statistical indicators for on-the-job injuries (e.g., severity rate, frequency rate, disabling injury index, and average days charged) showed a sharp, upward trend over the 1971–76 period.

Over that same six-year period sick leave usage (as measured by number of sick leave days used) rose by 136 percent. It was estimated that sick leave usage in 1976 cost the county $819,000 in lost productivity.

Responding to on-the-job injuries posed certain logistical problems that compounded the amount of time and money lost. Because of the lack of on-site health facilities, additional man-hours were lost to transport an injured worker to the county hospital or some other health care facility. The usual procedure was that a fellow employee would drive the injured worker to the appropriate health care facility and wait with him while he was treated. The county estimated that in 1976 this procedure alone cost the county 3,235 production hours and $14,600. In sum, sharp increases in on-the-job injuries, sick leave usage, and production costs led to the decision to expand the county's existing occupational health program.

*Adapted by permission from Paula R. Valente (in cooperation with the Public Risk and Insurance Management Association), *Current Approaches to Risk Management: A Directory of Practices*, Management Information Service Special Report No. 7 (Washington, D.C.: International City Management Association, November 1980) pp. 7–8. Reprinted with permission from the International City Management Association.

DESCRIPTION

The occupational health program for public works employees was initiated in December 1978. In addition to the health center operating at the county hospital, two new health centers were opened, one at each public works regional office. These offices were located at opposite ends of the county; approximately equal numbers of public works employees were assigned to each. Each health center is staffed by a registered nurse. The program is budgeted with the Department of Public Works, but the staff nurses report to the county hospital's director of quality assurance, who supervises the hospital's occupational health program.

The centers are responsible for providing on-the-job injury screening, preemployment physicals, documentation and follow-up of workers' compensation claims, annual physicals, health evaluations, and staffing of a minor complaint health clinic.

Workers injured on the job are seen first by the nurse at the health center, who gives first aid and determines the seriousness of the injury. Care of all minor injuries is provided at these centers; more serious injuries are referred to the county hospital or a private physician. The centers are also responsible for providing follow-up care for all minor injuries and for preparing appropriate reports to supervisors and department heads.

All documentation and follow-up on workers' compensation claims are handled through these facilities. The health center serves as the liaison between all parties involved in the claim: employer, employee, doctor, the county risk manager, and the county personnel board.

The centers also provide preemployment physicals for unskilled workers. The exam is administered after a supervisor has decided to hire the worker but before the final decision is made. The final hiring decision is contingent upon the successful completion of the exam.

The county also provides, free of cost, annual physicals for all county employees at these centers. An individual health profile is developed upon completion of the exam. Both the exam and the profile serve as mechanisms for identifying health problems, establishing health goals, and, in general, raising employee health awareness.

Each of these centers houses a minor complaint health clinic, where employees with minor health problems, such as colds, sore throats, and headaches, can receive basic, nonprescription medication at no cost. The idea is to encourage those employees with minor health problems to come into work rather than stay at home.

Health evaluations are conducted at these centers to monitor sick leave usage. Center personnel try to identify cases of chronic absenteeism, analyze the causes, and in those cases where health problems exist, help correct or eliminate them.

Total operating costs for the three health centers in 1979 was $74,000. This figure includes:

Salaries and employee benefits for three nurses and one clerk, at a cost of $50,000.

Costs of materials and supplies, totalling $19,000.

Capital outlay costs of $5,000 for such items as refrigerators, storage cabinets, typewriters, and medical equipment.

RESULTS

The county's risk manager estimates that for every dollar spent to implement this program, $3.37 is saved. Before the program's inception, the Public Works Department's average lost time per incident, computed for the first three months of 1978, was 29 percent *above* the average rate of other county departments. However, when the statistics were computed for the same three month period of 1979, public works was 13 percent *below* the average. The rate of improvement was 120 percent over the preceding year.

Seventy-five percent of all on-the-job injuries are now cared for at the health centers. Communication between the health centers, hospital physicians, and clinics is well established, enabling expeditious care of those workers who are referred for treatment.

Furthermore, the screening of on-the-job injuries performed by these centers provides a coherent, orderly mechanism for investigating the causes of injuries and for monitoring workers' compensation claims.

Before this occupational health program was started, unskilled laborers were not required to undergo physicals before being hired, even though all other prospective county employees were required to do so. The pre-employment physicals for unskilled workers have helped eliminate those job candidates whose existing health problems would become a liability for the county. Twenty percent of the candidates for unskilled jobs have been rejected for employment as a result of this health

screening. The program also has brought about a reduction in time lost from work due to injury or illness. The annual physicals and health evaluations have helped in many instances to identify and treat health problems, thus reducing the number of sick days used.

The program has been so successful that the county has opened another health center at the county courthouse, serving an additional 450 employees. The Jefferson County risk manager reports that county employees have responded very favorably to the occupational health program. The program has had a very positive effect upon employee morale and employer–employee relations within the Jefferson County government.

27

*Risk Management in Westchester County**

INTRODUCTION

In March, 1974, Alfred Del Bello became the county executive of Westchester County. This date also marks the birth of the Office of Risk Management. Historically, the insurance responsibility was handled by an individual in the Law Department. This individual had various other jobs and no authority, although it was needed, to develop and implement policy or a risk and insurance program.

The primary goals of the Office of Risk Management were and continue to be the analysis and reduction of risk that could cause Westchester County severe financial loss, thereby forcing a reduction in services to tax-

*By Robert M. Bieber, Ebasco Risk Management Consultants, Inc. The author is the former Director of Risk Management, Westchester County, New York.

payers. The objectives to help meet this goal were as follows:

- to establish a policy and procedure statement
- to inspect and examine county facilities to determine modes of operations and uncover employee safety problems
- to develop insurance and indemnification requirements and a system in which to monitor compliance with the above
- to develop a countywide safety program involving input from all departments
- to review security procedures at all county facilities
- to develop a countywide disaster plan
- to develop procedures for the solicitation and purchase of insurance
- to establish record-keeping procedures and reports for top management

to develop a working relationship with unions in order to air grievances in the area of safety and health

to develop a claims recovery system so the county may recover those monies from individuals found to have damaged county property

to review the county's Sick–Injured Employee Benefit Program which encouraged malingering

The formal "policy and procedure statement" was developed to inform all departments about the operation of risk management. It set down how the Office of Risk Management would interact with each county department. The procedural statement specifically described the goals the office had to attain and its methods for attainment. It outlined the method by which risk management was funded administratively, as well as for its insurance costs. It described risk management's interaction with all of the county's departments, specifically with respect to handling their property conservation problems and safety and health problems. It also outlined the specific types of information needed from each department for risk management's activities, for example, new construction, additions, and alterations to existing facilities; additions and deletions to the county fleet; damage to county property; changes in legislation and the continual awareness of court cases affecting municipal government; and county facilities collecting and/or handling large sums of money.

The statement also covered the methods by which to file claims for employees injured on the job. It outlined the notification procedures to the insurance company for such claims. The statement set down guidelines for the development of programs, one of which was the Safety-Loss Control Program. (See Exhibit 27.1.) The basis of the program was the selection of a middle management person from each department to have a safety function. This individual reported to both the department head and the director of risk management. One of the problems that existed

with this line of communications was that the department head would tell the safety director what he would or would not do in the safety area. This problem was alleviated by a directive from the county executive which stated:

I expect full implementation of this program by all employees at all levels. Our efforts must be directed toward preventing losses rather than straining to recover from them, and this is the logical approach to adopt.

With the forwarding of this statement, departmental management's ideas on safety were changed.

HOW TO CUT LOSSES

Another innovation under the safety program was the establishment of departmental safety committees and accident review boards. The committees review ongoing safety procedures for possible changes and additions. The accident review boards review departmental accidents to determine their cause and preventability. (See sample Accident Review Board report.)

Departmental management felt that the frequency and severity of accidents did not warrant setting up safety activities and that the innovation would be a waste of manpower. The problem was solved by forwarding departmental loss statements to all department heads and to the county executive advising them of their percentage of loss and the cost to the county in relation to the total dollars of loss. (See Tables 27.1 and 27.2.)

The accident review boards and the safety committees reduced the cost of loss within one year of implementation. Proof of their effectiveness was forwarded to those departments that were still somewhat hesitant to develop the safety programs. To date, the departments which are most able to contribute significantly to the county's loss experience have adopted the program.

Programs which grew out of the policy

EXHIBIT 27.1   Safety Director's Flow Chart.

and procedure statement included inspection and examination of county property. The assistant director of risk management, the insurance company's safety engineer, and the departmental safety director would inspect county facilities for hazards that could be injurious to the employee. They also would examine county property from a conservation point of view. This would include housekeeping procedures and water supply.

The problem had been that the departmental safety directors had no formal documentation with which to inspect the facilities since they were not safety engineers. Inspections had been made on a haphazard basis without the real knowledge of what to look for. To correct the problem, a formal inspection checklist was derived. This checklist was broken down into various areas, such as walking areas, storage areas, material handling, etc. Under each of these categories, specific questions were asked and the answers to those questions could determine if a hazard existed or a proper procedure were not being used. Upon completion of the inspection checklist by the safety director, a report with

ACCIDENT REVIEW BOARD (TYPICAL)

Reference:	Identify type of collision or injury, date and time, and person(s) involved directly or indirectly.*
Description:	Give pertinent details such as location, vehicle I.D. number, supervisor's name, injury sustained and/or damage incurred, and whether preventable or non-preventable.
Summary:	The board describes what events occurred to cause the collision, injury, or property damage. The description should be consolidated from both formal reports and interview information obtained at the board meeting.
Employee's Previous Accident Record	List a review of types of accidents, their dates, and a summary of days lost to date.
Conclusion:	Here the board concludes whether the employee was negligent, what the true cause of the accident was, and what unsafe act or condition brought it about.
Recommendations:	The board states what corrective action should be taken to prevent a recurrence and whether disciplinary action is recommended.
Signatures:	The report shall be dated and signed by the board (chairman and members).
Corrective Action:	The division or appropriate head reviewing the report shall indicate corrective action and disciplinary action taken and sign his name.

cc: Director of Office of Risk Management
       Personnel file
       Division file

Note: The Board shall also conduct a hearing on an employee whose actions resulted in an injury of a fellow employee. Board action and the report shall be processed in the same manner.

(*Any version of this report will be acceptable as long as the pertinent information is complete.*)

appropriate recommendations was sent to the department head and a copy to the Office of Risk Management. If no action was taken in a reasonably short period of time by the department head, the Office of Risk Management would follow up on the report.

PROTECTING THE COUNTY

A review of the county contracts, lease agreements, and permits indicated that the county was not properly protected and was assuming the liability of others. A statement of indem-

TABLE 27.1 County of Westchester: Losses by Department, 1977 and 1978

Department	No. of Comp. Accidents		No. of Non-Comp. Accidents		Total No. of Accidents		Total Incurred Losses	
	1978	1977	1978	1977	1978	1977	1978	1977
Comm. College	3	10	5	7	8	17	$ 5,316	$ 20,769
Correction	15	15	4	7	19	22	39,617	22,792
Envir. Facil.	34	23	48	49	82	72	249,268	36,865
Genl. Services	2	4	5	6	7	10	2,316	11,469
Health	9	5	6	4	15	9	16,770	6,227
Lab. & Res.	2	2	1	1	3	3	2,500	1,650
Med. Center	42	35	6	7	48	42	216,390	59,590
Mental Health	3	2	1	1	4	3	13,071	1,650
Parkway Police	13	7	13	23	26	30	59,012	40,921
P.R.C.	49	46	60	67	109	113	93,828	90,574
Playland	7	8	28	19	35	27	13,024	28,202
Probation	6	3	1	3	7	6	3,799	5,552
Public Works	41	42	25	34	66	76	60,566	94,709
Sheriff's Offc.	5	9	13	8	18	17	6,415	18,324
Soc. Services	37	49	21	17	58	66	63,567	66,184
Other Depts.	10	13	8	10	18	23	31,359	28,385
COMP. LOSSES	278	273					$865,282	$521,577
NON-COMP. LOSSES			245	263			$ 11,536	$ 12,386
TOTAL INCURRED LOSSES					523	536	$876,818	$533,963

TABLE 27.2 Sample Accident Analysis

Policyholder	COUNTY OF WESTCHESTER	
Location	WHITE PLAINS, NEW YORK	
Period Covered	1/1/78–1/1/79	
Date	July, 1979	By
	Compensation Cases	

WESTCHESTER COUNTY MEDICAL CENTER

CAUSE	Administration	General Services	Clinical Services	Ancillary Services	Laboratories	Other Prof. Services	Nursing Services	Non-Comp. Losses	Total No. of Cases	Total Incurred Losses
FALLS										
Steps & Stairs							1		1	$ 3,700
Floor	1	1							2	3,952
On Premises–Outside		2	1				1		4	16,202
Customers Premises							1		1	600
Falls – N.O.C.				1			1		2	2,050
HANDLING										
Inj. Manual Lifting		1	1				2		4	9,100
Wheeled Equipment		2					2		4	3,867
Back Strain							4		4	51,550
Assisting Patients			3				4		7	41,786
VEHICLES – AUTO										
Motor Vehicle Accident							1		1	1,166
CONTACT WITH OBJECTS										
Struck Against					1		1		2	3,370
INJURIES										
Heart Attack		1							1	55,000
Occupational Illness					1				1	5,750
Undefined Cause		1							1	25
MISCELLANEOUS										
Misconduct of Others							2		2	13,000
Miscellaneous – N.O.C.		1					4		5	5,253
NO. OF COMP. CASES	1	9	5	1	2	0	24		42	$216,371
NO. OF NON-COMP. CASES	1	1	1	1	0	1	1	$19	6	19
TOTAL NO. OF CASES	2	10	6	2	2	1	25		48	
TOTAL INCURRED LOSSES	$3,952	$71,094	$36,886	$1,000	$6,756	0	$96,702			$216,390

nification was developed which made all parties doing business with the county responsible for their own actions and, if their actions were subject to litigation and a court award, those persons would agree to protect and indemnify the interests of the county. To protect the indemnification clause, specific insurance requirements were placed into the contracts which acknowledged the existence of the indemnification clause and agreed to protect it financially. (See "Sample Indemnification Agreement.")

PLANNING FOR DISASTERS

Upon designation by the county executive, the Director of Risk Management was chosen to be a disaster manager. The position entailed the organization and management of disasters on county property. As part of the job, the disaster manager would have to outline a plan for communications through the county policy agency to all county officials having specific responsibility for disaster interaction.

The plan defined those disasters which would have a serious effect on people and property belonging to the county. Each department was asked to develop a specific plan relative to its own facility, i.e., a hospital disaster plan, a penitentiary disaster plan, an airport disaster plan, or a playland disaster plan. These plans were reviewed by the Office of Risk Management and the county police agency. The plan was also coordinated with the local Emergency Medical Services Council and facilitated availability of ambulances.

A list was compiled from throughout the county of all emergency equipment that could be available on a moment's notice, such as generators, lighting equipment, pumps, bulldozers, and cranes. The plans were again reviewed and disseminated to all departments for them to run mock disasters. As part of the overall disaster management response, the Office of Risk Management, along with the local public safety organizations, also developed and controlled fire drills and bomb evacuation programs.

The major problem with the plan was that there was no quick method by which to communicate with department heads. Officials were notified much too late to activate a functional program. The problem was resolved when each official was given a paging unit which was set off by the county police agency.

SAMPLE INDEMNIFICATION AGREEMENT

The following indemnification agreement shall be, and is hereby, a provision of the contract and shall be endorsed on the reverse sides of all certificates of insurance:

"The company agrees to indemnify the agency, the trustee, and the county from and against any and all liabilities (including liabilities arising under the strict liability doctrine in tort), losses, damages, costs, expenses of whatsoever kind and nature imposed on, asserted against or incurred by the agency or the county as a result of the act, failure to act, or omission of the company, its agents, employees, or independent contractors selected by the company in any way relating to (a) the construction, installation, and delivery of the project, or any part thereof; or (b) the ownership, possession, use, or operation of the project or any portion thereof to and including the actual acceptance date. Be it provided, however, that the company shall not be liable to the agency or county under the indemnity agreement in this section to the extent that any such liabilities, losses, damages, costs, expenses, and disbursements results solely from the act, failure to act, or neglect of the agency, its agents, or employees, or the county or any municipality, or their respective agent or employees, or for special or consequential damages of the agency or county."

SELECTING THE BEST INSURANCE

Another problem encountered by risk management was the way it bidded its insurance program. Once it was determined that the insurance was not subject to the legal requirement of bidding and that the need to bid would be based on poor service or mishandling of the account by the insurance company, a special insurance placement program was initiated.[1] The need for such a program was shown when 45 insurance brokers, agents, and companies were approached on a specific bid for insurance and only three responded. We learned that flooding the insurance marketplace with insurance proposals turned the majority of the insurance companies off the bid request.

After realizing that the insurance market did not want to participate in the insurance bidding procedure, the following legislation was passed. First, a Pre-qualification Board was established. This board was made up of three risk managers from the private sector, one broker, and one insurance company representative. The board prepared application forms, which were forwarded to firms wishing to bid on the insurance programs.

These forms requested information about the various insurance companies the agent/broker did business with and the premium volume generated by each company, the specific lines of business the broker specialized in, the types of services he or she could provide for the county, and the number of professionals working for that organization. The broker was asked to select three insurance markets to be approached in the solicitation process. From the information elicited, the board evaluated and selected three firms and assigned them designated markets. These firms were then invited to bid. Specifications were sent out by the Office of Risk Management to each of these designated firms. After the bids were received, they went to a selection board made up of the executive officer, county attorney, budget director, finance director, and the director of risk management. The selection board evaluated the bid proposals and made their recommendations for the purchase of the insurance.

(Note that 70 cents of the insurance premium dollar would go to the payment of losses, while the remaining would go for administration, that is, overhead and profit. If the claims during any one year exceed the 70 cents which was set aside as a loss reserve, the insurance company would have to raise its premium to cover the increase in losses. If losses remain at a reasonable level and the insurer can maintain its desired profit level, the premium doesn't necessarily increase.)

UNION MANAGEMENT AND ENVIRONMENTAL ISSUES

Risk management had the sanction from top management to develop recommendations for the handling of union–management problems concerning the safety and health of county employees. A committee was made up of various representatives who would provide input into solving safety and health problems, which include heating, ventilating, and the designation of smoking areas.

Another major problem was the lack of a line of communications from the existing facility with the problem to a local management person who had the authority to resolve it. Since it was determined that the Department of Public Works was responsible for the maintenance and upkeep of all county facilities, a high middle management person within Public Works was assigned the duty of receiving

---

[1]The concept of rebidding your insurance because you had bad losses is a fallacy. Each time you rebid, the insurer reviews at least five years of past loss experience and determines what the rates should be; so you don't necessarily benefit from continuous change. Plus, if you rebid your insurance too frequently, eventually no insurer will quote. The reason is that the first year with a new insurer is the most expensive because of policy issuance costs. It takes about three full years before they profit from the account. Failure to allow this profiting to take place gives you a bad name in the insurance marketplace.

complaints related to the environmental problems at county property. The plan indicated that these local facilities would notify the Department of Public Works immediately if there was a problem. Within a specific amount of time, the problem would be verified and evaluated to see if it could be rectified quickly. If it could not be, the department head was notified along with the county executive and a recommendation for temporary relocation for these employees was made.

DISCOURAGING MALINGERERS

One of the county's benefits was a sick–injured benefit plan. This plan could pay county employees injured on the job 100 percent of their salary up to a maximum of six months. The plan encouraged malingering, hence the problem. In order to reduce this possibility, a procedure was initiated where, upon filing a worker's compensation claim, the employee would immediately notify his or her supervisor of the accident and within 24 hours the employee would have to show medical evidence of an injury. The departmental safety director would maintain contact with the injured employee and encourage his or her return to work.

If it were determined that the employee seemed to be malingering, a medical examination of the employee could be ordered. If the examination showed that the employee could return to work and did not, sick–injured benefits would be stopped and personal sick leave would be charged. If the person were disabled, the county would continue to pay full income and the employee's recovery progress would be monitored by the departmental safety director.

THE FINANCIAL PAYOFF

As part of an annual report to the county executive, a letter of accomplishment was forwarded for his review. The letter described the techniques needed to establish a functional risk management program. It also detailed the various jobs taken over and completed by the Office of Risk Management, which helped to alleviate severe financial losses to the county.

In order to determine the success of the risk management program and how well each of the problems above helped to reduce financial loss to the county, a review of the financial impact of these programs was made.

It was shown that the county's severity of worker's compensation losses was reduced by over $200,000. By establishing proper techniques for purchasing insurance and insurance review, the county was able to save over $30,000 in the acquisition of its property insurance program and $600,000 on the casualty program. When the county did incur a fire loss, the net claims recovery was $40,000 more than it would have been under the old fire insurance plan because of the change in the fire insurance policy. The change was from an actual cash value policy with coinsurance to a replacement case policy with blanket coverage and agreed amount. The malingering prevention program and safety loss control program have reduced the loss in excess of $1,000,000 as of December, 1980.

As of January, 1981, the New York State Occupational Safety and Health Act was to take effect and all Government entities needed to comply. The act indicated a safe and healthful work environment must be provided to employees of government in line with established codes and standards. The law is a mirror image of the federal legislation. The financial impact of this law may be catastrophic to many municipalities. Because the county has preestablished safety loss control and property conservation programs, the financial impact of the new law will not be as severe.

Financial experts have determined that, if a government agency can maintain a risk and insurance program cost within one to two percent of their annual budget, the program would be financially effective. In 1980, the annual county budget was approximately $450 million and the cost to run the risk and insurance program should not exceed $3.6 mil- lion, which falls well within the guidelines for a financially stable risk management program. (See Table 27.3.)

TABLE 27.3   Cost of Risk Report

Cost of Risk	Current Year 1978	Last Year 1977	Average of Last 5 Years
1. Property and Crime Risk			
Uninsured (expensed) losses			
Self-insured (funded) losses			
Insurance premiums	$260,000	$150,000	$196,000
2. Liability Risks			
Uninsured losses			
Funded losses			
Insurance premiums	$2,800,000	$2,900,000	$2,235,000
3. Loss Control Costs		as part of premium	
4. Administrative Costs	$65,000	$62,000	$58,000
Cost of Risk as Percent of Budget	.7%	.7%	.6%

CHAPTER EIGHT

CREDIT AND CASH MANAGEMENT

Cash must be available to meet operating needs, and capital must be available to meet investment needs. To meet these needs, the professional practitioner today is expected to understand and manipulate cash receipts and disbursements, cash balances, and idle funds. Working relationships with financial institutions and the investment community are considered routine components of effective financial management. So, too, are marketing municipal securities and maintaining an acceptable credit position. The cases in this chapter present these subjects at the local level of government.

"How to Evaluate Short-Term Investment Performance," case no. 28, opens with an introduction to the topic of cash management. An evaluative mini-case, set in St. Mary's County, Maryland, is incorporated directly into the introduction to the case as an illustration of a successful cash management program. Centerdale City, a hypothetical jurisdiction, is the setting for exploring a relatively simple application of variance analysis for evaluating income earned from investment ("net investment return"). Centerdale City represents a model case.

"Bristol Goes to Market—General Obligation Bonds" is a two-part illustration of the fundamental issues and procedures involved in long-term borrowing from the perspective of the jurisdiction. The type of security is the general obligation bond, backed by the taxing power of the municipality. Debt policy, issuing, limitations, and capacity are among the topics considered. Some attention is given to disclosure obligations. Credit ratings, their development, what they mean, and their impact on interest costs are examined in detail in Section B. Whereas Section A is an evaluative case, laying out the bonding processes and circumstances in Bristol, Connecticut, Section B requires problem-solving with respect to credit ratings. It is supplemented by a glossary of terms.

28

How to Evaluate Short-Term Investment Performance*

INTRODUCTION

What Is Good Cash Management?

A good cash management system pools a local government's free cash, making funds available for short-term investment. Improved cash management is attractive because with little added cost it puts otherwise idle assets to work. The benefits spill over into all aspects of financial management. Cash management systems increase management's control of cash resources, often by merely reducing the number of bank accounts; they increase the accountability of cash information through improved reporting and forecasting, and they increase nontax revenue by making more cash available for investment at relatively high short-term interest rates.

Good cash management techniques enlarge the local money manager's knowledge and control of cash collections, disbursements, and bank accounts. Professional, formal banking agreements help local officials control the costs of financial services. Good cash management programs can even help local officials and citizens assess the social benefits of their cash management decisions and policies.

To assess a community's need for improved cash management practices, a local government official must first understand and then evaluate the city's present cash management system. (See "Symptoms of Inadequate Cash Management.")

The case of St. Mary's County, Maryland, shown in the following exhibit, demonstrates the real benefits of better cash manage-ment. St. Mary's County, with a population of approximately 52,000 and a fiscal year 1978 budget of $18 million, implemented new techniques in 1976 and experienced dramatic improvement. Eliminating unnecessary bank balances, establishing an accounts payable policy, planning and analyzing cash flows, and immediately buying short-term investments increased their investment income by almost 20% in spite of the fact that interest rates fell by 50% after the program started. (See "A Successful Cash Management Program.")

EVALUATING SHORT-TERM INVESTMENT PERFORMANCE

Investment performance can be measured against internal or external standards. Following is a simple method that communities can use to evaluate net investment return (the amount of income earned from investment operations). There are three factors that affect net investment return: the amount available for investment, the efficiency of investment, and the yield earned on investments. They determine the amount of investment income.

$$\begin{array}{c} \text{amount} \\ \text{available} \\ \text{for} \\ \text{investment} \end{array} \times \text{efficiency} \times \text{yield} = \begin{array}{c} \text{net} \\ \text{investment} \\ \text{return} \end{array}$$

The *amount available for investment* (AAI) is the average cash balance that is available for investment each day in interest-bearing accounts or securities, net of compensating balances and other requirements. The estimate of the upcoming AAI is the bottom line cash forecast.

*Adapted by permission from Nathaniel Guild, ed., *The Public Money Manager's Handbook* (Chicago: Crain Communications, 1981).

SYMPTOMS OF INADEQUATE CASH MANAGEMENT

The following list of questions should help local officials assess their communities' cash management programs. The answers will suggest areas in need of improvement.

Cash Management and Banking System

Does your community

delay disbursements beyond the date of vendor discounts for early payment?

incur unnecessary costs or lose goodwill because of significant bank overdrafts?

lack an active program to ensure the timely collection of significant receipts?

manually deposit large dollar collections rather than have those funds wired directly to the municipal account?

delay deposit of regular collections?

decentralize the responsibility for processing cash receipts and disbursements and for maintaining banking relationships?

maintain a large number of bank accounts?

lack current data on (1) deposits sent to the bank but not recorded by the bank or on (2) amounts deposited but not collected by the bank?

lack complete records on individual bank accounts that specify the purpose, activity, services, and average bank balances of each account?

produce irrelevant or untimely accounting information on the municipality's cash position?

Banking relationships

Does your community

maintain bank balances higher than necessary to compensate banks for the services rendered?

lack formal banking agreements?

use banks that lack bank wire facilities?

lack the current cost to the municipality of each banking relationship?

make limited use of bank administrative services, such as lock boxes, depository transfer checks and financial advisory services?

choose depository or collection banks on a noncompetitive basis?

Cash Forecasting

Does your community

rely on inaccurate undependable revenue estimates?

lack estimates of expenditures on capital projects?

lack adequate cash reserves for unforeseen cash emergencies?

make numerous and unpredictable trips to financial markets to borrow funds for short-term use?

Investment Policy

Does your community

lose revenue due to a noncompetitive return, compared with current money market rates, on short-term investments?

fail to invest a high proportion of idle cash?

sell investments prematurely?

buy and sell investments only on an overnight basis? fail to develop a formal, usable investment policy for day-to-day investment decisions?

A SUCCESSFUL CASH MANAGEMENT PROGRAM:
ST. MARY'S COUNTY, MARYLAND

The County

St. Mary's County, on Maryland's western shore, has a population of 52,000. Five part-time elected commissioners oversee an annual budget of approximately $18,000,000 (FY '78). In 1975 during a review of county bank deposits, Joseph P. O'Dell, Budget Officer, discovered that the county was losing large amounts of foregone interest income from uninvested cash. He initiated a process that convinced county officials to implement a new cash management program. It produced dramatic results for the taxpayers of the county.

The Results

Increased benefits:

In the first year the county earned $360,000 from the short-term investment of idle cash even though interest rates fell in that period by 50%. That alone saved taxpayers 17 cents on the tax rate.

The county continued to show improvement, earning $460,000 on interest income in FY 1979. It presently invests 98 to 99 % of its available cash balances, a remarkable rate of efficiency.

Increased costs:

To earn those benefits, the county expended little additional operating funds. Cash management operations were performed by reassigning the duties of current staff. The county did pay its outside auditors an additional $1,000 for oversight and evaluation reports of the cash management program.

Factors for Success

Mr. O'Dell credits success to the county's four-step process of research, education, and implementation. It (1) identified cash management problems, (2) planned a course of action, (3) centralized cash management responsibility, and (4) designed a system to review cash management performance.

Local officials faced the most difficult hurdle first — how to convince their commissioners that the county had a cash management problem. Like most people, St. Mary's commissioners were not immediately familiar with the sizable benefits and low costs in excavating interest income.

To win the minds of the commissioners, O'Dell prepared a working paper that detailed cash management problems and offered specific courses of action in areas such as internal organization, accounting systems, and local banking arrangements. The paper convinced the commissioners that every day that they delayed action, the county lost money.

Since cash management changes also affected local banks, the county presented each with a copy of the working paper. County officials met separately with each bank president, seeking comments and recommendations. Since county cash management improvements offered attractive returns, the banks also supported the plan.

The commissioners authorized county officials to eliminate all excess bank account balances, make timely payments on accounts payable, invest idle funds in repurchase agreements and savings accounts, and eliminate advances to spending units until money was needed.

What was the reaction of the community? The new cash management program was well publicized, much discussed, and well received.

Efficiency (EFF) is the percentage of available daily cash balance that the city invests in income-earning securities. Mathematically, efficiency is expressed as follows:

$$\text{efficiency rate} = \frac{\text{average daily investments}}{\text{average daily investment} + \text{average daily cash balances}} \times 100$$

Yield (YLD) is the rate of return that the municipality earns on its investments. The estimate for the upcoming year's yield depends on the community's prediction of interest rates and the type and maturity of proposed investment purchases.

An Example

To show investment evaluation in action, the following example describes the investment performance of Centerdale City for the 198x fiscal year. The upper line represents estimated figures, and the lower line represents actual ones.

AAI	×	EFF	×	YLD	=	net return
$4,572,300		95.00%		12.2%	=	$529,930
$4,322,650		96.30%		10.8%	=	$449,573
						$ 80,357 U

At the beginning of the fiscal year, the Centerdale City treasurer predicted that the Centerdale Investment program would produce $529,930 of nontax income for local coffers. At the end of the year, however, results were disappointing. Centerdale earned only $449,573, $80,357 less than predicted ("U" means an unfavorable variance), and the city council and news media wanted to know why. Generally, the treasurer could see that less cash was available for investment and interest rates were lower than predicted, but how and why did these factors affect the net investment return?

An Explanation of the Variance

The following method, which may be used annually for external reports or quarterly for internal performance reviews, helps explain the variance between the estimated and actual investment results. It may not provide definitive answers, but points to areas that require further investigation. There are many different ways to calculate variance; this one is standard.

The first variance calculation shows the amount of the $80,357 investment shortfall that is due to less cash being available for investment.

variance
due to   = (act. AAI – est. AAI)
lower   × (est. EFF) × (est. YLD)
AAI   or ($4,322,650 – $4,572,300)
             × (.9500) × (.122) = – $28,934U

Almost $30,000 of the $80,000 variance is due to lower available balances, which could be explained in a number of ways. For example, net payment levels could have increased from either spending that exceeded or revenues that fell short of budgeted amounts. Also, there could have been late payments of uncontrollable receipts from the state or federal governments. Finally the management of controllable receipts and disbursements could have lagged expected performance, giving the treasurer an opportunity to examine current systems for better cash management procedures.

The second calculation shows the amount of extra funds the community earned due to increased investment efficiency.

variance
due to   = (act. EFF – est. EFF)
efficiency   × (act. AAI × est. YLD)
           or (.9630 – .9500) × ($4,322.650)
               × (.122) = $6,856F

The favorable variance (F) means that the city earned an extra $7,000 due to the increased efficiency of its investment program. This is good news; however, the treasurer should see that the increased efficiency did not occur because too much cash was placed in investments while balances at banks were left below compensating levels or overdrawn.

The last calculation shows the amount of the variance that is due to lower investment yield.

variance
due to = (act. YLD − est. YLD)
yield × (act. AAI × act. EFF)
or (.122 − .108) × ($4,322,650)
× (.9630) = $58,278U

The largest variance is due to a disappointing yield. This could have happened if interest rates did not reach their forecasted levels. That would be apparent when actual yields are compared with forecasted yields for each type of investment.

A lower yield could also come from a lag in portfolio performance, which has three causes. First, the city could have purchased the wrong maturities. It could have bought six-month investments when cash was needed three months later, thereby forcing the city to sell investments prematurely. Second, the mix of investments might have caused a lower yield. For example, the city could have placed funds in a savings account at 5.25% rather than in U.S. T-bills at 9%. Third, the city could have miscalculated market timing. If it purchased a one-month investment at the be-

ginning of the year at 11% instead of a twelve-month investment at 10%, it would have earned a lower yield if rates later fell to 8%.

These three variance analyses help explain what portion of the investment process was responsible for an increase or decrease in actual results.

variance due to lower AAI	$28,934U
variance due to greater EFF	6,856 F
variance due to lower YLD	58,278U
net variance	$80,357U

The variance analysis is an internal comparison. Local governments can also compare investment performance with other local communities, although accounting problems can affect the analysis. They can also compare their performance with the return of their state's local government investment pool or with money funds as listed in the financial press. In these comparisons, local officials should compare apples with apples. The gross investment income earned by the community should be reduced by the cost associated with earning investment income, such as transaction fees and management expenses. The net investment return should serve as the basis for comparison.

29

*Bristol Goes to Market: General Obligation Bonds**

SECTION A: BONDING AND BRISTOL

Bristol is described in the 1980 Connecticut State Register and Manual as follows:

*By Russell E. Galipo, vice president and manager, Municipal Finance Department, and Maryann E. Romeo, formerly manager and officer, Municipal Credit Department, Connecticut National Bank, Hartford, Connecticut.

BRISTOL. Hartford County — (Form of government, mayor, city council.) — Town inc. May 1785; taken from Farmington. Town and city co-extensive, 1911. Area 26.6 sq. miles. Population, est., 55,100. Voting districts, 9. Children, 17,247. Principal industries, bulk printing and the manufacture of ball bearings, springs, clocks and watches, timing devices, brass products, paper boxes, screw machine products, cutting and creasing rules, syn-

chronous electric motors, variable transformers, automatic voltage regulators, electric connectors; brass, bronze and copper sheet, rod and wire; brass and aluminum forgings, wire forms, paper punches, various metal products to specifications, machine tools, metal stampings, counting devices; archery sets, ski poles, automobile parts, jewelry, etc. Transp. — Passenger: Served by buses of the Bonanza Bus Lines, Inc. from Hartford and Waterbury and from New York City via Danbury, and by Greyhound. Freight: Served by Conrail and numerous motor common carriers. Post office, Bristol, with classified station at Forestville. Three rural delivery routes.

According to the 1980 Census, Bristol's population was 57,370 up 3.4% from the 1970 census of 55,487. Bristol moved from 14th place in the 1970 census to 11th place in the 1980 census in Connecticut's population list.

Over the years Bristol has been a frequent issuer of debt, as evidenced in Table 29.1, which covers the last 20 years.

Bristol is one of the 98 Connecticut communities operating under a charter form of government. The charter created by legislative special act was approved in 1911 and made the Town and City co-extensive. Over the years, amendments to the charter have been made by legislative special act and more recently by charter revision under the home rule act. The roots of the present financial organizational structure come from a special act in 1933. The background for this act is included in an August 3, 1978, report of the "Mayor's Task Force for Revamping Fiscal Offices" as follows:

In August of 1925, the City Council appointed a Finance Committee composed of the Mayor, City Clerk and Treasurer. The committee acted on borrowings by the City for capital needs and tax anticipation loans. On April 21, 1932, the City Council created a Board of Finance consisting of seven members to hold office until July 15, 1933, or such time as a Board of Finance could be created by Special Act of the State Legislature.

The city, at that time, had incurred considerable short-term debt without a means of repayment. The depressionary period was adversely affecting tax collections and caused increased emergency relief and unemployment needs (a local major expense at that time).

The need for additional borrowings gave rise to a financial plan put together by Mr. DeWitt Page, President of New Departure Manufacturing Co., which included the condition that a Board of Finance be created. On April 5, 1933, Governor Cross signed House Bill #627 "An Act Creating a Permanent Board of Finance of the City and Town of Bristol." Charles Anderson was the first chairman of the interim council-created board as well as the legislatively created board, which set the membership at ten members plus the mayor.

The final resolution to the City's fiscal problems was an act which established a new fiscal year and authorized the issuance of funding bonds. An interim year of 12/1/32 to 6/30/33 was used to make the city uniform on July 1, 1933. The Board appointed the city's first comptroller, Allen Hall, effective 5/15/33. The council-created finance committee met on 5/17/33 and adjourned *"sine die."* Financial control, including the sole power to issue indebtedness, is vested with the appointed board of finance and not the elected city council, a very unique financial format when compared with other Connecticut communities.

Table 29.1 shows the debt issue frequency and purpose of issue. School debt was issued in the late 1950s and early 1960s to provide facilities for the increasing school enrollment, as shown in Table 29.2. Toward the end of the '60s, $5,615,000 of industrial park debt was financed. The project was part of a major program to develop an industrial park area in the northwest section of the city, where the New Departure Division of General Motors relocated its downtown Bristol and Meriden operations. The project was necessary in order to retain the city's largest taxpayer and employer.

As Bristol entered the recessionary period of the '70s, unemployment became a serious problem. Table 29.3 shows the extent

TABLE 29.1. Bonded Debt Issues — Last 20 Years

Date of Issue	Purpose	Coupon	Amount of Issue
11/15/61	School	3.10	$ 2,105,000
3/1/63	Municipal Building	2.90	1,690,000
11/1/64	Edgewood School	3.10	235,000
11/1/64	Improvement	3.10	815,000
11/1/64	Flood control	3.10	505,000
11/1/64	Sewer	3.10	185,000
7/15/65	Road	3.20	880,000
7/15/65	School	3.20	2,390,000
7/15/66	School	3.75	5,000,000
7/15/67	Industrial park	3.90	3,490,000
7/15/67	Industrial park water	3.90	1,600,000
7/15/67	Industrial park sewer	3.90	525,000
2/15/70	Sewer treatment plant	6.20	600,000
2/15/70	Sewer — 1970	6.20	225,000
2/15/70	Urban renewal	6.20	1,300,000
11/15/71	Redevelopment	4.30	700,000
11/15/71	General improvement	4.30	500,000
11/15/71	School — 1971	4.30	1,085,000
11/15/71	Sewer — 1971	4.30	205,000
3/15/76	Improvement bonds — Hoppers & Birge	6.20	225,000
3/15/76	School bonds — 1976	6.20	1,430,000
3/15/76	Improvement bonds — Stevens St. Standpipe — water	6.20	150,000
12/1/76	Sewer	5.20	560,000
		5.60	275,000
		5.80	165,000
12/1/76	Improvement	5.20	850,000
		5.60	250,000
		5.80	250,000
2/15/79	School	5.40	70,000
		5.90	770,000
		6.00	420,000
2/15/79	Improvement	5.40	25,000
		5.90	225,000
2/15/79	Urban renewal	5.40	50,000
		5.90	550,000
		6.00	250,000
2/15/79	Sewer	5.40	25,000
		5.90	200,000
Total			$30,775,000

of unemployment in comparison to the state of Connecticut. The severe unemployment problem had to be addressed for the 11/15/71 bond issue of $2,490,000. Moody's Investors Service, Inc. had rated previous issues Aa. The increasing debt load coupled with the unemployment issue were of concern to local officials for a rating on the upcoming issue. NBC did a nationally televised "white paper" on Bristol's unemployment problem. Consequently, a special brochure, entitled "The Bristol Unemployment Problem," was pre-

TABLE 29.2   Historical School Enrollment

Fiscal Year	Enrollment
1957–58	7,208
1958–59	7,659
1959–60	8,163
1960–61	8,612
1961–62	8,998
1962–63	9,494
1963–64	10,071
1964–65	10,334
1965–66	10,663
1966–67	11,086
1967–68	11,306
1968–69	11,559
1969–70	11,913
1970–71	12,102
1971–72	12,373
1972–73	12,232
1973–74	11,977
1974–75	11,530
1975–76	11,411
1976–77	11,004
1977–78	10,692
1978–79	10,262
1979–80	9,821
1980–81	9,383

Source: Bristol Board of Education

TABLE 29.3   Unemployment Rate Comparison

Month/Year	Bristol Labor Market[1]	State of Conn.
12/69	5.2%	3.7%
1/70	7.8	4.5
2/70	7.8	4.6
3/70	7.8	4.6
4/70	8.7	4.6
5/70	9.5	4.8
6/70	12.5	6.0
7/70	14.9	6.4
8/70	14.9	6.5
9/70	14.0	5.8
10/70	14.0	5.8
11/70	17.5	6.6
12/70	17.5	6.7
1/71	19.8	8.4
2/71	21.3	8.3
3/71	21.0	8.5
4/71	21.5	8.4
5/71	21.7	8.5
6/71	24.5	10.1
7/71	24.1	9.4
8/71	23.0	9.0
9/71	22.1	8.3

[1]The Bristol labor market was defined as the city of Bristol and the town of Plymouth at that time. Plymouth's 1970 census population was 10,321.

pared along with the standard financial information for a Moody's presentation. The presentation was successful and the Aa rating was maintained.

Debt was not issued again by the city until March of 1976. Moody's at this time revised Bristol's rating from Aa to A. Skipping A1 meant a two-notch drop. Reasons for the revision were heavy future financing needs, current revenue problems, minimal tax base growth, and a high unemployment trend. It has to be pointed out at this point that Standard and Poor, Inc. (S & P), another rating service, continued to rate Bristol AA.

Municipal Bond Market

The municipal bond market in the mid '70s was in a chaotic condition. In April and June of 1975, Congress passed amendments to the Glass–Steagall Act. One of the changes created the Municipal Securities Rulemaking Board (MSRB) as a self-regulatory agency under the Securities and Exchange Commission (SEC). The purpose of the MSRB initially was to promulgate rules governing the sale of municipal securities for SEC consideration and approval. In late summer of 1975, the New York City crisis hit the market with a severe blow—its inability to pay maturing notes. These events contributed to the volatility of the municipal bond marketplace. During this period the Municipal Finance Association of the U.S. and Canada (MFOA) was in the process of drafting voluntary guidelines covering the disclosure of information in the issuance of state and local government debt. This reaction by the MFOA was an attempt to keep the SEC out of direct control of municipal issues, such as is done for the corporate sector. Additionally, certain congressional leaders were attempting to pass legislation which would have required regulatory control over municipal debt issuance and/or reporting requirements. The state of the market can be shown by looking at the "Trend of the Bond Market" compiled by *The Bond Buyer*. (A recent version is shown in Exhibit 29.1)

Bristol city officials decided in mid-1980 that the issue of its Moody's rating should be addressed in an effort to regain part of the rating loss of 1976. In a meeting with their fiscal advisor, Hartford National Bank, strategy was planned to respond to the negative characteristics cited in the 1976 Moody's report. The role of the fiscal advisor is outlined in "Financial Advisory Agreement." The plan was to make a special presentation in the

EXHIBIT 29.1

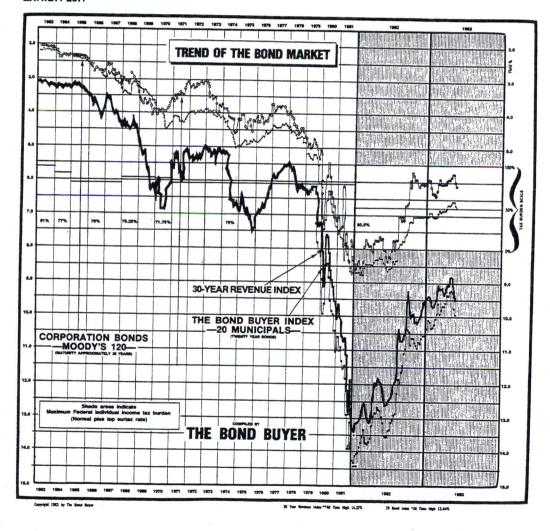

FINANCIAL ADVISORY AGREEMENT

This agreement between Hartford National Bank, hereafter referred to as the Financial Advisor, and _____ , hereafter referred to as the Municipality, defines the terms and conditions under which the Financial Advisor will render financial advisory services concerning the issuance of municipal securities by the Municipality.

I.   *Duties of Financial Advisor*
   A.   The Financial Advisor in all cases will
      1.   Pursuant to the Municipality's request, provide financial advice and recommendations concerning: financial feasibility; alternate methods of financing; project financing and costs; financial content of pre-authorization legal documents; pre-authorization estimates of bond and note terms and conditions; tax rate impact estimates; fact sheets, statistical and analytical materials; and other financial information relevant to the issue and/or the Municipality.
      2.   Arrange, schedule, and implement procedural steps for each style.
      3.   Recommend as to the various provisions, terms and conditions of the bond/note issues, including provisions as to the dates of the issue, interest payment dates, schedule of maturities, options of prior payment, and advise as to provisions designed to make the issues more attractive to prospective bidders.
      4.   Make recommendations regarding the financial content of resolutions, the notices of sale for the bond and other documents, if any.
      5.   Prepare official statements in the format, style and type face normally used by the Financial Advisor for each bond sale, which statements shall be descriptive of the bonds offered and shall contain information on the Municipality and its financial structure and condition.

   B.   With respect to each bond sale will
      1.   Reproduce, mail, and distribute the notice of sale, official statement and other documents, if any, to underwriters and institutional buyers to encourage the best competitive bidding for the bonds.
      2.   When requested, provide institutional bond buyers, dealers, dealer banks, and others with materials to encourage competitive bidding at the bond sales.
      3.   Assist the Municipality in obtaining bond ratings from Moody's Investors Service and/or Standard & Poor's Corporation.
      4.   Assist the Municipality in qualifying for municipal bond insurance, if requested to do so.
      5.   Assist the Municipality in calculating bids for the bonds, select the lowest bids at each sale and advise the Municipality as to the award of the bonds.
      6.   Arrange the bond closings and advise the Municipality concerning investment of bond proceeds.

   C.   The Financial Advisor shall pay its own out-of-pocket expenses.

fall of 1980, followed by a bond issue in early 1981. The presentation produced no results on a rating change. Moody's indicated that the city had been reviewed in the spring as a part of their normal review and update process. Since the city was planning a spring sale, a formal review would take place prior to the sale.

In the spring, a timetable was developed to sell various purpose, general obligation bonds totaling $1,795,000. A visit prior to the sale was made to Moody's, and information was provided to S & P. The city's official statement, dated March 19, 1981, and generally conforming to MFOA's 1979 disclosure guidelines for state and local governments, was distributed to the underwriting community. An ad was placed in *The Bond Buyer*, a trade publication for the municipal bond market, on March 19, 1981. The underwriting community normally puts together a syndicate, usually on an historical basis, to bid on issues that are offered in the marketplace. They develop an offering schedule (scale) which is the price at which the bonds will be offered to the public. This is usually done a day or two before the sale. At a final syndicate meeting, the manager will suggest a bid scale and profit margin for the account. Members of the syndicate decide whether to stay with the account or drop out. Once the final scale has been determined, it is multiplied by the number of bonds in each maturity and divided by the total issue to arrive at the average selling price. The dealer's spread (margin of profit) is deducted, resulting in the bid price for the bonds.

Sale Results

On March 31, 1981, Mayor Michael Werner, Finance Board Chairman Richard LaMothe, and Comptroller Theodore Hamilton represented the city of Bristol at the bond bid opening. Four bids were received and opened at 11:30 a.m. The bid results are described in Table 29.4, which shows the total interest cost over the life of issue based on each bidder's submission. In other words, the net interest to the city for the winning bidder was $1,104,056.60.

Although substantially higher than the net interest cost (NIC) of 5.9411% received on the last sale of 2/9/79, the rate was acceptable to the city officials. The BBI (20) for the '79 sale was 6.22% and for this sale 10.09% and trending upward numerically. (The Bond Buyer Index (BBI) is an index published by

The Bond Buyer, a trade publication, which measures market level and direction. It is a weekly average that measures the yield level of a group of 20 representative municipal bonds, all of which are assumed to have 20-year maturities and constant coupons. The 20 bonds range from Aaa obligations to Baa city bonds, and generally represent a crossection of actively traded general obligation bonds.) Other issues sold in the marketplace at that time with some comparable characteristics are shown in Table 29.5.

Upon acceptance by the city officials of the bid which was awarded to the bidder offering the lowest NIC, the winning underwriter was notified of the award. Bond counsel (Day, Berry & Howard) ordered the bonds from American Banknote Co.—the bond specimens had already been proofed—with the winning rates and an MBIA engraving. (The winning bidder elected to insure the deal through the Municipal Bond Insurance Association for $16,500.) The bonds were ordered to be delivered to the Signature Company in New York where they would be signed and delivered to the successful bidder. Refer to Exhibit 29.2 for the underwriters' reoffering scale.

Settlement

On April 15, 1981, the same city officials went to New York City. The bonds were signed, certified by Hartford National Bank, and delivered to the winning syndicate. For delivering the bonds, the city received in a federal funds check the following:

$1,795,000.00	Proceeds
148.40	Premium
6,503.27	Accrued interest (4/1 to 4/15)
$1,801,651.67	Total received

The funds were deposited at Bankers Trust Company in New York and immediately drawn down through the Federal Reserve System in Hartford and used to pay maturing notes (partially). The balance (new monies)

TABLE 29.4   Bid Summary, Hartford National Bank, for the City of Bristol, Connecticut $1,795,000 General Obligation Bonds, Dated: 4/1/81 — Due: 4/1/82-96

Maturity Year	Annual Maturity Amount (000's)	Cumulative Bond Years	Bidder Conn. Bank & Trust Co., Continental Illinois and McDonald & Co.	Bidder Roosevelt & Cross, Colonial Bank and Assoc.	Bidder United Bank & Trust Co.	Bidder Merrill Lynch, Hartford National Bank, Bache, E.F. Hutton, and Associates
1982	$225	225	9.50	9.40	9.25	9.25
1983	225	675	9.50	9.40	9.25	9.25
1984	220	1,335	9.50	9.40	9.25	9.25
1985	100	1,735	9.60	9.40	9.25	9.25
1986	100	2,235	9.60	9.40	9.25	9.25
1987	100	2,835	9.60	9.40	9.25	9.25
1988	100	3,535	9.60	9.40	9.25	9.25
1989	100	4,335	9.60	9.40	9.25	9.25
1990	100	5,235	9.60	9.40	9.25	9.25
1991	100	6,235	9.60	9.40	9.25	9.25
1992	85	7,170	9.60	9.40	9.25	9.25
1993	85	8,190	9.60	9.50	9.50	9.50
1994	85	9,925	9.60	9.60	9.50	9.50
1995	85	10,485	9.75	9.60	9.70	9.70
1996	85	11,760	9.75	9.60	9.70	9.70
GROSS INT. $			1,131,332.50	1,113,600.00	1,104,205.00	1,104,205.00
PREMIUM $			—0—	1,671.00	130.25	148.20
NET INT. $			1,131,332.50	1,111,929.00	1,104,074.75	1,104,056.60
NIC %			9.62	9.455181	9.40	9.388236

was deposited to city accounts. At that point the issue was concluded by the issuer (see Exhibit 29.3).

SECTION B: CREDIT RATINGS

Bond ratings indicate *creditworthiness*, which is a measurement of the ability of the issuer to repay the bond holder. Credit ratings are grouped in two major categories: investment grade and speculative. An investment grade rating greatly enhances the marketability of the issuer because it is less risky, and the higher the rating the lower the cost to the issuer.

There are two kinds of municipal bonds based on the security or repayment features involved: 1) general obligation bonds are secured by the ability of the issuer to levy taxes, 2) revenue bonds are repaid from a specific revenue source. This case study addresses general obligation bonds. It is important to remember that a rating is a *judgment* of credit quality based upon detailed analysis of specific data.

TABLE 29.5

Sale Date	Issuer	Purpose	Amount	Moody's	S & P	Maturity Dates	NIC	Number of Bids
3/26/81	Cuyahoga Falls, Ohio	Sewer-limit tax bonds	$1,500,000	Al	N/R	4/1/82- 11/1/96	9.1958%	5
3/31/81	Birmingham, Ala.	G.O. Refunding Warrants	8,300,000	Al	AA	4/1/83- 4/1/2001	9.8455%	8
3/31/81	Bristol, Conn.	Various	1,795,000	A	AA	4/1/82- 4/1/96	9.3882%	4
4/1/81	Harry Co. Sch. Dist., S. Carolina	Sch. Bldg. Bonds	3,500,000	A	A	6/1/82- 6/1/96	9.4103%	1*
4/2/81	Richland Co. Sch. Dist. #2, S. Carolina	Sch. Bldg. Bonds	5,900,000	A	A	5/1/83- 5/1/90	8.71665%	4

*Three bids were received late and not accepted.

Symbols

Rating symbols used by the two major rating agencies and their definition are as follows:

MOODY'S RATINGS

Aaa	best quality	
Aa	high quality	investment
A	upper medium grade	grade
Baa	medium grade	

Ba	has speculative elements
B	lacks desirable investment characteristics
Caa	poor standing — may be in default
Ca	highly speculative
C	extremely poor investment prospects

STANDARD & POOR'S RATINGS

AAA	extremely strong	
AA	very strong	
A	strong	investment grade
BBB	adequate protection	

BB		Least speculative
B	predominantly	↑
CCC	speculative	↓
CC		Most speculative

C	income bonds on which no income is being paid
D	in default

Bonds rated Aa, A, Baa, Ba, and B by Moody's which have the strongest investment prospects within the rating category are designated Aa1, A1, Baa1, Ba1, and B1, respectively. Standard and Poor's modifies its AA, A, BBB, and BB ratings by adding a plus or minus sign to indicate position within the rating category.

Rating Criteria

In analyzing municipal bonds, there are four principal rating criteria: debt, financial, economic, and management. Trends are ex-

EXHIBIT 29.2

The undersigned is pleased to have been a Joint Manager in the financing shown below:

New Issue   **Standard & Poor's Rating AAA#**
                                 Moody's Rating A

In the opinion of Bond Counsel, interest on the Bonds is exempt from Federal income taxes
under presently existing statutes.

$1,795,000
City of Bristol, Connecticut
General Obligation Bonds
(#Insured by Municipal Bond Insurance Association)

Dated: April 1, 1981   **Due: Serially April 1, 1982-1996**

Interest on the Bonds will be payable semiannually on the first day of October and April commencing
October 1, 1981. The Bonds will be coupon bonds in denominations of $5,000 each, registrable as to
principal only. The Bonds are not subject to redemption prior to maturity. The Bonds will be general
obligations of the City and will be payable, unless paid from other sources, from ad valorem taxes
levied on all taxable property in the City without limitation as to rate or amount, except as to certain
classified property. Each bond will have a single coupon attached for each installment of interest. Both
principal and interest will be payable at the Hartford National Bank and Trust Company in Hartford,
Connecticut, or at the Hartford Trust Company of New York (A Limited Purpose Trust Company) New
York, New York.

Amount	Due	Coupon	Yield	Amount	Due	Coupon	Yield
$225,000	1982	9.25%	7.25%*	$100,000	1990	9.25%	8.90%
225,000	1983	9.25	7.40*	100,000	1991	9.25	9.10
220,000	1984	9.25	7.60	85,000	1992	9.25	9.25*
100,000	1985	9.25	7.80*	85,000	1993	9.50	9.40
100,000	1986	9.25	8.00	85,000	1994	9.50	9.50
100,000	1987	9.25	8.25	85,000	1995	9.70	9.60
100,000	1988	9.25	8.50	85,000	1996	9.90	9.70*
100,000	1989	9.25	8.70				

* Not Available

Bonds of particular maturities may or may not be available from the undersigned or
others at the above prices on and after the date of this announcement.

The Bonds are offered for delivery when, as and if issued, subject to the approving opinions of Messrs.
Day, Berry & Howard, Bond Counsel, of Hartford, Connecticut. It is expected that delivery of the Bonds
in definitive form will be made on or about April 15, 1981.

Hartford National Bank

April 3, 1981
Telephone: 1-728-4780

EXHIBIT 29.3 A Public Debt Issue

A PUBLIC DEBT ISSUE   HARTFORD NATIONAL BANK
11/6/80

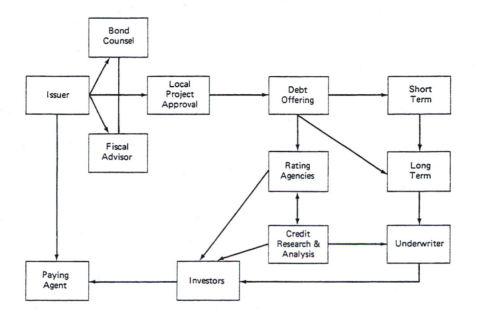

tremely important since they indicate an improvement or the deterioration of a credit.

The total debt of a community is broken down between long-term debt and short-term debt. Debt of overlapping entities must also be considered in the calculation of total debt. Long-term debt matures beyond one year, while short-term debt matures within one year. Deductions are made from total debt to account for self-supporting debt (not dependent upon the general taxing power for repayment) and grants from federal or state governments. The net result is overall net debt. This overall net debt figure is measured against the total population of the community plus the total wealth of the community, in terms of the value of taxable property and the income levels of its residents. These ratios indicate the debt burden on the community. Authorized but unissued debt has to be considered in terms of its effect on the total debt outstand-

ing. Bonded debt has usually been structured for repayment over a period of twenty years; however, during the last couple of years maturities have been shortened to ten years due to the high interest rate environment. The rapidity with which debt is matured is an important measurement. Usually the payment schedule will be structured to coincide with the useful life of the item being bonded.

The most frequently used fund in municipal accounting is the general fund, which is really the operating fund. Annual revenues and expenditures are matched against each other, and the annual operating results show the difference between revenues and expenditures. A shortfall occurs when expenditures exceed revenues. Sound financial operations dictate that revenues cover expenditures. Revenues are broken down into principal sources; and expenditures, likewise, are broken down into major expenditure items.

The principal source of revenue for a municipal entity is generally property taxes, although they have declined in recent years in an effort to decrease the dependence upon one revenue source. Another key source of revenue that must be examined is that amount which comes from other government entities, namely, the federal government and the state. Intergovernmental revenues are not reliable sources of revenue because there is no certainty that they will continue at the same or at greater levels in the future. Major expenditure items are usually for education, public safety, public works, general government, and debt service. Debt service is a fixed expense each year, and it is important to measure this expenditure item to total expenditures in order to determine how much of a burden this presents on each year's budget. The fund balance is the difference between total assets and total liabilities. This figure should be positive. A comparison of the actual revenues and expenditures to original estimates usually indicates the level of financial and managerial strength.

Property taxes are based on assessed values (property values for tax purposes) in the community. Tax collections relative to tax levies show the ability of the community to collect its taxes in a timely way. Slow tax collections and/or increasing tax delinquencies are negative credit factors and can easily lead to financial problems.

An historical study of the retirement system shows the trend in unfunded liabilities, the growth in assets, and the trend in the funded ratio. Unfunded liabilities are accrued pension benefits which exceed the value of assets accumulated to meet total costs. Assets should be set aside to provide for pension benefits according to the method suggested in the actuarial study. The ratio of accumulated assets to total pension liabilities shows the level of funding. The trends in asset growth and in funded ratios are significant in determining the soundness of the pension plan.

Various economic indicators are studied, such as population growth, employment trends, income levels, and the diversification and growth in taxable resources. The employment base is analyzed for any cyclicality or vulnerability to recession. A close examination of the tax and employment bases indicates whether a particular company (companies) dominates the economy. Population make-up, trends in income levels, building permit activity, land use, and age of the housing stock are important considerations.

The form of government is studied to determine the level of professionalism of the key officials. Constitutional limits (if any), the range of services provided, and the level of independence are assessed. A stable government is a valuable asset. A responsible, professional management will demonstrate the ability to keep debt under control, to produce sound financial results, and to aggressively collect delinquent taxes.

City of Bristol

Bristol, Connecticut is located in the northwestern part of the state approximately 18 miles southwest of Hartford. Its land area covers 26.6 square miles and population density equals 2,071 per square mile vs. 654 for the state. The city has a council–mayor form of government with a board of finance. Current population for 1980 equals 57,334, an increase of 3.2% between 1970 and 1980. The median age in Bristol, according to the 1970 census, is 27.5 years while the state median age is 29.2. School enrollment during the 1979–1980 year totaled 9,463, a decline from 14,800 during 1969–1970. Pertinent economic facts for Bristol compared to state figures appear in Table 29.6.

Specific socioeconomic statistics derived from the 1970 census are provided in Table 29.7 for further background. This is the most recent census information currently available, and it also is the basis upon which all ratings are made until new census data are available.

Table 29.8 shows a five-year trend of building permits and total dollar value with the number of residential and nonresidential permits segregated.

Bristol's overall net debt as of April 15, 1981, is $12,873,972, which is equal to $225

TABLE 29.6A   Economic Factors

	Bristol	Connecticut
1970 median family income	$11,835	$11,811
1977 per capita money income	$ 5,785	$ 6,564
1960-1970 population growth	22.0%	19.6%
1970-1980 population growth	3.2%	2.1%
January 1981 unemployment	10.1%	7.1%
July 1980 unemployment	9.6%	6.1%
1980 average unemployment	8.3%	5.9%
1980 full value per capita	$15,584*	$22,352
1979 full value per capita	$15,930*	$19,285
1978 equalized grand list per capita	$19,358	$26,444

*Revalued in 1977

TABLE 29.6B   Trend in Unemployment

Annual Average	Bristol	Conn.
1976	12.3%	9.5%
1977	7.2%	7.0%
1978	5.0%	5.2%
1979	5.5%	5.1%
1980	8.5%	5.9%

TABLE 29.6C   Trend in Employment

Annual Average	Bristol	Year to Year Growth	
		Bristol	Conn.
1976	22,557	—	—
1977	25,122	11.4%	5.2%
1978	26,556	5.7%	2.6%
1979	27,686	4.3%	4.7%
1980	26,946	(2.7%)	1.3%

TABLE 29.7   Comparative Figures on the 1970 Census

1970 Census	Bristol	State Urban Avg.	1970 Housing	Bristol	State Urban Avg.
% income below poverty level	3.7	5.8	% owner occupied	64.1	57.5
% income above $15,000	27.0	29.6	% 1-unit struct.	55.9	51.9
Median school yrs.	11.7	12.1	% blt. before 1939	40.7	47.0
% white collar	43.4	51.8	% blt. since 1959	25.7	20.1
% government	9.3	12.8	Owner occ. med. val.	$21,200	$25,100
% manufacturing	49.5	35.2	Median contract rent	$ 89	$ 104
% service	27.6	30.9			
% trade	17.3	19.0			

TABLE 29.8   Building Permits

	Total		Residential		Nonresidential	
1975	647	$9,550,664	437	$6,180,055	210	$3,370,609
1976	722	6,462,294	511	3,755,914	211	2,706,380
1977	715	13,386,668	566	5,669,789	149	7,716,879
1978	696	6,370,652	464	1,175,531	232	5,195,121
1979	904	13,877,766	671	10,056,507	233	3,821,259

per capita, 1.4% of estimated full value of the tax base, and 3.9% of income. Moody's Investors Service, a major rating agency, has calculated median debt ratios for cities of 50,000–100,000 population. The figures are $467 per capita and 3.6% of the full value of the tax base. Median ratios for 110 representative communities in the state of Connecticut equal $387 per capita, 2.8% of full value, and 6.1% of income. Debt service for the city as a percent of 1981 budgeted expenditures equals 6.6%, vs. a median of 7.6% for the 110 Connecticut towns. Median figures are usually lower than the average or mean statistic and are more conservative; consequently, analysts prefer to use the median.

Debt matures at the rate of 57.2% in five years and 85.6% in ten years. Generally speaking, an average rate of debt retirement (maturity) calls for redemption of 25% of total outstanding principal in five years, with 50% due in ten years. Rapid debt repayment means approximately 70% comes due in ten

years. A rapid retirement schedule is a stronger credit aspect than below average or slow payout. During the last 5 years, Bristol's total overall net debt has been declining, and the debt ratios have been trending downward also. A schedule of Bristol's debt repayment appears in Table 29.9.

Table 29.10 shows pertinent general fund financial results for the six-year period 1975–1980.

During this period, total revenues advanced 48% while total expenditures increased 34.8%. Year-end fund balance, as a percentage of total expenditures, increased steadily each year from 1.3% in FY 1975 to 8% in FY 1978, then dropped to 5.6% in FY 1979 and to 5.1% in FY 1980. Throughout this period total revenues generally exceeded total expenditures at each fiscal year end, and cash plus investments covered total liabilities by a comfortable margin each year.

The city maintains three pension plans for its employees. Annual actuarial evalua-

TABLE 29.9   Bonded Debt Maturity Schedule, as of March 15, 1981, Pro Forma

Due Fiscal Year Ended 6/30	Principal Payments	Interest Payments	Total Payments	This Issue	Pro Forma Cumulative Percents Principal Retired
1982	$ 1,485,000	$ 561,590	$ 2,046,590	$ 225,000	12.5
1983	1,455,000	496,335	1,951,335	225,000	24.8
1984	1,365,000	432,052	1,797,052	220,000	36.4
1985	1,365,000	370,197	1,735,197	100,000	47.1
1986	1,280,000	309,665	1,589,665	100,000	57.2
1987	1,145,000	252,702	1,397,702	100,000	66.3
1988	850,000	203,570	1,053,570	100,000	73.3
1989	515,000	166,195	681,195	100,000	77.8
1990	490,000	136,470	626,470	100,000	82.1
1991	385,000	108,220	493,220	100,000	85.6
1992	385,000	86,480	471,480	85,000	89.1
1993	325,000	65,805	390,805	85,000	92.1
1994	315,000	46,315	361,315	85,000	95.0
1995	225,000	27,445	252,445	85,000	97.3
1996	170,000	15,750	185,750	85,000	99.1
1997	120,000	5,650	125,650	—	100.0
	$11,875,000	$3,284,441	$15,159,441	$1,795,000	

**TABLE 29.10   General Fund Revenues and Expenditures
Fiscal Year Ended June 30 (000's omitted)**

	Audit 1980	*Audit 1979*	*Audit 1978*	*Audit 1977*	*Audit 1976*	*Audit 1975*
Total revenues						
Property taxes	$23,566	$20,996	$21,402	$20,356	$18,577	$16,657
Intergov't revenues	8,489	7,770	6,687	5,524	5,639	4,981
Other	1,933	2,281	2,128	1,732	1,531	1,327
Total	$33,988	$31,047	$30,217	$27,612	$25,747	$22,965
Total expenditures						
Education	$17,881	$16,310	$15,238	$13,752	$12,421	$11,895
Debt service	2,452	2,233	2,427	2,416	2,445	2,548
Other	13,687	13,119	12,185	10,890	9,980	10,796
Total	$34,020	$31,662	$29,850	$27,058	$24,846	$25,239
Operating results	$ (32)	$ (615)	$ 367	$ 554	$ 901	$ (2,274)
Fund balance	$ 1,729	$ 1,761	$ 2,375	$ 2,009	$ 1,323	$ 329
Fund balance/ total expenditures	5.1%	5.6%	8.0%	7.4%	5.3%	1.3%
Net cash balance	$ 163	$ 545	$ 1,314	$ 208	$ 623	$ 776
Property taxes receivable	$ 946	$ 751	$ 846	$ 719	$ 563	$ 428
Total receivables	$ 1,118	$ 893	$ 1,011	$ 817	$ 672	$ 482

tions are made and the city contributes each year to amortize its past service unfunded liability. Total unfunded liabilities for all three funds equal $4.2 million dollars, representing a modest $74 per capita and 0.4% of estimated full value. The three plans are well-funded at ratios of 95.2%, 70.8%, and 68.3%.

The data in Table 29.11 indicate that during FYs 1975–1978 the tax base grew, on average, 2.6% per year. This growth is slightly below average. Effective FY 1979, a revaluation of all taxable property increased the tax base 114.8%. Since that time, the tax base has grown approximately 1.3% per year. Annual tax collections are stable and have averaged a decent rate of 97.5% during the last 6 years. Collection of delinquent taxes is fairly prompt with just 0.2% remaining uncollected after 4 years.

The full value of the tax base on a per capita basis is equal to $15,930 which is below the state rate. The ten largest taxpayers in the city equal 12.9% of the tax base; however, 7.2% of that total is concentrated in the two largest taxpayers. Bristol's economic base is fairly dependent upon durable goods manufacturing which tends to be cyclical, fluctuating with the ups and downs in that industry. Information on the ten largest taxpayers appears in Table 29.12. Comparative statistics for other Connecticut towns and cities of similar size and makeup appear in Exhibit 29.4. Different ratings are accorded each community. Moody's rating was used because not every town is rated by Standard & Poor.

It is our opinion that Bristol's credit has improved over the last 5 to 7 years. A comparison of the city's economic and financial factors with other communities rated A and

TABLE 29.11   Tax Levies and Collections

Fiscal Year Ending 6/30	Net Taxable Grand List	Mill Rate	Annual Levy	Amount Collected Annually	Percent Uncollected as of 2/28/81
1981	$614,454,251	41.2	$26,344,151	In Process	
1980	599,061,870	38.5	23,493,224	97.5	1.6
1979	598,617,725*	34.9	20,892,798	97.4	1.2
1978	278,669,035	75.7	21,372,820	97.0	0.8
1977	272,373,269	75.7	20,302,629	97.3	0.2
1976	260,093,029	72.8	18,616,441	97.4	0.2
1975	258,428,950	65.4	16,639,660	98.1	0.1

*Revaluation

TABLE 29.12   Ten Largest Taxpayers

Name of Taxpayer	Nature of Business	Assessed Value 10/1/80	Percent of Total*
General Motors Corp.	Precision ball bearing mfr.	$33,262,830	5.2
Barnes Group, Inc.	Precision mechanical springs	12,476,080	2.0
Connecticut Light & Power Co.	Utility	9,168,350	1.4
Superior Electric Co.	Electrical equipment	7,882,770	1.2
Entertainment Sports & E.S.P.N.	Broadcasting	5,218,120	0.8
Carpenter Realty Co.	Comm. & ind. bldrs.	3,685,090	0.6
Bristol Shopping Plaza	Shopping center	3,592,210	0.6
W. A. Krueger	Printing	2,738,090	0.4
McGraw Edison & Co. d/b/a/Bussman	Clocks, watches, & timing devices	2,223,980	0.4
Florence Bergamini	Apartments	2,082,080	0.3
Total		$82,329,600	12.9

*Based on a net taxable grand list of $637,837,254.

A1 proves that Bristol's rating more realistically reflects attributes of an A1 credit.

PROBLEMS

1. Using the general information provided on credit analysis, the data provided for the city of Bristol, and the comparative statistics for the similar communities, what do you think Bristol should be rated? What are its strong points? Weak points?

2. What positive steps has Bristol taken since 1975 to improve its credit rating? Recommend further actions to be taken.

3. What is the value of a credit rating price differential? Calculate the value of the price differential attributable to the difference in credit quality. (Note that the 20–bond index is approximately equivalent in rating quality to a single "A" bond. An upward or downward movement is estimated to be equivalent to 25 basis points (.25%) for the 15-year Bristol issue.)

EXHIBIT 29.4 Comparative Statistics for Connecticut Cities and Towns

	BRISTOL	EAST HARTFORD	ENFIELD	TOWN OF GROTON	MANCHESTER	MERIDEN	MIDDLETOWN	WALLINGFORD	WEST HAVEN
Moody's Rating (current)	A	Aa	A	A1	Aa	A1	Aa	A1	A
HNB Rating (current)	solid A1	mid-range Aa	upper A	weak A1	lower-range Aa	solid A1	lower-range Aa	solid A1	mid-range A
Population 1978	55,400	54,300	45,500	37,800	48,400	56,800	37,700	36,000	53,700
1970-78 Pop. Growth %	(0.2)	(5.7)	(1.5)	(1.2)	0.8	1.5	2.1	0.8	1.6
1970 Median Income $	11,835	11,771	11,752	9,584	12,356	11,089	11,280	11,921	10,649
1975 Per Capita Inc.$	4,786	5,262	4,480	4,642	5,655	4,813	4,724	5,086	4,788
1978 Debt Ratios:									
Per Capita $	275	274	737	581	320	461	714	714	392
To Full Value %	3.6	1.8	6.8	4.5	3.3	5.6	6.7	5.9	4.3
To Income %	5.8	5.2	16.5	12.5	5.7	9.6	15.1	14.0	8.2
Debt Serv./Expend. %	8.1	6.8	11.9	7.9	3.8	6.6	13.5	8.9	11.0
1974 Debt Ratios:									
Per Capita $	314	388	508	446	88	374	822	685	337
To Full Value %	4.4	2.7	8.4	4.3	1.0	4.8	8.3	6.3	4.0
General Fund:1974-78									
Operations	2 deficits	positive	2 deficits	2 deficits	2 deficits	2 deficits	2 deficits	positive	4 deficits
Fund Bal./Expend.%	8.0	3.1	8.7	12.5	2.7	5.4	6.0	7.1	(1.5)
Fund Bal.Position	positive	positive	positive	positive	positive	3 deficits	positive	positive	1 deficit
Grand List:									
1974-78 Growth %	2.7	1.5	Reval.	7.4	3.6	2.1	3.2	3.9	1.9
% Commercial	14.0	28.8	13.7	29.6	15.2	14.1	24.7	18.4	21.2
% Chg.Mill Rate 1974-78	22.5	14.4	21.5 (4 yr.)	0.6	18.0	47.7	19.1	8.2 (4 yr.)	20.9
Tax Base:									
% Top 10	13.4	31.3	10.1	38.0	7.7	10.5	35.8	12.6	9.5
Full Value per Cap.$	15,448	15,261	11,176	13,429	16,114	15,206	20,314	13,488	9,424
Year Revaluation	1977	1971	1973	1972	1977	1965	1977	1970	1969
Sales Ratio per Cap. $	19,358	24,743	17,151	23,152	21,550	17,626	25,086	24,953	18,607
Characteristics	Top 1=6.2 (G.M.)	Top 1=22.6 (U.T.)	Broad	Top 2=32.9 (E.B.&Pfizer)	Broad	Broad	Top 2=28.3 (Util.&U.T.)	Broad	Broad
Tax Collections:									
Current 1978 %	97.0	98.7	96.8	96.4	98.6	94.0(9 mos.)	99.0	97.2	95.7
Annual Average %	97.6	98.9	96.5	96.9	98.2	94.3(9 mos.)	98.8	97.0	N/A
1974 Uncollected %	0.1	nil	1.2	0.4	nil	1.2	nil	0.2	0.2
Tax Burden %	8.1	8.6	7.6	6.9	6.8	7.6	8.5	7.6	6.9
Revenues per Capita $	545	652	506	549	515	631	553	638	447
Expend.per Capita $	539	636	495	551	512	603	538	602	453

FOR DISCUSSION

1. What factors, in your opinion, are the most crucial in determining the credit of a municipality?

2. What aspects are indicative of an improving credit? A declining credit?

GLOSSARY OF TERMS

Ad valorem tax A tax based on the value (or assessed value) of property.

Amortize Specific periodic payments which pay off a debt.

Assessed valuation The valuation placed on a property for purposes of taxation.

Assessment ratio The percentage of full value at which property is assessed. For example, an assessment ratio of 70% means that property is assessed for tax purposes at 70% of full value.

Bearer bond A bond which has no identification as to owner. It is presumed to be owned by the bearer or person who possesses it.

Blue list A daily list of dealers' municipal bond offerings, published by the Blue List Publishing Company.

Bond anticipation notes Short-term, tax-exempt municipal notes, available with maturity dates of three months to one year from original issue date. Bond anticipation notes are issued to finance project construction during the interim period between project approval (and receipt of all state and federal grants) and the permanent funding through the issuance of bonds.

Bond Buyer A daily trade paper of the municipal bond business. It also publishes "The Weekly Bond Buyer" which is devoted to money market news as well as being a wrap-up of municipal news of the previous week.

Callable bond A bond which is subject to redemption prior to maturity at the option of the issuer.

Certificates of Deposit Negotiable Certificates of Deposit (CD's) are issued by commercial banks as interest-bearing obligations which evidence their acceptance of a time deposit at a fixed rate of interest for a fixed period. Negotiable CD's are issued by commercial banks for periods from 30 days to 18 months. Certificates of deposit are considered high-grade, short-term investments, the security of which is based on the credit of the issuing bank. CD's are issued in amounts ranging from $25,000 to $10,000,000, subject to current market conditions.

Coupon That part of a bond which indicates interest due. Coupons are detached from bonds by the holders, usually on a semiannual basis, and presented for payment to the issuer's designated paying agent or deposited in his own bank for collection.

Coupon rate Percentage of principal or face amount of bond, representing the amount of funds to be paid as interest to bondholder.

Debt limit The statutory or constitutional maximum debt-incurring power of a municipality.

Debt service Required payments for interest and/or retirement of principal amount of a debt.

Default Failure to pay principal or interest promptly when due.

Dollar bond A bond which is quoted and traded in dollars rather than in yield.

Equalized grand list A formula comparing assessed values at fair market sales prices in each community. The ratio is used to provide comparable estimates of true (market) value for each locality.

Face value Par or 100% value of debt instrument.

Full faith and credit Issuer pledge to use all of its revenue-producing ability to pay interest and principal when due.

Full value Assessed value divided by the assessment ratio.

General obligation A bond secured by pledge of the issuer's full faith, credit and taxing power.

Interest Compensation paid or to be paid for the use of money.

Interest rate The interest payable each year, expressed as a percentage of the principal.

Investment grade The upper spectrum of the rating scale. Indicates the degree of certainty of interest and principal repayment. Investment grade bonds are generally regarded as eligible for bank investment.

Issuer A municipal unit which borrows money through the sale of bonds.

Legal opinion An opinion concerning the legality of a bond issue, usually written by a recognized municipal bond attorney specializing in the approval of public borrowing.

Limited tax bond A bond secured by pledge of a tax which is limited as to rate or amount.

Long-term debt Includes all bonds, serial notes, and long-term commitments.

Marketability The measure of the ease with which a bond can be sold in the secondary market.

Maturity The date upon which the principal of a bond becomes due and payable.

Municipal bonds Bonds issued by a state, territory, or possession of the United States; by any municipality, political subdivision (cities, towns, school districts, and special districts for fire prevention, water, sewer, irrigation, and other purposes); by public agency, or by instrumentality of one or more of the foregoing.

Net interest cost (NIC) Average rate of interest

over the life of a bond which the issuer must pay in order to borrow the funds.

New housing authority bonds A bond issued by a local public housing authority to finance public housing. It is backed by federal funds and the solemn pledge of the U.S. government to see that this payment is made in full.

New issue market Market for new issues of municipal bonds.

Overlapping debt That portion of the debt of other governmental units for which residents of a particular municipality are responsible.

Par value The full amount of a bond, $1,000 or $5,000.

Premium The amount paid, over and above the par value, to the issuer of municipal bonds sold at public sale as an incentive to the issuer to award its bonds to the low bidder on the basis of the lowest net interest cost to the issuing municipality. If two bidders specify the same rate, the low bidder is determined by computing total interest to be paid and deducting therefrom the premium. In this case, the premium serves as a "tie-breaker."

Principal The full amount of a bond exclusive of accrued interest.

Ratings These are designations used by investers' services, such as Moody's and Standard & Poor's, to give relative indications of municipal credit quality.

Registered bond A bond whose owner is registered with the issuer or its agents, either as to both principal and interest or as to principal only.

Revaluation Updating all taxable property to current values.

Revenue bond A bond payable from revenues secured from a project which pays its way by charging rentals to the users, such as toll bridges or toll highways, or revenues from another source which are used for a public purpose. It is not a pledge of the full faith and credit and taxing power of the issuer.

Self-supporting debt Debt incurred for a project or enterprise requiring no tax support other than the specific tax or revenue earmarked for the specific purpose.

Serial bond A bond of an issue which has matur-

ities scheduled annually or semiannually over a period of years.

Short-term debt Includes debt due to mature within one year.

Sinking fund A reserve fund accumulated by a municipality over a period of time for retirement of a debt.

Special tax bond A bond secured by a special tax, such as a gasoline tax.

Speculative Uncertainties or risk factors which outweigh the positive aspects of the credit and detract from the ability of the issuer to repay principal interest.

Syndicate A group of investment banks who buy (underwrite) a new bond issue from the issuing authority and offer it for resale to the general public.

Tax exempt bond Another name for a municipal bond. The interest on a municipal bond is exempt from federal income tax.

Term bond A bond or a bond issue which has a single maturity.

Trustee A bank designated as the custodian of funds and official representative of bondholders.

Unlimited tax bond A bond secured by pledge of taxes which may be levied in unlimited rate or amount.

U.S. Treasury Bills U.S. Treasury Bills are direct obligations of the U.S. Treasury, backed by the full faith and credit of the U.S. Government, pledged to their payment. For all practical purposes, there is no credit risk, only a money market risk on U.S. Treasury Bills. U.S. Treasury Bills are non-interest bearing obligations, issued at a discount, which have a maturity of one year or less. They are regularly issued on a 3-month, 6-month, 9-month and one-year basis. U.S. Treasury Bills have greater liquidity with a broader secondary market than any other type of short-term investment.

U.S. Treasury Notes and Bonds U.S. Treasury Notes and Bonds are long-term debt obligations of the U.S. Government, which are secured by the full faith and credit of the U.S. Government. Treasury Notes can be issued to mature in not more than seven years and Treasury Bonds can be issued to mature from 7 to 30 years.

CHAPTER NINE

FINANCIAL CONDITIONS AND FORECASTING

Assessing the fiscal viability of a jurisdiction consumes more time and effort now than ever before.[1] Although the drama unfolding around cities such as New York City and Cleveland were in part responsible for triggering some concern, something less extreme than crisis or default is behind the widespread interest. It is that the threat of fiscal stress is the result of structural conditions and is related to general economic conditions. There is the recognition today that an "appreciation of potential problems for the next five years will enable municipal leaders to make sound fiscal policies today."[2] That the same point applies at all government levels is illustrated by some of the information requirements introduced into the federal budget process by the Congressional Budget and Impoundment Control Act of 1974 (P.L. 93–344).

What has happened simply is that we have extended our managerial and analytical time horizons. The analysis begins with an assessment of the current situation and the identification of emerging problems (case no. 32). The process involves anticipating imbalances between revenues and expenditures (no. 30) and estimating the budgetary impacts of changes in policy or the legal and macroeconomic environment. The latter may require a systematic or sophisticated forecasting effort (no. 31). The process and its resulting assessment enable decision makers to establish a reasonable link between solvency and services and between the annual budget and its long-term fiscal implications.

The three cases in this chapter introduce the issues and techniques associated with assessing financial conditions and forecasting. These cases emphasize the interplay between budgeting and planning and the role information plays in decision making. Evaluations, projec-

---

[1] The interest is reflected in the growing body of literature on the subject. See, for example, MFOA's *Governmental Finance* 7,4 (November 1978) on forecasting and 9,12 (June 1980) on fiscal stress.

[2] Roy Bahl, with assistance from William Montrone, *A Handbook for Forecasting Municipal Revenues and Expenditures* (Boston, Mass.: Coalition of Northeast Municipalities, September 1979), Preface.

tions, and forecasts direct attention forward, in contrast to the traditional viewpoint succinctly described by a state budget director, who quipped, "Short-term planning is the next budget; long-term planning is the next election."

"Confessions of a Budgeteer," case no. 30, examines state budget projections in terms of appropriate professional and public expectations. (See also case no. 2.) It makes an argument for the disaggregation of data because an aggregate forecast "may be less inaccurate than the forecasts of components of the total."[3] Substantial deviations between budgeted amounts and projections on the one hand and actuals on the other may be washed out at the aggregate level. How this happens and with what consequences are explored in this evaluative case.

Assumptions about economic conditions are one source of deviations. These assumptions are examined in case no. 31 (and also in no. 36, Section A). "Multi-Year Forecasting in San Antonio" lays out the major policy and technical issues surrounding the effective use and production of forecasts. Design issues focus attention on how prospective users determine the appropriate forecasting approach. The case takes the reader through some of the major technical issues relating to generating forecasts by posing problems (especially in the area of constructing revenue projections). Applications require the less complex techniques, such as trend analysis, and are supplemented by a variety of discussion questions at the conclusion of the case study. The locale is the eleventh largest city in the United States. This city has adopted the decentralized approach and uses a combination of expert judgment, trend analysis, and deterministic equations in forecasting revenues and an incremental approach to forecast expenditures.[4]

"Indicator analysis" is based upon qualitative measures of financial conditions expressed as ratios, which are merged into a systematic display of fiscal relationships.[5] This method is used in case no. 32 to assess the current fiscal condition of a hypothetical community and to identify its potential problems. The decision-forcing component is incorporated directly into the case itself. "Smithville" adopts an expansive definition of financial condition by extending it beyond an assessment restricted to cash and budgetary matters to include long-run and service-related considerations.

Case nos. 31 and 32 include bibliographies and introductions to

[3]Congressional Budget Office, U.S. Congress, "A Review of the Accuracy of Treasury Revenue Forecasts, 1963–1978" (Washington, D.C.: Staff working paper, February 1981), p. ix. Note that Treasury revenue estimates deviated from total collections over the period by an *average* of about 4%.

[4]For a review of the experiences of other communities, see Public Technology, Inc., "Multi-Year Revenue and Expenditure Forecasting: Report of National Workshops" (Washington, D.C.: Office of Policy Development and Research, U.S. Department of Housing and Urban Development, 1980).

[5]Sanford M. Groves, W. Maureen Godsey, and Martha A. Shulman, "Financial Indicators for Local Government," *Public Budgeting and Finance* 1,2 (Summer 1981), pp. 5–19.

the specific topic.[6] Related cases include no. 36 on economic assumptions and the role of projections; no. 2 on professional expectations for the effect of information on decision making; no. 8 on uncertainty; nos. 19 and 20 on personnel costs; and nos. 21 and 22 on price change and the techniques for allowing for this factor. In addition, case no. 34 treats planning and budgeting, and case no. 29 examines the type of financial assessment associated with generating a credit rating.

[6]Other bibliographies are available in: Philip M. Dearborn, "Urban Fiscal Studies," in John E. Petersen, Catherine Lavigne Spain, and Martharose F. Laffey, eds., *State and Local Government Finance and Financial Management: A Compendium of Current Research* (Washington, D.C.: Government Finance Research Center, Municipal Finance Officers Association, August 1978), pp. 156–164; Larry D. Schroeder, "Forecasting Revenues and Expenditures" and Sanford M. Groves and W. Maureen Godsey, "Managing Financial Condition," both in J. Richard Aronson and Eli Schwartz, eds., *Management Policies in Local Government Finance* (Washington, D.C.: International City Management Association, 1981), pp. 66–90 and 277–301, respectively; and "Measuring Governmental Financial Condition," no. 5 in series Elements in Financial Management (Washington, D.C.: Government Finance Research Center, Municipal Finance Officers Association, May 1980).

30

*Confessions of a Budgeteer**

When the state concludes a fiscal year in the administration of a $2.4 billion budget virtually on target, with the zero year-end surplus that the legislature anticipated when the budget was enacted, we have to acknowledge that as a remarkable feat.

Based on the September 1 final report for the 1979–80 fiscal year issued by state Comptroller J. Edward Caldwell, that is exactly what has happened. The year ended with an operating surplus of less than $1 million. Technical adjustments raised that figure to $3.1 million.

As the finance commissioner Gov. Thomas J. Meskill used to refer to as "the architect of the deficit," I speak with an outrageous self-serving conflict of interest when I say that fortune, good or bad, usually ranks alongside administrative skill in managing the year-end surplus statement.

Since 1957, no finance commissioner has completed his term without overseeing at least one year-end deficit with the exception of Jay O. Tepper. And in 1976, God knows he tried.

To the critics of the state fiscal scene, the administration that permits the state to slide into a deficit position is ineffective, wild-spending, and mismanaged. The administration that produces a surplus has overtaxed the people, been niggardly with social programs, and is probably planning an election-year tax cut. Then there are those who contend that either a substantial surplus or deficit reflects hopeless fiscal ineptness.

Well, what of the administration that

*By Leo V. Donohue, Democratic State Auditor, State of Connecticut, and former state Finance Commissioner. Reprinted courtesy of the author. This article appeared in *The Hartford Courant,* September 9, 1980, p. 15.

hits it right on the nose? It must really know what it's doing. It must be faithfully executing responsibilities without playing to the voters at the expense of the taxpayers or those dependent on state programs. Without offending my friends in the Office of Policy and Management, I can say that in 1979–80 I think they were good, but I know they were lucky.

Let's take a look at just how it was that they hit the year-end bottom line on the nose in 1979–80 to try to determine just how big a role fortune played in the final outcome.

Actual expenditures for the year were $37 million greater than in the original budget plan. Revenues are coming in at about $38 million more than the legislature anticipated. So we have two variances that total $75 million, but because one is a minus (expenditures) and one is a plus (revenues) they net out to $1 million.

Further, the $38 million in increased revenues represents $69 million in overruns and $31 million in shortfalls for a cumulative variance of $100 million in the specific taxes and sources of revenues on which the original budget was based.

The $37 million in excess spending really reflects $57 million in greater spending than anticipated for some functions of government and $20 million less than planned for others — a total variance of $77 million.

So this budget that came out right on target had overruns and underruns of $100 million in revenues and $77 million in expenditures.

Isn't it unusual that you can be wrong by $177 million and still be right? I don't think so. The diverse nature of the state's revenue structure and the sensitivity of expenditures to economic conditions beyond the state's control have more often than not made the original legislative budget plan hardly recognizable when the comptroller issues his year-end statement.

This does not minimize, but rather, emphasizes the importance of the efforts of the Budget Division in overseeing budget adjustments necessary to accommodate a wildly careening economic and fiscal situation.

My concern is with those critics to whom I earlier referred, who believe that an unbalanced budget reflects either incompetence or scheming. My concern is that they will seize on the 1979–80 experience as a demonstration that fiscal experts, if they really want to, can hit the budget right on the nose. Yes, the bottom line was right but for a lot of wrong reasons.

It now appears from taxes deposited in July from June retail sales that the three-month plummet of the sales tax may have been temporary. This four-month experience with the state's leading revenue producer is a dramatic demonstration that revenue projecting is a precarious undertaking.

It is also an example of the pressures to which the legislative budget for 1980–81 has already been subjected. We can expect that the comptroller's monthly reports on the progress of the budget plan will continue to show drastic adjustments to the original estimates. These changes should be fully documented and explained.

But let's not live in the make-believe world that there are those who know precisely where the budget is headed—what the bottom line surplus or deficit will be on June 30, 1981.

I'm reminded of Damon Runyon's tough guy, Rusty Charlie, who never lost at craps because he rolled the dice in the bottom of a derby, announcing when he made his point. The only safe way to predict a surplus or deficit is to keep your predictions under your hat until the books are closed.

31

*Multiyear Fiscal Forecasting in San Antonio**

I. INTRODUCTION

During the latter half of the 1970s, especially in the wake of the New York City "fiscal crises," interest in projecting the likelihood of

*Larry D. Schroeder, Metropolitan Studies Program, the Maxwell School, Syracuse University. The author would like to acknowledge the assistance provided by the Department of Budget and Research in San Antonio, especially S. Marcus Jahns, Director; Rick Naylor, Chief Management Assistant; and Stu Summers, Senior Budget Analyst. None is responsible, however, for what is contained in this case. This material was prepared with the support of the National Science Foundation, grant (contract) No. DAR78–20256. Any opinions, findings, conclusions, or recommendations expressed herein are those of the author and do not necessarily reflect views of NSF.

future revenue gaps in other cities became increasingly popular. More and more cities began to wonder if they, too, were liable to experience large deficits in the face of such events as continuing rampant inflation, increased taxpayer resistance, and tightened budgets at the state level. These questions remain today with the additional concern that policies made in Washington will adversely affect the local fisc.

While forecasting by itself is incapable of altering federal policies or of changing red ink to black, it does allow policymakers to prepare in advance for potential difficulties. At the same time it raises both conceptual *policy issues* relating to how the forecast can be produced and used most effectively, as well as *technical issues* concerning how the forecasted numbers are to be generated. These issues have been faced and responded to in San Antonio, Texas, where for the past several years multiyear forecasts of revenues and expenditures have been produced, published, and ultimately used for both policymaking and managerial decisions. This case reviews that experience.

In 1980, San Antonio was the eleventh largest city in the United States. It has a city manager form of government with a city council consisting of ten district representatives plus the mayor. San Antonio provides a set of services commonly found in urban governments, such as police, fire, parks and recreation, and sewerage services (an organization chart is provided in Exhibit 31.1). The city does not, however, assume the education responsibility.

The city's principal revenues include both the real property tax and a sales tax. San Antonio also derives revenues from the City Public Service (CPS) based upon gross receipts of this city-owned, but independently operated, utility.

While San Antonio is located in the rapidly growing "sunbelt" and can take advantage of the liberal annexation laws of Texas, it is not without problems. As in the case of cities located in the Northeast and North Central States, it contains an old capital infrastructure. This, when combined with the capital requirements associated with annexation, has made planning, especially capital-facility planning, extremely important.

The city is dependent, to a considerable extent, upon periodic changes in federal defense policies because San Antonio is the location of five military installations. (This may aid the city during the next few years as the

EXHIBIT 31.1

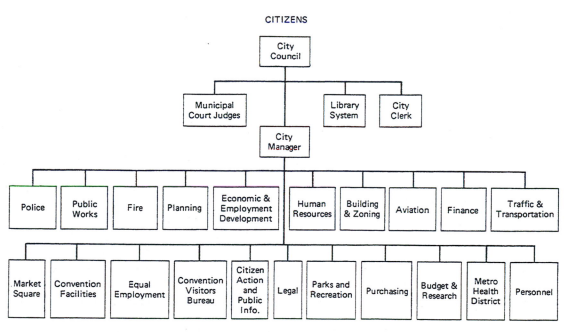

ORGANIZATIONAL CHART
AUGUST 1, 1979

Adapted from City of San Antonio, *Proposed Consolidated Annual Budget,* Fiscal Year 1979-80.

military budget expands.) On the other hand, its nonpublic economic base is not especially tied to any single industry other than, perhaps, tourism; therefore, San Antonio is less likely than major industrial centers to suffer from cyclical fluctuations in national economic activity. (A more complete discussion of San Antonio's economic base is contained in the Appendix, pp. 286–299.)

The first serious effort to develop a long-range forecast began in 1977 after the appointment of a new city manager and a new director of the Department of Budget and Research. They were both interested in developing a systematic, continuous financial planning process—one portion of which was the multiyear forecast. Since there is a set of questions which they, as well as any jurisdiction contemplating a similar effort, had to answer, we begin by discussing these general issues. Section III considers several specific and more technical issues that arise in most forecasting efforts. The fourth section addresses uses of these forecasts.

II. DESIGN ISSUES

No matter how small, any jurisdiction that has decided to produce a multiyear forecast must consider several basic design issues before a forecast can be generated. These include the questions as to *what* is to be forecast, *by whom* it is to be forecast, *when* it is to be forecast, *how* it is to be forecast, and policymakers' roles in producing the forecast. In what follows, alternative "answers" to these issues are provided, as well as the approach ultimately chosen by San Antonio.

A. What Is To Be Forecast?

As in most cities, the revenues and expenditure activities in San Antonio are accounted for in several funds with the principal fund being the General Operating Fund. (Table 31.1 lists the city funds maintained as of 1979.) While a large percentage of all spending under the direct control of the city takes place from the general fund (over 80 percent of operating fund revenues in FY 1980), the fund obviously excludes some important activities. The first question then is: just how extensive is the forecast to be, or, in other words, should the forecast concentrate only upon the general fund or should all funds (or at least a major subset) be projected?

By projecting all funds, the city can obtain a more complete picture of its financial position; furthermore, since there are transfers between the general fund and other funds, these transfers will, at the very least, have to be forecast even if the general fund is the focus of the effort. Still, since San Antonio does not have the benefit of a computerized approach to forecasting (or at least did not during its early history), every additional fund means greater costs in terms of time and effort to produce a forecast.

San Antonio opted for a complete set of forecasts on all funds. In addition, the city adopted the rule that surpluses in any single fund were to be carried over into the subsequent forecasted year, while negative fund balances would be set to zero under the assumption that such a situation could not continue into the following year.

B. Who Is To Produce the Forecast?

Responsibility for producing the forecast can be given to a budget department, finance department, an economic analysis or other special agency, or even to an office set up under the guidance of the city council. Preparation of the annual budget in San Antonio is the task of the Department of Budget and Research. At the same time, the Office of Revenue and Taxation within the Finance Department has traditionally played an important role in estimating revenues for the annual budget and the Planning Department is responsible for long-range planning. Thus there are several possible locations for the production of the forecast. In addition there is always the alternative of creating an entirely new unit in direct liaison with the city manager and council. In San Antonio the multiyear fore-

TABLE 31.1   Financial Funds, San Antonio

I. *Operating Funds*
General Operating Fund
Departments:
Budget and Research
Building and Zoning
Centro 21
Citizen Action and PIO
City Clerk
City Manager
Convention Facilities
Economic and Employment
   Development
Finance
Fire
Health—SAMHD
Hemisfair Plaza
Human Resources
Legal
Library
Market Square
Mayor and Council
Parks and Recreation
Personnel
Planning
Police
Public Works
Purchasing
Traffic and Transportation
Utilities Supervisor
	Nondepartmental Funds:
	Airport Revenue Fund
	Airport Administration Fund
	Stinson Airport Fund
	Convention and Visitors Bureau
	   Fund
	Parking Facilities Revenue Fund
	Sewer Revenue Fund
	Insurance Reserve Fund
	
	II. *Trust and Agency Funds*
	Expanded Health Services Fund
	Home Health Agency Fund
	Family Planning Fund
	Memorials and Gifts Fund
	Public Library Memorials and Gifts Fund
	
	III. *Debt Service Funds*
	General Obligation Debt Service
	Convention Center Arena Debt Service
	Sewer System Revenue Bonds
	Parking Structure Debt Service
	International Airport Revenue Bonds
	
	IV. *Intragovernmental Service Programs*
	Central Stores
	Automotive Maintenance
	Radio Maintenance
	Motor Pool

Source: City of San Antonio, "Five-Year Financial Forecast Manual" (San Antonio: Budget and Research Department, 1980), pp. 5–6.

casting responsibility was placed within the Department of Budget and Research.

C. When Is the Forecast To Be Produced?

Annual budget preparation is a hectic period in all cities. The question therefore arises whether the long-range forecast (especially if placed in the Budget Office) should be produced concurrently with the annual budget or sometime else during the year. With concurrent production, the results will be up-to-date during debates on the proposed budget and the multiyear implications of specific budget initiatives can be shown explicitly. Furthermore, the latest information concerning the long-term outlook for the economy can be utilized in this forecast. At the same time, there is the possibility that participants in the production of the multiyear forecast will not be as serious about their efforts if they are simultaneously preparing the annual budget.

The city of San Antonio opted for an "off-season" preparation of the multiyear forecast. Although the fiscal year runs from August 1 to July 31, with the annual budget presented to council in early June, the multiyear projection is released in December or January. Preparation of this forecast begins in September or soon after the current fiscal year has begun.

D. How Is the Forecast To Be Produced?

There are numerous methods by which revenues and expenditure projections can be made. Two overriding considerations, however, are (1) the degree to which the process is centralized or decentralized (departmental inputs are used) and (2) the specific techniques to be applied in generating the forecasted revenues and expenditures.

Centralization. No matter who has ultimate responsibility for the forecast, the degree to which that agency relies upon other agency inputs is open to question. At the one extreme, the forecasting agency can (a) decide upon the assumptions to be used in the forecast, (b) carry out the necessary computations of both revenue and expenditure projections, and (c) produce the necessary report(s). At the other extreme, the agency can rely entirely upon each department or budget unit to carry out each of the three steps mentioned. Although neither of the extremes is likely to be totally acceptable, the final forecasting procedures are likely to emphasize one or the other of the approaches.

Some degree of centralization may always be necessary. Obviously, it is appropriate for a single unit to derive the assumptions underlying the analysis lest various assumptions be made by different agencies. An economics-oriented group may be the most reasonable unit to carry out this task. Likewise, only a single group is likely to be able to produce the necessary documents in a timely manner and in a readable style. Gathering data can, however, be either a centralized task or decentralized.

In San Antonio, data-gathering is generally decentralized. Although deriving the initial assumptions and producing the final report are the responsibility of the Department of Budget and Research, many of the computational steps and preparation of data are the responsibility of the individual departments. This is true for the departmental expenditures, as well as revenues that are collected by individual departments; e.g., the Department of Building and Zoning collects fees for several of the inspection activities it carries out.

Techniques. There are at least four alternative approaches possible for producing revenue and expenditure forecasts. These include (a) expert judgment, (b) trend, (c) deterministic, and (d) statistical or econometric techniques.[1] While most cities use each of these to some degree, cities rely primarily on one or two of the methods.

Under the expert judgment approach the forecaster or someone to whom the forecaster goes uses her or his own best judgment as to what the revenues and/or expenditures are likely to be in the future. While cheap, the approach is no stronger than the skills of the expert or the ability of the forecaster to seek advice from the "correct" expert. Intergovernmental aids are often forecasted in this manner since there may be no better model for predicting the political actions of elected officials at a higher level of government.

Trend techniques extrapolate revenues or expenditures based purely on recent history. Most commonly linear trends or linear growth rates are used as the underlying "model." Again, while relatively low cost in terms of its data and computational costs, the approach is incapable of forecasting downturns if the recent past is characterized by continuous growth.

Deterministic approaches involve two mathematical computations—multiplication and addition. Total collections of a revenue source are the product of a base times the rate. Thus, under a deterministic approach, all one needs to do is to derive some estimate of both of these factors for each of several revenue sources and add the resulting products. Nearly all cities, including San Antonio, use basically a deterministic method to forecast spending. Again, total expenditures on any

[1]Ray Bahl and Larry Schroeder, "Forecasting Local Government Budget," Occasional Paper No. 38, Metropolitan Studies Program, The Maxwell School (Syracuse, New York: Syracuse University, 1979).

particular item will be equal to the product of the price per unit of the item times the number of items, e.g., average annual salary times the projected work force. In San Antonio, while the price assumptions are made centrally, departments are requested to produce documented projections of how many units of the several types of inputs will be required to produce services over the forecast period. But even here the individual department is not given free rein with respect to the derivation of these projections but, instead, is required to show how these inputs are necessary in light of centrally imposed assumptions concerning population growth, annexation activity, etc., as well as planned new capital facilities and state or federal mandates.

Finally, statistical or econometric methods can be employed to produce forecasts. While the details associated with this forecasting technique are beyond the scope of this case, suffice it to say that the approach involves estimating a statistical relationship between a revenue source and a set of one or more independent, explanatory variables using linear regression techniques. (Most introductory statistics books explain the basics of regression analysis.) Once such a relationship has been estimated, projected values for the independent variables can be used to produce forecasts of the revenue series under the assumption that past functional relationships will hold in the future.

This approach has the capability of yielding forecasts which vary systematically with business conditions and which can be evaluated in a more "scientific" manner than those derived from any of the previous methods. However, the approach is considerably more costly in terms of time, data, and personnel requirements and, possibly, computer inputs than the other alternatives. Furthermore, for most expenditures, other than those which fluctuate in response to economic conditions, e.g., many transfer programs, the technique is probably not sufficiently fine tuned to capture the subtleties of the annual budget process.

In general, San Antonio has used the deterministic approach to project expenditures, and trend analysis for its revenue forecasts. In part, the latter may be attributable to its apparent isolation from major business cycles, although lack of computerization probably contributed to the initial choice of technique.

E. Role of Policymakers

As noted above, multiyear projections are often produced for both the policymaker as well as the internal manager. The degree to which the makers of policy have a role in the production of the forecast can, however, vary from none at all to an integral one. The San Antonio method relies quite heavily upon policymakers, not in the details associated with generating the numbers, but in constructing the underlying assumptions. Obviously, forecasting of any sort requires the use of assumptions. But this, in turn, means that the output from any forecast can be attacked on the grounds that the assumptions are "improper." So as to minimize this possibility, the forecasting technique used in San Antonio employs an approval process by the city council before the forecasts are produced. The Department of Budget and Research prepares a memo stating the set of assumptions to be employed in the forecast. This is then approved or altered by the council.

The set of assumptions which the council debates includes: assumptions about population growth rates over the projection period; economic assumptions, including assumptions about the role of federal installations within the city; assumptions about tax rates and other fees (usually the assumption is of no change in these rates); assumptions about inflation over the forecast period; assumptions about service levels (usually that service levels, however defined, will remain "constant"); assumptions about the self-sufficiency of particular enterprises, i.e., that rates will be altered to insure that revenues meet expenditures; assumptions indicating that the city will respond to any state and federal mandates imposed; and even policy assumptions such as the assertion that federal revenue sharing will be used in a specific way.

Whether the approval of assumptions is necessary for high quality forecast is debatable; however, it probably does have the advantage of dividing the debate over the forecasts. Debate about the adequacy of the assumptions can occur at one point in time leaving discussion of the results as the exclusive topic for council consideration once the forecast is completed.

These questions, then, are basic to the design of any forecasting system and should be addressed before the first number is collected or the first memorandum to a department head is sent. While the approaches can be altered over time, e.g., the process may become more decentralized or different techniques may be used to project revenues, a thorough debate of the pros and cons of the several choices provided may help eliminate future surprises and yield a forecast with maximum utility.

III. SPECIFIC TECHNIQUES

San Antonio, then, has opted for a decentralized approach to forecasting using basically trend techniques to project revenues and a deterministic approach to the projection of expenditures with assumptions made centrally by the Department of Budget and Research, but approved by the city council. In this section, two different aspects of the process are presented—examination of centrally made assumptions and derivation of a departmental forecast of both revenues and expenditures. The data and information contained here were those used in late 1979 to prepare the 1980–85 long range financial forecast.

A. Assumptions

The Department of Budget and Research has prepared the set of assumptions. (See Exhibit 31.2 and Table 31.2.) Ms. Oversight of that department has the responsibility to present it to the council. The following is a hypothetical, partial transcript of the proceedings:

Madam Mayor: We have been joined by Ms. Olivia Oversight of the Department of Budget and Research, who will now explain the rationale behind the assumptions she and others in Budget and Research prepared for our deliberation tonight. The approved assumptions will then be used as members prepare the next long-range financial forecast. Ms. Oversight.

Ms. Oversight: Thank you. Since we have distributed these assumptions to you in advance, I will be brief. I will simply highlight our thoughts regarding several of these assumptions.

For our general assumptions we assumed an average population growth rate of 1.5 percent, since that is about as rapid as our growth has been during the past five years. Since there are no major annexations currently under consideration, we have assumed no new annexations beyond the one passed last September. While the next five years may see a push for increased military operations, we have no idea whether San Antonio will share in this expansion and therefore have made assumption 3.

All of our revenue assumptions are essentially those of nothing new. That is, we are not attempting to predict what you as a council might do over the next five years to alter the revenue structure of our city. While this might be an overly conservative assumption, we feel it is justified for a baseline projection. We can produce alternative forecasts under different scenarios concerning revenue policies; but in order to be most informative they should be comparable to some baseline forecast and the one suggested here would seem to be the most appropriate baseline.

EXHIBIT 31.2

PROPOSED ASSUMPTIONS FOR FY 1980–1985 FIVE-YEAR FINANCIAL FORECAST

I. General Assumptions

1. An annual population growth rate of 1.5 percent (Table A).
2. Except for the proposed annexations currently under city council consideration (Ordinance No. 51272, passed September 20, 1979), there will be no other major annexations.
3. No major change in local military operations.
4. No major shortage of energy supplies, but an understanding that the cost of petroleum and petroleum-related products will be subject to extraordinary increases.

TABLE A. Planning Department's 1979–1985 Population Projections

Year	San Antonio Projected Population (with Proposed Annexation)
1979	845,100
1980	858,700
1981	872,300
1982	885,800
1983	899,400
1984	913,000
1985	926,600

II. Revenue Assumptions

1. Actual property tax revenues will grow only as a result of the proposed annexations, new construction, and property improvements added to the tax rolls. Any change due to reappraisal will be offset by a change in the assessment ratio and/or tax rate.
2. Unless there is proven evidence to the contrary, federal and state categorical and entitlement grants will continue at the current level of funding.
3. The following activities will continue to be self-sustaining from user charges or special revenue sources:
    — Building and Zoning
    — Garbage Collection
    — Sewers
    — Airports
    — Parking Facilities
    — Golf Courses
    — Convention and Visitors Bureau
4. All other revenue rates, fees, and service charges will be held constant. No new revenue sources will be utilized.
5. Revenue projections will assume moderate economic expansion and development and the absence of severe, traumatic changes in the local economy.
6. No substantial utility rate inceases.
7. An amount equal to 26 percent of the annual property tax revenues shall continue to be allocated to the Debt Service Fund. The remaining amount shall be allocated to the general fund.

III. Expenditure Assumptions

1. Debt service requirements will be given first expenditure priority.
2. Assume that the proposed 1980 general obligation bond issue and the proposed revenue bond issues (airport, sewers, etc.) will be approved and that the Financial Forecast includes expenditures for the operation and maintenance of the proposed capital improvements projects.
3. Operating programs will be maintained at the current level of service, as provided for in the FY 1979–80 budget.
4. Rates of inflation for expenditures shall be based on projections of economic indicators furnished by the U.S. Congressional Budget Office. Specific inflation rates, by year and type of expenditure, are shown in Table 31.2.
5. The city will adhere to the federal mandates for scheduled increases in Social Security contributions.
6. Revenue sharing appropriations shall be used for capital projects and nonrecurring expenditures unless additional financial resources are required to balance the general fund.

You will note that our economic assumption, number 5, is neither terribly optimistic or pessimistic about the state of the local economy. While we would like to hope that the economy will pick up and outperform the past several years, we are unwilling to make such an assumption for these projections.

Turning now to our expenditure assumptions, here again we are basically assuming nothing new. This is stated most explicitly in assumption 3, which is essentially a "constant service level" assumption. You will see in the accompanying table of inflation rates that we are being slightly optimistic. On the other hand, if we underestimate inflation on the expenditure side, our revenues, at least the sales tax and very possible the utility receipts, should also expand in response to more rapid price increases.

That, then, is a brief idea of what we were thinking about when we put together this set of assumptions. Are there any questions?

Mr. J. R. Pennyman: Yes, I have a couple of questions. First, where have you people been? Obviously not in the business world. Those inflation rates that you are proposing are entirely too low as long as the current administration remains in office in Washington. I'd be willing to bet that you've underestimated inflation by at least 50 percent.

Second, we all know that there are going to be additional annexations of substantial amounts of land into the city over the next five years. Just because this council is not currently debating them does not mean that they are not going to happen. Why my associate, Mrs. Pennyman, is herself preparing an application to add 45 more acres of prime commercial and industrial space to the city and should have the necessary options and papers drawn up within the next year and a half. Why not include these in the forecast?

Ms. Oversight: I appreciate your concern, Mr. Pennyman, for the inflation rates that we have used. We ourselves had considerable debate concerning these numbers but, in the end, chose those that are shown here since we felt they would be consistent with the rest of our assumptions. Furthermore, they were not invented by our group in Budget

TABLE 31.2.   Projected Expenditure Inflation Rates

Expenditure Classification	Indicator	Rates				
		FY 1980-81	FY 1981-82	FY 1982-83	FY 1983-84	FY 1984-85
I. *Personal Services*						
General salary adjustments, cost-of-living, merit, and position reclassifications	Consumer Price Index (all items, all urban)	8.6%	7.7%	7.5%	7.4%	7.4%
Health Insurance	Consumer Price Index (medical care)	7.8	8.3	9.8	9.2	9.2
Social Security contributions	Budget & research formula based upon legal mandates	14.0	11.7	8.0	7.2	10.7
II. *Contractual Services*						
All services	Consumer Price Index (services)	8.7	7.7	8.1	8.2	8.2
III. *Commodities*						
Energy petroleum-based products, and energy intensive products	Wholesale Price Index (fuel, power, and related products)	16.4	13.5	10.5	10.5	10.5
IV. *Capital Outlay*						
All capital items	Wholesale Price Index (all commodities)	9.0	8.8	8.3	7.7	7.7

and Research, but, instead, were based upon projections of economic indicators furnished by the U.S. Congressional Budget Office.

Mr. Pennyman: Sure, a group with the same philosophy as the current administration.

Ms. Oversight: Be that as it may, we would prefer a consistent set of assumptions to a totally *ad hoc*, and possible inconsistent, set.

With respect to your second question, the underlying philosophy of our forecast is that we make no predictions as to what you, as policymakers, will decide in the future. While this may mean that, ultimately, our revenue and/or expenditure forecasts are in error, we feel it is inappropriate to make such projections. You may also like to know that, in general, the other cities with which we have discussed multiyear forecasting also used this same methodology.

Mr. Pennyman: Well, okay; but I still think that you're going to be mistaken.

Ms. Oversight: Are there other questions? Yes, Mr. Cruz.

Mr. José Cruz: But what about all of the unregistered aliens currently living here in San Antonio? We know that it is a substantial number.

Ms. Oversight: You are probably correct, Mr. Cruz. However, there are two reasons why we do not or cannot include these individuals. First, no one knows with certainty how many there really are, or at least they are not telling. Secondly, if the number of aliens grows at the same rate as the observed population, the proportions will remain constant, and although our population estimates will be undercounts, they will remain proportionately constant over the projection period and therefore for projection purposes should not create difficulties. Obviously, however, it is the first factor that is the more important for this omission. Are there other questions?. . .

The debate then continues but ultimately the council, somewhat grudgingly, accepts the assumptions as presented by the Department of Budget and Research.

B. Deriving Projections[2]

As an analyst in the Department of Building and Zoning, you have been given the responsibility to derive the revenue and expenditure estimates for the department. You have been provided with the council-approved general assumptions shown previously (Exhibit 31.2 and Table 31.2), as well as some historical data.

Revenue projections. The Building and Zoning Department collects user fees from businesses and individuals using their services. The only additional information that has been made available to you for projecting Building Permit revenues is found in Exhibit 31.3 and the upper portion of Table 31.3. In addition, based upon the first four months of the fiscal year, you are willing to increase the FY 1979–80 budget estimates from $838,766 to $840,766 (also shown in Table 31.3). While you know that permit revenues will be most directly affected by building activity, the lack of more explicit information concerning the future has prompted you to use a simple trend-projection technique.

Expenditure projections. To prepare expenditure projections several different tasks must be completed, with many requiring the inputs of other departmental personnel, especially the department head and division chiefs. Appendix B (p p.287–297) provides the overall set of instructions for completing this task.

1.   *Program description*. Exhibit 31.4 provides the centrally prepared draft of the description of the Building and Zoning

---

[2]The information contained here is a variant on the actual projections made by this department for the FY 1980–85 forecast.

EXHIBIT 31.3.

REVENUE PROJECTIONS

In preparing a long-range financial forecast, the initial step will be the projection of revenues for FY 1980 through FY 1985. Departmental input in this process is necessary to assure the accuracy of the revenue projections. Accordingly, we ask that each department responsible for city revenue sources complete and forward the enclosed revenue survey forms to the Budget and Research Department by October 25, 1979.

Information for Projection Revenues

1. All city revenue sources that have yielded revenues over the last few years are included on the survey forms. We realize that some revenue sources will be very difficult to project due to dependent factors outside the department's control. If it is determined that a particular revenue source cannot be projected, leave the provided spaces for the projections blank. The Budget and Research Department will project the revenue source based on the best available information. In addition, enter zeros in the projection spaces for any revenue source which has been discontinued or unlikely to yield future revenues and provide a brief explanatory note.

2. In projecting revenues, the department should consider historical trends as indicated by previous years' actual figures (FY 1974–75 to FY 1978–79), as well as the department's knowledge of factors that influence revenues. Such factors could include pending administration/policy changes, city council direction, anticipated change to current trends, etc..

3. The assumptions in Exhibit 31.2 and Table 31.2 should be used as a guide in determining the extent of internal and external factors influencing city revenues.

4. Please add any existing revenue source which was omitted from the attached forms, along with the projection of revenues. If a department has any questions or requires assistance, please call the Budget and Research Department, or the budget analyst assigned to your department.

TABLE 31.3 Historical and Projected Revenues

Fiscal Year	Revenues
1975	$275,816
1976	505,155
1977	566,075
1978	627,414
1979	864,935
1980 (budget)	838,766
1980 (extrapolated from first 2 months of FY 1980)	840,766
1981	- - -
1982	- - -
1983	- - -
1984	- - -
1985	- - -

Department: Building and Zoning
Revenue Source: Building Permits

Department. The Building and Zoning Department consists of eight different divisions, including overall administration. The department decided to accept this draft as final.

2. *Department goals and objectives.* As an analyst you feel that it is inappropriate for you to attempt to set any final goals and objectives. You may, however, be asked to prepare a draft of these goals and objectives. You begin by looking at the last two years' forecasts and find that the goals and objectives were identical in each:

to maintain a code enforcement program which is effective and efficient
to provide adequate admin-

EXHIBIT 31.4

DRAFT OF THE PROGRAM DESCRIPTION FOR BUILDING AND ZONING

Program description

The Building and Zoning Department is responsible for enforcement of construction-related City Codes. These include the Building; Electrical; Plumbing, Heating, and Air Conditioning; and Minimum Housing Codes, as well as the Zoning, Dangerous Premises, and Home Improvement Contractor ordinances. Additionally, the department is responsible for enforcing the Junk Vehicle and Junk Yard Ordinances, as well as Mobile Home Park Regulations. The Department also jointly enforces several provisions of the Fire Prevention Ordinance, issues permits in accordance with the city's Master Plan to ensure an orderly development of the city, processes applications for zoning changes, and conducts area studies to be used as guides by the Planning Commission and the City Council when considering zoning changes. Historic review, activities, planned building groups, planned unit development and mobile home park plans are also under the jurisdiction of the department.

Divisions administered by the department include Administration, Building Inspection, Heating and Air Conditioning, Electrical Inspection, Plumbing Inspection, Minimum Housing, House Number and Permits, and Zoning Administration.

---

istrative support for the inspections program to include the maintenance of records which will provide current information concerning building construction in San Antonio to ensure the timely processing of all zoning, Board of Adjustment, and historic preservation cases.

It is apparent that these goals could be made more specific. Furthermore, the department head has expressed considerable interest in moving the department towards a greater ability to maintain automated records and the ability to write permits and reports using an automated system.

3. *Critical issues.* Again, it may be beyond the responsibility of an analyst to specify these issues independently, so that in a meeting with the department head and division chiefs the following list of issues is enumerated:

Internal

In order to keep the Building and Zoning Department a self-sustaining activity, license and fee rates will have to be raised an average of 9 percent per year.

The proposed development of permit writing capability in four geographical areas of the city would necessitate computer programming, and computer-related equipment, at a total estimated cost of $59,200. The amount of direction of normal city growth and the scope of projected annexations would dictate the best possible locations for the electronic permit writing capability.

External

Curtailment of CETA funding for the three positions in the Historical Preservation Section, would necessitate city funding at an estimated cost of $24,400.

Future federal monetary policies, as indicated by interest rates, may have an adverse impact on building activity within the city.

4. *Adjustments to current services.* The department currently has 95 positions.

In order to maintain current service levels it is felt that the addition of one clerk (II) is necessary in FY 1980–81 with that position continued throughout the projection period. While Table B–1 (see Appendix) shows that staffing *could* be increased in the later years, it is felt that such increases would be hard to justify at the present time. Table 31.4 contains the initial entries necessary for computing the personal services and commodities costs associated with the proposed clerk (II).

5. *Departmental service improvements.* In the same meeting as was held for the discussion of critical issues, the following set of departmental service improvements was devised:

House numbering and permits: In order to improve the permit writing capability of this department and to offer a greater service to the builders, contractors, and citizens, it is proposed that electronic permit writing facilities be established in the northeast, northwest, and southwest sections of the city. Such a system, in addition to improving service, would elim-

TABLE 31.4   Form FF-A, Worksheet for Calculations Adjustments to Current Services and Departmental Service Improvements

Character	Year						
	1979-80	1980-81	1981-82	1982-83	1983-84	1984-85	Total
Personal services	$8750	$	$	$	$	$	$
(multiplier)	(Base)	(1.086)	(1.170)	(1.257)	(1.350)	(1.450)	
Contractual services							$
(multiplier)	(Base)	(1.087)	(1.171)	(1.265)	(1.369)	(1.481)	
Commodities	250						$
(multiplier)	(Base)	(1.090)	(1.186)	(1.284)	(1.383)	(1.5)	
Other							$
(multiplier)	(Base)	(1.087)	(1.171)	(1.265)	(1.369)	(1.481)	
Capital outlay							$
(multiplier)	(Base)	(1.09)	(1.186)	(1.284)	(1.383)	(1.5)	
TOTAL	$	$	$	$	$	$	$

Brief Description:

Analyst: _____   Date: _____

Circle one: Adjustment   Improvement
Department: Building and Zoning
Section: House Numbering and Permits
Year to take effect: 1980–81

inate the present requirement for builders, contractors, and citizens to come to the downtown area to obtain required permits. This system would cost nearly $60,000 and have annual operational costs of $33,000.

Rather than filling out another Form FF–A, the department has included what they consider to be the necessary information directly within the previous paragraph. They realize that the request is currently little more than a "wish," but it represents an improvement which might be pursued more aggressively in the future. Since they are not highly serious about it at this time, they feel little need to complete the supplemental forms.

6. *Program statistics.* Someone must decide which three-service indicators would be most useful for your department.

7. *O & M costs associated with the CIP.* The department has no major capital facilities planned for the next five years and therefore does not have to fill in Form FF–B. (See Table B.3 on p. 292.)

8. *5-year capital equipment forecasts.* The additional clerk (II) noted in (4) will require an electric typewriter, a desk (45" x 30"), and a stenographic posture chair in 1980/81. Based upon this information, together with the other data listed in the memorandum from Ms. Oversight (see Appendix B), the Form FF–C (Exhibit 31.5) can be completed.

The tasks associated with the multiyear projection project are then completed.

EXHIBIT 31.5   Form FF–C

—————LONG RANGE FINANCIAL FORECAST—————

CAPITAL EQUIPMENT BUDGET SCHEDULE

Fund	Department	Division	Section	Act No.

CAPITAL EQUIPMENT BUDGET*

Capital Equipment Detail	No.	R/A	Projected Amount	No.	R/A	Projected Amount	No.	R/A	Projected Amount	No.	R/A	Projected Amount	No.	R/A	Projected Amount

*R denotes Replacement, A denotes addition.

IV. PRESENTING AND USING THE FORECAST

After the Departmental projections have been submitted and checked for accuracy and reasonableness, adjusted, if deemed necessary, and aggregated, the forecasts of total revenues and expenditures by fund can be derived. These forecasts for 1980–85 are for the general operating funds and the general fund. (See "Revenue and Expenditure Trends by Major Fund" and "General Fund Revenue and Expenditure Trends.") Appendix C contains the detailed revenue and expenditure projections that lie behind these totals. This is then presented to the council for debate and also is released to the press and the public, including potential political candidates.

One might anticipate that, as the city enters into the next annual budget season, some very hard decisions will need to be made so as to avoid these projected revenue shortfalls. Among the options that might be considered are cutbacks in current services, generation of additional revenues through new revenue sources or higher rates on existing sources, delay in some capital equipment spending, especially those projects that will likely generate large operating and maintenance costs, appeals to Austin and/or Washington for greater intergovernmental assistance, or some combination of the above. The

EXHIBIT 31.6

REVENUE AND EXPENDITURE TRENDS BY MAJOR FUND

Presented below are projected total revenues and expenditures for the General Operating Funds for fiscal years 1980–85.

General Operating Funds are comprised of the city's general fund (Exhibit 31.7), general revenue sharing, the administrative portion of community development block grants, Comprehensive and Employment Training Act, and categorical grants. As reflected in the assumptions, revenue sharing was utilized for capital improvements unless additional resources were required to balance the general fund. Community development funds were divided between administration and the capital improvements program.

Revenues are projected to increase by 48.7 percent, and expenditures are projected to increase by 49.6 percent over fiscal years 1980–85. Although nearly all of the revenue sharing funds were included in the forecast of general operating revenues, it is projected that this fund category will still incur a deficit in four out of the next five years. Generally, the projected deficits result from general fund operating expenses increasing at a faster rate than available revenues.

General Operating Funds* (in thousands of dollars)

	FY 80	FY 81	FY 82	FY 83	FY 84	FY 85
Revenues	$170,383	$182,712	$198,578	$219,160	$235,840	$253,328
Expenditures	169,843	187,787	202,893	219,160	236,138	254,175
Difference	540	− 5,075	− 4,315	− 0 −	− 298	− 847

*Includes fund balances and unallocated reserves.

EXHIBIT 31.7

GENERAL FUND REVENUE AND EXPENDITURE TRENDS

Presented below are projections of general fund revenues and expenditures for fiscal years 1980–85. Revenues are projected to increase by 53.5 percent over the six-year period, while expenditures are projected to increase by 54.3 percent. The table below indicates that expenditures are projected to outpace available revenues in four out of the next five fiscal years. Substantially larger deficits are projected for fiscal years 1981 and 1982 than fiscal years 1984 and 1985, due primarily to an anticipated higher rate of inflation.

It is important to note that, in accordance with the forecast assumptions, two significant revenue adjustments (an increase in service fees and the utilization of revenue sharing) were included in the general fund revenue totals. Thus, the removal of these revenue adjustments would produce a substantially larger deficit for each fiscal year over the forecast period. The increase in revenue from service fees ranged from $1.2 million in FY 1981 to $5.4 million in FY 1985. The inclusion of these revenues are needed to keep the self-supporting basis of specific general fund activities. Average annual revenue rate increases of 9.0 percent for Building and Zoning licenses and permits, 11.3 percent for golf course fees and golf cart rentals, and 9.3 percent for the residential waste collection fee (excluding alleys) were included in the revenue totals.

In addition, general revenue sharing was utilized to supplement the general fund in an attempt to balance revenues and expenditures. However, in all but one of the succeeding fiscal years, the shortfall between revenues and expenditures exceeded the total amount of revenue sharing available. The amount of revenue sharing funds utilized in the general fund was $10.0 million for each fiscal year, except FY 1981 ($9.6 million).

As an alternative, if property taxes were to be utilized as a substitute to revenue sharing or the increased service fees, respective additional tax rate increases of $.39 and $.12 would be required for each fiscal year. However, if property taxes were to be utilized only to balance revenue and expenditures in FY 1981–82, a temporary increase of $.20 would be needed for those years. Other alternatives include further adjustments in current revenue rates, fees, and service charges; additional revenue sources; and/or a reduction in the current level of city services.

General Fund (in thousands of dollars)

	FY 80	FY 81	FY 82	FY 83	FY 84	FY 85
Revenues	$153,221	$165,581	$181,647	$201,826	$218,149	$235,145
Expenditures	152,681	170,656	185,962	201,826	218,447	235,992
Difference	540	−5,075	−4,315	−0−	−298	−847

multiyear forecasting model should play a major role in these decisions.

BIBLIOGRAPHY

The available literature on long-term fiscal forecasting is not extensive, since much of what is done is not distributed widely. A brief introduction to the issues is found in Roy Bahl, "Revenue and Expenditure Forecasting by State and Local Governments," in John E. Petersen and Catherine Lavigne Spain, eds., *Essays in Public Finance and Financial Management, State and Local Perspectives* (Chatham, N.J.: Chatham House Publishers, Inc., 1980), pp. 120–26. A more extensive discussion is contained in Larry Schroeder, "Forecasting Revenues and Expenditures," in *Management Policies in Local Government Finance*, J. Richard Aronson and Eli Schwartz, eds., (Washington, D.C.: International City Management Association, 1981), pp. 66–90. Some of the more technical aspects of forecasting, with a comparison of how several cities approach the problems, are discussed in Roy Bahl and Larry Schroeder, "Forecasting Local Government Budgets," Occasional Paper No. 38, Metropolitan Studies Program, The Maxwell School (Syracuse, N.Y.: Syracuse University, 1979), while San Antonio's efforts are documented in some detail in Roy Bahl, Larry Schroeder, and Marla Share, "Local Government Revenue and Expenditure Forecasting: San Antonio," Occasional Paper No. 48, Metropolitan Studies Program, The Maxwell School (Syracuse, N.Y.: Syracuse University, 1981).

FOR DISCUSSION

Design Issues — Section II

1. Discuss the appropriateness of carrying forward fund surpluses but setting fund deficits to zero. What alternative might one offer?

2. Where might a forecasting unit be placed within the city? What might be the pros and cons of such a placement?

3. What are the principal advantages in a decentralized approach to forecasting and what might you recommend for your own city?

4. Is it only a "fluke" that cities experiencing growth (e.g., San Antonio and Dallas) use a decentralized approach to forecasting while more "stagnant" cities (e.g., New York City, Washington, D.C., and New Orleans) have used a more centralized approach?

5. It is sometimes stated that the "expert judgment" approach often used in deriving annual budget revenue estimates is more accurate than more complex techniques such as econometric forecasting. On the other hand, the more complex approaches seem to do better for multi-year forecasts. Why might this be?

6. If you were to estimate the costs of a "constant services" budget, why might you use the deterministic approach outlined in the case rather than a statistical or econometric technique for traditional urban services?

7. Explain in detail how you would go about forecasting sales tax receipts five years into the future using statistical regression analysis if you have data for the last 15 years on sales-tax revenue, the sales tax rate in effect during those years, a measure of local personal income (in nominal terms), a price index, and a population history for that same time period.

Specific Techniques — Section III

8. What are some of the practical problems faced when applying simple time-trend techniques to revenue projections?

9. What purpose(s) do the goals and objectives of the building and zoning department serve? How would you evaluate them for purposes of the forecast? Suggest more specific goals and objectives for the department.

PROBLEMS

Design Issues — Section II

1. Examine the fund structure of a city and make a recommendation as to which fund(s) would be included in a fiscal forecasting project.

2. San Antonio produces its forecast during the "off-season." Prepare an advisory statement for a local jurisdiction with respect to a new forecasting effort. When would you recommend it carry out this forecast?

3. Develop in detail a method for forecasting sales tax receipts (along the lines of discussion question no. 7).

Specific Techniques — Section III

4. Develop a new set of assumptions, including more explicit economic assumptions. Be prepared to justify your choices. (The Congressional Budget Office makes 5-year projections, as does the Office of Management and Budget in the president's annual budget.)

5. Use simple time-trend techniques to derive the revenue projections and complete Table 31.3. (See discussion question no. 8.)

6. Complete Table 31.4 (by multiplying the base year amount for 1979–80 by the relevant multipliers and deriving the totals).

7. Derive alternative and/or additional program indicators. (Those used in San Antonio include: number of inspections, number of permits and licenses, and number of zoning cases.)

8. Complete Form FF-C (Exhibit 31.5).

9. Design and carry out a forecasting exercise for a local jurisdiction.

Presenting and Using the Forecast — Section IV

10. Based upon the information in the boxes: "Revenue & Expenditure Trends by Major Fund" and "General Fund Revenue and Expenditure Trends" and Appendix C (pp. 298–299), write a brief memorandum outlining the kinds of policy options that are available to a city's policymakers with respect to using the forecast.

31

*Appendix**

APPENDIX A: DEMOGRAPHIC AND ECONOMIC TRENDS IN SAN ANTONIO

This appendix provides some background concerning the economic, demographic, and fiscal features of San Antonio and also reviews the organization of the government. The information is useful since the approach and focus of the multiyear projections in a municipality are often tailored to the conditions and needs of that city.

This appendix is drawn from Roy Bahl, Larry Schroeder, and Marla Share, "Local Government Revenue and Expenditure Forecasting: San Antonio, Texas," Occasional Paper No. 48, Metropolitan Studies Program, Maxwell School (Syracuse, New York: Syracuse University, 1981).

The growth patterns in San Antonio parallel those in other major sunbelt cities — it has been experiencing a higher level of economic activity, business expansion, and population growth than the nation as a whole. But unlike some younger sunbelt cities, San Antonio is also confronted with problems typically associated with older cities (e.g., deterioration of the capital infrastructure).

San Antonio is located within Bexar County, Texas, and constitutes approximately 91 percent of the total county population. In 1972 the city expanded its boundaries by incorporating an additional 50 square miles. Annexation has occurred at fairly regular intervals in the past, and another annexation was anticipated around 1980. The city recognizes the direct impact of annexations on the city's budget (responsibility for the provision of basic services such as sewers to the incorporated territory and the generation of additional tax revenues) and attempts to account for this in the forecasting exercise.

Population was estimated by the City to be 831,700 in 1978, up from 708,582 in 1970.[1] If current trends continue, San Antonio's population is expected to increase to 800,000 by 1984.[2] This represents an average annual increase of nearly 2 percent.

Employment trends in the San Antonio SMSA[3] parallel the population growth pattern. Total employment increased by 4.5 percent during the first half of 1978 and was estimated to be 400,000 by the beginning of 1979. The total workforce is projected to increase at a rate of 3 percent annually between 1975 and 1985. Unemployment for the SMSA has averaged 6.4 percent in 1978 as compared to 7.0 percent in 1977. The declining trend in unemployment is expected to continue through 1979.[4]

[1]U.S. Bureau of the Census, *County and City Data Book 1977* (Washington, D.C.: Government Printing Office, 1977), Table 4, p. 756.

[2]*Long Range Financial Forecast FY 1979–84, City of San Antonio,* p. 9.

[3]The Standard Metropolitan Statistical Area includes Bexar, Comal, and Guadalupe Counties.

[4]*Long Range Financial Forecast FY 1979–84*, City of San Antonio, p. 7.

Government, services, and trade represent the three largest components of the local economic structure. Together, the three sectors accounted for 70 percent of area employment in 1975 (see Table A.1). Government alone was responsible for 27.6 percent of all wages paid to the local labor force in 1978. This percentage is the result of five military installations which surround the city and which contribute an estimated $1 billion to the local economy annually.[5]

[5]*Ibid.*, p. 8.

TABLE A.1   Employment for San Antonio SMSA 1975 (in thousands)

Total Nonagricultural Employment	310.8
Mining	1.6
Contract construction	18.7
Manufacturing	37.0
Durable goods	16.6
Nondurable goods	20.4
Transportation & public utilities	13.9
Wholesale & retail trade	78.2
Finance, insurance, and real estate	21.7
Services	54.0
Government	85.7
Federal	39.3

Source: U.S. Department of Labor, *Employment and Earnings,* States and Areas, 1973–75.

APPENDIX B

CITY OF SAN ANTONIO
Interdepartment Correspondence Sheet

To: All budget analysts

From: Mary Oversight

Subject: Review of departmental input for long-range financial forecast

                           Date: November 1, 1979

It is requested that as you review the subject, you keep the following objectives and criteria in mind:

---

1. *Program description*

   Julie has already inserted the first "draft" program descriptions into the word processor. These drafts are attached. Please make any appropriate corrections or additions and return the drafts to Julie.

2. *Departmental goals and objectives*

   These should be brief, clear sentences. When practical, state the proposed deadline for completing each goal. Every effort should be made to include some goals and objectives, but if a department can't come up with some meaningful goals, it would probably be best to leave this section blank.

3. *Critical issues*

   This will be a very important part of the forecast! The city exists in and serves a constantly changing environment, and this critical issues section should be used to anticipate the departments' problems in adjusting to that environment. Consider here the future of federally funded programs, the aging fleet of fire trucks, etc. Hopefully, your departments will not withhold potential problems, but if you know of some critical issues that were not submitted by the department, you may want to add some.

4. *Adjustments to current services*

   a. The total requested positions for any year may not exceed the numbers on Table B.1 of maximum allowable positions for each department for each year. That table has been prepared to show the maximum staffing levels allowable consistent with the assumed levels of city population growth. However, these staffing levels are *not* automatic. The requests for positions and equipment must be, in your opinion, necessary for the department to maintain the current level of services.

   b. The departments should be submitting cost estimates for each adjustment in "current" (not inflated) dollars. You will have to adjust these figures for inflation, for each character, and for each year. Costs should be rounded to the nearest thousands of dollars for each year, and the cumulative costs should also be shown. Table B.2 should contain your calculations of these costs. To complete the worksheet, show in the first column the current cost of the character; then for each year applicable enter the product of the cost times the particular multiplier shown in parentheses. (These multipliers are based on our assumed inflation rates.) Then sum the rows and columns.

   c. All adjustment requests must be for activities currently performed by the department.

   d. If a requested adjustment does not comply with these guidelines, it may be necessary to transfer some positions and/or associated expenses to the service improvement section.

   e. All equipment associated with an acceptable adjustment to current services must also be listed in a five-year capital equipment schedule.

   f. All O&M costs associated with CIP should be summarized as an adjustment.

5. *Departmental service improvements*

   a. Generally, any reasonable and practical request may be included in the service improvements section. However, if you judge a request to be unrealistic or frivolous (a six-man fireboat??), the request should be omitted.

   b. As with "adjustments," you will have to inflate the annual costs of the improvements, but since the costs of service improvements are not included in the forecast summaries, you don't have to be as accurate as you need be in calculating adjustments. These, too, should be entered on another copy of Table B.2

   c. The purchase of capital outlay equipment for service improvements should *not* be included in the 5-year capital equipment schedules.

6. *Program statistics*

   Select the 3 most meaningful indicators.

7. *O&M costs associated with CIP*

   a. You will have to complete the "Worksheet for Calculating Capital Improvement Projects O&M Costs" (Table B.3) as you receive them from your departments. Generally, you will be using the annual inflation rates approved by the council. Use the current pay plan in determining the current salaries for additional positions. Use Step *D* as your base salary and inflate by the council-approved "General Salary Adjustments."

   b. Check the capital equipment outlay associated with the CIP for reasonableness and accuracy.

8. *5-Year capital equipment forecasts*

   a. There should be a separate form FF–C for each section.

   b. If necessary, spread the schedule out so that the quantity and cost of equipment is evenly distributed for each year. Only the most essential equipment should be listed for FY 1980–81.

   c. Check the forms for reasonableness and accuracy. Be sure that equipment associated with adjustments is included.

   d. For each department with more than one section, add up the figures by classification (i.e., "Office Furniture and Equipment"), and show these on a blank form which you will entitle "Departmental Summary."

   e. The typing load for these forms will be extremely heavy, so please make sure the forms are legible and accurate before you turn them in. Also, please complete them as soon as possible so that we don't fall too far behind.

   f. The projected prices for capital equipment are shown in the attachment to this memo, Table B.4.

TABLE B.1 Personnel Staffing by Department by Year
Maximum Staffing Level to Maintain Per Capita Service Level

	79-80 Budget	80-81 Budget	81-82 Budget	82-83 Budget	83-84 Budget	84-85 Budget
Mayor & Council						
City Clerk	9	9	9	9	10	10
Library	208	211	214	217	220	223
Manager	14	14	14	15	15	15
Legal	44	45	45	46	47	47
Finance	109	111	112	114	115	117
Municipal Cts.	72	73	74	75	76	77
Budget	18	18	19	19	19	19
Personnel	40	41	41	42	42	43
Purchasing	11	11	11	11	12	12
DEED	62	63	64	65	66	66
Police	1,713	1,737	1,762	1,786	1,811	1,835
Fire	885	898	910	923	936	948
Public Works	1,164	1,181	1,197	1,214	1,231	1,247
Parks & Recreation	1,367	1,387	1,406	1,426	1,445	1,465
Building & Zoning	95	96	98	99	100	102
Traffic & Transp.	90	91	93	94	95	96
Health	425	431	437	443	449	455
Human Resources	100	101	103	104	106	107
Convention Fac.	86	87	88	90	91	92
Hemisfair Plaza	50	51	51	52	53	54
Planning	34	34	35	35	36	36
Market Square	19	19	20	20	20	20
EEO	18	18	19	19	19	19
Citizen Action	15	15	15	16	16	16
Utility Supvr.	4	4	4	4	4	4
Centro 21	2	2	2	2	2	2
Total Gen. Fund	6,654	6,748	6,843	6,940	7,036	7,127
Employees per Capita	.00786	.00786	.00786	.00786	.00786	.00785
Convention Bureau	53	54	55	55	56	57
Aviation	222	225	228	232	235	238
Sewers	340	345	350	355	359	364
EMS	209	212	215	218	221	224
IGS	218	221	224	227	230	234
Parking	23	23	24	24	24	25
Grand Total	7,719	7,828	7,939	8,051	8,161	8,269
Employees per Capita	.00912	.00912	.00912	.00912	.00912	.00911

TABLE B.2 Worksheet for Calculation of Adjustments to Current Services and Departmental Service Improvements

Character	1979-80	1980-81	1981-82	1982-83	1983-84	1984-85	Total
				Year			
Personal services	$8750	$	$	$	$	$	$
(Multiplier)	(Base)	(1.086)	(1.170)	(1.257)	(1.350)	(1.450)	
Contractual services							$
(Multiplier)	(Base)	(1.087)	(1.171)	(1.265)	(1.369)	(1.481)	
Commodities	250						$
(Multiplier)	(Base)	(1.090)	(1.186)	(1.284)	(1.383)	(1.5)	
Other							$
(Multiplier)	(Base)	(1.087)	(1.171)	(1.265)	(1.369)	(1.481)	
Capital outlay							$
(Multiplier)	(Base)	(1.09)	(1.186)	(1.284)	(1.383)	(1.5)	
TOTAL	$	$	$	$	$	$	$

Brief description:

Analyst: _____ Date: _____

Circle one: Adjustment   Improvement

Department: Building and Zoning

Section: House Numbering and Permits

Year to take effect: 1980-81

TABLE B.3 Form FF-B, Worksheet for Calculating Capital Improvement Projects O and M Costs

DEPARTMENT _____ *PROJECT NAME* _____

Beginning Year of Operation and Maintenance Costs _____ *Project Number* _____

Personnel:

Job Class	Position Title	Salary Range	1980–81		1981–82		1982–83		1983–84		1984–85	
			# of Pos.	Amount	# of Pos.	Amount	# of Pos.	Amount	# of Pos.	Amount	# of Pos.	Amount
Total Personal Services												

(1979–80 dollars)

Other annual operating costs

Contractual services	$ _____	$ _____	$ _____	$ _____	$ _____
Commodities	$ _____	$ _____	$ _____	$ _____	$ _____
Other	$ _____	$ _____	$ _____	$ _____	$ _____
Total operating	$ _____	$ _____	$ _____	$ _____	$ _____
Capital outlay	$ _____	$ _____	$ _____	$ _____	$ _____
Grand total	$ _____	$ _____	$ _____	$ _____	$ _____

292

EXHIBIT B.1   FORM FF-C

LONG RANGE FINANCIAL FORECAST

CAPITAL EQUIPMENT BUDGET SCHEDULE

Fund	Department	Division	Section	Act No.

CAPITAL EQUIPMENT BUDGET*

Capital Equipment Detail	No.	R/A	Projected Amount	No.	R/A	Projected Amount	No.	R/A	Projected Amount	No.	R/A	Projected Amount	No.	R/A	Projected Amount

* R denotes Replacement, A denotes addition.

TABLE B.4 Projected Price List for Selected Equipment for Fiscal Years 1979–80 through 1984–85

Item	Description	Prices: 1979–80	1980–81	1981–82	1982–83	1983–84	1984–85
Class: Vehicle and Service Equipment							
Automobile	Administrative, four-door, six-cylinder, automatic transmission, air-conditioned (compact)	$ 4,950	$ 5,396	$ 5,871	$6,356	$ 6,846	$ 7,425
	Administrative, four-door, six-cylinder, automatic transmission, air-conditioned (intermediate)	5,775	6,295	6,849	7,415	7,987	8,663
	Police, four-door, eight-cylinder, automatic transmission, air-conditioned	6,550	7,140	7,768	8,410	9,059	9,825
Trucksters	Three-wheel	4,600	5,014	5,456	5,906	6,362	6,900
Truck	Pick-up: 1/2 ton	5,275	5,750	6,256	6,773	7,295	7,913
	3/4 ton	5,780	6,300	6,855	7,422	7,994	8,670
	Standard cab and chassis, GVW 8,500	7,785	8,486	9,233	9,996	10,767	11,678
	Standard cab and chassis, GVW 10,000 (1 ton)	6,710	7,314	7,958	8,616	9,280	10,065
	Standard cab and chassis, GVW 22,500 (2 ton)	8,410	9,167	9,974	10,798	11,631	12,615
	Tilt cab—add $1,645		1,793	1,951	2,112	2,275	2,468

Item						
Standard cab and chassis, GVW 25,500 (2-1/2 ton)	11,955	13,031	14,179	15,350	16,534	17,933
Tilt cab—add $1,645		1,793	1,951	2,112	2,275	2,468
Standard cab and chassis, GVW 27,500 (2-3/4 ton)	12,475	13,598	14,795	16,018	17,253	18,713
Tilt cab—add $1,645		1,793	1,951	2,112	2,275	2,468
Tilt cab and chassis, GVW 34,000 w/automatic transmission (garbage truck)	21,175	23,081	25,114	27,189	29,285	31,763
Cabinet file Letter size:						
4-drawer with lock	180	196	213	231	249	270
5-drawer without lock	195	212	231	250	270	293
5-drawer with lock	210	229	249	270	290	315
Legal size:						
4-drawer without lock	185	202	219	238	256	278
4-drawer with lock	200	218	237	257	277	300
5-drawer without lock	220	240	261	282	304	330
5-drawer with lock	240	262	285	308	332	360
Cabinet, storage, metal						
4-shelves 78" x 36" x 18"	160	174	190	205	221	240
4-shelves 78" x 36" x 24"	170	185	202	218	235	255
5-shelves 78" x 36" x 18"	170	185	202	218	235	255
5-shelves 78" x 36" x 24"	180	196	213	231	249	270
Calculators						
Electronic, printing, 12-digit, 4-function	150	164	178	193	207	225
Electronic printing, 12-digit, 4-function w/memory	175	191	208	225	242	263
Typewriter Manual:						
Carriage width 15" or 16"	345	376	409	443	477	518
Carriage width 20"	360	392	427	462	498	540

TABLE B.4 — continued

Item	Description	Prices:1979–80	1980–81	1981–82	1982–83	1983–84	1984–85
Typewriter	Electric:						
	Carriage width 20"	675	736	801	867	934	1,013
	Element type, width 15"	675	736	801	867	934	1,013
Chair, steel	Straight, upholstered w/arms	70	76	83	90	97	105
	Straight, upholstered without arms	55	60	65	71	76	83
	Revolving, upholstered w/arms	120	131	142	154	166	180
	Revolving, upholstered without arms	110	120	130	141	152	165
	Stenographic posture	115	125	136	148	159	173
Chair, steel	Drafting	100	109	119	128	138	150
	Metal folding	12	13	14	15	17	18
Desk, steel							
Contemporary:	Executive w/overhang	180	196	213	231	249	270
	Clerical, double pedestal, 60" x 30"	165	180	196	212	228	248
	Clerical, single pedestal, 45" x 30"	135	147	160	173	187	203
	Typewriter, 60" x 30"	230	251	273	295	318	345
Traditional	Executive	280	305	332	360	387	420
	Clerical, 60" x 30"	225	245	267	289	311	338
	Clerical, 45" x 30"	200	218	237	257	277	300
	Typewriter, 60" x 30", 'L' Shape	330	360	391	424	456	495
	Typewriter, 60" x 30", w/platform	270	294	320	347	373	405
Table	Steel, office: 60" x 30", contemporary design	125	136	148	161	173	188

72" x 36", contemporary design	140	153	166	180	194	210
60" x 30", traditional design	165	180	196	212	228	248
72" x 36", traditional design	180	196	213	231	249	270
Steel, conference:						
72" x 36"	175	191	208	225	242	263
96" x 34"	210	229	249	270	290	315
96" x 36", w/drawers	230	251	273	295	318	345
Drafting table	275	300	326	353	380	413
Auxiliary drawer unit	140	153	166	180	194	210

Class: Radio and Communications Equipment

Radio

Two-way mobile units:						
2-channel — truck or automobile	880	959	1,044	1,130	1,217	1,320
4-channel — truck or automobile	1,000	1,090	1,186	1,284	1,383	1,500
2-channel — motorcycle	1,200	1,308	1,423	1,541	1,660	1,800
4-channel — motorcycle	1,400	1,526	1,660	1,798	1,936	2,100
2-channel — portable	800	872	949	1,027	1,106	1,200
6-channel — portable UHF	1,500	1,635	1,779	1,926	2,075	2,250
8-channel — portable UHF	2,050	2,235	2,431	2,632	2,835	3,075

APPENDIX C: REVENUE PROJECTIONS FISCAL YEARS 1980–1985 (THOUSANDS OF DOLLARS)

PART I

Revenue Category	FY 1980	FY 1981	FY 1982	FY 1983	FY 1984	FY 1985
City Operating Funds						
General Operating Funds						
Beginning Balance	$ 4,613	$ 2,540	$ 2,250	$ 2,500	$ 2,750	$ 3,000
Taxes						
Property taxes	44,164	36,370	37,370	39,617	42,188	44,945
City sales tax	29,035	32,981	36,970	41,283	46,315	51,706
Liquor by the drink	789	900	1,018	1,149	1,299	1,658
Business franchise	2,723	3,102	3,574	4,047	4,507	5,005
License & permits	2,498	2,691	3,009	3,100	3,303	3,524
Revenue from CPSB & CWB	45,090	52,151	60,280	71,190	76,096	80,934
Revenue from Bexar County	393	495	573	617	668	716
Revenue fr. federal agencies						
General revenue sharing	0	10,008	10,008	9,648	10,008	10,008
Comm. develop. block grant	635	408	408	408	408	408
Comp. employment act	4,912	5,335	5,746	6,173	6,630	7,122
Other st. & fed. grants	11,615	11,388	10,777	10,753	10,653	10,653
Charges for city services	14,564	15,950	17,162	18,381	19,692	21,187
Fines	2,694	3,016	3,378	3,783	4,239	4,796
Revenue fr. use of money/prop.	519	356	372	387	389	392
Sales	302	328	362	399	438	480
Other revenue	2,330	1,129	1,163	1,193	1,229	1,265
Transfers	3,507	3,564	4,158	4,532	5,028	5,529
Total revenues & transfers	$165,770	$180,172	$196,328	$216,660	$233,090	$250,328
Total funds available	$170,383	$182,712	$198,578	$219,160	$235,840	$253,328

PART II

Expenditure Category	FY 1980	FY 1981	FY 1982	FY 1983	FY 1984	FY 1985
City Operating Funds						
General Operating Funds						
Departmental expenditures						
Budget & Research	$ 925	$ 747	$ 790	$ 838	$ 889	$ 946
Building & zoning	1,852	2,030	2,359	2,436	2,639	2,856
Centro 21	78	84	91	99	106	114
Citizen action	323	369	397	428	461	495
City clerk	282	400	346	451	496	523
City manager	399	436	472	507	545	588
Convention facilities	3,181	3,584	3,993	4,302	4,670	5,022
Economic & employment dev.	1,729	1,808	1,926	2,052	2,085	2,231
Equal employ. opportunity	340	369	398	430	461	497
Finance	4,254	4,678	5,026	5,447	5,893	6,337
Fire	20,187	22,529	24,385	26,025	28,192	30,128
Health	7,607	8,298	8,709	9,493	10,205	10,963
Hemisfair plaza	1,596	1,761	1,930	2,092	2,260	2,466
Human resources	10,622	10,916	11,249	11,564	11,973	12,273
Legal	1,155	1,299	1,398	1,551	1,656	1,785
Library	3,963	3,793	4,273	4,555	4,887	5,232
Market square	573	735	803	855	902	958
Mayor & council	178	198	206	221	238	257
Municipal courts	1,277	1,379	1,487	1,660	1,786	1,922
Parks & recreation	15,034	17,194	18,919	20,587	22,276	24,236
Personnel	1,156	1,298	1,400	1,472	1,579	1,699
Planning	1,075	1,171	1,252	1,331	1,412	1,503
Police	36,720	40,279	43,208	47,364	50,962	55,196
Public works	30,207	34,382	37,087	40,036	43,493	46,789
Purchasing	230	293	304	319	345	370
Traffic & transportation	7,649	8,856	9,813	10,724	11,747	12,877
Utility supervisor	120	132	143	152	162	174
Other appropriations	15,131	16,519	18,029	19,419	20,918	22,488
Unallocated reserve	2,000	2,250	2,500	2,750	3,000	3,250
Total expenditures & transfers	$169,843	$187,787	$202,893	$219,160	$236,138	$254,175
Ending balance	$ 540	$ (5,075)	$ (4,315)	$ 0	$ (298)	$ (847)

32

Evaluating Financial Condition: City of Smithville*

INTRODUCTION

What Is Financial Condition?

The term "financial condition" has many meanings. In a narrow accounting sense, it refers to whether a government can generate enough cash or liquidity over thirty or sixty days to pay its bills. This is referred to here as "cash solvency." Financial condition also refers to whether a city can generate enough revenues over its normal budgetary period to meet its expenditure obligations and not incur deficits. This is referred to here as "budgetary solvency."

In a broader sense, financial condition can refer to the long-run ability of a government to pay *all* the costs of doing business, including expenditure obligations that normally appear in each annual budget, as well as those that show up only in the years in which they must be paid. Examples of these latter expenditure obligations are: pension costs; payments for accrued employee leave; deferred maintenance; and replacement of capital assets, such as streets, equipment, and buildings. Although these costs will eventually show up in a budget or will otherwise make themselves known, a short-run analysis of one to five years may not reveal them. Therefore,

this long-run balance between revenues and costs warrants separate attention and is referred to here as "long-run solvency."

Finally, financial condition can refer to whether a government can provide the level and quality of services required for the general health and welfare of a community as desired by its citizens. For want of a better term and for the sake of consistency, this will be referred to here as "service-level solvency." A lack of such solvency would be seen, for example, in the case of a government that in all other respects had sound financial condition but was not able to support an adequate level of police and fire services, and it would suffer from cash, budgetary, or long-run solvency problems if it did provide them.

Therefore, financial condition is broadly defined as the ability of a city to pay its way on a continuing basis. Specifically, it refers to a city's ability to:

1. maintain existing service levels
2. withstand local and regional economic disruptions
3. meet the demands of natural growth, decline, and change.

The Financial Trend Monitoring System

Evaluating a jurisdiction's financial condition can be complex. It is a process of sorting through a large number of pieces, including the national economy, population level and composition, local business climate, actions of the state and local government, and the character of the internal finances of the city itself. Not only is there a large number of these factors to evaluate, but many are difficult to isolate and quantify. In addition, no single piece tells the whole story.

*By Carl F. Valente and Maureen Godsey Valente, courtesy of International City Management Association, Washington, D.C. Introduction from Sanford M. Groves, *Evaluating FInancial Condition*, Handbook No. 1 (Washington, D.C.: ICMA, 1980). Reprinted by permission of International City Management Association. The case describes a hypothetical community that represents a composite overview of the many indicator trends in cities in which ICMA worked on evaluating financial condition.

The Financial Trend Monitoring System (FTMS) is a system that identifies the factors that affect financial condition and arranges them in a rational order so that they can be more easily analyzed and, to the extent possible, measured. It is a management tool that pulls together the pertinent information from a city's budgetary and financial reports, mixes it with the appropriate economic and demographic data, and creates a series of local government financial indicators that, when plotted over a period of time, can be used to monitor changes in financial condition.

The FTMS does not provide specific answers to why a problem is occurring, nor does it provide a single number or index to measure financial health. What it does provide are:

1. flags for identifying problems
2. clues to their causes
3. time to take anticipatory action.

The FTMS (see Exhibit 32.1) is built on twelve "factors" that influence financial condition. These financial condition factors are associated with thirty-six "indicators" that measure different aspects of seven of these factors. (See Exhibit 32.2.) Once developed, these indicators can be used to monitor changes (increasing or decreasing) in the factors or to monitor changes in financial condition.

Many aspects of financial condition cannot be measured explicitly, but there is much that can be done. By quantifying the thirty-six indicators and plotting them over a period of

EXHIBIT 32.1. Financial Condition Factors.

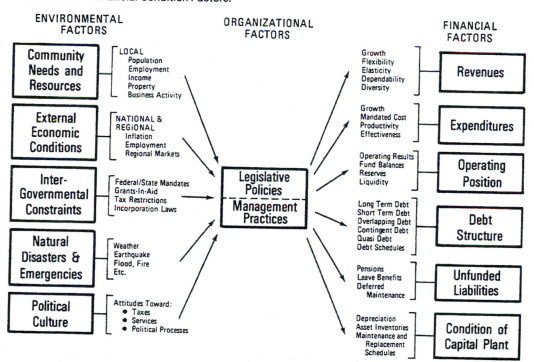

Source: Sanford M. Groves, *Evaluating Financial Condition*, Handbook No. 1 (Washington, D.C.: ICMA, 1980), p. 6. Reprinted by permission of International City Management Association.

EXHIBIT 32.2. Financial Trend Monitoring System.

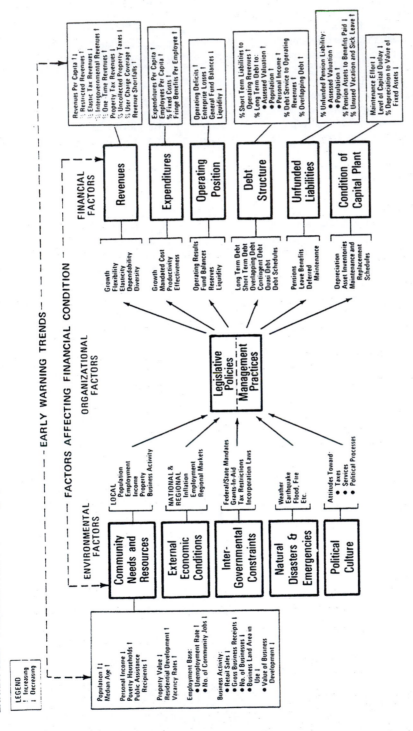

Source: Sanford M. Groves, *Evaluating Financial Condition*, Handbook No. 1 (Washington, D.C.: International City Management Association, 1980), p. 8. Reprinted by permission of International City Management Association.

302

at least five years, city officials can begin to monitor their government's financial performance. The use of these indicators will not provide answers to why a problem is occurring or what the appropriate solution is, but it may provide the opportunity to make an informed management response.

CITY OF SMITHVILLE

Population	30,000
Current annual budget	$14 million
No. of employees	127
Major local tax source	Property tax
Major federal grants	Revenue sharing, CDBG, Section 8 housing

John Q. was recently hired as the City Administrator of Smithville, USA. John replaced the administrator who had been with the city only 18 months. Over the last 10 years no city administrator has worked for Smithville more than 30 months. This was generally due to the relative noncompetitive salary Smithville has paid its city administrator. The result has been a lack of long-range financial planning. However, the city council is committed to having a professional administrator and recently raised the administrator's salary to make it competitive with similar communities.

Smithville is a suburban metropolitan community whose population has been growing about 2-3% per year since 1970. While there is a small segment of low-income families on the south side of town, Smithville is predominantly middle and upper-middle income families. There are well-organized neighborhood groups in Smithville, which, for the most part, have been supportive of the town leaders. Recently these groups have been pressing for increased police protection and improved road maintenance.

Smithville relies on the property tax as the major revenue base, with 35% of the property taxes coming from commercial prop-

erty and 65% from residential property. The commercial tax base had grown fairly rapidly until the mid-70s but has been relatively stable since that time. An upcoming property revaluation (the first in 7 years) will likely shift more of the tax burden to the residential property owners. Generally the housing stock is older, but well maintained by the owners. The city owns large amounts of vacant land in town. Over the last few years city officials have sold tracts of this land to developers. However, because of a slowdown in the regional economy this land has not been developed.

Smithville is a full-service community except for education and electricity which is provided by the county. City employees unionized in 1972 and have won substantial increases in salaries and benefits since that time. While they are not overpaid compared to workers in adjacent towns, their benefits package is substantially better. Their pension system is administered by the state.

The city is presently building a new police station and resurfacing 2.3 miles of road as part of its Capital Improvements Program. In addition, a number of city buildings are being renovated to make them more energy efficient. Smithville is also building a water treatment plant, which was required by EPA in order to meet water quality standards. Total debt service (interest and principal payable in current year) is 13% of operating revenues this year.

The city has been relatively prosperous over the last 10 years, maintaining a large fund balance. However, the city had to use portions of its fund balance to balance the last two years' budgets. As the year comes to a close, John Q. finds that the city will have to draw on the fund balance again because estimated revenues are running less than projected. Both property tax revenues and fees for building permits are lower than projected. Fund balance at the end of the current year is projected to be $530,000.

One problem John Q. has already identified is in the Finance Department. Because it lacks established procedures, Smithville is probably not collecting all taxes due to the city. Furthermore, because it lacks accurate historical data, the city has been overestimating revenues for each of the last three years.

The city administrator, finance director and department heads are now in the early stages of planning next year's budget. In order to rebuild the city reserves and to offset the effect of inflation, John Q. will recommend an increase in the property tax rate — the first in 6 years. He will also recommend reductions in a number of services. Based on his informal conversations with the city council, John Q. feels that there will be a good deal of resistance to his proposed tax increase and service reductions. However, he also feels now is the time to get a better hold on the city's finances. John has four months before he presents his budget recommendations to the council. After the budget year begins, he would like to begin some long-range financial planning for the community and has assigned his assistant to work with him on this project. John feels he will need a good deal of information before he makes his budget and long-range financial planning recommendations. As a start John, his assistant, and the finance director, have begun to compile financial information about Smithville (see Exhibits 32.3A–D).

PROBLEMS

Assume that you are a consultant hired by the city administrator to advise the city on financial matters.

1. In the space below list three indicators (from Exhibit 32.3) which are of *immediate* concern to Smithville. Give one reason that might explain why each indicator may have moved in an unfavorable direction. Where possible, *use other indicators or information from the case study to support your reasoning.*

INDICATORS OF IMMEDIATE CONCERN

Indicator Name	Indicator Number	Reason
1._____	_____	_____
		_____
		_____
2._____	_____	_____
		_____
3._____	_____	_____
		_____

2. In the space below identify three indicator trends (from Exhibit 32.3) which should have their direction reversed over the *long-term* if Smithville is to achieve good financial health. Give one reason that could explain why each indicator may have moved in an unfavorable direction. Where possible, use other indicators or information from the case study to support your reasoning.

INDICATORS TO BE ADDRESSED FOR THE LONG TERM

Indicator Name	Indicator Number	Reason
1._____	_____	_____
		_____
		_____
2._____	_____	_____
		_____
		_____
3._____	_____	_____
		_____
		_____

3. John Q. feels that he needs additional financial information about Smithville. However, because of time constraints, he can only develop *three* additional indicator trends. Which indicators (or what other financial information) would you

urge John Q. to develop? Why? See "Summary of Indicator Formulas" in Exhibit 32.3D for all indicators.

ADDITIONAL INFORMATION TO DEVELOP

Indicator Name	Indicator Number	Reason
1. _____	_____	_____
		_____
		_____
2. _____	_____	_____
		_____
		_____
3. _____	_____	_____
		_____
		_____

BIBLIOGRAPHY

TERRY N. CLARK et al., *How Many New Yorks?*, Comparative Study of Community Decision-Making, Report No. 72 (Chicago: University of Chicago, April 22, 1976).

SANFORD M. GROVES, W. MAUREEN GODSEY, MARTHA A. SHULMAN, "Financial Indicators for Local Government," *Public Budgeting & Finance* 1,2 (Summer 1981), pp. 5–19.

Municipal Financial Officers Association, *Is Your City Heading for Financial Difficulty?: A Guidebook for Small Cities and Other Governmental Units* (Chicago: MFOA, 1979).

GEORGE PETERSON et al., *Urban Fiscal Monitoring* (Washington, D.C.: The Urban Institute, 1978).

U.S. Advisory Commission on Intergovernmental Relations, *City Financial Emergencies: The Intergovernmental Dimension* (Washington, D.C.: GPO, 1973).

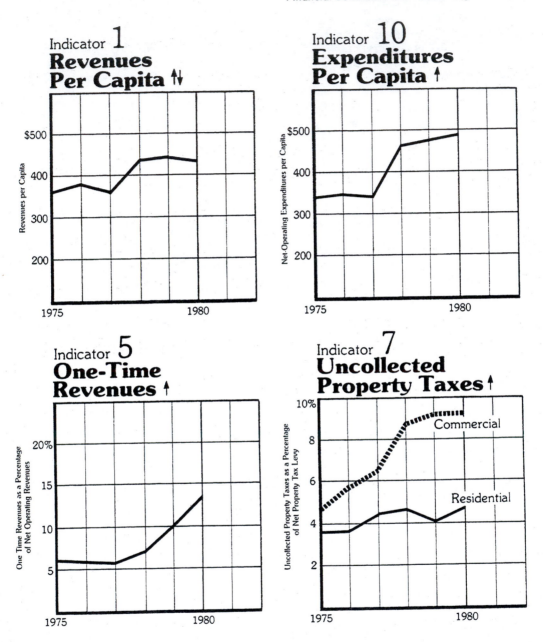

EXHIBIT 32.3A.   A City of Smithville — Selected Indicators.

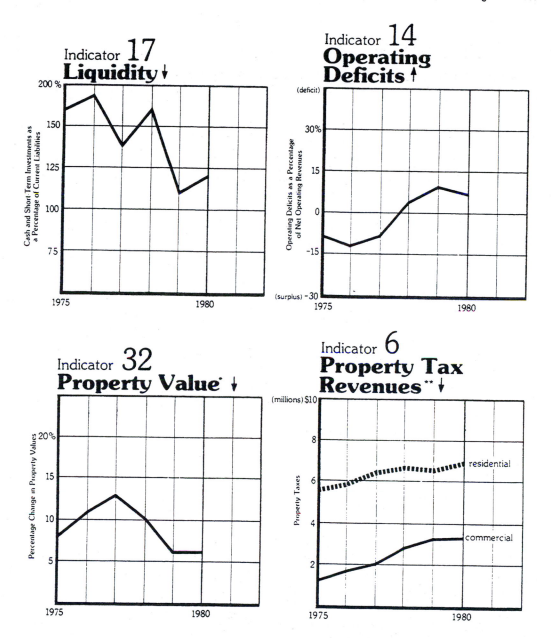

Indicator 17
Liquidity ↓

Indicator 14
Operating Deficits ↑

Indicator 32
Property Value˙ ↓

Indicator 6
Property Tax Revenues˙˙ ↓

*Warning Trend: declining GROWTH in market value of residential, commercial, or industrial property (constant dollars).

**Warning Trend: declining GROWTH in property tax revenues (constant dollars).

EXHIBIT 32.3B.

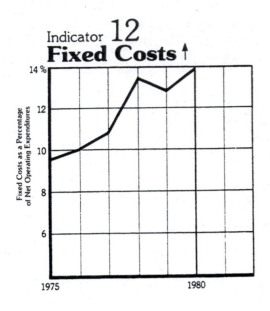

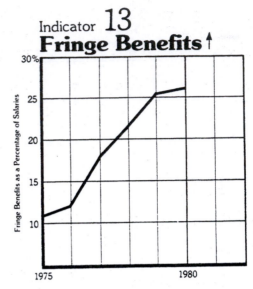

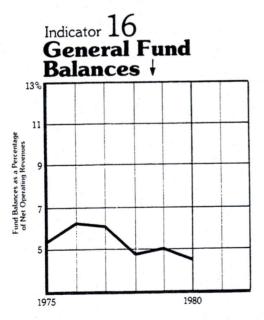

EXHIBIT 32.3C.

No.	Indicator Title	Formula
1.	Revenues Per Capita	Net Operating Revenues in Constant Dollars / Population
2.	Restricted Revenues	Restricted Operating Revenues / Net Operating Revenues
3.	Intergovernmental Revenues	Intergovernmental Operating Revenues / Gross Operating Revenues
4.	Elastic Tax Revenues	Elastic Operating Revenues / Net Operating Revenues
5. **	One-Time Revenues	One-Time Operating Revenues / Net Operating Revenues
6. **	Property Tax Revenues	Property Tax Revenues in Constant Dollars
7. **	Uncollected Property Taxes	Uncollected Property Taxes / Net Property Tax Levy
8.	User Charge Coverage	Revenues from Fees and User Charges / Expenditures for Related Services
9.	Revenue Shortfalls	Revenue Shortfalls / Net Operating Revenues
10.**	Expenditures Per Capita	Net Operating Expenditures in Constant Dollars / Population
11.	Employees Per Capita	Number of Municipal Employees / Population
12.**	Fixed Costs	Fixed Costs / Net Operating Expenditures
13.**	Fringe Benefits	Fringe Benefit Expenditures / Salaries and Wages
14.**	Operating Deficits	General Fund Operating Deficit / Net Operating Revenues
15.	Enterprise Losses	Enterprise Profits or Losses in Constant Dollars
16.**	General Fund Balances	Unrestricted Fund Balance of General Fund / Net Operating Revenues
17.**	Liquidity	Cash and Short-Term Investments / Current Liabilities
18.	Current Liabilities	Current Liabilities / Net Operating Revenues
19.**	Long-Term Debt	Net Direct Long-Term Debt / Assessed Valuation
20.	Debt Service	Net Direct Debt Service / Net Operating Revenues
21.	Overlapping Debt	Overlapping Long-Term Debt / Assessed Valuation
22.	Unfunded Pension Liability	Unfunded Pension Plan Vested Benefits / Assessed Valuation
23.	Pension Assets	Pension Plan Assets / Pension Benefits Paid
24.	Accumulated Employee Leave Liability	Total Days of Unused Vacation and Sick Leave / Number of Municipal Employees

No.	Indicator Title	Formula
25.	Maintenance Effort	Expenditures for Repair and Maintenance of General Fixed Assets / Amount of Assets
26.	Level of Capital Outlay	Capital Outlays from Operating Funds / Net Operating Expenditures
27.	Depreciation	Depreciation Expense / Cost of Depreciable Fixed Assets
28.	Population	Population
29.	Median Age	Median Age of Population
30.	Personal Income	Personal Income in Constant Dollars / Population
31.	Poverty Households or Public Assistance Recipients	Poverty or Public Assistance Households / Households in Thousands
32.**	Property Value	Constant Dollar Change in Property Value / Constant Dollar Property Value Prior Year
33.	Residential Development	Market Value of Residential Property / Market Value of Total Property
34.	Vacancy Rates	Vacancy Rates
35.	Employment Base	. Rate of Unemployment . Number of Community Jobs
36.	Business Activity	. Retail Sales . Number of Community Businesses . Gross Business Receipts . Valuation of Business Property . Business Acres Developed

**Indicators developed by Smithville.

EXHIBIT 32.3D. Summary of Indicator Formulas

CHAPTER TEN

BUDGET REFORM

Any substantial change in budget process or format is likely to be labeled "reform," a term which elicits a variety of positive connotations. It conjures up the rational, the progressive, better and more efficient management, and the public good. Perhaps the usefulness and frequency of the claim to reform explain why the literature on budgeting and financial management dwells upon this topic. Yet, so too do politicians and professional practitioners. It is not simply a political device or polemical tool but a shared ideal. The theme of reform reflects a common concern and real commitment to providing more useful information for "better" decision making. This professional norm extends well beyond the confines of public budgeting in the United States.[1]

"Reform" remains, however, less an analytic than a political term. Acknowledging the political core of budget reform is critical for understanding the lineup of adherents and opponents, their goals, and the chances for successful implementation. Allocational, distributional, and power relationships and issues are involved. Reform is not a purely technical undertaking with neutral consequences, although it is frequently couched in these terms. Aaron Wildavsky zeroed in on the political aspect when he wrote that "any effective change in budgetary relationships must necessarily alter the outcomes of the budgetary process. Otherwise, why bother?"[2] It follows that any assessment of budget reform should look at budget outputs and systemic outcomes, along with the usual array of procedures, deadlines, guidelines, classificatory schema, and the like. (Case no. 33 illustrates this point.)

This essentially political perspective on budget reform is supplemented logically by next targeting more narrowly on matters internal to budgeting and financial management. Allen Schick has identified three successive stages of budget reform based on shifts in functional emphasis.[3] He argues that reform alters the balance among the three

[1]XVIIIth International Congress on Administrative Sciences, "20 Years of Budgetary Reform: A Tentative International Stocktaking," General Report of the Working Group in Integrated Budget Systems, International Institute of Administrative Sciences, Brussels, 1982.

[2]Aaron Wildavsky, "Political Implications of Budgetary Reform," *Public Administration Review* 21 (Autumn 1961), p. 183.

[3]Allen Schick, "The Road to PPB: The Stages of Budget Reform," *Public Administration Review* 26 (December 1966), pp. 243–58.

functional orientations in budgeting: control, planning, and management. Analysis in these terms has come to dominate the literature, is used as a unifying, thematic element in this casebook, and appears directly in case no. 34.

Over the last several decades, the descriptive literature has scrutinized a series of reform efforts and proposals that must appear as cryptograms to the uninitiated—PPBS, MBO, ZBB. Some general lessons have emerged. Woodrow Wilson provided one almost a century ago: "Wherever regard for public opinion is a first principle of government, practical reform must be slow and all reform must be full of compromises."[4]

The normative literature has generated a number of prescriptions, just as expected. One is courtesy of George Bernard Shaw, who directly contributed to the literature of budgeting.[5] In his "Man and Superman," he warns, "You can be as romantic as you please about love, Hector, but you mustn't be romantic about money." Another is attributed to Napoleon, who judged that "outside a budget there is no salvation."[6]

The impetus behind reform shapes its target and type. The strongest single impetus behind contemporary changes in process and format is the attempt to "control"—contain or reverse—growing public expenditures (cases nos. 35 and 36). The fact that a high level of executive commitment marks successful implementation suggests that some executives may use reform to leave their mark. It certainly is a useful way of informing members of one's own bureaucracy and the legislature, as well as the public, that a new administration has arrived. Reform may also represent a relatively easy and inexpensive substitute for substantive policy or a means by which to really transform allocation or distributional outcomes. The budget process, including budget reform, is one of the battlegrounds on which executive–legislative conflict historically has been fought. (See cases nos. 6 and 15.) Alternatively, and especially when there is an effort underway to integrate budgeting with the planning process (no. 34) or management process (no. 24), the reform effort may reflect a growing recognition of the changing role of government and, derivatively, of the budget.

The cases in this chapter describe three attempts at budget reform. "A Council Member Looks at Performance Measurement" is an evaluative case drawn from Iowa City's experience with a new budget technique explicitly designed to meet the council's needs. The council member sums up the reform by concluding, "As an elected body, our decisions are political ones . . . . If they also happen to be rational and logical, so much the better." This case views reform from a purely political perspective.

Case no. 34, "How Can You Plan When You Can't Even Budget," traces the U.S. Department of Commerce's experiences in terms of basic public management concepts (e.g., organization theory) and budget reform principles (e.g., executive commitment). Here, the

[4]Woodrow Wilson, "The Study of Administration," *Political Science Quarterly* II, 2 (June 1887), p. 208.

[5]George Bernard Shaw, *The Common Sense of Municipal Trading* (Westminster: A. Constable & Co., Ltd., 1904).

[6]J. Herold, *The Mind of Napoleon* (New York: Columbia University Press, 1955), p. 137.

budget process is viewed through an organizational perspective as a management mechanism. The planning component is especially important in this large, complex, and highly decentralized department.

"Budgeting in Columbus" examines a decentralized budget system that is designed to control departmental spending. This evaluative case describes the response to the deficit projected in the quarterly general fund status report. The case introduces two different approaches to municipal budget preparation (centralized vs. decentralized) and alternative priorities (spending control vs. services/output). It concludes with a series of discussion questions.

It has been said that "[t]he field of budgeting is experiencing future shock."[7] Because change and reform are such broad and pervasive topics, many of the cases in this casebook touch upon budget reform. Many are cross-referenced in this introduction.

Some readers may note a common thread running through these cases. No reformer lays claim to immediate or short-term cost savings unless economy itself is the objective. In fact, considering the costs of starting up and sustaining even refinements in procedure and technique—everything from printing new forms to staffing and training needs—one may find reform costly. The decision may not be cheaper; one can only hope that it will be better.

[7]Thomas D. Lynch, ed., *Contemporary Public Budgeting* (New Brunswick: Transaction Books, 1981), Preface.

33

A Council Member Looks at Performance Measurement*

Prior to July 1976, the Iowa City Council had a continuing concern that its budget process was woefully inadequate. The budget was impossible to read in a meaningful way because it dealt only in numbers. The council had no basis on which to make funding decisions other than how much money had been allocated the previous year and whether or not it "liked" what was going on within a particular city department. The council felt that if department heads could present a plan for the upcoming budget period, it would be better able to decide a department's budget on what was projected to occur within the coming year. As a body, the council was inexperienced with performance measurement. The city administrator responded appropriately: management by objectives—performance standards and measurement—were implemented in Iowa City.

The city started with a performance program budgeting technique that attempted to answer the questions of the city council. That process began with goals and objectives being set by department heads in conjunction with the city manager. However, the council wanted, as policymakers, to establish its own goals and objectives.

Realistic performance measurement is a continuing process that reflects the consolidation and accommodation of a large number of "cues" received by the originator of the budget in question. Perceptions of community needs

from administrative and legislative points of view may be diametrically opposed. The administrator responding to "cue" stimuli often opts for both budget program and performance measurements that co-opt the "middle ground" in the decision-making process, thus satisfying, albeit moderately, as many "cue" givers as possible, especially if those "cue" givers have or can gain political influence. To the administrator, the budget process and the establishment of performance measurements often become satisfaction oriented, rather than product oriented, as perceptiveness to "cues," coupled with observed needs, becomes a partial basis for budgeting, as well as the ensuing performance measurements that rate a portion of the budget process. This process is at once both rational and political, but it is subject to so many variables that it is less than compatible with carefully arrived at, and subscribed to, planning efforts.

Determining that the city council wasn't offering enough initial "cues" early enough in the budget process, it modified the plan. The council collectively arrived at a set of goals and objectives which were then used by the department heads as a guide in the preparation of their fiscal-year budgets. This is now an annual occurrence by the council, with its goals and objectives serving as the directives for the priorities within each of the departments, as well as for the city as a whole. Further modification has brought about the issuance of quarterly reports by the individual departments which provide the council with a step-by-step assessment of the goals and objectives of each department throughout the fiscal year. These quarterly reports enable the council to change periodically the programs of the departments to coincide with changes in service demands.

*Excerpts from a presentation by Carol deProsse, council member, City of Iowa City, Iowa, at a colloquium sponsored by the Government Finance Research Center (Municipal Finance Officers Association) entitled "Performance Measurement in Local Government," May 18, 1979, Washington, D.C. Reprinted by permission from *Resources in Review* 1,4 (May/June 1979), pp. 4–5.

After several years of moving in a direction of measuring work productivity and program effectiveness, it is now easier to determine which departments are unable to meet their goals and what adjustments need to be made in order to bring about the desired result.

A major benefit of this system is the increased awareness the council now has of the amount of work being undertaken by each of the departments. This new sensitivity has helped to ease the unreasonable workload the council often puts on its staff. When the council had no idea how many projects were underway in any given department, or their status at any particular moment, or the number of hours of manpower that those projects were expected to utilize, many items were referred to the staff with directions to "report back as soon as possible." There were no priorities except what a majority wanted done at any given moment.

In addition, to examine the quantity of service without being concerned with its quality is to lose sight of the meaning of performance measurement.

Prior to FY 78, Iowa City departmental operations were on a day-to-day basis and the council was unable to assess projects and programs because there was no plan of action. Since that time the council has been able to go to the budget document, along with the quar-

terly reports, and see where certain projects or programs have failed to meet a proposed service level. Performance standards and measurement in Iowa City serve to make the various departments accountable to the city manager, with the city council as the final body of review.

Performance management in Iowa City is based on 1) the quarterly reports that are part of our management-by-objectives system, 2) citizen input as to service delivery, 3) economic constraints on service delivery, and 4) political considerations in providing services. The political considerations play the largest role in the city council's decision of the performance of each department.

As an elected body, the council's decisions are political ones—or at least perceived as political. If they also happen to be rational and logical, so much the better. In a local government setting, the more performance measurement you have, the more constraints are placed on the council's decision-making process. Performance standards and measurements must be flexible enough to produce an improvement in efficiency and effectiveness, but at the same time permit the democratic process to work. In general, the implementation of performance management, therefore, is tied to upper-, middle-, and lower-level management more than to the legislative body.

34

*How Can You Plan When You Can't Even Budget?**

On August 5, 1979, a group of 15 senior management officials from the Department of Commerce gathered at the Smithsonian Insti-

*Alan P. Balutis, Director, Office of Policy and Systems, U.S. Department of Commerce. The views expressed here are solely the author's.

tution's Belmont Conference Center in the rolling hills of Maryland. Their task was to determine what was needed to get a newly conceptualized planning and management system underway in the department. The group that assembled during those humid three days included the "best and the brightest" in the Office of the Assistant Secretary for Administration at Commerce:

Clifford J. Parker—director of the Office of Budget and Program Evaluation (OBPE), acting director of personnel, a savvy career bureaucrat, and one of the major designers of the department's new "system," dubbed integrated planning and management (IPM).

David S. Nathan—co-designer of IPM with Parker and his alter ego in OBPE and personnel. Nathan had served as budget director and controller and worked at the old Bureau of the Budget (BOB), where he was one of the authors of BOB Bulletin 66–2, the directive that established PPBS in the federal government.

Mitch Levine, Nancy Richards, Mark Brown, Enzo Puglisi, and Howard Dendurent—senior officials in the Commerce Budget Office. The budget process was one of the few centralized mechanisms available in the department and IPM was to be built around it.

Vicki Emerson, Dick Schnurr, Steve Roman—senior officials in the Commerce Personnel Office. Personnel systems, existing and planned, were to be linked in as well.

Various other representatives from key staff offices—Lucille Reifman, Rob Hull, and myself, from Program Evaluation; Len Sweeney, acting controller; and Hugh Brennan from the Office of Organization and Management Systems.

The effort to develop a new approach emanated from a number of sources. One of the most significant was the passage of the Civil Service Reform Act (CSRA), which mandated that appraisal of performance be based on both individual *and* organizational performance. But a number of other forces were at work as well. The overall budget climate within the federal government had forced a concern with "doing more with less" and improving the management of agency re-

sources. The Office of Management and Budget had been pressuring the department to improve program performance measures and develop a long-range planning capability.

Even without all these external factors, however, the department would have proceeded with an integrated planning and management-like approach, for it had recognized the need to improve the ability to plan for, budget for, and monitor organizational performance. The passage of the CSRA was only one manifestation of the increased emphasis on accountability in government—budget reform, the introduction of sunset legislation, and increasing congressional oversight being others. This had been recognized by departmental officials, as had the increased amount of collaboration required to bring the various resources of the department to bear on target populations or industries in a more coordinated fashion to achieve major outcomes. Finally, there was a widely held notion that Commerce was a bureaucratic backwater, a poorly managed, badly run department. This was so prevalent a notion that when Juanita Kreps stepped down as secretary, she was praised in the press for "having taken a third-rate department and made it second rate."

IPM was intended to be more than a complex management agenda or a planning schedule. It was meant to provide an overall framework within which all the machinery and activities of the department could function in concert. It was hoped that it would also institutionalize some new values in Commerce. For example, it emphasized the importance of planning and the desire to have budgets built on the basis of plans and not vice-versa. It sought to bring administrative staff into the planning process in its very earliest stages on the assumption that program planning should give a great deal of weight to the problems support staff were facing in management areas (e.g., personnel, procurement, ADP, etc.)

Also fundamental to the IPM effort in the department was an informed realism which accepted the necessity for both integration and diversity in administration. On the one hand, Commerce had historically functioned as a holding company, a loosely run confederation of 12 major operating components, which existed as relatively autonomous fiefdoms. (See Exhibit 34.1.) In fact, Commerce has often been called the "attic of government" in recognition of that fact. Juanita Kreps borrowed a familiar observation: that there is a great similarity between Commerce and Noah's Ark. The difference between them, she said, is that Commerce has just one of everything. On the other hand, Assistant Secretary for Administration Elsa Porter and Under Secretary Luther Hodges had been trying to develop the view that there was indeed a Department of Commerce and that it needed to change if it was to accomplish its basic missions and meet the challenges now confronting it—to increase foreign and domestic trade, to achieve balanced regional development, to encourage industrial innovation, etc.

Thus, there was a recognition of the need for differentiated processes suited to diverse agency situations and for decentralization. But there was also an integrative drive for unity of purposes and for coordination. IPM had to be designed, therefore, to be flexible in approach so as not to try to impose a monolithic system on the entire department. Over those three days and in the weeks that followed, the IPM approach was developed and a strategy for implementing it in the department was agreed to.

DEVELOPING THE CONCEPT

IPM as a concept was simple, perhaps deceptively so. One of its chief merits was that its key elements could be quickly listed in plain English and were understandable to most managers.

The key elements of integrated planning and management were as follows:

1. Setting goals, objectives, and priorities in terms of results to be accomplished in a given time.

2. Developing plans for the accomplishment of results (long-range planning).
3. Allocating resources (personnel, money, space, equipment, etc.) in terms of established goals, objectives, and priorities (resource allocation).
4. Involving support staff in the development and implementation of program plans (operational planning).
5. Tracking or monitoring progress toward goals and objectives, with specific immediate milestones (monitoring).
6. Evaluating results in terms of effectiveness (including quality), efficiency, economy, and impact (evaluation).
7. Generating and implementing improvements in program objectives and results (feedback).

Exhibit 34.2 outlines the IPM process. The objectives of this effort were to:

1. Establish an environment for better planning and management by having an ongoing year-round process for top level program and administrative discussion and interaction.
2. Establish a mutual understanding between program and administrative officials in the bureaus and within the department of what the major objectives were in each bureau and in the department.
3. Identify who was responsible for particular objectives and assure administrative support where appropriate.
4. Provide appropriate methods for evaluating overall department performance, bureau performance, and the performance of key individuals.

Underlying the relatively simple elements of IPM reviewed above were several basic concepts of contemporary management theory and practice. These were the following:

1. Acceptance of the necessity for integration *and* diversity in administration.

EXHIBIT 34.1. Organizational Chart of the U.S. Department of Commerce.

U.S. DEPARTMENT OF COMMERCE

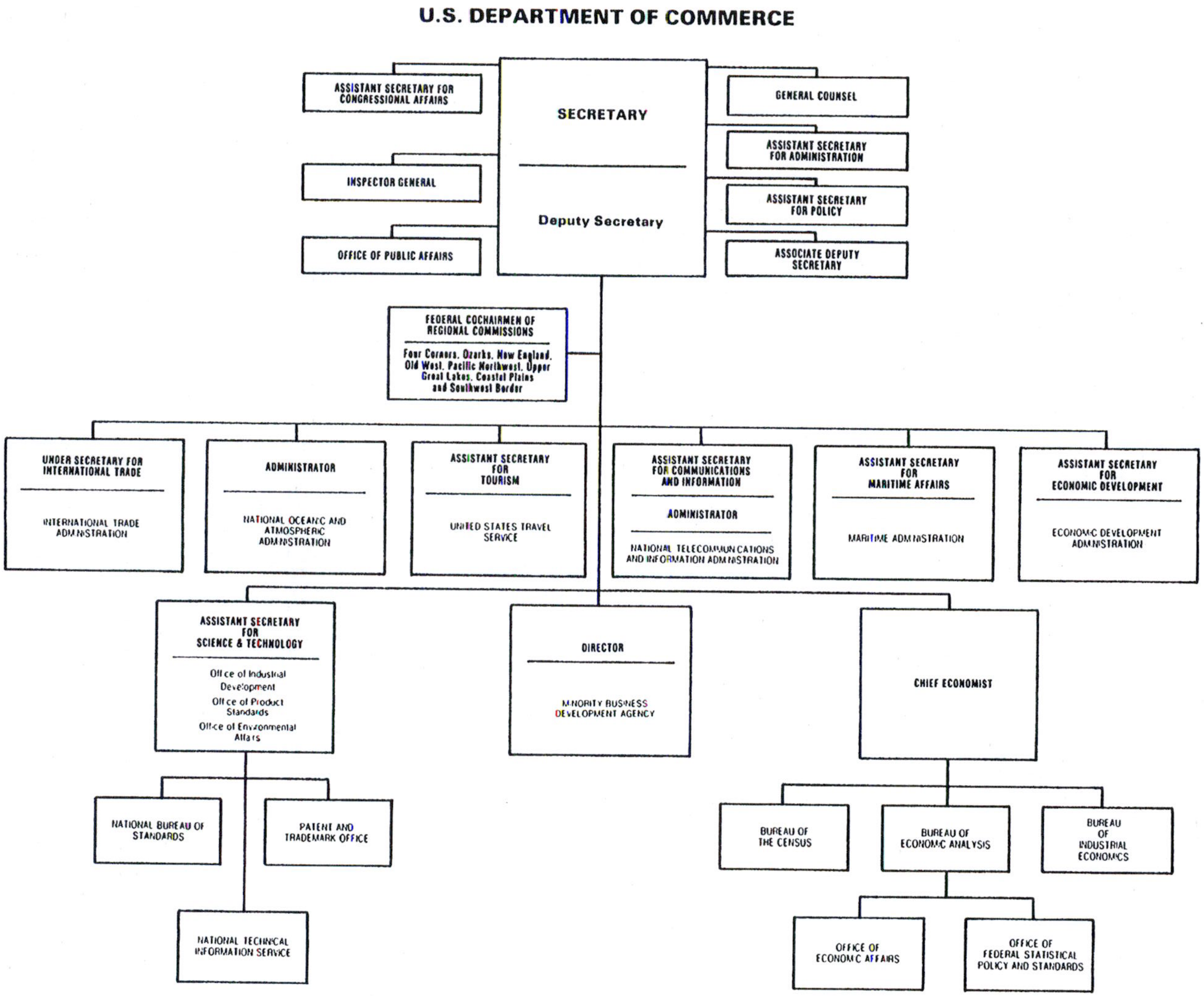

EXHIBIT 34.2.   The IPM Process.

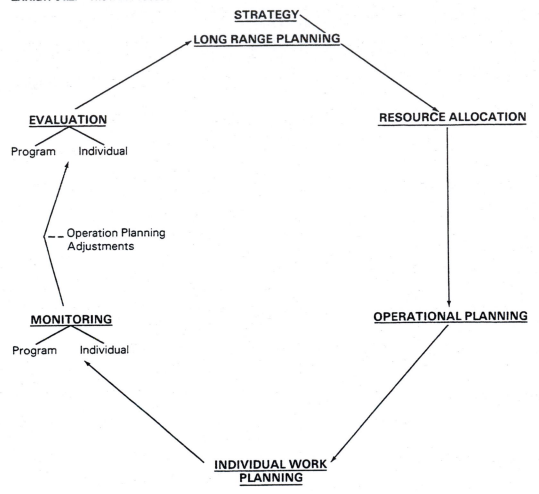

2. Reliance on systemic approaches, focusing on organizations as social systems.
3. Recognition of both production and human needs.

Let's examine each of these in turn.

Integration and Differentiation

Under the IPM approach, great leeway was to be given to bureaus with respect both to their management and planning systems and to their formulation of objectives. It is noteworthy that the Office of the Secretary did not present a manual to the bureaus on how the effort was to operate. Instead, each bureau was urged to think carefully about what its own unique characteristics were, what comparable efforts were underway (in the bureau and the department), and what would work for them. The role of the office of the Secretary was to provide assistance in outlining possible approaches, to develop an internal capacity (if help was desired), and to serve in an advisory capacity.

Systems Approaches

Integrated planning and management, in contrast to mere objective-setting, was to be a systemic approach. That is, IPM, as a management approach, focused on organizations as social systems. Attention was directed to how functions—especially program planning and administrative support—interrelated with one another and to a total system and to how organizations interacted with and coped with their environments. Once again, the budget process was to be the major mechanism for forcing that interrelationship.

Production and Human Needs

IPM was generally defined as an approach to managing an organization which involved broad participation of managers and subordinates in objective-setting and evaluation of results. Its focus was on goals, objectives, and priorities and on managing to achieve results; but that focus included both production and human needs.

IPM was not to be a "system" imposed on the department. Instead, it was to be the aggregate of several systems and processes already in existence (e.g., budget) or under development (the senior executive service and merit pay provisions of the Civil Service Reform Act) within the department. In many respects these notions of situational flexibility, a phased approach keeping the logic simple, and building on existing systems, were based on the years of experience of senior managers (especially Parker and Nathan).

The Nathan involvement with PPBS was especially important. Nathan felt that PPB had failed because it grew overly complicated as we forgot the most salient features—identification of program objectives and the execution of cost-effectiveness analyses. Moreover, it had sought to impose a single system over a diverse group of departments and agencies, with no attempt to tie it into existing ways of doing business. Finally, PPB was a monolithic "system," that is, it allowed for no digressions from the established forms and procedures. Nathan argued loudly against even calling IPM a "system." Noting that government managers had grown inured to new management systems—PPB, MBO, ZBB—to the point that they were considered almost faddish, he asserted that we should sell IPM as a discipline, an integration of existing systems, or a selective process. As he said:

> What we should stress is that IPM is an approach which consciously stresses setting goals, objectives, and priorities and then managing to achieve the defined results. It's a way of doing what we are supposed to do. If it's going to succeed—and I really think this is our last chance—we've got to get across that it's not a new system, it isn't a bunch of reports, it isn't a new set of meetings. This is basic administration—Management 101.

At the close of the Belmont meeting, after reaching agreement on the elements of IPM, several subcommittees were formed to accomplish the following:

> Identify all the tasks which must be carried out in order to implement these elements and assign a priority for each.
> Identify the necessary resources and assign individuals responsibility for each task.
> Develop a strategy for explaining and implementing IPM in the department.
> Develop a schedule for accomplishment of each task and for overall implementation of IPM.

One of the most important tasks was the third item noted above—explaining and implementing IPM. That was determined to involve the following steps:

> obtaining the under secretary's approval
> establishment of the process by the under secretary

discussing the concept with people inside and outside the department, to explain and thereby "sell" the IPM approach.

IMPLEMENTING AND MARKETING IPM

Over the next several weeks, meetings were held with key staff in the Office of the Assistant Secretary for Administration (AS/A) and aides in the Office of the Secretary. Bureau administrative officers, the senior management people in each of the operating components in the department, were briefed. Finally, the deputy secretary, the associate deputy secretary, and their special assistants were briefed on September 15.

On November 1, 1979, Under Secretary Hodges formally instituted IPM in the department and established a system to monitor a number of major program and administrative objectives. These objectives included 17 FY 1980 operational planning initiatives and 9 long-range planning issues. The objectives were developed jointly by analysts from the Office of Budget and Program Evaluation and by staff from the operating units. They were selected on the basis of their importance to the secretary, their political sensitivity, and their importance to such outside groups as the Congress, OMB, and so on. This new system was basically a management-by-objectives (MBO) effort.

Sessions were then held with OMB staff, congressional aides, and key senior administrative officials to gain their support and cooperation. In January 1980, the newly designated secretary, Philip M. Klutznick, was briefed by Parker and Nathan on IPM and the department's FY 1982 budget. While speaking highly of the IPM concept, Mr. Klutznick warned that "management improvements shouldn't be viewed as ends in themselves." He indicated that he felt that the real audience for our efforts should be program managers in the bureaus and asked Parker and Nathan to begin a "marketing campaign" for IPM with

senior executives in each of the operating units.

Sessions were held with each bureau's senior executives and program managers between mid-March and June 16. Approximately 300 of the 459 senior executives in the Washington metropolitan area—or 65 percent of the members of the senior executive service (SES)—attended one of the briefing sessions. The sessions were also attended by a number of mid-level program managers.

In addition, one staff member was scheduled to attend Commerce Management Training Center seminars scheduled during 1980 to make a presentation on IPM to the mid-level executives (GS–13 through GS–15) attending. As a result, about 200 or so mid-level executives were also reached with the marketing effort.

In all the bureaus, an attempt was made to tailor the presentation to make the general concept of IPM more relevant, understandable, and meaningful. Several bureaus were considered to be receptive to near-term IPM implementation, and presentations specifically tailored to those bureaus' management activities and programs were prepared.

Objectives of the Campaign

The IPM marketing campaign was designed to achieve several objectives. First, the briefings were conducted to raise the level of awareness of senior executives about the need for and the merit of IPM. The sessions were to be used to describe the IPM concept—its underlying assumptions and purpose—and to explain what was being done in the Office of the Secretary (specifically, in the Office of the Assistant Secretary for Administration) to facilitate IPM. Second, the briefings would demonstrate how IPM was likely to have an impact on the department in general and each bureau in particular over the next several years. Third, the individualized sessions were to provide senior executives with a demonstration of IPM practices in their bureau as a motivational tool. Fourth, the presentations were structured to provide Bureau executives with a low-key assessment of where the department stood, as well as where that particular bureau stood, relative to the IPM components and/or expectations. Finally, it was hoped that the sessions would elicit expressions of interest in, support for, or commitment to the department's IPM implementation effort.

Overall Assessment

Two consulting firms—Middlesex Research Center, Inc. (MRC) and Management Analysis Center, Inc. (MAC)—were asked to prepare a description of the IPM marketing campaign and an evaluation of its effectiveness. It was their conclusion that the first three objectives of the campaign were met fully, while the last two were moderately achieved.

Mark J. Versel, vice-president of Middlesex Research, noted in his report on the IPM marketing campaign that:

At the completion of each briefing session it was apparent that most of the audience:

Was aware of the need for improving the linkages between bureau and departmental planning, budgeting and operations management.

Expressed their understanding of the potential benefits of more tightly linked planning and management processes.

Was generally supportive of the planning and management linkages described.

While there were numerous positive indications of the campaign's effectiveness, there were other, less favorable attitudes expressed which underscored the need to continue additional IPM marketing activities. Again, to quote from the MRC report, Versel also witnessed:

A fair degree of skepticism about the Department's role as the leading edge of IPM.

Characterizations of past departmentally initiated management initiatives as single-purpose, burdensome, and not useful to bureau-level managers and fears that the IPM "requirement" had the potential for the same outcomes.

Perceptions that IPM, robed in "Management 101" garb, was either too abstract to take seriously or too simple/basic to require much change.

Opinions that bureau-level management processes and systems were already quite suitable for real decision making.

Related opinions that strategic long-range planning and formal program evaluation were beyond the reach of bureau-level program managers and not too useful given changing political winds, shifts in departmental priorities, and managerial changes.

Roger Coates of MRC argued that while this year's IPM initiative appeared well underway and at least modestly successful, there was now a need to sharpen our project focus. He said:

The problem with the implicit project purpose—"marketing IPM"—is that it resembles selling motherhood: almost everyone is for it in general, but almost no one takes it seriously until it is likely to change his/her life. We are, after all, trying to change DOC employees' lives; it remains to translate IPM concepts into the sort of specific, appropriate, and individualized actions that managers are likely to take seriously.

Impact on Selected Bureaus

It was apparent that there was a dichotomy between IPM acceptance in those bureaus with which some previous contacts existed (e.g., NTIA, NTIS, PTO, and MBDA) and the rest of the department.

In those agencies in which the department achieved the most receptive response, the actual IPM presentation had been preceeded by a considerable amount of contact. In NTIS, PTO, MBDA, and so on, the department had passed through a "courtship" and had built a relationship of trust. They had been able to link IPM concepts with bureau management needs, tapping into the self-interest of bureau leadership for the energy needed to define, plan, and kick off a genuine management improvement effort.

In NTIS, for example, several meetings had been held with the director, Melvin Day, and the associate director for financial and administrative management, Ellie Clark; and OBPE staff were working with NTIS staff to develop a long-range planning system for the agency. Based on these efforts, a solid foundation had been built for the presentation to NTIS senior managers.

At NTIA, the active interest in and support for IPM on the part of Stan Cohn, the deputy administrator for operations, was a major factor in the success of the marketing presentation. Once again, the department was building on a previously established relationship which was a major factor in focusing discussion on specific steps to improve existing management processes.

In those bureaus where SES members were neutral or hostile (e.g., MarAd, Office of the Chief Economist), the department had moved rather abruptly into the planning/action stages without a proper "courtship," without building client trust, without determining the client's needs. As a result, they gained only a courteous audience for their presentation.

In the department, Clif Parker and Dave Nathan used their governmental experience to reflect on these experiences and create the integrated planning and management concept. However, they had *not* translated this IPM concept into specific, appropriate, individualized actions that managers were likely to take seriously. They had not developed IPM guidelines, a list of "best practices," or a "how to do it" manual—anything that would tell managers what they must (or could) do day-to-day to achieve the goals of IPM. These managers needed, and many asked for, a detailed description of the activities necessary to attain those goals.

Only in those bureaus where managers had seen what IPM meant as applied to a specific situation or problem (the long-range planning process in NTIS, the administrative assessment of ITA, the need to improve the program memoranda and related budget formulation processes in NTIA) were significant inroads made.

One other point deserves mention. A number of bureau senior executives and program managers stated their view that the department should "put its own managerial house in order" in such areas as procurement, personnel, and long-range planning before attempting to proceed with new management initiatives, to "push IPM on the bureaus," or to judge the management capability of the bureaus in terms of an idealized IPM process. Put less harshly, it was obvious that AS/A needed to "lead by example," and they couldn't expect the bureaus to undertake significant projects unless they first saw the results of IPM in the Office of Administration.

SUMMARY

According to the two consulting firms, the overall results of the IPM marketing campaign were:

Approximately 300 senior executives and Program Managers in the Department are highly aware of the need for IPM, the general concept of IPM, and the advantages of the approach. Many of them also recognize that a number of the components of an IPM-like system are present in their own Bureau.

An additional set of perhaps 200 to 400 mid-level managers in DOC have been exposed to a similar marketing campaign and are aware of IPM and its objectives.

The Department is committed to improving IPM by parallel actions at the bureau level and improvements in department-wide systems and processes.

The Department has stated that it will provide technical assistance and performance incentives (i.e., the Secretary's bonus pool for senior executives) to bureau executives to facilitate enhanced planning and management capabilities along the lines of the IPM design.

The Department is committed to an ongoing exchange of information about IPM and a gradual, yet discernible, enhancement and linkage of bureau and departmental planning and management processes over the next two to five years.

ACCOMPLISHMENTS

The implementation of IPM was thought to be a three- to five-year endeavor. In the first 15–18 months, a reasonable beginning to the improvement of the planning and management of Commerce programs was made. Among the projects undertaken in the first year were the following:

An experiment in long-range planning was conducted as part of the FY 82 Spring Preview process. This led the Secretary to decide to implement a uniform long-range planning process as a basic management system in FY 81 and to commit additional resources to carry out this function.

An ADP Planning System was established to identify the need for and plan the acquisition of ADP resources.

A major revision of the Department's "Budget and Program Analysis Handbook" was undertaken to incorporate certain aspects of IPM into the budget process.

From a list of OMB administration initiatives, the Assistant Secretary for Administration developed a list of Management Improvement Activities to be initiated during FY 80 and 81.

A procurement planning system and a procurement tracking system were developed.

The IPM effort was tied to the Department's implementation of the Civil Service Reform Act.

An Issues Monitoring System was established to monitor a number of major program and administration objectives for the Secretary.

A series of management reviews were conducted, focusing on seven major management/administration thrusts initiated or being monitored by the Office of Administration.

Considerable progress was made in institutionalizing the program evaluation function, including the preparation and publication of the first annual evaluation plan and a set of Evaluation Guidelines.

Technical assistance or "institution-building" efforts were conducted in a number of Bureaus to improve and coordinate existing planning, management, monitoring, and evaluation capabilities.

The Information Management Committee began to identify those administrative data elements critical to the proper functioning of the Office of the Secretary.

In order to provide needed information on the work force and Equal Employment Opportunity, a Department Personnel Data System was implemented.

Efforts were made to improve communication and collaboration between administrative staffs through "linkage management."

At the beginning of FY 1981, a plan for the institutionalization of IPM in the Department was developed. There were five major components to this plan:

Strategy Development and Implementation Planning—Based on the management reviews, specific bureau-level planning and management improvement initiatives were to be developed for FY 81.

Information Exchange—AS/A staff were to assume the role of catalysts, gatekeepers of information. Another product of the management reviews was to be a list of Bureau "best practices" to be shared throughout the Department and used as the foundation for a "how to do it" work on IPM.

Drawing on Bureau practices would also make the suggestion more palatable to many managers. They would not be confronted with a specific set of instructions from the Office of the Secretary (OS) on how to do IPM; instead, they would have a range of options, found useful by their peers, to consider, adapt, and adopt.

Department Process/Systems Enhancements—The staff was to continue to develop and enhance such basic department-wide systems as procurement planning and monitoring, ADP planning, personnel management evaluation, and so forth.

Technical Assistance—Since we had been most successful in those Bureaus in which we had already established a base through our technical assistance efforts, we intended to continue and expand these efforts.

Incentives—We intended to develop the IPM-related incentives available in AS/A so that we had something to offer individual Bureaus. This entailed utilizing such "carrots" as the Secretary's SES bonus pool, technical assistance contract resources, Departmental recognition, etc., and the few "sticks" available *in budget, personnel, and so on. This called for developing not only the incentives themselves, but a willingness to use them.*

THE DEMISE OF IPM

In November 1980, the voters cast their ballots and overwhelmingly rejected the Carter Administration. As transition groups moved into federal departments and agencies, Parker and Nathan scanned the members of the Commerce transition team for familiar names and faces. Their aim was to sell them early on the IPM aproach and to package it as a concept developed, marketed, and being implemented by career managers in the Office of the Secretary for their counterparts in the bureaus. Their argument was that IPM was a neutral tool that could be used by any secretary or deputy secretary of the department to plan, manage, and control Commerce programs. Drawing on their knowledge of operations in other departments (e.g., HUD and Health and Human Services), they held the view that the only way a management innovation would "take" in a large, complex organization would be to give it several years. In other words, it needed more time than the average term of an assistant secretary or a deputy secretary (18–24 months) or even of an administration (4 years).

While members of the Commerce transition team were receptive to the IPM concept (and praised it, along with Parker and Nathan, in their report), none of them remained at the department when the president made his new appointments. Instead, they were offered positions in other departments/agencies or returned to private life. As a result, Parker and Nathan were faced with a brand new audience. This time they failed, mainly because IPM had come to be viewed as the initiative of the previous administration. The endorsement of the outgoing secretary (Klutznick) and the retiring assistant secretary for administration (Porter) only served to taint it

further in the minds of the incoming Reagan appointees and sound the death knell for IPM in spite of efforts to sanitize it. One wag on the staff even suggested that we rename IPM; it would become, instead, the resource overview network (RON)—perhaps more appealing to the new leadership.

On April 14, 1981, Deputy Secretary-designate Joseph R. Wright issued a memorandum establishing a new management planning system to improve the department's performance in accomplishing major policy, programmatic, and management initiatives. Efforts to include some reference to IPM or to indicate that this new system was built upon the IPM foundation were rejected by the new political leadership. With that failure, IPM became an "unsystem" in the Department of Commerce.

Yet, there was a very real question as to whether or not this death notice was a blessing in disguise, that is, salvaging IPM from a "living death," breached in letter and spirit, but kept on the books. For IPM was beginning to fail even before the election and the arrival of the new political appointees.

Some of the attitudes noted earlier were causing problems for IPM. Perhaps the most troubling was the view that "marketing IPM" resembled "selling motherhood" and that all there was to IPM was "good management" generalities. The attitude in many bureaus and even in AS/A itself might be categorized as one of general acceptance and receptivity, along with a sense of expectation that IPM would soon be more fully developed and defined. Even after the extensive marketing effort, few people had a clear notion either of what it was meant to achieve or the range of weapons available to make its critical rhetoric stick.

The parable of the blind men and the elephant is often used in discussing certain aspects of public management. The image conveyed is of a number of sightless individuals with their hands on various portions of the elephant. One, with his hand on the tail, thinks he's holding a piece of rope. Another, with his hand on the side of the animal, thinks he's standing next to a large wall. A third, sitting on the elephant's back, believes he's on top of a hill. Still another, holding the trunk, pictures a large snake. The parable is meant to illustrate those aspects of management theory in which different individuals, while talking about the same thing, "see" very different things in it. IPM was coming to be seen as "all things to all people." In our effort not to impose "a system" on the bureaus, we had left things so open that many bureaus either claimed that they had instituted IPM already or that they were awaiting further direction. As two administrative officers noted:

We fully support IPM as a concept. But now we need to see what it is we're expected to produce. What does Parker want us to produce? We're really waiting for the "how to."

I don't have any problem with what Clif has proposed. If that's all there is, it's only doing what any good manager is already doing or knows he's supposed to do. But I'm sure there's more. And we're waiting to see it.

The bureau staffs also translated IPM's principles of phased implementation and flexibility to mean that they didn't have to do anything.

There were certain other major barriers to the implementation of IPM that existed as well. These were:

lack of commitment and follow-through by key executives
taking too long to install the system
inadequate supply of change agents
installation of a few pieces of the system without installing the supporting pieces
failure to allocate resources according to the values built into the system
ignorance

Let me discuss each of these in turn.

Lack of commitment and follow-through by key executives. The first problem in ac-

complishing any major organizational change is the posture of the key executives. If they are perceived as enthusiastic, as advocating and using the changes being made, a major hurdle is overcome in getting the changes accepted. Many managers find themselves caught up in the hassle of day-to-day emergencies and lose sight of their long-term agendas. Theirs is a failure of organization, one that precludes the successful installation of the innovations because the energy required to reinforce and sustain those innovations is drained off by the latest fire that needs their personal attention.

The continuous effort of key executives is essential because they are the major holders of power and authority in their organizations. Furthermore, in their behavior they have to be models for the behavior they expect from other members of the organization.

We were surprised to find that resistance among mid-level employees was not among the major barriers to installation of the system. After the orientation sessions on IPM conducted as part of the Commerce Management Training Center seminars, we asked the attendees about their receptiveness to this new management approach. They indicated overwhelmingly that they were enthusiastic about it but doubted that their supervisors and senior managers would actually use it. In spite of our efforts, we were never able to spread the commitment to the IPM approach far beyond the initial group that gathered at Belmont.

Taking too long to install the system and inadequate supply of change agents. These two factors are considered jointly because they are interrelated. People don't like to feel that they are in a state of always becoming, but never being. They want to feel that they will, at some known future point, be able to use the system and derive the benefits from it rather than always building that system.

During the first year of so, we were not able to install all the basic elements of IPM. A major problem was that our implementation efforts, in our desire to avoid the pitfalls of PPBS, were essentially a two-man operation.

Since we had stressed that IPM was only basic "good management," that it built on existing systems, and so on, Parker and Nathan wanted to avoid all trappings of a system, such as a central staff unit dedicated to IPM implementation. As a result, however, we were trying to develop, market, and install a comprehensive planning and management system in a department of over 40,000 employees, with 12 major operating components, over 800 programs, and an annual budget of $3.4 billion—all with two staff people.

Installation of a few pieces of the system without installing the supporting pieces. The parts of a system like IPM are so interrelated that to install one part without the supporting ones limits the likely effectiveness of the installed part. An effort like the issues monitoring system, for example, could prosper only if the supporting work planning, appraisal, financial monitoring, and reward allocation are installed simultaneously or very soon afterward. Since we were working with such a small staff over an extended period, these mutually supporting mechanisms were not in place.

Failure to allocate the resources according to the values built into the system. If budgetary decisions are not shaped by the plans, planning will not be taken seriously. If rewards are not based on appraisals, and appraisals are not based on assigned responsibilities and objectives, the objectives will not be taken seriously. Managers need constantly to be reminded of these facts; otherwise, they have a tendency to regress to more traditional (and, some would add, bad) habits.

A few examples illustrate the problem. At the Belmont retreat, we said that one of our priorities was to tie together personnel planning and budget formulation (i.e., to link position management and job classification with the budget review). The Budget and Program Analysis Handbook was revised to incorporate this concept. Steve Roman and his staff worked to develop procedures for such a review. But when they actually sought to participate, they were told that the budget staff would let them know if they were needed. They were told that "it is too damn difficult to integrate," that "it takes too much time," and that "the budget staff doesn't have the time to work with the Office of Personnel people." Several of the people I spoke with in personnel raised this matter and wondered how serious we were about IPM.

This experience with the issues monitoring system was a similarly unsatisfactory experience for many. Monitoring was to be the responsibility of budget and program evaluation analysts. But, early in the reviews, the budget staff announced that they were too busy to engage in the process. There were no words of praise for the evaluation staff who carried out their responsibilities over the year; there were no recriminations against the budget staff for their refusal to participate. Again, a basic theme in implementing organizational change was ignored: key executives have to use their power and authority to weld together the disparate parts of their organizations and to sanction those who would go in incongruent directions if the innovations they advocate are to be accepted. The failings noted above were particularly troublesome because they occurred in units Parker supervised and involved the crucial foundation of IPM—the budget process.

The conventional wisdom in public administration has always been that budgets are also instruments of coordination, control, and planning.[1] What IPM tried to do was to recast budgeting at the department from a repetitive process for financing permanent programs into an instrument for deciding, monitoring, and coordinating the activities of the department. IPM was designed with the budget process and with budget outcomes in mind. New systems were designed and enhancements of existing systems made so that they would be

[1]See, for example, George Berkley, *The Craft of Public Administration* (Boston: Allyn and Bacon, 1975), pp. 254–84, and Nicholas Henry, *Public Administration and Public Affairs* (Englewood Cliffs, N.J.: Prentice–Hall, 1975), pp. 158–83.

compatible with the budget cycle. But IPM failed to penetrate the vital routines of putting together and justifying a budget. Always separate but never equal, IPM had little influence over the form or content of the budget. Allen Schick's explanations for the demise of PPB are equally relevant to IPM:

> *PPB failed to penetrate because the budgeters didn't let it in and the PPB'ers didn't know how to break down the resistance. But even if the leadership, data, analytical capability, resources and support, interpersonal and institutional sensitivity, and all the factors which worked against PPB had been favorable, there still would have been the antianalytic thrust of the budget process to contend with.* [2]

Thus, while it is clear that every budget system contains planning, management, and control features, the control orientation has been preponderant. This has meant the subordination of planning and management functions.

Lack of knowledge. Individuals who do not understand or are not knowledgeable about various aspects of IPM obviously cannot use the system effectively. There were many managers and employees who were not aware of the IPM initiative or, if they were aware of it, were waiting for further direction.

CONCLUSIONS

The efforts to implement integrated planning and management in the Department of Commerce disclose a distressing gap between theory and practice. As with other administrative reforms, it is difficult to convince senior managers to try something different or to get them to persist with new ways of doing things when they yearn for the "old, familiar, comfortable" ways in spite of evidence to the contrary. Managers continue to pay lip service to principles which no longer operate.

Budgeting has long been the focus of reform efforts. The problems caused by doing so have been spelled out in the literature. These pitfalls have only been intensified by recent events that are quickly changing the rules of the budgeting game. These new and unexpected events are making the task of public budgeting infinitely more complex, complicated, and worrisome. More and more public administrators find themselves working in conditions of fiscal stress in which they must try to accomplish unlimited goals with fewer real resources. As Naomi Caiden notes:

> *With potential resource levels more variable and objectives more complex, past experience is less relevant in budgeting. Meantime competition for resources intensifies among pressure groups, levels of government and public agencies. Alignments disintegrate, shift and reform with baffling fluidity. The budget game is being played with more conflict and the rules are giving way under the strain. It becomes more difficult to agree on and stick to budgets.* [3]

If the mistakes of the past are to be avoided in future efforts designed to accomplish management, coordination, and planning in the budget process, existing budget reform principles need to be replaced with ones that better suit the new reality.

---

[2]Allen Schick, "A Death in the Bureaucracy: The Demise of Federal PPB," *Public Administration Review* 33 (March/April 1973), p. 149.

[3]Naomi Caiden, "Public Budgeting Amidst Uncertainty and Instability," *Public Budgeting and Finance* 1 (Spring 1981): 10.

35

*Budgeting in Columbus**

INTRODUCTION

The city charter of Columbus provides for a mayor–council form of government. The mayor is the chief elected official and a seven-member city council elected at large serves as the legislative body for the city. An organizational chart for the city is presented in Exhibit 35.1.

There are a number of major participants in the Columbus budget process. In addition to the city agencies which prepare individual budget requests, the major actors are the mayor, Department of Finance, city auditor, and city council. The mayor of Columbus has overall responsibility for preparation of the mayor's recommended budget. The mayor is assisted by the Department of Finance. The Department of Finance actually prepares the annual budgets, monitors expenditures, forecasts revenues, and coordinates debt issues. The department also coordinates public investments in major local investment projects and provides administrative services to the city departments. The third major actor in the formal budget process is the city auditor. The auditor is an elected official. The responsibility of the auditor's office is to provide complete and accurate financial information to the city, record all receipts and disbursements, maintain general ledgers, and audit all revenues received and vouchers for payment for the city. The auditor's major role in the budget process is a legal obligation to provide the city with general fund revenue estimates which set the legal limit on budgeted expenditures for the city. The auditor is also required to give the city revised estimates during the year. The

*By Mark Weinberg, Ohio University, and Lee Holmer, senior budget analyst, Department of Finance, City of Columbus.

final actor in the budget process is the city council. The council approves all appropriation ordinances.

Preparation of the budget starts in April of the year preceding the coming budget year. Columbus's fiscal year corresponds to the calendar year. Under the new budget process the equivalent budget is prepared from April 16 to June 5. The equivalent budget presents service levels to be provided if a department is funded at its current budget level. From April 16 to July 2, departments prepare their expansion and reduction budget requests. Administrative hearings take place from August 10 to August 28, with finalization of the budget document occurring from September 15 to October 1. Until 1982 the annual and capital budgets appeared in one document. Separate annual and capital budgets were presented for fiscal year 1982.

INNOVATIONS IN THE BUDGET PREPARATION PROCESS: 1978 TO 1982

In 1978 Columbus changed its process of budgeting with the adoption of a system called "budgeting by financial responsibility centers" (FRC). City agencies that were supported in full or in part by the general fund were grouped into fifteen financial responsibility centers. These centers generally corresponded to organizational departments. The general fund revenue for 1978, $94,500,000, was then allocated to the fifteen centers under a block grant system. Each center received a certain proportion of these funds and were not allowed to receive supplemental appropriations. Each center was given authority to make the final decisions on divisional operational budgets for recommendation to the city council.

EXHIBIT 35.1. Organization Chart of City Government, City of Columbus, Ohio.

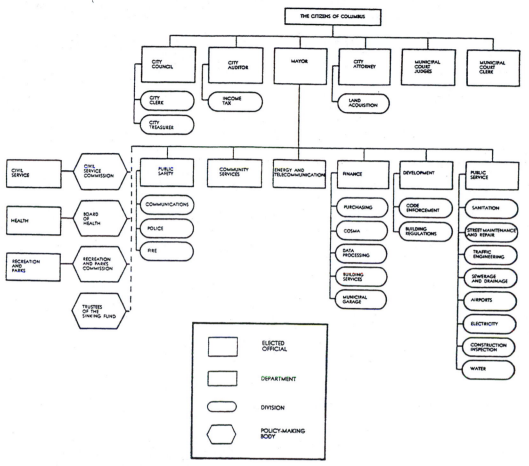

Source: Operating budget for 1982, City of Columbus.

Table 35.1 shows the fifteen financial responsibility centers and fund distribution for 1978. Allocations were determined based on weighted fund expenditures.[1] All revenue from the revised auditor's estimate was to be carried over to the next fiscal year and not reallocated to departments.

[1]These are the weighted average percentages of the total general fund expenditures incurred by each FRC for the last three years.

1978 also saw a second major innovation in the budget process. This was the adoption of a computerized information management system for the budget called FAMIS II. The FAMIS II system allowed the city to include greater detail in the budget and to group expenditures by functions, as well as by traditional departments, and by programs within functions so that expenditures could be analyzed in terms of performance criteria.

With the adoption of the FRC system

TABLE 35.1. Financial Responsibility Centers and Fund Allocations, City of Columbus, 1978

Dept. No.	Department	General Fund Allocation
030	Mayor (030)	$ 247,831
080	Finance (080, 084, 270, 770)	3,133,650
090	Community Service (090)	428,859
180	Civil Service (180)	688,411
220	Development (220, 440)	2,301,335
280	Public Utilities (280)	131,001
300	Public Safety (300, 340, 360, 370, 410)	55,379,636
320	Recreation and Parks (320, 790)	7,909,095
500	Health (500)	3,337,030
600	Public Service (600, 480, 610, 670)	11,262,604
010	City Council (010, 020, 025, 050)	1,309,859
040	City Auditor (040, 110)	1,852,011
060	City Attorney (060, 065)	1,735,206
120	Court—Judges (120)	2,531,380
130	Court—Clerk (130)	2,242,092
	TOTAL	**$94,500,000**

Source: Budget instructions, City of Columbus, 1978

the central budget office (Department of Finance) became responsible for applying the allocation formula, providing the FRC's with their allocations and necessary budget information, e.g., budget instructions, narratives, and data, and helping the FRC's in budget preparation through the provision of technical assistance. The FRC became responsible for establishing its own budget and most importantly, for finishing the year with a surplus. Deficit spending was not to be allowed. To ensure this, an incentive system was created. If the FRC finished the year with a surplus, that surplus would be returned to the FRC in the following year. If the FRC finished the year with a deficit, that deficit would be deducted from the FRC's following year appropriation. The FRC system was designed to produce "good management" and avoid costly "failures." It was thought that by allowing for highly decentralized management, financial responsibility would be matched with line operating responsibility, which would give line managers the ability to realize economies in the budget and improved performance.

The general response of the departments to the FRC system was favorable. They liked the reduced role of the central budget office in questioning departmental spending, regardless of whether or not they liked their actual allocations.

The FRC system was modified in 1979 for the 1980 budget year. The FRC manager was asked to make priority choices among diverse requests among the units in the FRC. This process was to involve preparation of two budget requests—a base budget request and a supplemental budget request. The base budget request was a current services budget, while supplemental requests included possible enhancements. The supplemental requests were ranked in order of priority at the division level and submitted to the FRC manager, who in turn ranked the requests for the FRC as a whole. All supplemental requests were then forwarded to the Department of Finance for evaluation and budgeting according to available funds. The major change then in the "modified" FRC system was that general fund estimates were not allocated among the divisions in the preliminary stages of the budget process. This modification was initiated so that FRC managers could pay more attention to choices "between various service levels with less attention placed on total dollars available."

The other significant change in the preparation of the 1980 budget was the increased importance of the budget narrative in the formal budget document. All departments and divisions were asked to complete budget narratives which included a "division overview," a discussion of the department's primary service mission, accomplishments in the previous year, priorities for the coming year, and "section objectives," listing specific objectives identifying operational priorities of each section within a division. The increased focus on the budget narrative represented a greater emphasis on looking at the budget in terms of program and performance criteria.

Transition to a New Process

In 1981 the city started to move away from the FRC system as initiated in 1978. Instead of proving to be an effective budget management tool, the FRC system was plagued with problems. First, the "arbitrary" allocation system was unable to respond to "changing service demands across departments." Second, good management became identified with the ability to control spending and took no account of the quantity or quality of services provided. For example, departments facing pressing demands for service also faced the possibility of being penalized by budget overruns if they sought to meet the demand, while at the same time they could "save" money by failing to provide needed services and then be rewarded with extra money for the next year's budget. Third, because the formula for the allocation of funds was based on previous years' expenditures, each department received the same share each year. This led to a budgetary decision-making system where no priorities were set or allowances accorded for service demands and cost factors. Fourth, the FRC formula did nothing to reinforce efforts to improve productivity or efficiency. In reality, agencies which had been "fat" in the past or who provided a lower quality service or quantity of service per dollars spent were assured of continuing generous budgets. In contrast, agencies which provided a high level and quality of service were "locked" into tight budgets. Finally, the "FRC system did not work" when it "became obvious" that "its keystone incentive system could not be enforced." Agencies routinely received supplemental appropriations from city council to cover cost overruns, and city council refused to reappropriate agency carryovers.

Starting in 1981 the Department of

Finance initiated efforts to collect and utilize service demand and delivery information in order to increase the central budget office and mayor's control over departmental spending. Agencies were required to provide data on the quantity and unit costs of primary services which could be delivered within the base-level funding. Information was required on the improved performance which would result from supplemental funding. The benefits of this improved information system included increased focus on service-delivery effects of funding decisions, the ability of agencies to gain needed support for programs, and a greater possibility of agency managers to identify program priorities and potential efficiency improvements within their own agencies.

The new system was implemented with some difficulty and confusion for the 1982 budget year and is being used for preparation of the 1983 budget as well. Agencies are now required to prepare a budget submission package which includes three "major elements": an equivalent budget, discussed earlier; a reduction budget; and an expansion budget. The equivalent budget is intended to identify, by cost center,[2] "the quantity and quality of services to be provided given a specified allocation." This budget then becomes the basis for the reduction and expansion budgets, which show the impact on services of a spending reduction or expansion. The reduction budget asks divisions to prepare requests totalling 20 percent reductions from the equivalent budget. The expansion budget presents ranked supplemental requests documenting service level increases if the division receives funding above the equivalent level. This new system thereby resembles certain elements of a zero-based budgeting system.

In addition to the confusion which normally accompanies any budgetary change, the movement to this new process has generated

---

[2]A cost center is an organizational unit within a division which provides related services. Generally, the division's cost centers correspond to its sections as defined under the organizational hierarchy system of FAMIS II. See Table 35.2.

TABLE 35.2.   Illustration of Cost Center Structure

Model	Example
Cost Center I	Pollution control services
Index A	Pollution control
Activity A_i	Household sewage disposal inspections
Activity A_{ii}	Swimming pool inspections
Index B	Environmental lab services
Activity B_i	Sewage sample testing
Cost Center II	Environmental health education
Etc.	

Source: Budget manual for the preparation of the mayor's recommended budget, 1982.

some departmental resistance. The departments now have to tell what they are doing with their money. Many oppose having to justify expenditures and the increased central review of their budgets.

The city is committed to the new budget process. As indicated in the mayor's budget memo to all department and division heads (April 22, 1982) the new system is designed to:

> allow the administration to develop a budget which functions as a citywide plan of action in setting priorities and

responding to revenue and cost contingencies throughout the year

focus budgetary choices on services provided and the resulting public benefits rather than on expenditure items

present a budget through which both we and the public can better understand what difference our funding recommendations intend to make in terms of the quality of community life.

FOR DISCUSSION

1. What were the problems with FRC system? Did the financial incentive system work? Why or why not?

2. In what ways was the new equivalent budget system a direct response to the problems above?

3. Under the FRC system the city council ignored the FRC allocation set by the Department of Finance and mayor and gave agencies supplemental appropriations. How might the Department of Finance use the equivalent budget system to increase its influence with city council?

4. What type of control mechanism is used to assure that departments do not overspend? What mechanisms could be used?

5. What mechanism is used to evaluate administrators, and is budget solvency part of this evaluation process?

CHAPTER ELEVEN

CUTBACK MANAGEMENT

Cutback management encompasses designing and implementing effective retrenchment strategies to deal with an unusually acute imbalance in the budget. In his nineteenth-century novel *David Copperfield*, Charles Dickens frames the issue with arithmetic simplicity: "Annual income twenty pounds, annual expenditure nineteen nineteen six, result happiness. Annual income twenty pounds, annual expenditure twenty pounds ought and six, result misery." Mr. Micawber is hardly the first to have noticed the need for fiscal integrity via a balanced relationship between revenues and expenditures. Marcus Tullius Cicero (106–43 B.C.) applied the same principle, albeit in normative terms, to the public budget: "The state budget must be balanced, the state treasury should be filled."[1] The fact of permanent, universal resource scarcity suggests that this is an area of ongoing intellectual interest; the newsworthy experiences of Cleveland, Washington, D.C., New York City, and Detroit and current economic conditions suggest that this is an area of immediate practical concern.

Recent literature on the subject draws upon organization theory, human resource management, fiscal stress concepts, and more. (See bibliography.) The political constraints in fiscal policy making indicate that retrenchment exacerbates political conflict. Organizational incentives generate considerable reluctance to cut budgets and to lay off public employees. Although remarkably little is known about management responses to cutback, recent research suggests that effective retrenchment is related to coherent, centralized government authority. (The executive's role in Minnesota's case is, therefore, especially instructive.) At issue is the government's capacity to recognize a problem and take action to resolve it. As for its impact on the field of public budgeting and financial management, Charles Levine and Irene Rubin note: "The brunt of the burden of adjusting governments to the pressures of fiscal stress falls on their budgetary and management systems."[2]

The last case in this casebook takes a close look at that burden in actuality. It describes first the discovery and then the response to an

---

[1]We appreciatively acknowledge the courtesy of Howard Reiter and Henry Krisch of The University of Connecticut for providing the Dickens and Cicero quotes, respectively.

[2]Charles H. Levin and Irene S. Rubin, eds., *Fiscal Stress and Public Policy*, Sage Yearbooks in Politics and Public Policy, vol. 9 (Beverly Hills: Sage Publications, 1980), p. 14.

immediate cutback challenge in the state of Minnesota. Section A illustrates that timely and adequate information and particularly financial information are a large part of government capacity. It applies concepts such as fund balance, biennial budgets, encumbrances, and revenue estimation (and its acceptable parameters). It explores the interplay between economic conditions and a state's budget. It concludes with two problems about fund accounting and a series of discussion questions. Related cases include those in Chapter 9 and cases nos. 9 and 10.

Section A provides the background for Section B, an evaluative-type exploration of Minnesota's retrenchment strategy. It scrutinizes the application of "equity" and introduces concepts such as fixed costs and essential services. The case material enables the reader to examine allocational, distributional, and intergovernmental issues. It brings professional, political, economic, and humane perspectives to the problem and explores the magnitude of that problem. Minnesota's General Fund Reduction Program for FY 1981 confronts one of the most critical, perplexing, and conflict-ridden issues of this decade.

Bibliography

CHARLES H. LEVINE, ed., *Managing Fiscal Stress, the Crisis in the Public Sector* (Chatham, N.J.: Chatham House Publishers, 1980).

———— and IRENE S. RUBIN, eds., *Fiscal Stress and Public Policy*, Sage Yearbooks in Politics and Public Policy, vol. 9 (Beverly Hills: Sage Publications, 1980).

————, IRENE S. RUBIN, and GEORGE G. WOLOHOJIAN, "Resource Scarcity and the Reform Model: The Management of Retrenchment in Cincinnati and Oakland," *Public Administration Review* 41,6 (November/December 1981), pp. 619–28.

CAROL W. LEWIS and ANTHONY T. LOGALBO, "Cutback Principles and Practices: A Checklist for Managers," *Public Administration Review* 40,2 (March/April 1980), pp. 184–88.

LESTER THUROW, *The Zero-Sum Society* (New York: Basic Books, 1980).

36

General Fund Budget Reduction Program, Fiscal Year 1981, State of Minnesota*

INTRODUCTION

On July 11, 1980, the Minnesota Department of Finance issued a monthly financial status report for state government. That report indicated that by June 30, 1980, state revenues had fallen $90.5 million behind the pace required to fully realize the resources necessary to support the spending authorized through June 30, 1981, by the 1979 and 1980 sessions of the legislature.

On that same day Governor Quie convened a public meeting of state agency heads, to which legislative leaders and news media representatives were also invited, and announced the following actions.

1. The Department of Finance was directed to prepare a revised revenue ("fund balance") forecast for the balance of the current biennium to incorporate the dramatic change in economic conditions reflected in the June revenue data.
2. The Department of Finance was also directed to prepare a contingency plan to reduce state expenditures in the event that a revised revenue forecast indicated such reductions to be necessary.
3. State agency heads were directed to exercise maximum restraint in hiring, pro-

curement, and other expenditure commitments to preserve flexibility to accommodate such budget reductions as might prove to be necessary.
4. Local government and school district officials were put on notice that a significant shortfall in state revenues would require reduction in state aid to cities, counties, towns, and school districts.

On August 21, 1980, the Department of Finance issued a revised forecast which indicated that for the two-year period ending June 30, 1981, the state of Minnesota will realize $195.1 million less in tax receipts than required to fully fund all expenditures authorized by the legislature. On the basis of that forecast, Governor Quie approved a reduction of state expenditures in the amount of $195.1 million to meet the constitutional and statutory requirements that the state conclude the biennium with a balanced budget.

The purpose of this report is to provide all interested parties with reasonably detailed information on the shortfall of revenue in comparison to projected levels and on the specific measures adopted to achieve the needed $195.1 million expenditure reduction. Section A seeks to provide a context for the budget reduction program through the concise background presentations on state budgetary and revenue forecasting procedures. Section B provides extensive information on how the budget reduction required of state government operating units was allocated to individual departments and agencies.

*By James Mallory, director of training for the National Association of State Budget Officers. Appreciation is extended to Val Vikmanis, acting commissioner of the Department of Finance, state of Minnesota, who, as state budget director, was the chief architect of the plan and budget reduction documentation.

SECTION A:
GENERAL FUND BALANCE
AND REVENUE ESTIMATION

Background

The state of Minnesota budgets its revenues and expenditures on a biennial basis. In January of each odd-numbered year, the governor proposes and the legislature acts on a budget for the two-year period to begin on July 1 of that year and end on June 30 two years later.

The state's budget is based on fund accounting principles, i.e., certain revenues and expenditures are segregated into "funds" established for specific purposes. The Trunk Highway Fund, for example, is made up of revenues from gasoline tax receipts and motor vehicle registration fees and is dedicated to programs which support the state's road system. The bulk of state revenues and expenditures, however, occurs in the multipurpose "General Fund." This report is limited to the current status of that fund.

The status of the fund is expressed in terms of an "unrestricted fund balance" projected for the close of the current budget period, June 30, 1981. That balance represents the resources available after accounting for all payments made by that date and after sufficient funds have been set aside to pay all obligations incurred but not yet paid. Additionally, funds must be set aside for expenditure authorizations which are available for specific purposes until expended (e.g., funds appropriated for land acquisition where lengthy condemnation proceedings are common). A positive fund balance represents an anticipated budget surplus, a negative balance, a deficit.

It is important to note that the fund balance does not represent "cash on hand," which, while a very important matter, is a separate issue. To understand the distinction, consider the analogy of the typical citizen attempting to determine the status of his/her finances on June 30, 1981. If that citizen calls the bank, he or she will be informed of the "cash on hand" in his or her checking account. This single piece of information, however, is misleading unless combined with the following additional considerations:

deposits made by the citizen before June 30 but not yet recorded by the bank
checks written by the citizen which have not yet cleared the bank

Anyone with a checking account is familiar with these considerations. What most citizens are not aware of are two additional restrictions which apply to government financing. If state government were balancing the above "checkbook," it would be required to deduct two additional amounts from the cash balance shown by the bank:

sufficient funds to pay for goods and services ordered before June 30 and which must be paid for after June 30 with funds earned before June 30
sufficient funds to pay for purchases *authorized* before June 30 (even though actual procurement has been delayed) but which must be paid for after June 30 with funds earned before June 30

These restrictions are necessary to insure that government financial statements properly disclose and provide for *all* obligations attributable to a particular budget period. Moreover, these actions are required by generally accepted accounting principles (GAAP). Auditors express their opinion on the fairness of presentation of the state's financial state in conformance with these principles. The state's credit and bond ratings can be adversely affected if these principles are not properly applied.

With these considerations as background, we can review the fund balance analysis recently issued by the Department of Finance. Table 36.1 provides that analysis for fiscal year 1981.

TABLE 36.1. Analysis of Projected Changes, General Fund Balance

Resources	Amount (in thousands)
A. Balance forward 6/30/80	$ 64,127.7
B. Prior year adjustments	15,000.0
Adjusted balance forward	79,127.7
C. Revenue	3,770,235.3
D. Transfers from other funds	39,701.6
Total resources	3,889,064.6
Estimated Expenditures	
E. Direct expenditure authorizations	2,549,991.7
F. Open and standing authorizations	1,410,668.2
G. Anticipated cancellations	(32,500.0)
Total expenditures	3,928,159.9
H. Transfers to other funds	131,782.5
Total expenditures and transfers	4,059,942.4
Unreserved fund balance	− 170,877.8
I. Less appropriations carried forward	(24,245.0)
Unrestricted fund balance (Projected 6/30/81)	− 195,122.8

A concise review of each component of Table 36.1 follows.

A. *Balance forward* represents the unrestricted resources remaining after the previous fiscal year obligations have been met.

B. *Prior year adjustments* represent that portion of resources reserved in past years for future obligations which current information indicates will not in fact be required. This reduction in previously reserved monies "frees" them for current year use.

C. *Revenue* represents tax and fee receipts to be realized during the current year. (A detailed review of such receipts is contained in the next section of this case.)

D. *Transfer from other funds* represents reimbursements received from the Trunk Highway, Game and Fish, and other funds for services performed by general fund-financed programs.

The above four components account for the general fund resources now projected as available during the current fiscal year. Those resources, however, will not be sufficient to provide for the following estimated expenditures:

E. *Direct expenditure authorizations* represent those amounts the legislature has appropriated for *direct* expenditures, i.e., for a specific purpose, in a specified amount, and usually for one fiscal year.

F. *Open and standing authorizations* represent current estimates of the amounts necessary to cover the expenditures authorized by the legislature for a specific purpose but where the appropriation is not limited to a specific sum. The cost of tax refunds is an example of an open and standing authorization.

G. *Anticipated cancellations* reflect the fact that not all expenditures authorized by the legislature will occur. Thus, authorized expenditures are reduced accordingly.

H. *Transfers to other funds* represent mandatory transfers such as those made to the debt service fund.

The above four expenditure components exceed the resources projected as available for the period ending 6/30/81 by $170.9 million.

I. *Appropriations carried forward* represent those amounts of current year funds which must be reserved to finance authorizations made by the legislature in previous years.

This brief summary indicates the complexity of accurately projecting the unrestricted fund balance which will be available at the end of a particular year. In addition to the problems associated with projecting current-year revenues (a matter discussed in the next section), the estimator must also attempt to project the resources to be used pursuant to open and standing expenditure authorizations, the portion of direct expenditure authorizations to revert as a result of underexpenditures, and the adjustments that will occur in the funds reserved for prior year obligations. The results of our analysis of all the factors described above lead to a projected "unrestricted fund balance" for the fiscal year of a negative $195.1 million.

Revenue Estimating

As indicated at the beginning of the previous section, the state budgets on a two-year basis. Thus, the revenue estimates used to prepare the current biennium's budget (July 1, 1979–June 30, 1981) were made in December of 1978, or *two and one-half years* before the conclusion of this biennium.

The December 1978 forecast was, however, revised in January of 1980 to reflect the fact that the long expected national recession did not arrive as expected despite the efforts of the national administration to slow down economic activity to counter inflation. Thus, it is useful to examine the changes which have occurred in the forecast for the projected balance at the end of the 1979–81 biennium.

TABLE 36.2.

	Amount (in thousands)		
Resources	December 1978	January 1980	August 1980
Balance forward 6/30/79	$ 311,653.0	$ 288,731.0	$ 286,731.0
Gross personal income tax	3,667,045.3	3,705,080.0	3,686,725.0
Gross corporate income tax	749,302.0	814,512.0	745,309.7
Sales tax	1,361,620.0	1,405,100.0	1,371,335.7
Other taxes and fees	1,580,412.3	1,583,543.4	1,539,132.7
Transfers from other funds	120,060.6	117,122.3	113,224.1
Total resources	$7,790,093.2	$7,914,088.7	$7,742,458.2
Expenditures			
Direct expenditures	$4,671,902.4	$4,927,396.7	$4,926,114.2
Open and standing	2,897,564.5	2,769,944.7	2,800,556.5
Anticipated cancellations	(40,000.0)	(64,568.8)	(65,500.0)
Total expenditures	7,529,466.9	7,632,772.6	7,661,170.7
Transfers to other funds	227,507.2	253,342.4	252,165.3
Total expenditures and transfers	$7,756,974.1	$7,886,115.0	$7,913,336.0
Unreserved fund balance	33,119.1	27,973.7	(170,877.8)
Less appropriations carried forward	(1,427.3)	(24,245.0)	(24,245.0)
Unrestricted fund balance (Projected 6/30/81)	31,691.8	3,728.7	(195,122.8)

TABLE 36.3.

	Impact on Projected 6/30/81 Fund Balance
Projected 6/30/81 Fund Balance after 1979 session	$ 31.7
Revisions by Department of Finance (1/15/80)	
Increase in net revenues projected	122.2
Decrease in expenditure estimates	55.6
Increase in debt service transfer	(89.2)
Increase in transfers to other funds/appropriations carried forward	(35.6)
Revised fund balance forecast	84.7
Actions by 1980 Session	
Appropriations measures	(86.7)
Tax relief measures	(16.1)
Increased revenue measures	7.2
Revision of education aid cancellation estimate	14.6
Revised fund balance forecast	3.7

Table 36.2 indicates changes in projections occurring from the December 1978 to the current (August 1980) forecast. Note that the figures are adjusted to reflect actions taken by the 1979 and 1980 sessions of the legislature. The $28 million decrease from the $31.7 million balance left by the 1979 session to the $3.7 million balance projected after the 1980 session had concluded its work was due to the information considered in Table 36.3.

A fund balance of $3.7 million meant that if revenues and/or expenditures deviated by more than *one-tenth of one percent* from estimates, a budget problem was possible.

The accuracy of revenue estimates is a function of two key considerations:

1. How accurately the revenue estimator predicts what will happen to the economy of the state (particularly personal income, corporation profits, and retail sales) during the projection period.
2. How accurately the revenue estimator translates the economic developments anticipated into the tax receipts to be realized by the state.

There is a critical distinction between these two considerations. Perhaps the best way to make that distinction is as follows: If the state's revenue estimator had *perfect knowledge* of what developments to expect in the state's economy over a projection period and still seriously over- or underestimated state tax revenues, the basic model is clearly in need of revision. On the other hand, a perfect model for translating economic developments into tax receipts is to no avail if the economy deviates sharply from expectations. In such circumstances, however, it is legitimate to ask whether the state revenue estimator's economic prognosis was consistent with that of reputable economic forecasting services and established economists.

To illustrate the sensitivity of state tax revenues to economic developments, the following table indicates the various sources of tax and fee revenues and their percentage of the net receipts now anticipated for the current fiscal year.

	Revenues (in millions)	Percent
Individual income tax	$1,471,403	44.9
Corporation income tax	339,800	10.4
General sales tax	718,900	22.0
Other revenues	743,935	22.7
Total	$3,274,038	100.0

Included within "Other revenues" is $93.4 million in motor vehicle excise tax, which represents 2.9% of net state revenue. When these receipts are added to individual, corporation, and general sales taxes, the four constitute 80.2% of total revenues. All four sources are directly affected by general economic developments.

Additionally, it must be recognized that the federal government can cause significant developments in the economy through changes in budgetary, tax, and monetary policies. We have little or no control over the consequences of such changes.

FOR DISCUSSION

1. Should budget officers plan to have an ending balance and/or conservatively estimate revenues?
2. What degree of accuracy should be expected in state revenue estimates?
3. State revenues are quite sensitive to general economic conditions. To what extent and how can a state influence its own economy?

PROBLEMS

1. (a) Assume the Department of Natural Resources made a $200,000 equipment order in April 1980 for delivery in October 1980. To which fiscal year would this expenditure be charged?
   (b) Now further assume that the equipment order is cancelled in July 1980. What changes must be made to the figures in Table 36.1?
2. Assume that in January 1981, the Department of Transportation notifies the Department of Finance that, contrary to previous expectations, a particular Rail Service Improvement Grant for $750,000 will not be made during fiscal 1981. What adjustment must be made to the figures in Table 36.1?

SECTION B: BUDGET REDUCTION PROGRAM

Constitutional and Statutory Mandates

Once the magnitude of the potential revenue shortfall/fund balance deficit was determined, it was necessary to take action to eliminate the deficit, i.e., balance the budget. This necessity arose from the Minnesota constitution, which, in effect, requires a balanced budget by the end of each biennium. While the constitution does not explicitly state "the budget shall be balanced," it effectively mandates that result by limiting the purposes for which the state may incur debt. Thus, while the constitution permits bonding for capital projects and authorizes short-term certificates of indebtedness to manage cash flow needs *during* a biennium, it provides no mechanism for deficit financing of operating expenses past the end of a biennium.

Given this constitutional mandate, two courses of action were open to the governor:

1. Increase revenues by convening the legislature to increase taxes and/or defer tax cuts previously enacted.
2. Reduce state expenditures by the amount of the projected revenue shortfall.

After consideration of the economic difficulties being faced by Minnesota citizens, the governor chose to reduce expenditures. Under these circumstances, Minnesota statutes require that the budget reduction be developed by the commissioner of finance and approved by the governor.

Scope and Equity of the Reduction Program

Once the decision was made to balance the budget through expenditure reductions rather than tax increases, the first issue to be resolved was to identify those areas of state expenditure which *could* be considered for reduction. For this purpose, state expenditures were classified into the categories in Table 36.4.

The total in Table 36.4 exceeds the $4,059.9 million in FY 1981 expenditures shown in the fund balance analysis by $124.1 million for the following reasons:

1. It includes $67.3 million of FY 1980 and previous year appropriations which will carry forward into FY 1981.
2. It includes the $32.5 million of cancellations anticipated on the fund balance analysis.
3. It includes the $24.3 million in appropriations anticipated to carry forward into FY 1982 by the fund balance analysis.

In simple terms, the above amount represents the *gross appropriated dollars available for allotment* in FY 1981, regardless of the year they were appropriated or in what year they will, in fact, be disbursed.

The first four categories were excluded from the budget reduction program for the following reasons:

1. *Tax relief and mandatory payments* include funding for such items as the Homestead Credit, Property Tax Refund, Debt Service Payments on state bonds, and payments to various retirement funds. These payments represent obligations which must be met.
2. *Tax refunds* represent payments which must be made to comply with the tax laws of the state.
3. *Income maintenance/medical assistance* payments, while legally reducible, were excluded by the governor. This exclusion was made for two reasons. First, the governor did not believe it proper to have the state's revenue difficulties result in a direct reduction of aid and services to people almost entirely dependent on state programs for subsistence or medical care. Second, these programs are experiencing cost increases which may result in *existing* levels of funding being inadequate by the end of FY 1981.
4. *Legislative, judicial, and constitutional officer* budgets were excluded from the program. Minnesota statutes explicitly

TABLE 36.4.

	FY 1981 Appropriations Available (in thousands)	Percent of Total Budget
1. Tax relief and mandatory payments	$ 961,969.3	23.0
2. Tax refunds	341,186.0	8.2
3. Income maintenance medical assistance	467,047.9	11.2
4. Legislative, judicial, and constitutional officers	67,482.1	1.6
Subtotal	$1,837,685.3	44.0
5. State agencies and institutions	579,479.5	13.8
6. State educational institutions and programs	433,597.6	10.4
7. Aid to school districts	1,081,300.2	25.8
8. Aid to local units of government	251,942.8	6.0
Subtotal	2,346,320.1	56.0
Total	$4,184,005.4	100.0

exclude the legislative and judiciary from the governor's budget reduction authority. In the case of the constitutional officers, it was the governor's judgment that, as elected officials, they should be in a position to make their own determination as to whether they wish to reduce their budgets. The governor's office budget, however, was reduced by the full percentage levied against other components of the budget, i.e., no portion of the governor's budget was exempted from the cut.

The last four categories of state expenditures listed in the preceding table were determined to be open for consideration in preparing a budget reduction program. The $195.1 million budget reduction required represented 8.3% of the $2,346.3 million budgeted for these categories.

After careful consideration of these and other issues, the governor ordered preparation of a budget reduction program based on the following principles:

1. The budget reduction must be equitably distributed among state agencies, education, and aid to local units of government.
2. Within the educational component, aid to school districts and support for state operated institutions and programs must be treated in an equitable manner.
3. Within state agencies reductions must be applied in a manner which reflects

the nature of the services performed by each agency and the type of expenditures necessary to provide those services.

A "first cut" at implementing an equitable general distribution yielded the results indicated in Table 36.5.

A closer examination of the appropriation accounts within the state agency listing surfaced two special appropriations of $3,360,700 and $61,400 to the Minnesota State Retirement Association and the Public Employment Retirement Association, respectively. These appropriations were to compensate the pension funds for benefits granted to legislative and judicial branch participants. More significantly, $1,200,000 and $6,900 of the respective appropriations are *known* to be unnecessary. Since these accounts were not intended for current operating needs of state agencies, there was no basis for "crediting" those agencies with the $1,206,900 "savings" known to exist. Thus, these accounts were deducted from the state agency base, and the $1,206,900 was used to reduce the total deficit from $195,122,800 to $193,915,900. This amount was then allocated to the various components as indicated in Table 36.6.

State Agencies and Institutions

The above process established an equitable distribution of the total reduction among the four components to be reduced. The next issue addressed was how to allocate the total re-

TABLE 36.5

	FY 1981 Appropriation Available (in thousands)	8.3161 Percent Reduction
State agencies and institutions	$ 579,479.5	$ 48,190.1
State educational institutions and programs	433,597.6	36,058.4
Aid to school districts	1,081,300.2	89,922.0
Aid to local units of government	251,942.8	20,951.8
Total	$2,346,320.1	$195,122.3

TABLE 36.6.

	FY 1981 Appropriation Available (in thousands)	8.2768 Percent Reduction
State agencies and institutions (adjusted)	$ 576,051.1	$ 47,678.6
State educational institutions and programs	433,597.6	35,888.0
Aid to school districts	1,081,300.2	89,497.0
Aid to local units of government	251,942.8	20,942.8
Total	$2,342,891.7	$193,916.4

duction required of state agencies and institutions *among* those agencies and institutions. This was accomplished through the following measures:

1. Program reductions. A number of agencies were scheduled to implement new programs in FY 1981 or significantly expand existing programs. A few agencies had access to program appropriations carried forward from previous biennia. A decision was made that it would be inequitable to allow some agencies to proceed with full funding for new programs or program expansion while requiring others to reduce existing levels of expenditure. Thus, all funding for new, expanded, or carry forward programs was examined to determine whether some or all of that funding could be reduced. Funding for some programs, particularly those with direct impact on citizens, was left intact. In other instances, funding was reduced to allow slower implementation than originally contemplated. Finally, funding for some programs was deferred entirely.

It is important to note that the above decisions relate to *funding* and did not constitute "directives" to agency heads to defer the programs in question. Each agency head has been asked to evaluate his or her agency's priorities and FY 1981 work plan to reflect the impact of the *total* reduction program. Based on this evaluation and the priorities which emerge, agencies may well proceed to fully implement new programs while reducing efforts in existing ones.

2. Mandatory cancellations. A second equity consideration was the past expenditure history of individual agencies. Some agencies consistently cancel (do not expend) significant portions of their appropriation; others expend virtually the total funding available. To a larger extent, these differences are a function of the nature of each agency's budget, e.g., agencies with a high percentage of resources budgeted for high-turnover classes of employees will normally experience higher than average salary savings.

Quite obviously, agencies with a history of large cancellations are in a better position to absorb a budget reduction than those with little or no cancellations. To compensate for this factor, a "normal" cancellation was computed for each agency (based on recent-year experience) and taken "off-the-top" as a *mandatory cancellation*. It is important to note that this does not constitute a simple counting of "normal" cancellations before they occur; it is an *immediate* budget reduction which must be implemented at this time. "Normal" cancellations will still occur (and are planned on in the fund balance analysis) because after agencies implement the budget reduction program, the same factors which generated "normal" cancellations in the past will still be at work. Thus, state agencies are not receiving credit for dollars which would have reverted to the treasury in any case; rather, they are being assessed a flexibility equalization charge at this time. A second element in the mandatory cancellation process was the appropriation available as a "salary supplement" to fund salary and fringe benefit increases to occur after July of this year.

Rather than allocate that appropriation to agencies (and state-funded educational institutions and programs) and then recover a like amount through the reduction program, that portion of the appropriation budgeted for agencies and institutions was simply cancelled. This reduction to state agencies is no less than if the appropriation had been allocated and budgets *then* reduced; the agencies must still fund the salary and fringe benefit increases due their employees in FY 1981.

Finally, two state agencies were found to have resources budgeted for special purposes in FY 1981 which could in fact be cancelled on an accelerated basis without disruption of the current level of services. A total of $3,450,000 was cancelled from the Department of Transportation for the following reasons:

> $1,500,000 of the "performance funding" appropriation for MTC will be cancelled. While it is anticipated that MTC could earn the full appropriation, they have agreed to utilize a portion of their working reserve. This action is based upon current estimates of costs, ridership, etc. and will not require any reduction in the level of services provided by MTC.
> $1,300,000 of the "social fares" appropriation for MTC will be cancelled. Of this amount, approximately $1,200,000 is currently estimated to be excess appropriation based upon ridership estimates. The balance will come from utilization of a portion of MTC's working reserve.
> $650,000 of the "projected mobility" appropriation for MTC will be cancelled. This amount was determined to be available after full allowance was made for continued provision of all current service and planned implementation of service increases to meet the needs of handicapped and disabled citizens.

An additional $1,386,000 was cancelled from the Department of Health's budget. This amount represents dollars appropriated as a subsidy (match for federal funding) for a water treatment plan at Cloquet. Current information indicates there is virtually no possibility of federal funding for this project in FY 1981, and thus this appropriation can be cancelled. If Cloquet receives the federal funds and decides to proceed with this project, this amount will be restored to the Health Department's budget from the general contingent fund.

The total reduction accomplished through this process was $25,503,000 of which $7,567,500 came from the salary supplement appropriation.

3. January 1981 cost-of-living adjustment. By a contract and law, state employees are entitled to a cost-of-living salary increase in January of 1981. That increase will be based on changes in the Consumer Price Index. With inflation exceeding all expectations over the last twelve months, however, a previous cost-of-living adjustment (granted this July) substantially depleted the appropriation provided for this purpose for the current biennium. (The 1980 session of the legislature rejected a request to increase the funding available.)

Given this situation, state agencies and educational programs were notified this spring that they would have to absorb the January 1981 cost-of-living adjustments from within existing agency resources, i.e., salary savings and other internal budget reductions.

Since the mandatory cancellations outlined in the previous section effectively removed such internal flexibility as each agency may have had to plan for the January 1981 COLA, the estimated cost of the January 1981 COLA was returned to each agency from its mandatory cancellation. For those agencies where the January 1981 COLA cost *exceeded* their mandatory cancellation, the cancellation was reduced to zero. The dollars returned to agencies for this purpose totalled $3,951,400.

At this point in the process, the results shown in Table 36.7 had been achieved.

TABLE 36.7.

	Base (in thousands)	Reduction (in thousands)
FY 1981 appropriation available	$579,479.5	—
Program reductions	(15,161.7)	$15,161.7
Mandatory cancellations	(25,503.0)	25,503.0
Return on January, 1981 COLA cost	3,951.4	(3,951.4)
Net results	$542,766.2	$36,713.3

To reach the total of $49,743,000 required of state agencies and institutions, an additional reduction of $13,029,700 was necessary. The question was one of how to allocate this amount to the various agencies and institutions in an equitable manner. The process adopted was to classify the $542,766,200 still available after the above reductions had been made into the categories listed in Table 36.8.

The first three categories in Table 36.8 consist of items we found to be virtually impossible to reduce in any short-term budget adjustment program:

TABLE 36.8

	Amount (in thousands)	Percent
Fixed costs	$ 40,918.1	7.54
Essential services	148,970.1	27.45
Special cases	75,664.1	13.34
Subtotal	$265,552.3	48.93
Semi-fixed costs	9,610.6	1.77
Direct services	39,203.1	7.22
Additional special cases	44,750.9	8.24
Subtotal	$ 93,564.6	17.23
"Residual budget"	183,649.3	33.84
Total	$542,766.2	100.0

Fixed costs include items such as heating and utility payments for state facilities, workman's and unemployment compensation payments, lease costs, and other contracted expenses. While these costs can be controlled over the long-term (e.g., leases can be broken, contracts can be terminated), 7.54% of state agency budgets are committed for such items over the short term.

Essential services include direct patient care in state hospitals, inmate care in correctional institutions, and resident care in veterans' facilities. These three items account for $142.2 million of the $149.0 placed in this classification. The balance represents modest sums in five additional state agencies. These sums do not include administrative and support service costs for the institutions involved, only those costs *directly* necessary for patient/inmate care.

Special cases include fee revenues of the various self-supporting boards, recovered costs of regulatory bodies, "hard" matching funds for federal grants, and grants and payments already legally committed for FY 1981. In the first three instances reductions would be counterproductive since they would lead to a loss of revenue; in the fourth they are not legally possible.

The sum of these three categories— 48.93% of state agency and institution budgets—was classified as excluded from whatever level of reduction might be necessary; the costs involved are ones that simply must be funded.

The second three categories were established to recognize costs which *can* be reduced under severe circumstances, but such reductions would pose the following particular problems for the agencies required to do so:

Semi-fixed costs, for example, include contracts with termination clauses which would allow work (and payments) to stop after notice, telephone service (excluding toll charges), security contracts, refuse removal, and building repair costs.

Direct services represent costs associated with providing direct services to a non-residential clientele or transfer payments to other units of government for that purpose (e.g., Department of Health, Community Health Services Grants).

Additional special cases are largely grants and transfer payments which can be prorated or otherwise reduced if necessary, but such reductions or prorations would directly impact services.

With all of the above categories excluded, the "residual" budget of state agencies and institutions totalled $183,649,300. This amount was then reduced by a uniform 7.0948% for each agency to achieve the final $13,029,700 of reductions required of state agencies and institutions.

The above process was designed for the sole purpose of allowing a rational and equitable distribution of the 8.3% budget reduction required of state agencies and institutions *among* those agencies and institutions. It had no impact on the broader equity issue of the proper allocation of the total reduction amount among state agencies, school aids, and local government aids.

TABLE 36.9.

	FY 1981 Appropriation	Percent of Education
Department of Education	$ 18,431.7	1.22
Higher education coordinating board	55,558.9	3.67
State university system	79,607.1	5.25
Community college system	38,524.2	2.54
University of Minnesota	232,463.7	15.35
Minnesota Education Computing Consortium	4,065.7	0.27
Subtotal	428,651.3	28.30
Department of Education-M.I.S.	3,410.0	0.23
Mayo Medical School	1,536.3	0.10
Subtotal	4,946.3	0.33
Education aids	1,026,484.2	67.75
Agricultural tax aid	50,790.0	3.35
Non-public school aid	4,026.0	0.27
Subtotal	$1,081,300.2	71.37
Total	$1,514,897.8	100.0

State-funded Educational Institutions and Programs

To provide equity among all components of education, the budget reduction process segregated state appropriations for education into three categories and applied an equal 8.3% (8.276) reduction to each category. The three categories include elements in Table 36.9.

To provide equity *within* the first category—state-funded institutions and programs—a process virtually identical to that used to analyze the budgets of state agencies was utilized. That process was adjusted to reflect the following three considerations unique to education:

Direct instructional costs were identified and excluded from the base on which the reduction was computed. Such costs, however, were limited to teaching faculty salaries and direct classroom supplies. Salary dollars budgeted for student employees who are provided work opportunities as part of a financial aid "package" were also excluded from the base used to compute the reduction.

While only *appropriated* resources were reduced by 8.3%, tuition and other operating receipts were included in the analysis to insure equity in terms of resources available for operating purposes.

A parallel analysis to that presented for state agencies must first adjust the total budget to include tuition and other operating receipts as follows:

	Amount (In thousands)
FY 1981 appropriated funds	$428,651.3
Tuition and operating receipts	125,056.6
Total budget	$553,707.9

From this total, the program deferrals in Table 36.10 were found to be possible.

TABLE 36.10.

Department of Education	Balance of ESV Computer Council Out-of-school youth study	$ 132,900
	Deferral	33,000
	Subtotal	165,900
Higher Education Coordinating Board	B.E.O.G. replacement funds	$1,600,000*
	Deferral of AVTI governance study	28,000
	Phasing of data processing dev.	198,600
	Subtotal	$1,826,600
Minnesota Education Computing Consortium	Defer Ortonville microcomputer study	100,000
	Balance of telecommunications study	64,000
	Subtotal	$ 164,000
Total program deferrals		$2,156,500

*This sum represents a part of the excess FY 1980 grant and scholarship funds carried forward into FY 1981. HECB intended to fund a $50 per student aid adjustment to compensate for a corresponding reduction in federal Basic Educational Opportunity Grants. Such funding, while desirable under normal circumstances, can be foregone this year.

TABLE 36.11

Department of Education	Normal cancellation	$ 874,000
Higher Education Coordinating Board	Normal cancellation	225,000
	Tuition reciprocity (result of renegotiation)	4,100,000
	Normal revision of grants and scholarships	3,710,100
	Unused balance of work–study program	200,000
	Subtotal	$ 8,235,100
State university system	Normal cancellation	478,200
Community college system	Normal cancellation	275,000
Minnesota Computing Consortium	Normal cancellation (Telecommunications)	325,000
Total cancellations		$10,187,300

The second step in the process was to identify mandatory cancellations for each educational unit. These cancellations are delineated in Table 36.11.

Note that the University of Minnesota does not "cancel" funds to the state treasury at the end of a fiscal year; it retains all balances for future use.

The third step in the process was to return $870,800 to the educational systems and Department of Education for the January 1981 cost-of-living adjustments on the same basis as was done for state agencies. At this point in the process, the results shown in Table 36.12 had been achieved.

To reach the total of $34,621,100 required of state funded educational institutions and programs, an additional reduction of $23,148,100 was necessary. As in the case of state agencies, the remaining base budget of $542,234,900 was allocated to the six categories listed in Table 36.13.

To achieve the total reduction required, a uniform reduction of 12.0771% was necessary for each unit's "residual budget." This figure is, of course, almost double that assessed the residual budget of state agencies because the educational units were not in a position to defer a significant dollar amount of new or expanded programs. This outcome is,

TABLE 36.12

	Base (in thousands)	Reduction (in thousands)
FY 1981 budget available	$553,707.9	0
Program reductions	(2,156.5)	$ 2,156.5
Mandatory cancellations	(10,187.3)	10,187.3
Return of January 1981 COLA cost	870.8	(870.8)
Net results	$542,234.9	$11,473.0

TABLE 36.13

	Allocation (In thousands)	Percent (in thousands)
Fixed costs	$ 69,099.0	12.74
Essential services	15,762.6	2.91
Special cases	5,678.9	1.05
Subtotal	90,540.5	16.70
Semi-fixed costs	35,684.9	6.58
Direct services	223,567.5	41.23
Additional special cases	772.7	0.14
Subtotal	$260,025.1	47.95
"Residual budget"	191,669.3	35.35
Total	$542,234.9	100.00

however, equitable in that both components absorb the 8.3% overall reduction in appropriated dollars.

School Aids

School aids will be reduced by a uniform 8.2768%. The Department of Education is now in the process of refining a model which is based on the fundamental concept of the aid program and takes into consideration local effort. Preliminary data indicate that the 8.3% reduction in state aid will result in a 5.3% net reduction in total operating resources for each district.

The actual impact on individual districts will, of course, vary based on the following considerations:

The extent to which a district has an unappropriated fund balance (surplus) available from previous years. The sum of such fund balances was $241 million statewide at the end of fiscal year 1979. Some districts, however, have no fund balances, and a few are in statutory debt status.

The nature of the "normal" change a district was to experience in state aid between FY 1980 and FY 1981. It would appear that districts experiencing significant growth *or* decline in pupil units will be in a more favorable position than those with little change in enrollment.

The extent to which a district has current vacant positions or will experience staff turnover during the course of the year.

It is the governor's hope that school boards will first work to reduce expenditure in whatever ways are possible without adverse impact on instructional services. To the extent actual spending reductions and use of unappropriated fund balance monies do not allow some districts to fully balance their budgets, it is recognized that operating debt may result. The Department of Education and the Governor's Office are now reviewing statutory provisions which apply to school district financing to identify avenues of possible relief which might be proposed as interim measures to the 1981 session of the legislature.

Local Government Aid

Aid to local units of government will also be reduced by a uniform 8.2768%. The Department of Revenue is now in the process of developing an equitable procedure to adjust actual aid payments. As part of that process, the department is examining the consequences of the fact that local units of government operate on a calendar fiscal year as opposed to the July 1 to June 30 fiscal year of the state.

As in the case of school districts, it is the governor's hope that local government will attempt to reduce actual expenditures to the extent possible before utilizing existing unappropriated fund balances. For those cities able to do so, it is hoped that an increase in the local property tax levy will be a course of last resort.

CONCLUSION

Since some of the elements of the reduction program are based on estimates of balance to be brought forward into fiscal year 1981 from prior years, as well as estimates of program requirements, those elements are subject to revision as actual data become available. To the extent such revisions are necessary, they will be made in a manner which insures that the basic objective of a balanced budget is met.

There should be no doubt that the budget reduction program outlined in this report will result in a decrease in services to the citizens of Minnesota. There is no way that a budget reduction of $195 million can have any other result. Given the fact that the state must live within a reduced amount of total resources for the balance of this year, it is necessary to recognize that virtually *any* reduction will result in consequences some will find undesirable. It is also necessary to recognize that specific budget reductions can be avoided only through identification of other programs where an equal amount might be reduced instead. (See Table 36.14.)

FOR DISCUSSION

1. Why was the budget reduction necessary? What facts were presented in support of the need for reduction? What information do you think was lacking, and why?

2. What other approaches to reducing programs might have been taken? What types of expenditures are easiest to cut? More difficult to cut? How are cuts classified and tiered?

3. Were the cuts really applied in the most equitable manner in this case? How would you define "equity" when it comes to budget reductions? What judgmental factors would you apply to making significant budget cuts?

4. What groups are most affected by these reductions? How are the reductions to be implemented?

5. Why was an across-the-board approach to reductions used? What are its advantages and disadvantages?

6. What is the size of the problem as a percentage of the General Fund budget? As a percentage of controllable expenditures? How else can the problem's magnitude be measured?

7. How would you design a budget reduction program detailed to the level of major state agencies? Consider alternative philosophical premises, competing priorities and political objectives, and different approaches to the concept of "equity."

8. What authority does the governor have to make reductions? What other approaches to retrenchment are possible in lieu of executive initiative and development? What advantages are there to an executive-led budget reduction program? Disadvantages?

TABLE 36.14 Extract from Budget Reduction Detail (in thousands)

	(1) Avail. for Allotment	(2) Fixed Costs	(3) Essential Services	(4) Special Cases	(5) Semi-fixed Costs	(6) Direct Services	(7) Additional Spec. Cases
Dept. of Transportation	36,716.2	0	2,346.0	13,194.9	0	547.5	14,074.1
Dept. of Public Welfare	161,247.0	7,314.2	108,097.5	2,687.8	1,707.7	59.2	449.0
Dept. of Revenue	25,984.9	1,068.6	0	5,448.0	454.7	0	100.0

	(8) Program Reductions	(9) Mandatory Cancels.	(10) Cost-of-living Adj.	(11) Adjusted Base	(12) 7.09% Reduction	(13) Total Reduction	(14) Balance Available
Dept. of Transportation	2,107.1	3,450.0	0	996.6	70.7	5,627.8	31,088.4
Dept. of Public Welfare	441.4	1,600.0	1,600.0	40,490.2	2,872.7	3,314.1	157,932.9
Dept. of Revenue	0	1,001.0	341.0	18,253.6	1,295.1	1,955.1	24,020.8

INDIVIDUAL CONTRIBUTORS

Alan P. Balutis, Director, Office of Policy and Systems, U.S. Department of Commerce.

Robert M. Bieber, Ebasco Risk Management Consultants, Inc., and formerly Director of Risk Management, County of Westchester, New York.

Anthony Brown, Assistant Professor, Political Science Department, Oklahoma State University.

James D. Carney, Principal, Peat, Marwick, Mitchell and Company.

Mark R. Daniels, Assistant Professor, Department of Political Science and Master of Public Affairs Program, The University of Connecticut.

Carol deProsse, past member of city council, Iowa City, Iowa.

Leo V. Donohue, Auditor of Public Accounts and formerly Finance Commissioner, State of Connecticut.

Paul D. Epstein, Manager, Citywide Productivity Program, City of New York, and formerly Productivity Analyst, Division of Government Capacity Building Program, Office of Policy Development and Research, U.S. Department of Housing and Urban Development.

Kenneth J. Euske, Assistant Professor of Accounting, Administrative Sciences, Naval Postgraduate School.

Charles Falvey, Program Director, Financial Management Curriculum, Management Sciences Training Center, U.S. Office of Personnel Management, Washington, D.C.

Russell E. Galipo, Vice-President and Manager, Municipal Finance Department, Connecticut National Bank, Hartford, Connecticut.

John Garmat, Deputy Director, Office of Budget and Program Analysis, U.S. Department of Treasury.

John R. Gist, Associate Professor, College of Architecture and Urban Studies, Virginia Polytechnic Institute and State University.

Andrew Glassberg, Associate Professor, Department of Political Science, University of Missouri–St. Louis.

Sanford M. Groves, Assistant City Manager, Paramount, California, and formerly Project Director, International City Management Association.

Nathaniel Guild, Vice-President, Rousmaniere Management Associates, Brookline, Massachusetts.

William J. Haga, Adjunct Professor of Administrative Sciences, Naval Postgraduate School.

John M. Hardesty, Captain, United States Army.

Lee Holmer, Senior Budget Analyst, Department of Finance, Columbus, Ohio.

Jamil E. Jreisat, Professor of Public Administration, University of South Florida.

Francis J. Leazes, Jr., doctoral candidate, Department of Political Science, The University of Connecticut.

Donald Levitan, Professor of Public Management, School of Management, Suffolk University.

Carol W. Lewis, Associate Professor, Department of Political Science and Master of Public Affairs Program, The University of Connecticut.

Thomas D. Lynch, Professor, Department of Public Administration, Florida International University.

James Mallory, Director of Training, National Association of State Budget Officers.

Edward Murphy, Director of Financial Management Curriculum, Management Sciences Training Center, U.S. Office of Personnel Management, Washington, D.C.

Frank M. Patitucci, President, Relocation Consultants, Inc., Mountain View, California, and Lecturer, Graduate School of Business, Stamford University.

Brian W. Rapp, President, Telluride Corp., Telluride, Colorado.

Maryann Romeo, account executive for a brokerage firm and formerly manager and officer, Municipal Credit Department, Connecticut National Bank, Hartford, Connecticut.

Peter F. Rousmaniere, President of Rousmaniere Management Associates, Brookline, Massachusetts.

Stanley Schoenfeld, Principal, Peat, Marwick, Mitchell and Company.

Larry Schroeder, Professor of Public Administration and Economics and Senior Research Associate, Metropolitan Studies Program, The Maxwell School, Syracuse University.

Michael J. Scicchitano, doctoral candidate, Department of Political Science, University of Georgia.

John W. Swain, Assistant Professor of Public Administration, University of Nebraska–Omaha.

Carl F. Valente, Director for Financial Management, International City Management Association, Washington, D.C.

Maureen Godsey Valente, Freelance consultant in Alexandria, Virginia, specializing in assisting public and private organizations in managing human and financial resources.

Paula R. Valente, Project Director, International City Management Association, Washington, D.C.

Lisa Weinberg, graduate of the Master of Public Affairs Program, The University of Connecticut.

Paul R. Woodie, Assistant City Manager, Dayton, Ohio.

Carol W. Lewis is an Associate Professor in the Department of Political Science and Associate Director of the Institute of Urban Research at The University of Connecticut, where she teaches public budgeting and urban management in the Master of Public Affairs Program. She received her B.A. from Cornell University and her Ph.D. from Princeton University. She is author and coauthor of several monographs on budgeting and has published in *Public Administration Review, Policy Studies Journal, Municipal Year Book, Comparative Urban Research,* and other sources.

A. Grayson Walker, III is the Director of Systems and Programming, Hoffmann-La Roche Inc., Nutley, New Jersey. Prior to joining Hoffmann-La Roche Inc., Mr. Walker was the Director of Loan Office Software at Beneficial Data Processing Corporation in Peapack, New Jersey. He is a former member of the Graduate Faculty of Fairleigh Dickinson University's College of Business Administration, where he was also Director of the Public Administration Institute's Computer Center. Walker received his Ph.D. from the University of Georgia. He is the author and coauthor of a variety of monographs, and has published in the *Public Administration Review.*

INDEX